Gandhi, Truth, and Nonviolence

Gandhi, Truth, and Nonviolence

The Politics of Engagement in Post-Truth Times

Edited by

VINAY LAL

OXFORD
UNIVERSITY PRESS

OXFORD
UNIVERSITY PRESS

Great Clarendon Street, Oxford, OX2 6DP,
United Kingdom

Oxford University Press is a department of the University of Oxford.
It furthers the University's objective of excellence in research, scholarship,
and education by publishing worldwide. Oxford is a registered trade mark of
Oxford University Press in the UK and in certain other countries

Published in the United States of America by Oxford University Press
198 Madison Avenue, New York, NY 10016, United States of America

British Library Cataloguing in Publication Data

Data available

Library of Congress Control Number: 2024944431

ISBN 9780198936626

DOI: 10.1093/9780198936657.001.0001

Printed and bound in India by Replika Press Pvt. Ltd.

Acknowledgements

Around half of the papers included in this volume emerged from an am-bitious conference that I organized at the University of California, Los Angeles (UCLA), where I have been a member of the history faculty since July 1993, on the occasion of the 150th birth anniversary of Gandhi. The conference, which took the title 'Truth and Nonviolence in Post-Truth Times', was held over the course of four days and was organized much in the same way in which I have orchestrated other academic meetings in the past. Only four to five papers were slotted each day, and, what is increas-ingly rare even in the academy, each participant was given nearly an hour to deliver the paper, followed in each case by half an hour of discussion.

A large number of departments and other academic units at UCLA contributed to the success of the conference, either in the form of financial support or material assistance, and I would like to thank the Division of the Social Sciences and its then Dean, Professor Darnell Hunt; the Asian American Studies Center and its Director, Professor Karen Umemoto; the Center for the Study of Religion and its Director, Professor Carol Bakhos; the UCLA International Institute and its Vice Provost, Professor Cindy Fan; and the Bedari Kindness Institute. Additional funding came from the University Religious Conference and the Interdisciplinary Cross-Campus Affairs Committee. The Young Research Library (YRL) provided event space, courtesy of Suzy Lee and the librarian, Matthew Johnson. My thanks to all.

Special thanks are due to two units of the university which played a central role in facilitating the conference. The Center for India and South Asia (CISA) provided initial seed funding and its Director at that time, Professor Akhil Gupta, was extremely helpful throughout, and the then Assistant Director, Sumita Mitra, gave timely help in enabling the Sambhi Endowed Lecture delivered by Gopalkrishna Gandhi. My home depart-ment, History, provided not only additional funding but its staff, and in particular Khris Go, Jay Jang, and above all Drew Soucie were especially helpful. The then-Chair of the Department of History, Professor Carla

Pestana, was enthusiastic about the initiative and contributed to the conference with funds from the Joyce Appleby Endowed Chair of America in the World that she holds. Though the Academic Senate at UCLA does not fund conferences, I am grateful to it for some grants in previous years that made possible some of my own research which was important in helping me frame the intellectual parameters of the conference.

The Los Angeles-based Sambhi Foundation, named after the late Dr Mohinder Sambhi, a UCLA physician with an abiding interest in Indian classical music, was set up to promote some causes that Dr Sambhi championed. Nearly half of the funding for the conference was provided by the Sambhi Foundation, and I am especially grateful to my friend and one of its trustees, Daniel M. Neuman, Executive Vice Chancellor Emeritus at UCLA, for facilitating the magnanimous gift. I am also thankful to one of its other trustees, Dr Vikram Kamdar, for his support of the conference. And, finally, I owe to my then research assistant, Erica Neighbors, the success with which the conference was held. She worked indefatigably in facilitating the visits of the speakers, coordinating with various university departments and units to ensure the flawless execution of the myriad tasks that are required to host a large conference. Erica also set up the conference website [https://gandhi2020ucla.weebly.com/] and prepared the requisite publicity materials. I cannot thank her adequately enough.

It would be superfluous of me to thank the conference participants, if only because most of them are represented in the conference volume which itself is testimony to their fellowship in a common cause. I cannot, however, conclude without mention of three other individuals. Priyanka Venkatesh, who has since gone on to earn a doctorate in musical arts at UCLA, kindly agreed to play a composition by Sirish Korde on her violin on the opening night. She played with her characteristic grace and skill, and I am grateful to her for her generosity, for adding an artistic touch to the opening night, and for introducing me to the oeuvre of this unusual composer. Gopalkrishna Gandhi's delivery of the Sambhi Endowed Lecture was memorable as much for its delivery as for the gravitas of his remarks and the insights he brought to his understanding of Mohandas Gandhi. In private conversations, he gave freely of his time and was remarkably undemanding, notwithstanding the lofty positions he has occupied in his lifetime.

This volume is dedicated to the memory of Reverend James M. Lawson, who was a dedicated theorist and practitioner of nonviolence in the United States for over seven decades. He is rightly referred to by many in the US who are in the know as a 'national treasure', and I had the remarkable privilege, and sweet and often rapturous pleasure, of his friendship for a decade. He was the principal spokesperson for, and exponent of, the idea of nonviolence in American history and retained, until his death at 95 years of age in June 2024, a vigorous schedule of talks and lectures that would have been a feat for someone half his age. Reverend Lawson delivered the conference's opening address, 'Gandhi and the Long, Bitter, Beautiful Struggle for Justice and Truth', and left an ineradicable impression on everyone, not least on Gopalkrishna Gandhi. This volume is but a small tribute to a tireless advocate of nonviolence who moved from being the architect of the Nashville Sit-ins to a major force in the labour movement in Los Angeles. He, putting it plainly, inspired us all, and I do not doubt that his spirit will continue to move future generations of thinkers and activists who tread the path of truth and nonviolence.

Vinay Lal
Los Angeles
November 2023

Contents

Contributors

Leilah Danielson is Professor of History, Northern Arizona University, Flagstaff: AZ, USA

Faisal Devji is Professor of Indian History, University of Oxford, Oxford, UK

Charles R. DiSalvo is Woodrow A. Potesta Professor of Law, College of Law, West Virginia University, Morgantown: WV, USA

Yohanan Grinshpon is Professor Emeritus of Indian Studies at the Hebrew University of Jerusalem

Sudipta Kaviraj is Professor of Indian Politics and Intellectual History, Columbia University, New York: NY, USA

Vinay Lal is Professor of History, University of California, Los Angeles (UCLA)

Rev. James M. Lawson (1928–2024) was Pastor Emeritus of Holman United Methodist Church, Los Angeles

Karuna Mantena is Professor of Political Science, Columbia University, New York: NY, USA

Uday Singh Mehta is Distinguished Professor of Political Science, Graduate Center, City University of New York, New York: NY, USA

Sumathi Ramaswamy is James B. Duke Distinguished Professor of History, Department of History, Duke University, Durham: NC, USA

Neelima Shukla-Bhatt is Professor of Religion and South Asia Studies, Wellesley College, Wellesley: MA, USA

Ajay Skaria is Professor of History, Department of History, University of Minnesota, Minneapolis: MN, USA

Tridip Suhrud is Professor and Provost, CEPT University, Ahmedabad, India

Introduction

The Measure of a Man: The Many Enigmas and Strange Journeys of Mohandas Gandhi

Vinay Lal

Just how does one take the measure of a man known the world over as Mahatma Gandhi? So much has been written on him: the British spoke of 330 million gods and goddesses in India, not that, notwithstanding their proclivity towards an enumerative world and their investment in that tool of insidious intent called the census, they ever conducted a census of Hindu deities, and so perhaps I might with good reason casually throw around the comparatively modest figure of 1,000 to suggest how many biographies there are in English alone of the Mahatma. This is apart from certainly thousands more in Indian, European, and other languages, and besides this there are scholarly studies or the more specialized works known as 'monographs'. (Banish that word from your lexicon, a learned friend advised me, if you wish to sell your books to the public.) And yet Gandhi remains inexhaustible, or why else this edited book? And yet, too, India lately seems to have had enough of him and seems to be exhausted by one who was felled by three bullets and remains the target of many assassinations. In the Indian epics, the Ramayana and the Mahabharata alike, the heroes are banished. It appears that Gandhi is being banished from India, slowly being excised from the nation's consciousness. It remains to be said that this book is not an attempt on the part of the editor, and I daresay the contributors, to make Gandhi 'relevant': perhaps some of the contributors may think otherwise, but there is something rather banal in trying to render Gandhi 'relevant'. That work can safely be left to the government institutions and to the (often) self-appointed Gandhians.

Vinay Lal, *Introduction* In: *Gandhi, Truth, and Nonviolence*. Edited by: Vinay Lal, Oxford University Press.
© Oxford University Press 2025. DOI: 10.1093/9780198936657.003.0001

Every year, at least on his birthday, there are multiple conferences, hosted by the mandarins in power, held with the explicit aim of pronouncing his 'relevance', though those with some degree of discernment would surely have noted that, with every such conference, the hope is that he will be pushed deeper into his grave. (And, lest the technical-minded should snort with the rejoinder that Gandhi was burnt on the funeral pyre rather than buried, that fact has not escaped me.)

It is something like the conundrum with the statues of Gandhi. Every town in India has at least one, and one presumes that statues are there to remind Indians that such a one as Gandhi did walk in flesh and blood upon this earth. But what is it that the eminent Austrian novelist and essayist Robert Musil had to say about statues? The 'most striking feature of monuments', he wrote, 'is that you do not notice them. There is nothing in the world as invisible as a monument. Like a drop of water on an oilskin, attention runs down them without stopping for a moment.'[1] Statues may be designed, in fact, to make one forget as much as remember the person being commemorated—which is, perhaps, one reason we might be grateful alike to the miscreants and political radicals who, in recent years, have been vandalizing statues of Gandhi. They have succeeded remarkably well in making Gandhi alive once again. The Mahatma, I would go so far as to say, might even have been pleased at the desecration and removal of his statues: as he once wrote in the pages of *Harijan*, 'It will be a waste of good money to spend Rs. 25,000 on erecting a clay or metallic statue of the figure of a man who is himself made of clay and is more fragile than a bangle . . .'[2]

In 1969, on the 100th anniversary of his birth, the Indian Institute of Advanced Study at Simla, a rather more purposeful institution those days than the sinecure largely for obscure BJP academically inclined apparatchiks that it has become today, published a hefty volume on Gandhi's thought and political praxis. One of the more memorable contributions came from the pen of T. K. Mahadevan, an iconoclastic thinker

---

[1] Robert Musil, 'Monuments', in *Posthumous Papers of a Living Author* (New York: Archipelago Books, 2006), 61–3.

[2] M. K. Gandhi, 'Mahatma's Statue', *Harijan*, 11 February 1939; also in *The Collected Works of Mahatma Gandhi* [hereafter *CWMG*], 2nd rev. ed., 100 volumes (New Delhi: Publications Division, Ministry of Information and Broadcasting, Government of India, 2000), 75: 44–5, also online at http://www.gandhiashramsevagram.org/gandhi-literature/mahatma-gandhi-collected-works-volume-75.pdf. References henceforth to the *CWMG* will be to the online edition.

who offered 'an approach to the study of Gandhi', essentially an intellectual framework that revolved, not surprisingly, around his notions of
ahimsa (nonviolence) and *satya* (truth). Mahadevan took recourse to the
Upanishads and the Mahabharata to expound on Gandhi's forays into
Indian intellectual traditions. Since the time that Mahadevan engaged in
an exercise, akin to what in those days was called 'the history of ideas', that
was eminently useful, our understanding of Gandhi has considerably
deepened, and this brief introduction, resting as it does on many works
that remain unacknowledged, offers a different framework for the study
of Gandhi, his thought, and the histories of nonviolence. I may appear at
times to be speaking in riddles, but I will suggest that Gandhi cannot be
approached merely as someone who is 'relevant', or a peacemaker, or as
someone who is there to remind us of our better selves. He may be all of
those things, but he is, even more so, a necessary provocation, a disrupter
of the consensus, someone who, if we take the measure of the man even
lightly, is there to unsettle us—to comfort the afflicted and afflict the com-
fortable. Hence, the subtitle of this introduction, 'The Many Enigmas and
Strange Journeys of Mohandas Gandhi'.

Let us begin with the particular anomaly presented by 2 October. It is
one of the three, and only three, national holidays mandated by law in
India. I suspect few in the country know about the National and Festive
Holiday Act under which all establishments and institutions, whether
private or public, are required to be closed on 26 January (Republic Day),
15 August (Independence Day), and 2 October (Gandhi's Birthday, or
'Gandhi Jayanti'). Now, 2 October is not unimportant, of course, and
the UN General Assembly in 2007 passed a resolution declaring it the
International Day of Nonviolence, but for someone such as myself it is
30 January that is the most important day of what we may provisionally
call the 'Gandhi calendar'. On 30 January 1948, some minutes after five
o'clock in the evening, Gandhi was shot dead while he was walking to
his evening prayer meeting at Birla House in New Delhi. His assassin, a
Chitpavan Brahmin from Pune by the name of Nathuram Godse, harboured many a grudge against him, and he would go on to elaborate his
views at some length in a statement which was subsequently proscribed
by the Government of India. I will not enter into a discussion of Godse's
statement at this juncture, but the *shahaadat* or martyrdom of Gandhi is
for many such as myself, as I've noted before, the more critical date. The

late Ramachandra Gandhi, one of Mohandas's grandsons and an eminent thinker and philosopher in his own right, put the matter thus in his
characteristically inimitable fashion: 'Gandhi stopped three bullets on
their deathly trajectory of hate.'[3] *Difficult as is the art of living, Gandhi
knew the yet more demanding art of dying.*[4]

Gandhi took the bullets on his chest and, it has been said, brought to
an end the violence that had gripped India and led neighbours to kill
each other and many more people to jettison the ties that had informed
their lives. It was a strange time, a time of madness famously captured
in the biting and sardonic voice of the gifted storyteller Saadat Hasan
Manto. But Gandhi's chest was evidently not as wide as the chest of the
present Prime Minister,[5] not capacious enough to neutralize the bullets
which have resumed their deathly trajectory of hate once again. We are at
a peculiar, some will say (with good reason) perilous, juncture in modern
Indian history. The country has been roiled, oddly enough even blessed,
in recent years by protests and dissenting movements, none more significant than the remarkably disciplined nonviolent dissent against state
authoritarianism shown by Muslim women, some of them illiterate
and others semi-literate, in the south Delhi neighbourhood of Shaheen
Bagh,[6] and just months later by the 'Farmers Movement'. I use the word
'blessed' advisedly, if only because such movements have been necessitated by the precipitous decline of democracy in India: things would certainly not have come to this pass had the Indian state, and its vast number
of acolytes and foot soldiers in the burgeoning middle class, not shown a
frightening intolerance for views that deviate from what has been dished
out as national interest and patriotism. It is comforting that India can still
claim heroes and heroines, but we would do well to recall the exchange
from Bertolt Brecht's *Life of Galileo*: 'pity the nation', says a character,

---

[3] Cited by Gopalkrishna Gandhi, Introduction to *Gandhi Is Gone: Who Will Guide Us Now?*,
ed. Gopalkrishna Gandhi (Ranikhet: Permanent Black, 2007), 14.

[4] For further elaboration, see Vinay Lal, 'On the Art of Dying: Death and the Specter of
Gandhi', in *Experiments with Truth: Gandhi and Images of Nonviolence*, ed. Josef Helfenstein
and Joseph N. Newland (Houston: Menil Collection, 2014), 329–36.

[5] Readers will recognize, I hope, the implied reference to the boast by Narendra Modi that he
had a 56-inch chest. It is not clear when he first made the claim, but it was in the campaign before
the 2014 election. See Veenu Sandhu, 'Who can boast about a 56-inch chest?', *Business Standard*
(31 January 2014), https://www.business-standard.com/article/beyond-business/who-can-
boast-about-a-56-inch-chest-114013101063_1.html [accessed 25 October 2022].

[6] For a more detailed discussion, see Vinay Lal, 'The Grandmothers of Shaheen Bagh: An
Indian Muslim Women's Protest and the Future of Satyagraha', *Protest* 3, no. 1 (2023), 1–27.

'that breeds no heroes', to which Galileo replies, 'pity the nation that needs a hero'.[7] Gandhi is very much present in these demonstrations of resistance to state authoritarianism, even if the demonstrators have not always thought through carefully what it means to offer satyagraha, and even if the very idea of satyagraha is sometimes not present to them—but if he can nonetheless be invoked as an icon of Hindu–Muslim unity, it suffices.

It is for a different if related reason that, in the present climate of opinion, it appears imperative that we do take a measure of the man and his extraordinary and unusual place in world history. The same government that in India has showered encomiums on Gandhi has done everything possible to reduce him—if I may use his own language—to zero. Most of the luminaries who are part of the present government, now in power for more than a decade, and their innumerable camp followers have nothing but intense dislike for Gandhi—though they make a public show of reverence, as they must by protocol, for the 'Father of the Nation'. Official functionaries are also astute enough to realize not only that, nearly seventy-five years after his death, Gandhi is still the most well-known Indian name in the world but also that he earns the country a good share of the cultural capital that it might have. His detractors in the middle class, however, can openly declare that they have no use for Gandhi, and even call him a traitor to the nation, usually without any consequences. In the 2019 general election, a woman who is implicated in terrorist cases and who has pronounced Gandhi's assassin a *desh-bhakt*, or lover of the nation, was elected to Parliament.[8] Nathuram Godse has been apotheosized not only by this Member of Parliament but by many

---

[7] The lines are drawn from Scene 13 of the play: there are numerous translations and I have settled upon what appears to me the most felicitous expression of the ideas at stake. The edition I have most often used—Bertolt Brecht, *Life of Galileo*, trans. John Willett (New York: Arcade Publishing, 1994), 98—offers the most common translation: when Andrea says, 'Unhappy the land that has no heroes!', Galileo replies, 'Unhappy the land where heroes are needed.'

[8] 'Pragya Singh Thakur calls Nathuram Godse a patriot', *The Hindu* (16 May 2019), https://www.thehindu.com/elections/lok-sabha-2019/pragya-singh-thakur-calls-nathuram-godse-a-patriot-bjp-disagrees/article61672105.ece; see also Vinay Lal, 'Pragya Thakur and the Glorification of Gandhi's Assassin' (18 May 2019), https://vinaylal.wordpress.com/2019/05/18/lovers-of-the-motherland-pragya-thakur-and-the-glorification-of-gandhis-assassin/ [both accessed 20 October 2022]. Predictably, she then delivered an 'apology' and, just as predictably, repeated the offence months later when the storm had died down. See 'Pragya Thakur Calls Godse a 'Deshbhakt' Again, This Time in Parliament', *The Wire* (27 November 2019), https://thewire.in/politics/pragya-thakur-calls-godse-a-deshbhakt-again-parliament [accessed 20 October 2022].

in the ruling party as a great patriot, as an intensely masculine figure who knew what it takes for a nation state to become respected in this world and who therefore had no choice but to remove the effeminate Gandhi from the political scene. Some in the country have even proposed that Vinayak Savarkar, one of the principal ideologues of Hindu nationalism who mentored Godse and whose own role in the assassination of Gandhi has been the subject of numerous inquiries, be conferred the Bharat Ratna—the country's highest civilian honour, awarded to fewer than fifty people in the nearly seventy years of the existence of the Indian Republic. The day when the Bharat Ratna is proposed to be awarded to Godse is likely not far behind.

I might go on in this vein—describing, that is, the scurrilous, virulent attacks on Gandhi in social media—ad infinitum. Some of these are juvenile: as an illustration, I have encountered on social media, as passed on to me by my own children, posts and messages which state that Gandhi was a friend and ally of Hitler. This is on the grounds that he addressed two letters to Hitler which begin with the salutation, 'Dear Friend'. I have addressed this question elsewhere and it would be superfluous to rehearse details that are elementary, except to say that the letters in question, neither of them delivered to the intended recipient on account of the state censor's intervention, were written by Gandhi as a plea to Hitler to abandon the course of violence.[9] Let us leave aside the consideration that the epistolary art in English has, for some centuries, proceeded according to some protocols, among them the fact that it is customary to begin a letter, even to one's adversaries, with the salutation, 'Dear Friend'. Many among the young are clueless about writing letters, evidently under the impression that tweet-length messages and emojis are more than adequate to carry out an exchange of views. What is, of course, far more pertinent and disturbing is that there is no awareness here of Gandhi's view that the ontological argument for ahimsa precludes one from supposing that there is a single human being without some spark of divinity. Gandhi doubtless thought that Hitler's acts were monstrous, but everything in his thinking would have rebelled at the idea that Hitler was nothing but a monster. Gandhi was also equally beholden to the idea that to believe

---

[9] Vinay Lal, 'Gandhi and Palestine', *Critical Muslim 6: Reclaiming Al-Andalus* (April–June 2013), 171–90.

that the truth resides entirely with oneself, and that not an iota of it resides with the other, is not merely arrogance but itself a species of violence. How such a worldview could lead to the conclusion that Gandhi was a friend of Hitler—a friend as the word is ordinarily understood—beggars the imagination.

Criticisms of Gandhi, it should be clear, are rife. That is how it should be, unless we desire only a hagiographic representation of Gandhi. But a critical lens on Gandhi may yet be available in an idiom which would differ from the criticisms that one has now come to expect—those which excoriate him for racism, sexism, casteism, and so on. In the midst of these criticisms, I would like to offer a vision of Gandhi as a player of infinite games. I begin these reflections with the African American activist Bayard Rustin, widely recognized as a key player in the civil rights movement and as the master organizer who worked to make possible the famous March on Washington in 1963. In my late teens, I had the unusual pleasure of meeting him and spending an evening with him over a private dinner, and the impress that he left on me is perhaps part of the warrant for taking his life as a starting point for some of my ruminations. Rustin was a lifelong student of the life and work of Gandhi and, along with Reverend James M. Lawson (see Chapter 10), had a large hand in shaping Martin Luther King's understanding of satyagraha and bringing nearly the entire arsenal of Gandhian ideas of mass nonviolent resistance to the fore in the struggle for civil and political rights. His most prominent biographer, John D'Emilio, says unhesitatingly that 'more than anyone else, Rustin brought the message and methods of Gandhi to the United States'.[10]

Rustin's eyes were turned upon the anti-colonial struggle in India and he was firmly of the view that 'no situation in America has created so much interest among negroes as the Gandhian proposals for India's freedom'. King was but a schoolboy when Rustin had already established a reputation as a 'one-man nonviolent army' working on behalf of the Fellowship of Reconciliation (FOR), an international religious organization that advocated radical pacifism and that in the US sought a distinctive and revolutionary approach to the race problem. Rustin sought

[10] John D'Emilio, *Lost Prophet: The Life and Times of Bayard Rustin* (New York: Free Press, 2003), 1.

to desegregate lunch counters in the Deep South and on a bus ride from Louisville to Nashville in 1942 moved to the section reserved, by both law and custom, for whites: when he refused to vacate his seat, the police were summoned and he was verbally abused and pummelled with blows. Rustin also assumed an avuncular role as chief advisor to the Congress of Racial Equality (CORE), an organization founded in 1942 with the intention of bringing Gandhi's ideas to the struggle against racism. 'Consciously dressing themselves in the garb of Gandhian philosophy,' writes D'Emilio, CORE's young activists 'made nonviolence a spiritual road to follow'.[11]

Rustin embraced an outlook that most of Gandhi's own associates in the Congress Party rejected, viewing nonviolence as not 'just a policy' but as 'a way of life', a way of being in the world.[12] Yet it is striking that Rustin, besides being a Quaker and a pacifist, was also a conscientious objector (though in popular parlance that amounted to being a draft dodger), an avowed homosexual who was sexually prolific, and a communist for a few years until the Nazi invasion of the Soviet Union in 1941 led him to reverse course. None of this was calculated to earn him goodwill in good old America, considering that, as the rap artist H. Rap Brown once put it, 'violence is as American as cherry pie'.[13] We may say of Rustin that he was also, in many of the respects that I have outlined, everything that Gandhi emphatically was not. Rustin's flirtation with communism may have been relatively brief, but it is worth pointing out that communism held no at-traction for Gandhi at all—not necessarily because, as some imagine, he would have been opposed to the radical redistribution of wealth, but be-cause he saw communism beholden both to violence and to the industrial modernity of which he was a critic. Similarly, it is not Ruskin's homosexu-ality that would have repulsed him, even if he had found it disagreeable,

---

[11] Ibid., 51–4.

[12] Ibid., 39–71, especially 54.

[13] H. Rap Brown's famous aphorism is drawn from a speech that he gave at a press conference in Washington, DC, on 27 July 1967. As has been pointed out by scholars, it is the condensed version of a lengthier comment which reads as follows: 'I say violence is necessary. Violence is a part of America's culture. It is as American as cherry pie. Americans taught the black people to be violent. We will use that violence to rid ourselves of oppression if necessary. We will be free, by any means necessary.' See S. C. Stanko and G. A. Crews, 'Violence is as American as Cherry Pie: Mass Incarceration and Juvenile Violence', in *Handbook of Research on School Violence in American K-12 Education*, ed. G. A. Crews (Hershey, PA: IGI Global, 2019), 305–17, https://scholarworks.utrgv.edu/cj_fac/58/?.

but rather his sexual promiscuity. Indeed, Rustin's sexual escapades—on one occasion, the police found him having oral sex in a car with one of two young white men in Pasadena, California—brought him such notoriety that, in the interest of protecting his friends and associates in the civil rights movement, and to ensure that his own moral laxity would not be used by white supremacists to discredit the movement, he worked from behind the scenes.[14]

What is also indubitably true is that Rustin, as everyone who worked with him over the decades admitted, had a masterful understanding of Gandhi and appeared to have imbibed his spirit at least in his capacity as a nonviolent political activist. The sceptic might be inclined to say that Rustin did what many others did, namely instrumentalize nonviolence as an efficacious mode of instigating and organizing African American resistance to racism and its brutally oppressive outcomes, and remain indifferent, if not hostile, to everything else in Gandhi. Such an argument is ignorant of Rustin's deep and unwavering commitment to nonviolence—and, rather more importantly, of his more expansive understanding of Gandhi. But the case of Rustin points to a puzzle that, after decades of Gandhi scholarship, is far from being resolved. Just how is it that Gandhi gathered around him, whether in person or from far afield, an extraordinarily large and disparate crowd of followers, disciples, and admirers? And what a motley crowd it was, including the daughter of an English admiral who gave up a life of privilege to come and clean latrines in Gandhi's ashrams; a Kashmiri Brahmin and his father, thoroughly anglicized in their fashion and habituated to an aristocratic lifestyle; a lumbering giant of a Pathan whom Gandhi would describe as the perfect exponent of satyagraha; a Tamil Christian economist who would go on to furnish the framework for Gandhian economics; a Gujarati Patidar lawyer who, as Sardar or the Iron Man, was honoured to be called Gandhi's right-hand man; and countless others from nearly every walk of life, speaking in myriad tongues, sometimes engaging in conduct that was anything but

---

[14] D'Emilio, *Lost Prophet*, 191–2, *passim*. See also Samantha Schmidt, 'Arrested for having sex with men, this gay civil rights crusader could finally be pardoned in California', *Washington Post* (21 January 2020), https://www.washingtonpost.com/history/2020/01/21/bayard-rustin-gay-pardon/; and Dylan Matthews, 'Meet Bayard Rustin, the gay socialist pacifist who planned the 1963 March on Washington', *Washington Post* (28 August 2013), https://www.washingtonp ost.com/news/wonk/wp/2013/08/28/meet-the-gay-socialist-pacifist-who-planned-the-1963-march-on-washington/ [both accessed 21 October 2021].

unimpeachable, often embracing worldviews wholly at odds with the subject of their affection and often reverence.[15]

The sociologists and political scientists of previous generations had a word for this phenomenon: charisma. I am tempted to say that that theory has, for a variety of reasons, run its course, but in any case few who knew Gandhi thought that he was possessed of charisma. Some who met him thought him rather ugly, but of course charisma was never only a theory based on physical appearance or 'looks'. As the late American political scientists Susanne and Lloyd Rudolph argued, the roots of Gandhi's charisma lay in his, as they saw it, uncanny ability to work Indian 'traditions' and speak in a voice which permitted villagers to claim him as one of their own.[16] That may explain, perhaps, why Gandhi was able to gain the following of the Indian masses, but it would not tell us why he was able to elicit the sympathy of thousands of Britons, the mill workers of Lancashire, and intellectuals and artists from around the world. Another school of thought holds that it was Gandhi's sincerity that was gripping to others, and this in turn took many forms. He never subjected anyone to a task that he did not first set for himself; he demanded nothing of others that he did not first demand of himself. I have often related one of my favourite anecdotes from his life, which I first encountered in a little booklet written by one of his closest associates, Kaka Kalelkar: it tells the story of a little boy whose grandmother was agitated by the fact that he ate too many sweets, and whom Gandhi counsels to give up sweets—but only after Gandhi had himself gone for a month without sweets. He made

[15] The daughter of the English admiral who gave up everything to join Bapu in India was Madeleine Slade, better known to the world as Mirabehn. See her *The Spirit's Pilgrimage* (New York: Coward-McCann, 1960). Readers will recognize the Kashmiri Pandit and his father as none other than the Nehrus, Jawaharlal and Motilal, and the Pathan leader who formed a nonviolent army of resistance, which he called Khudai Khidmatgars, was Badshah Khan, also known as Abdul Ghaffar Khan or by the moniker 'Frontier Gandhi'. There is a growing literature on Badshah Khan, but still charming and informative in equal measure is the early work by Eknath Easwaran, *Nonviolent Soldier of Islam: Badshah Khan, A Man to Match His Mountains*, 2nd ed. (Tomales, CA: Nilgiri Press, 1999 [1984]). Rajmohan Gandhi has written biographies of both Badshah Khan and Sardar Patel ('Iron Man of India'). The economist who produced critically important agricultural surveys for Gandhi and later worked with Mirabehn in the areas of forest conservation, ecological water management, and organic agriculture has received the scholarly attention of Mark Lindley, *J. C. Kumarappa, Mahatma Gandhi's Economist* (Mumbai: Popular Prakashan, 2007). A shorter assessment is available in Mark Lindley, 'Kumarappa: A Giant or a Midget?', *Economic and Political Weekly* 42, no. 21 (26 May 2007), 1975–81.
[16] Susanne Hoeber Rudolph and Lloyd I. Rudolph, *Gandhi: The Traditional Roots of Charisma* (Chicago: University of Chicago Press, 1983).

the Kantian ethical formula his own: 'So act as to treat humanity, whether in your own person or in another, always as an end, and never as only a means.'[17] I suspect that the founders of religion would have agreed with all this, but Gandhi was no founder of a religion—even if, at his death, printmakers and artists placed the martyred Gandhi, in one print after another, in the company of Jesus and Buddha.[18]

Perhaps it is Gandhi's inclusiveness, some have suggested, that endeared him to so many. His encounters and exchanges with Christian missionaries, which commenced in South Africa, are instructive. The Christian missionaries and preachers who came into contact with him might have thought at first of seeking to convert him but soon recognized that the attempt would be futile, not so much because Gandhi was a devout Hindu—that he was, having declared himself a believer in *sanatan dharma* and *varnasrama dharma*—but because he was a better Christian than any they had ever encountered. From pulpits across America, beginning with John Haynes Holmes's sermon at the Community Church of New York in 1921 where he pronounced Gandhi 'the greatest man in the world', the word went out that a new Christ had been incarnated in the East. 'When I think of [Romain] Rolland . . . I think of Tolstoi,' Holmes

---

[17] Immanuel Kant, *Groundwork of the Metaphysics of Morals*, trans. James W. Ellington, 3rd ed. (Indianapolis: Hackett Publishing Co., 1993), 36. I am grateful to the external reviewers for engaging with this paper thoughtfully. One expressed disagreement with my suggestion that Gandhi had made Kant's categorical imperative his own, noting that 'in Kant, the deontological axiom does not admit of any change and secondly his axiom has its origin in the Kantian view of human beings as primarily autonomous and rational. I don't think Gandhi would agree to this. To my mind his moral axiom comes from the Gita's notion of *nishkama karma* which he interprets as *anasakta karma*.' I cannot respond to this at great length, but a few succinct observations may be in order. I do not, of course, dispute the importance that *nishkama karma* held for Gandhi. But at the same time it must be admitted that the sources of Gandhi's actions and ethical thought were many, and even as he was perhaps partial to certain texts, Gandhi cared little for where ideas that he stood by came from. The Kantian categorical imperative is often expressed in this first formulation: 'Act only according to that maxim whereby you can at the same time will that it should become a universal law' (*Groundwork*, 30). This is a purely formal or logical statement, a moral maxim not subject to any dilution by contingencies; it could be applied to any rational being. The second formulation that I have invoked is not weaker as such, and indeed derives from the first; but, nevertheless, it speaks to the humanity of others, insisting that one has a duty not to instrumentalize either oneself or others in the pursuit of some end. I can't see Gandhi as disagreeing with the fundamental moral thrust of this formulation; if the Kantians think otherwise, Gandhi would scarcely have been bothered with the presumed authority of the philosopher.

[18] See Vinay Lal, *Insurgency and the Artist: The Art of the Freedom Struggle in India* (New Delhi: Roli Books, 2022), especially the concluding chapter; and Edwin Neumayer and Christine Schelberger, *Bharat Mata: India's Freedom Movement in Popular Art* (New Delhi: Oxford University Press, 2008). By 'print' I mean a nationalist print, or art work, generally an oleograph or chromolithograph.

had said, adding: 'When I think of Lenin, I think of Napoleon; But when I think of Gandhi, I think of Jesus Christ.'[19] Similarly, it is doubtless true that Gandhi never lacked English friends, and indeed the most distinctive aspect of the anti-colonial struggle that he waged was that he sought to liberate not only India from British rule but also the British from their own worst tendencies. Before the English colonized Indians, they colonized the Irish, the Scots, and the Welsh; and, acting on the notion that colonial violence is homologous to sexual violence, Gandhi almost took it as axiomatic that the English colonized their own womenfolk. What part Gandhi played in liberating the British, in awakening them to their excesses, and in attracting them to the freedom struggle in India is far from being fully explored.[20] A man who had the gumption to address Hitler, 'the Führer', as 'Dear Friend' was nothing if not inclusive. But something in this argument, too, rankles: talk of 'inclusiveness', much like talk of 'diversity', is self-consciously modern and also lends itself easily to the anodyne ways of corporate culture and the managerial elite. Dictators, war criminals, sexual profligates, corporate hawks, misogynists: all have had to undertake diversity training these days. The Roman historian Tacitus said they make war and call it peace: today they call it diversity.

Not everyone is, furthermore, sold on the idea of Gandhi's 'inclusiveness'. Indeed, there is these days a minor industry committed to establishing that a great many people did not fall within his moral orbit. Gandhi's South African years are taken as the most glaring exhibit of his bigotry and narrow-mindedness. The record indicates that for some years he referred to black people in derogatory terms, and Charles Di Salvo, in this volume, may be read as offering a rigorous indictment of Gandhi on this account. The chorus of voices denouncing him for racism has become louder in recent years, and the broken statues to which I have previously alluded suggest that some of his critics have taken to throwing

---

[19] The sermon can be accessed online: https://www.harvardsquarelibrary.org/biographies/mahatma-gandhi-who-is-the-greatest-man-in-the-world-today/ [accessed 22 October 2022].
[20] A beginning has been made in books such as Jeffrey Paine, *Father India: How Encounters with an Ancient Culture Transformed the Modern West* (New York: HarperCollins, 1998), 22–7 and 227–68, and Nico Slate, *Colored Cosmopolitanism: The Shared Struggle for Freedom in the United States* (Cambridge, MA: Harvard University Press, 2012). But we are still considerably removed from understanding how Gandhi—who had become an assemblage of ideas and images, far more than a name—impacted everyday social relations, and the conception of the self, in the United Kingdom and the West more broadly.

brickbats at him. Gandhi also, his critics argue, pointedly refused to invite them to join the struggle on the supposition that they would not have had any comprehension of the purpose, technique, or utility of nonviolence, though it is also on record that many black commentators, for instance in the United States, expressed a strong conviction that Gandhian nonviolence with its emphasis on fasting, purity, and asceticism would have no appeal for the African American population.[21] Nor is there any reason to believe that black South Africans expected or invited Gandhi to render the struggle he was waging on behalf of the rights of Indians in South Africa more inclusive. In the matter of class, Gandhi is thought to have subscribed to similarly retrograde views, though when the criticism comes from the left there is in their opprobrium at least a touch of the preposterous. The Indian communist parties, which historically have rarely shown any ability to think for themselves, content to take their marching orders from the communist parties in countries that have had what they call 'real' revolutions, were resolutely of the view that there was no room for the working class in Gandhi's thinking. His 'inclusiveness' only extended to the capitalists, whom he sought to save and legitimize, on this view, with his foggy theory of trusteeship. The Dalit grievances against Gandhi are extensive and would fill a catalogue, and the view persists among them that Gandhi was never able to accept them within his fold except on the most patronizing terms.[22]

Despite all this, we must persist with the question: what made Gandhi so singularly attractive to so many people? The ideas of *satya* (truth), *ahimsa* (nonviolence), *dharma* (conduct; duty), *aparigraha* (non-possession), *asteya* (non-stealing), *brahmacharya* (celibacy), and *sadhana* (discipline) were the bedrock of his being. While his grounding in these fundamental ideas is clear enough, they remain crucially open to interpretation—often in the most unexpected ways. Consider, for example, the idea of *asteya* or theft. Climate change activists, environmentalists, and others to whom ethical thinking is not foreign are rightly agitated that the world is being depleted of natural resources by crushing levels of consumption, and they have called attention to how future

---

[21] Vinay Lal, 'Gandhi, the 'Colored Races', and the Future of Satyagraha: The View from the African American Press', *Social Change* 51, no. 1 (2021), 51–69.

[22] For further discussion, see Vinay Lal, 'The Gandhi Everyone Loves to Hate', *Economic and Political Weekly* 43, no. 40 (4–10 October 2007), 55–64.

generations are being robbed of clean air, soil, water, indeed of the very possibility of life itself. But Gandhi, by the standards of most mortals of what it means to be human, appeared to have taken his understanding of theft to absurd levels. His parsimonious habits of eating are put down to his rigid adherence to a disciplined life, but to him the inability to control one's palate signified more than indiscipline; if one ate, or indeed used anything at all, strictly beyond one's bare needs, one was committing theft. 'We should be ashamed of resting or having a square meal', he wrote in 1921, 'so long as there is one able-bodied man or woman without work or food',[23] but there are scores of such passages found in his writings over several decades, many expressing his apprehensions in much sterner language. His letter to Maganlal Gandhi, later the Manager at Sabarmati Ashram, is clear enough even if in some circumstances one may find cause for differing interpretations: 'If I need only one shirt to cover myself with, but use two, I am guilty of stealing one from another. For a shirt which could have been of use to someone ese does not belong to me. If five bananas are enough to keep me going, my eating a sixth one is a form of theft.'[24]

Thus, Gandhi's oft-stated ambition to reduce himself to zero and gradually strip himself down to such clothing as was necessary to cover himself with a modicum of modesty was inspired not only by the desire to attain a state of emptiness, all the more so that he might become a receptacle for God's love, but also by the thought that it would be criminal for him to have on him clothing beyond what the poorest Indians could afford. His friends and fellow ashram dwellers have left behind a mound of stories testifying to his—as it first seemed to others—punishing outlook on consumption and his obsessive insistence on maximizing the use of every object. There is a story that is told of ashram dwellers searching on their hands and knees for a pencil stub that was barely 2 inches long, and another story of Gandhi sending his adolescent grandniece, Manu, through a dense forest on a several-hour long journey to recover a rough

[23] M. K. Gandhi, 'Notes', *Young India*, 6 October 1921, in *CWMG* 24: 364; also online at http://www.gandhiashramsevagram.org/gandhi-literature/mahatma-gandhi-collected-works-volume-24.pdf [accessed 21 October 2021].

[24] M. K. Gandhi, 'Letter to Maganlal Gandhi', sometime after 14 March 1915, in *CWMG* 14: 383–5 at 384, also online at http://www.gandhiashramsevagram.org/gandhi-literature/mahatma-gandhi-collected-works-volume-14.pdf [accessed 21 October 2021].

stone with which he cleaned his feet and which Manu had apparently for-gotten at the previous stop during his tour of riot-torn Noakhali.[25]

If the principal ideas that informed Gandhi's thinking lend themselves to varying interpretations, he remains elusive in other respects: just when one thinks one has begun to get a grasp on him and take the measure of the man, he startles and surprises. I would venture to suggest that Gandhi was, to borrow the language of the American philosopher of religion James Carse, a player of infinite games. Carse has written that 'there are at least two kinds of games. One could be called finite, the other infinite. A finite game is played for the purpose of winning, an infinite game for the purpose of continuing the play.'[26] The American attitude towards sports, which has been nearly universalized to all sports, although the test form of cricket still shows some signs of obduracy, best exemplifies the notion of 'finite games'. No American sport can be played without a decisive finish: if, at the end of regulation time, the game is drawn, it must go into overtime, and if necessary into further overtime so that an un-disputed winner can emerge. Though the protocols of supposed sports-manship require an acknowledgement of the heroic efforts of the loser, the culture of American sports is even more insistent that there be clear winners and losers. Nothing is as dreadful as ambiguity: the evil is out there, and one must be either for Osama bin Laden or against him, just as one cannot be both for and against America. I cannot here elaborate on the increasing loss of ambiguity under conditions of modernity, but it is necessary to add that there are cognate terms or what Wittgenstein called family resemblances for ambiguity: thus one can also think of states of in-betweenness, liminality, and so on.

The subject matter of finite and infinite games, needless to say, is far more than sports. Indeed, Carse is least interested in sports as such, and eschews—whether wisely or not can be debated—the example with which I have sought to illustrate the tenor of his argument. For instance, nearly all of 'education' is a finite game; there are a number of smaller

---

[25] See, for example, Kaka Kalelkar, *Stray Glimpses of Bapu*, 2nd rev. ed. (Ahmedabad: Navajivan Publishing House, 1960), but a more complete insider's view is found in the massive four-volume biography by Narayan Desai, *My Life is My Message*, trans. Tridip Suhrud (New Delhi: Orient BlackSwan, 2009), and *The Diary of Manu Gandhi, 1943–44*, trans. and ed. Tridip Suhrud (New Delhi: Oxford University Press, 2019).
[26] James P. Carse, *Finite and Infinite Games: A Vision of Life as Play and Possibility* (New York: Free Press, 1986).

finite games within its boundaries. We commence playing these games from childhood, with a graded hierarchy of schools, and this continues through secondary schooling, college, higher education, and professional schools: at every step, there are games—winners advance, gain accolades and titles, while losers drop out and must settle for the crumbs. Within higher education, there are tiers of schools, and within each tier further demarcations arise as title holders—'Distinguished Professor', Nobel Laureate, Infosys Prize winner, Field Medal winner—begin to outstrip the pack of lecturers, senior lecturers, assistant professors, and so on. 'It is not uncommon for families', Carse notes, 'to think of themselves as a competitive unit in a broader finite game for which they are training their members in the struggle for societally visible titles.' Yet a finite game is far more than an exemplification of the 'competitive spirit', since finite players, which is nearly all of us, inhabit the world in a certain way. Finite players may rearrange the elements, as in a picture frame, but they still play within the boundaries; infinite players, by contrast, play with boundaries. The very idea of 'society' is a finite game, it may be argued, though that would lead most leaders to conclude that Carse, in vindicating infinite players, is only offering approbation to those who become outsiders—renunciates, most prominently perhaps, or those who entirely opt out of the 'rat race'. The player of infinite games, in fact, does not seek to stop the play, or to opt out of the play, or reposition himself within the assigned rules of the game, but rather to continue the play and play in such a fashion that the game continues and has no discernible end.

In characterizing Gandhi as a player of infinite games, we may turn to any domain of his life or thinking, be it politics, sexuality, or religion, or—to take only a few subjects—his ideas of history, the nation state, rights and duties, and so on. Donald J. Trump, to take the most obvious example, knows no language other than that of winners and losers. He derives his manliness, his very identity, from being, or imagining himself as, a winner; there is nothing as 'pathetic', in his worldview, as a 'loser'. But he is only the most vulgar instantiation of 'normal politics', rather than, as many would like to believe, an exception to the world of civilized politics with its tolerable levels of compromise, deceit, and the jockeying for power. Uday Mehta in this volume has offered a perceptive analysis of Gandhi's blunt disavowal of normal politics, and here I seek only to explain what he means in somewhat different language. The Engler brothers, Mark and Paul, have introduced Gandhi's ideas to the wider American public, and they are committed advocates of the idea that the time for organized and principled nonviolent resistance is in the here and now, but it appears to me that there is something seriously amiss in their piece 'How did Gandhi win?', which is on the transformative impact of the Salt March.[27] Nowhere in the vast corpus of Gandhi's writings do we find any reference to 'winners' and 'losers', though of course this is the least of the ways in which we may understand his thoroughgoing critique of political rationality, his instinctive dislike of the jejune language of 'winning' and 'losing', and his complete disavowal of zero-sum politics. Gandhi had little use even for the language of 'victory' and 'defeat': we cannot say that he would necessarily have agreed with Nietzsche's insight that 'human nature finds it harder to endure a victory than a defeat; indeed, it seems to be easier to achieve a victory than to endure it in such a way that it does not in fact turn into a defeat',[28] but he certainly had intimations of the idea that victory is more catastrophic for the victor than it is for the defeated. It is, in any case, of signal importance that *the notion of satyagraha altogether abdicates normal politics* and its notions of political rationality, which is precisely why liberals, constitutionalists, communists, Ambedkarites, Hindu nationalists, and others belonging to well-known political constituencies have not merely been uncomfortable with Gandhi's worldview but at various times thought it fit to dismiss Gandhi as a crank and as someone whose time was long up.

The literature of the official British and European encounter with Gandhi, commencing in South Africa and concluding with the negotiations that would lead to the bifurcation of India, is rife with examples of colonial officials who simply could not comprehend the nature of Gandhi's politics. What was one to do with a man whose notion of chivalry entailed that one was not to take advantage of the 'enemy' (not that this word was part of Gandhi's lexicon), and that if the opposition was weakened owing to some extraneous factor, the action against the opposition was to be called off? Gandhi represented a form of opposition that

---

[27] Mark and Paul Engler, 'How did Gandhi win?', *Open Democracy* (14 October 2014), https://www.opendemocracy.net/en/transformation/how-did-gandhi-win/ [accessed 22 October 2022].

[28] Friedrich Nietzsche, *Untimely Meditations*, Cambridge Texts in the History of Philosophy, ed. Daniel Breazeale and trans. R. J. Hollingdale (Cambridge: Cambridge University Press, 1997), 3.

was inconceivable to those steeped in constitutional and conventional revolutionary politics alike. When Gandhi left South Africa, his principal adversary, General Jan Christian Smuts, remarked in a letter to a friend, 'the saint has left our shores – I sincerely hope for ever'.[29] I suspect that Smuts had had enough of Gandhi: had he been a dissenter or rebel of the usual sort, petitioning higher authorities, wielding a gun, sabotaging government properties, shouting platitudes about 'justice, liberty, and equality', or pronouncing the readiness of the 'coloured' man to assume the responsibilities of living according to democratic norms, Smuts would have known what to do with him.

It wasn't only the British or Europeans who found Gandhi unfathomable. His fellow Indians were baffled by his political choices and privately many declaimed against his idiosyncrasies. They could not make much sense of his frequent decisions to forgo hard-won political advantages. Nearly everyone, including his closest admirers and colleagues in the Congress, fumed at his decision to call off the non-cooperation movement in March 1922, at a time when the colonial state seemed to be on the back foot and British administration in parts of north India appeared to be paralysed, merely because a mob had killed twenty-three Indian policemen.[30] Many thought that he had returned from the Second Round Table Conference in 1931 empty-handed: despite all the international brouhaha over the Salt March, this was a pyrrhic victory. There is a near consensus, to which his most ardent admirers are equally a party, that on at least a few occasions he displayed poor if not disastrous political judgment. They admit that such occasions provide evidence of his deleterious influence on the course of Indian politics, even if, as his admirers insist, he may have been well-intentioned. His support of the Khilafat Movement, for which Gandhi stands condemned by everyone, is unquestionably one of the most notable cases in point. It is supposed that Gandhi argued for the restoration of the caliphate in the hope that he could extract from Indian Muslim leaders their support for a ban on cow-slaughter.

[29] Ramachandra Guha, *Gandhi before India* (New York: Alfred A. Knopf, 2014), 529.

[30] Shahid Amin, *Event, Metaphor, Memory: Chauri Chaura, 1922–1992* (Delhi: Oxford University Press, 1995), remains the best book on the incident and on the ways in which the name of Chauri Chaura has resonated in India. See also my 'Chauri Chaura and the Destiny of India', *ABP Live* (5 February 2022), https://news.abplive.com/blog/chauri-chaura-and-the-destiny-of-india-mahatma-gandhi-100-years-of-chauri-chaura-1511039.

This is a wholly erroneous argument, for which there is not the slightest shred of evidence, and one, more importantly, that is wholly contrary to everything that Gandhi understood as an ethical politics. He would have deplored this form of quid pro quo as 'normal politics' and one that militated against his conception of the gift. In a similar vein, his advocacy of Hindu–Muslim unity cannot be reduced to a cold calculation on his part that it was bound to lead to more fruitful forms of anti-colonial resistance or traduce the British for perpetuating the lie that they were indispensable to keeping the peace between adherents of different faiths. The question of 'Hindu–Muslim unity', whatever the intellectual problems with its framing, was for Gandhi intrinsic to the notion of selfhood in India. I would go so far as to say, at the risk of sounding like a heretic in modern-day India with its politics of xenophobia and virulent forms of majoritarianism, that for Gandhi the Hindu was incomplete without the Muslim just as the Muslim was incomplete without the Hindu. But none of this has ever been comprehensible to those who live and swear by 'normal politics'.

Gandhi's general disinclination towards conversion, which is not often discussed, may be—and has been—adduced as evidence of his Hindu chauvinism and may appear to controvert my claim that he strikes a wholly anomalous figure on the Indian scene. His dislike of the very idea of conversion stemmed not even remotely from any feeling of superiority he might have harboured about his Hindu faith: his assassin, we should take pains to remember, held Gandhi responsible for betraying the Hindu community. There is nothing in common between Gandhi and the advocates of Hindutva in their mutual opposition to conversion. The opposition of Hindu nationalists arises from apprehensions about the rise of Christianity and Islam, objections to economic inducements offered to potential converts, the real or imagined threats to Hinduism, the frequently unsavoury history of proselytization, and other such considerations. Conversion in India, which has become exceedingly difficult in some Indian states where anti-conversion legislation has been passed in recent years, arouses immense controversy and often invites abuse, since under the present political dispensation the view is that India is for the first time on course to repudiate 1,200 years of slavery. There has in any case been little time of the day given to Gandhi, and, in the matter of conversion, the nuances of his thought are invisible or, if at all apprehended, dismissed as charlatanism. Gandhi took the rather unusual position that the person who converts almost invariably does so from a poor comprehension of his or her faith, and therefore from a mistaken conception of the comparatively fecund possibilities of the other faith: every faith, he took the view, is fully endowed with the pharmacopeia for leading the ethical life, howsoever that may be conceived. But there were circumstances under which the idea of conversion could be countenanced—when, for instance, 'one changed one's religion with deliberate knowledge and in a sincere spirit in order to cultivate more detachment and attain God sooner',[31] and never more so than when the decision passed the litmus test of the conscience. Gandhi could not be opposed to conversion in toto, recognizing as he did the sovereignty of the individual as a morally autonomous being.[32] It is also important to recognize that, as in some other matters, Gandhi's views on conversion evolved: those seeking consistency in his views might recall his injunction to the reader in 1933 that

> in my search after Truth I have discarded many ideas and learnt many new things. . . . What I am concerned with is my readiness to obey the call of Truth, my god, from moment to moment, and therefore, when anybody finds any inconsistency between any two writings of mine, if he still has faith in my sanity, he would do well to choose the later of the two on the same subject.[33]

Thus, if in a discussion with C. F. Andrews in 1926 he averred that 'proselytization will mean no peace in the world', six years later we find him apparently allowing for the possibility that a person may want to give up their faith, especially if they should think of their religion as 'false': 'Regarding conversion, I don't mean that it is never justified'.[34]

---

[31] M. K. Gandhi, letter to Kantilal Gandhi, 1 December 1936; in *CWMG* 70: 136–8 at 137, also online at http://www.gandhiashramsevagram.org/gandhi-literature/mahatma-gandhi-collected-works-volume-70.pdf.

[32] The literature on Gandhi's thoughts on conversion is slim, and even books focused on his views on religion, for instance studies by J. T. F. Jordens and Kathryn Tidrick, are silent on the subject. For further elaboration, see Vinay Lal, 'Gandhi's Religion: Politics, Faith, and Hermeneutics', *Journal of Sociology and Social Anthropology* 4, nos. 1–2 (2013), 31–40.

[33] M. K. Gandhi, 'Inconsistencies?', *Harijan*, 29 April 1933; in *CWMG* 61: 22–4 at 24, also online at http://www.gandhiashramsevagram.org/gandhi-literature/mahatma-gandhi-collected-works-volume-61.pdf.

[34] M. K. Gandhi, 'Discussion with C. F. Andrews', *Harijan* (28 November 1926), 70: 58–60 at 60, also online at http://www.gandhiashramsevagram.org/gandhi-literature/mahatma-gandhi-collected-works-volume-70.pdf; Letter to Premabehn Kantak, 22 April 1932,

The 'litmus test of conscience' is no easy phrase and itself sets a high bar. Gandhi's reverence for Tulsidas's *Ramacaritmanas* did not blind him to passages—most notoriously, *dhol ganwar shudra pashu naari, sakal taadana ke Adhikari,* 'Drums, the illiterate, Shudras, animals, and women are all deserving of a beating'—within it which he thought highly objectionable and which, whatever their origin and whatever the conflicting interpretations to which they may have been subjected, had been deployed to suppress women. If one's conscience rebelled against such palpable misogyny, then the offensive passage perforce had to be discarded. Gandhi was similarly unimpressed by arguments about the infallibility of the Quran and the hadiths and famously refused to concede the ground to Maulvis who during a debate with him in the 1920s insisted that stoning to death was part of the sunnah. In this matter his views may not seem altogether distinct, having something in common with the worldview of the enlightened liberal, but the exceptionality derived from the larger position he staked on the contentious question of secularism suggests the very awkward difficulties of reading him mainly through the registers of liberalism. While Gandhi unquestionably shared with avowed secularists such as Nehru (who had no appetite for public displays of religiosity) and Jinnah (who made a show of being a Muslim in public but was as good a non-believer as any) the view that the state had no business in transacting religion, he derived his secularism from his practices as a devout Hindu. He would have fully understood how Maulana Azad, similarly, could be wedded to the creed of the secularist precisely because he was an observant Muslim. Where is the risk, or should we call it play, except in being a secularist who is at the same time devoutly 'religious'?

Turning back to Bayard Rustin, and to the motley crowd of Gandhi's followers, admirers, and devotees, I have long thought that Gandhi's attractiveness to others, some of it doubtless for reasons that I have adumbrated, arises from the tacit awareness that he was a player of infinite games. There are elements of the common narrative that I have not touched upon, such as the whiff of saintliness that hangs around Gandhi, for instance among peaceniks and many social workers. But, for reasons that should be amply clear, there are an equally large number of people who would be outraged at any rendering of Gandhi as a saint. It was possible to be a saint in the time of Francis of Assisi and Teresa of Ávila, or Jnaneshvar and Guru Nanak, but saintliness has become obsolete under our regimes of scrutiny, surveillance, and savage scurrilousness. Gandhi at least passes muster as a player of infinite games, besides the fact that he would have been the first person to be relieved of the burden of being a saint. Though his followers themselves were nearly all players of finite games, at least a few of them saw in Gandhi the vision of life as play and possibility. It is my hope that readers will encounter the essays in this book as aids in the pursuit of that vision.

1

The Topography of Nonviolence

Faisal Devji

Seen as the father of his nation, Gandhi remains a territorial icon located firmly within the boundaries of India. We all recognize that he was also an imperial and international figure in politics, even one of the first global celebrities of newsreel film. But this role tends to be understood as incidental to the Mahatma's real achievement, which was the founding of a nation state. Gandhi not only conceived of his own struggle as potentially global in scope but also was not particularly interested in the state and even critical of its modern form. He understood that India's freedom could not be won without engaging with the world in which it was placed, one whose reality was defined largely in maritime terms.

The British Empire, after all, was a maritime power, and India's role within it was defined by the sea as much as it was by land. For India was not simply the object of imperial desire in its own right, but a base from which to provision territories overseas with labour and raw materials, as well as to secure them by the cheap and easy dispatch of troops. From the Arabian to the Caribbean Sea, and from the Indian Ocean to the Pacific, Indian manpower and natural resources held the empire together. Gandhi realized, therefore, that colonialism would have to be fought on land and sea if it was to be truly defeated, and I want in this chapter to describe how he conceptualized the relations between these two arenas.

Like the international order that succeeded it, imperialism entailed a specific relationship of land to sea, the former representing the realm of legal and social particularity and the latter of a boundless universality. In economic terms, this relationship was defined as that between protectionism and free trade. Laissez-faire had been the ideological form that Britain's naval supremacy took, while controls and restrictions of various kinds were upheld as the realm of domestic sovereignty. Similarly, the

Faisal Devji, *The Topography of Nonviolence* In: *Gandhi, Truth, and Nonviolence*. Edited by: Vinay Lal, Oxford University Press. © Oxford University Press 2025. DOI: 10.1093/9780198936657.003.0002 universality of international law held sway over the seas, in contrast to the sovereign particularity of the territorial state. This difference is what allowed Indians to be treated as equals in Britain but unequally at home.

Indian nationalists were divided about this dual character of the imperial and later international order, demarcated is it was by the relationship of sea to land. They tended either to want a laissez-faire universalism in which India and England were equals, or a protectionism which retained the former's distinctiveness in a positive rather than negative way. Nehru, for instance, spoke in *The Discovery of India* about the 'two Englands', one the land of liberty and John Stuart Mill, and the other an oppressive colonial power.[1] He wanted England to remain true to its better self, but Gandhi understood that the two Englands were in fact one and the same, each made possible by the other, just like the particular and universal.

The Mahatma called the universal claims of capital and law 'modern civilization', which he thought destroyed even the particularities it was meant to preserve in forms like sexual or racial difference. While Britain, Europe, or the West might think of themselves as the originators of this civilization, in other words, they could not, he argued, hold possession of it for very long, soon being reduced to particularities and exploited in their own right. By pointing out the risks involved in such a dualistic conception of imperial order, Gandhi recognized its fundamental weakness. His German contemporary the jurist Carl Schmitt elaborated the problem this caused precisely by considering the relationship of land and sea.[2]

Britain's world empire was scattered across the surface of the earth, lacking any spatial integrity. Its amplitude could not be grasped except by attending to the smallest land and water bridges that linked one portion of the empire to another. This is why the British were fixated with the security of otherwise minor bodies of water, from the English Channel and the Suez Canal to the Straits of Gibraltar, Hormuz, and Malacca. Many of these maritime locations, including bases and coaling stations like Aden, Singapore, and Hong Kong, remain crucial to global politics and

---

[1] Jawaharlal Nehru, *The Discovery of India* (New Delhi: Jawaharlal Nehru Memorial Fund, 1999), 284–8.
[2] See Carl Schmitt, *Land and Sea: A World-Historical Meditation*, trans. Samuel Garrett Zeitlin (New York: Telos Press, 2015).

capitalism into our own day, but for Schmitt they served as illustrations of the British Empire's lack of territorial integrity and inability to manage its own plenitude in any spatially coherent way.

Not only was the empire's amorphous universality represented by the sea; for Schmitt it was also put into practice there in the form of humanitarianism. British imperialism, he maintained, expressed its universal claims in the language of what we might today call humanitarian intervention, whose exemplary manifestation came to be the abolition of slavery. As part of a humanitarian imperative, the Royal Navy could break all legal conventions by boarding and impounding even foreign vessels on the high seas that were suspected of carrying slave cargo. Linked to this practice, and with us to this day, was the navy's use of sanctions and blockades, again for ostensibly humanitarian reasons. Clearly, these forms were only possible across maritime rather than territorial borders.

Humanitarianism, of course, was crucial in the legitimization of empire because it took precedence over popular consent and political representation. Conceptualized as a gift to colonized subjects who might not even be able to appreciate it, the humanitarian understanding of imperialism dispensed with their agreement even as it sought to save some categories of people like women, children, and minorities from others. If the empire's universality was made possible by the sea, then, it was given subjective shape in the figure of humanity. In other words, humanitarianism, like free trade and international law, permitted the British Empire to elaborate a universal mission in maritime terms, and at the same time to tolerate or protect exceptions to its logic in territorial ones.

The British Empire worked by establishing a distinctive relationship between land and sea, one that possessed economic, juridical, and ethical dimensions. In order to win India's freedom, therefore, the Mahatma had to break this relationship, and I want here to describe the way in which he did this. Gandhi struggled to understand and dismantle the relation of land and sea throughout his career, and I want to focus in particular on how he thought about it by way of three sea voyages he made. These were his journey as a student to London in 1888, as a lawyer to South Africa in 1893, and as a nonviolent preacher returning to India in 1914. But I shall begin with the sea's curious absence from Gandhi's account of his childhood in the port city of Porbandar and later in the inland city of Rajkot that was also intimately connected to seaborne trade.

A Lost World

Gandhi's native Gujarat was famous for the important role it had always played in India's seaborne trade, and he was himself born and brought up in one of its most famous ports. But Gujarat was not only part of the Bombay Presidency but also divided between patches of British territory and hundreds of princely states, thus like a miniaturized version of the British Empire lacking any geographical or administrative integrity of its own. This absence of territorial fixity meant that its links with the Arabian and African settlements where Gujaratis lived were as important in defining the region as the towns and villages from which they hailed. And it was this absence of territorial integrity that would eventually allow Gandhi to abandon India for a lawyer's position in South Africa when he couldn't succeed in Bombay. For Durban and Johannesburg were, like Bombay, more intimate to Gujarati commerce and memory than other parts of India. Yet never once in the many pages dedicated to his years in Porbandar and Rajkot does the future Mahatma even mention the sea, to say nothing about Gujarat's economic dependence on it.

The only sense we get of this maritime world is when Gandhi describes his father discussing religious and philosophical matters with the Hindu, Muslim, Parsi, and Jain friends who represented the region's mercantile history. It is almost as if Gujarat's dispersed geography was mirrored in such fragmentary examples of an unthought and barely visible oceanic universe. And this was perhaps because it was a universe that had been occluded by a colonial vision of the sea and its relationship with the land. Indeed, the cosmopolitanism of overseas Indian trade had been reduced to a defensive fixation on maintaining caste rules and restrictions. As with the Indian Mutiny of 1857, which sought to uphold caste and community distinctions that the British were seen as wanting to eradicate, the hierarchical cosmopolitanism of native society had been narrowed down to interdictions regarding food and sex.

The mutineers had feared what they saw as British attempts to interfere with their sexual and dietary laws. These included conversions to Christianity, miscegenation, and, famously, breaking the caste and religious identities of Hindus and Muslims by having them bite bullet cartridges thought to have been greased with cow and pig fat. They imagined that such practices would destroy their plurality and turn Indians into undifferentiated slaves of the British, without any identities and therefore sovereignty of their own. The Mutiny, in other words, brought upper-caste Hindus and Muslims together in a partnership of equals for the first time, in order to prevent rather than encourage their subordination to a single identity, which they could only understand as a servile one.

The Mutiny's defence of India's plurality still possessed a political form and mode of thinking, as embodied by the last Mughal emperor and the precolonial order of Mahratta supremacy that he represented. But following its crushing defeat, even the memory of such an order was smashed, with the social regulations of endogamy and commensality serving as the depoliticized vestiges of this past. Food and sex, in other words, had become the last remnants of an unequal yet cosmopolitan world, one that could be glimpsed only as a set of irrational particularities within the universal mission of imperialism. The same was true for Gandhi, too, whose understanding of Gujarati society was defined by interdictions around bodily pleasure as much as transgression.

From his childhood in Porbandar and Rajkot to his student days in London, Gandhi grappled with the twin interdictions of food and sex, which should not simply be seen as a peculiarly traditional inheritance. For Gandhi well understood that they were among the last defences against the wholesale naturalization of colonial universality in the form of 'modern civilization'. He was first tempted to abandon these restrictions by a friend whom he doesn't name, but who we know was Sheikh Mehtab, whose reasoning, like that of many Indian reformers, had to do with emulating the habits of Englishmen in order to become their equals if not superiors. In his autobiography, Gandhi quotes doggerel by the poet Narmad to this effect:

> Behold the mighty Englishman
> He rules the Indian small,
> Because being a meat-eater
> He is five cubits tall.[3]

---

[3] M. K. Gandhi, *An Autobiography or the Story of my Experiments with Truth*, trans. Mahadev Desai (Ahmedabad: Navajivan Publishing House, 2009), 18.

Mehtab himself, Gandhi tells us, was an object of envy for his fearlessness and physical strength, but rather than attributing these qualities to some native if nevertheless spurious source like Islam, he understood them only in colonial terms as the results of imitating the British. In doing so, Mehtab provided the perfect illustration of the workings of imperialism, because he was unable to understand the relations between different kinds of Indians without their mediation by colonialism. Unlike the Mutiny, whose sepoys could conceive a partnership between Hindus and Muslims against the British, Sheikh Mehtab, like many other Indians, was unable to visualize such a relationship because it had been rendered impossible by colonial rule.

As an adult, Gandhi would theorize this voiding of relations between Indians belonging to different castes and communities as an aspect of Britain's policy of 'divide and rule'. But rather than seeing it as a deliberate strategy, he understood this process as the logical corollary of imperialism construed as a specific relationship between the universal and the particular. For its seaborne universality invested the colonial state with the liberal attributes of neutrality and therefore fairness as a rational third party there to adjudicate between territorial Indian interests consigned by their passion, prejudice, and partiality to the realm of pure particularity. In this sense the colonial and liberal states were the same, and the former even the latter's truest form in representing neutrality far better than it.

The Mahatma would argue later in his career that freedom meant, among other things, reconstituting the social relations among Indians by refusing their mediation and so effective voiding by the state. For any state that functioned according to the relationship of universal and particular would remain a fundamentally imperial institution, one that depended on robbing its subjects of their agency and reducing them to particularities unable to enter into any relationship with one another apart from itself. But since the state was unable to mediate every relationship all the time, it reduced the units of Indian society to relations of permanent enmity, whose violence required constant recourse to the police and courts and so strengthened them more and more.

Sheikh Mehtab induced Gandhi to break the dietary rules of his religion by eating meat as a kind of anti-colonial duty rather than pleasure. He also tried to break sexual taboos by taking Gandhi to a house of prostitution, but there his friend's shyness overcame the pleasure he was meant to enjoy and prevented any lapse into sin. Yet these transgressions tormented Gandhi into adulthood, and his dealings with them tell us how the Mahatma understood imperialism as a relation of sea to land and universal to particular. Gandhi, after all, was forbidden to embark on the voyage to London by the elders of his caste, who feared crossing the waters not for any metaphysical reason but because he would be unable to maintain his dietary as well as sexual restrictions, and therefore Hindu identity, there.

Hinduism had not yet been reshaped as a Protestant religion for these men and resided not in inner belief so much as outer practice, with the head of the caste telling Gandhi that '[i]n the opinion of the caste, your proposal to go to England is not proper. Our religion forbids voyages abroad. We have also heard that it is not possible to live there without compromising our religion. One is obliged to eat and drink with Europeans!'[4] Having refused to obey his caste leaders, Gandhi was duly cast out by them, but nevertheless continued to observe Hinduism's sexual and dietary rules even as the latter were immediately put into question on his journey out. Afraid of accidentally eating something forbidden, and embarrassed by his table manners and painful shyness, Gandhi ate the food he had brought on board in his cabin. He also followed custom in asking English passengers to provide him with certificates attesting to his vegetarianism, until he found out that these were to be had for a price even for those who had not observed any dietary restrictions.

The arguments against vegetarianism as a religious practice were all universalistic in character. Not only were Hindu and for that matter Muslim dietary restrictions understood as irrationally territorial particularisms by those speaking on behalf of 'modern civilization', but animal protein was seen as essential in colder climes and sometimes even medically required. Initially, Gandhi's justification for refusing to give in to such universalistic reasoning had to do with the promises to abstain from meat that he had made to his mother. Instead of confirming his loyalty to a religion defined as the very instantiation of particularism, in other words, Gandhi undercut the rationale of universalism by referring

---

[4] Gandhi, *Autobiography*, 34.

to a purely moral commitment that could be defined in neither one way
nor the other.

Sex, Food, and Humanity

In London, Gandhi joined a vegetarian society and started thinking
about his food habits in more scientific ways. But he never made of them
simply an alternative form of universal reasoning and in fact expanded
his conception of moral duty precisely to undo the relationship of particular and universal, land and sea, that defined both imperialism and
'modern civilization' more generally. Diet, therefore, became a site of
moral rather than merely cultural difference, its restrictions illustrating,
just as in the Mutiny, the Indian subject's sovereign agency, not his un-
thinking obedience to some archaic superstition:

> For me the question of diet was not one to be determined on the au-
> thority of the Shastras. It was one interwoven with my course of life
> which is guided by principles no longer depending upon outside au-
> thority. I had no desire to live at the cost of them.[5]

As we know, the Mahatma would go much beyond vegetarianism to
experiment with different kinds of dietary restriction, including the fasts
for which he became famous, and which re-politicized eating for the
first time since the Mutiny's response to cartridges greased with animal
fat. But if he broke food's links with Indian particularity and so political passivity by invoking duty, Gandhi approached sex by referring to
providence. Of the four instances of illicit sexual temptation Gandhi describes in his autobiography, at least two are associated with the sea as a
boundless site of promiscuous mixing. Here is his description of one such
encounter:

> During the last year, as far as I can remember, of my stay in England, that
> is in 1890, there was a Vegetarian Conference at Portsmouth to which
> an Indian friend and I were invited. Portsmouth is a sea-port with a

---

[5] Gandhi, *Autobiography*, 376.

large naval population. It has many houses with women of ill fame, women who are not actually prostitutes, but at the same time not very scrupulous about their morals. . . . We returned from the Conference in the evening. After dinner we sat down to play a rubber of bridge, in which our landlady joined, as is customary in England even in respectable households. Every player indulges in innocent jokes as a matter of course, but here my companion and our hostess began to make indecent ones as well. I did not know that my friend was an adept in the art. It captured me and I also joined in. Just when I was about to go beyond the limit, leaving the cards and the game to themselves, God through the good companion uttered the blessed warning: 'Whence this devil in you, my boy? Be off, quick!' I was ashamed. I took the warning, and expressed within myself gratefulness to my friend. Remembering the vow I had taken before my mother, I fled from the scene. To my room I went quaking, trembling, and with a beating heart, like a quarry escaped from its pursuer.[6]

As with his justification of dietary restrictions, Gandhi refers to vows given his mother when describing sexual temptation here. But unlike his firm refusal to compromise on the question of food, Gandhi is adamant that he was saved from sexual degradation not by his own will but by that of God. Already in his first encounter with a prostitute, to whom Sheikh Mehtab had taken him in Gujarat, the young Gandhi was saved by what he then despised as his shyness, only to realize much later that it was in fact a sign of divine providence:

I sat near the woman on her bed, but I was tongue-tied. She naturally lost patience with me, and showed me the door, with abuses and insults. I then felt as though my manhood had been injured, and wished to sink into the ground for shame. But I have ever since given thanks to God for having saved me. I can recall four more similar incidents in my life, and in most of them my good fortune, rather than any effort on my part, saved me.[7]

---

[6] Gandhi, *Autobiography*, 60.
[7] Gandhi, *Autobiography*, 20.

Important about providence was the fact that it was unwilled and so constructed the moral self differently from the way duty did. And for Gandhi providence was crucial because it presented a limit to the kind of moral calculus that sought to draw all action into a framework of prediction and control. As a reader of the *Bhagavad Gita*, of course, Gandhi was set against this highly instrumental way of understanding moral action, since that text famously counselled doing one's duty without any consideration of its result. By conceptualizing moral action as a sacrifice without recompense, the *Gita* sought to free it from the law of karma's endless cycle of cause and effect.

Gandhi, however, was also interested in how, by disdaining its result, action left the future open by preserving many moral ends rather than simply one in a zero-sum game. He understood that even if moral action achieved its desired result, it was unable to predict or control the consequences that followed. This was why he refused to sacrifice means for ends: not only because of the violence it entailed but also because ends could never truly be determined in advance. By leaving such ends aside, then, moral action and duty welcomed and made providence possible in the form of the incalculable, which Gandhi frequently described as the incarnation of Vishnu on earth. And it was precisely the incalculable that came to Gandhi's aid when he was about to succumb to sexual temptation.

Now the sharing of food and sex, along with communication, are also the conventional markers of human as much as political solidarity. Yet Gandhi realized that language or reason, which constitutes one of the classic definitions of humanity, is notoriously unreliable in creating solidarity because it is unequally distributed and recognized. Meanwhile, sexual and commensal relations are as likely to promote violence as its opposite. He was also suspicious of such biological conceptions of humanity, which simply expanded racist and other forms of exclusionary reasoning to the whole of mankind. Unsurprisingly, the Mahatma was more interested in moral definitions of humanity, especially those that repudiated any vision of its undifferentiated universality.

In his 1909 manifesto, *Hind Swaraj or Indian Home Rule*, written aboard the *Kildonan Castle* as she sailed from England to South Africa, Gandhi argued, 'I am so constructed that I can only serve my immediate neighbours, but in my conceit I pretend to have discovered that I must with my body serve every individual in the Universe. In thus attempting the impossible, man comes in contact with different natures, different religions, and is utterly confounded.'[8] Appearing in a chapter on railways and the hubris of world mastery they, like all technology, created, Gandhi's refusal of humanitarianism's universal mission was clearly directed at the role it played in imperialism. But it also pointed to the way in which such universalization made social particularity a problem.

Schmitt had argued that by making humanity the object of its politics, the British Empire eventually ended up dealing with its enemies by dehumanizing them. As a political ideology, in other words, humanitarianism led to the exclusion and even annihilation of some of its members, something that was by no means unfamiliar under colonial rule. And it is from here that Gandhi's worry about the humanitarian being 'confounded' by social difference understood as a territorial particularity came. For it was always the particular that could be made into an exception and eliminated from the oceanic embrace of the human race. It was against this logic that he defended the dietary and sexual restrictions that made for India's pluralism, but without consigning them to the realm of the particular.

The Mahatma did not define humanity as a self-enclosed identity, with humanitarianism as its narcissistic counterpart, but instead sought to open it up to the non-human as a promise rather than a threat. The Hindu practice of cow protection provided one site at which this opening could occur, and Gandhi chose it precisely because the cow had become such a flashpoint for Hindu–Muslim violence.[9] Instead of simply presenting it as an example to follow, in other words, Gandhi defined cow protection as a nonviolent practice capable of tolerating rather than eliminating social difference. And he did so by pointing out its moral as opposed to biological character, one that rejected the humanitarian ideal of a shared language, sexuality, and alimentation.

The cow stood for all non-human life, and for Gandhi her care was truly humanitarian because it allowed men to exit their own species by creating a moral relationship with life forms that did not depend upon their similarity to us. Only because no generalized sexual, linguistic, or

---

[8] M. K. Gandhi, *Hind Swaraj or Indian Home Rule* (Ahmedabad: Navajivan Publishing House, 2008), 42.

[9] See, for this, Faisal Devji, 'Gandhi, Hinduism and Humanity', in *The Oxford History of Hinduism: Hindu Practice*, ed. G. Flood (Oxford: Oxford University Press, 2020), 375–97.

dietary communion could exist between humans and animals, in other words, might their relations become truly moral and therefore nonviolent. Our care for animals as much as fellow human beings, he thought, occurs in the absence of any sure knowledge about or identity with them, revealing its most pure manifestation in sacrifice for the other. And in this way Gandhi managed to break open colonial humanitarianism without proposing an alternative universality.

Impossible Indians

While his voyage to London allowed Gandhi to rediscover India outside the colonial relationship of universal and particular, the journey to South Africa permitted him to question what it was to be an Indian. Upon arriving in Durban, he discovered a Gulliver's world of topsy-turvy relations, where a Gujarati elite composed of Muslim merchants and their Hindu and Parsi clerks struggled to distinguish themselves from the South and North Indian indentured and freed labourers who comprised the majority of the Indian population. Regularly identified with these latter by South African whites, the upper-caste traders and their employees insisted on taking on new identities:

> In the course of these two or three days I could see that the Indians were divided into different groups. One was that of Musalman merchants, who would call themselves 'Arabs'. Another was that of Hindu, and yet another of Parsi, clerks. The Hindu clerks were neither here nor there, unless they cast in their lot with the 'Arabs'. The Parsi clerks would call themselves Persians. These three classes had some social relations with one another. But by far the largest class was that composed of Tamil, Telugu and North Indian indentured and freed labourers.[10]

And yet the more Indians in South Africa emphasized their assumed identities, the more tenuous these became. In his autobiography, Gandhi describes how his compatriots resented the use of terms like 'sammy' and

[10] Gandhi, *Autobiography*, 89–90.

'coolie' for them, trying to wheedle white South Africans into identifying them in other ways:

> Whenever, therefore, an Indian resented being addressed as a *sami* and had enough wit in him, he would try to return the compliment in this wise: 'You may call me *sami*, but you forget that *sami* means a master. I am not your master!' Some Englishmen would wince at this, while others would get angry, swear at the Indian and, if there was a chance, would even belabour him; for *sami* to him was nothing better than a term of contempt.[11]

Gandhi himself adopted forms of dress that would distinguish him from the others. His first struggle in South Africa was to be admitted to court wearing the 'Bengali puggree' that he thought marked him out as a modern Indian. And in 1896, when he returned to South Africa after a trip to India bringing his family with him, the future Mahatma describes how he insisted on prescribing what they were to wear:

> I therefore determined the style of dress for my wife and children. How could I like them to be known as Kathiawad Banias? The Parsis used then to be regarded as the most civilized people amongst Indians, and so, when the complete European style seemed to be unsuited, we adopted the Parsi style. Accordingly my wife wore the Parsi sari, and the boys the Parsi coat and trousers. Of course no one could be without shoes and stockings. It was long before my wife and children could get used to them. The shoes cramped their feet and the stockings stank with perspiration. The toes often got sore.[12]

When describing his return as a newly minted barrister from London in the *Autobiography*, Gandhi had already made the first of several comparisons between a storm at sea and a tumult on land, whether physical or psychological in nature. On that occasion he compared the rough seas that brought him to Bombay with the news of his mother's death and other troubles that awaited him in India.[13] Similarly, a storm at sea

[11] Gandhi, *Autobiography*, 90.
[12] Gandhi, *Autobiography*, 155.
[13] Gandhi, *Autobiography*, 73.

as he returned from India to South Africa with his family attired in Parsi style came to be seen as a foreboding of the trials that awaited him on land. But more than this, life on board a ship also struck Gandhi as an experimental model of what might be accomplished on land. This is why he used sea voyages to study languages, as he would go on to do in the various prisons in which he ended up being incarcerated, and which represented another kind of laboratory for morality and politics in the world beyond. The storm's very danger, it seemed to Gandhi, offered an opportunity for the reform of social relations and religious devotion, if only it could be made to endure on land:

> But as though to warn us of the coming real storm on land, a terrible gale overtook us, whilst we were only four days from Natal. . . . All became one in face of the common danger. They forgot their differences and began to think of the one and only God—Musalmans, Hindus, Christians and all. . . . The ship rocked and rolled to such an extent that it seemed as though she would capsize at any moment. It was out of the question for anyone to remain on deck. 'His will be done' was the only cry on every lip. . . . At last the sky cleared, the sun made its appearance, and the captain said the storm had blown over. People's faces beamed with gladness, and with the disappearance of danger disappeared also the name of God from their lips.[14]

What awaited these passengers in Durban was a fired-up crowd at the docks and hostile public opinion among whites, who saw Gandhi as the leader of a move to bring more Indians to settle in South Africa and in so doing threaten both the demographic basis of white supremacy and commercial dominance there. Since Gandhi had spoken to the international press before leaving India about the worsening treatment of Indians in South Africa, he was greeted by a mob upon disembarking in Durban and nearly lynched before being spirited away to the house of a friend. But the crowd followed him there, and Gandhi had to escape in order to save his family, who had been brought there separately. At the suggestion of Durban's police superintendent, he donned a disguise and so assumed

---

[14] Gandhi, *Autobiography*, 156.

yet another identity in what makes a frightening event seem like a piece of burlesque theatre:

> As suggested by the superintendent, I put on an Indian constable's uniform and wore on my head a Madrasi scarf wrapped around a plate to serve as a helmet. Two detectives accompanied me, one of them disguised as an Indian merchant and with his face painted to resemble that of an Indian.[15]

What all of these incidents demonstrate is the fact that Indian identities were both fluid and transient things. That did not make them superficial, though Gandhi did suggest this was the case for his own sartorial experiments, but it certainly revealed how irrelevant all such claims and expressions were politically. The problem was not that such forms of identification were either weak or inauthentic, only that their assumption for the reason of gaining some material advantage was wrong and therefore unviable. And so, he would go on to reconstruct the Indian subject in a quite different way.

Gandhi began by suggesting that the discrimination upper castes faced in South Africa was a punishment for their own treatment of lower castes in India, making a moral issue of it that, typically, turned actual victims into prospective agents. But while he was keen to have them all identify as Indians, Gandhi did not argue that such unity would save his compatriots from their predicament. For one thing, he would never abandon the discrete castes and communities by whose names Indians identified each other, not least because these were the only groups that possessed some measure of political agency in the colonial state.

When the Mahatma launched his first mass movement in India after the First World War, he called upon the country's communities and castes to non-cooperate with the state, since they were the only social groupings that could administer themselves without reference to it. For as Indians alone they were defined by the colonial state and therefore unable to act without it. But Gandhi also distrusted the self-interest that gave all identities their political meaning. In *Hind Swaraj*, he pointed out the ambiguity of interest, itself the fundamental category of liberal

---

[15] Gandhi, *Autobiography*, 162.

thought, describing how Indians had come to be colonized precisely by self-interest, because they wanted the goods and services the British provided.[16] And in his autobiography Gandhi went on to link self-interest to cowardice and the lack of principles, writing that '[t]he average Englishman believed that the Indian was a coward, incapable of taking risks or looking beyond his immediate self-interest'.[17]

Similarly, he realized that Indian traders in South Africa were willing to put up with the racial discrimination they faced out of self-interest, as long as they gained from it financially. He was struck by these men's rueful statements about 'pocketing insults' as they pocketed the cash of white South Africans enough to repeat it several times in his autobiography. Interest, after all, was also a capitalist category describing both material and psychological forms of ownership. One could only have an interest in something from which some advantage could be derived, and so it became a kind of property even as an identity. This is why voting rights in Gandhi's day were restricted to owners of physical or intellectual property, who were understood as being invested and so having an interest in politics.

Like the imperial idea of humanity as a universal form made possible by the technologies of conquest, interest in its most basic unit as self-interest was considered a universal and so natural quality. It was, however, part of an economic theory about human behaviour, seen as being motivated primarily by the maximization of self-interest. Even altruism, in the utilitarian philosophy that undergirded so much of the colonial enterprise, was understood as creating the optimal context for self-interest to operate. Acts of disinterestedness and sacrifice that could not be folded into this theory, as many examples of Indian 'superstition' were not, had therefore to be defined as irrational, unnatural, and territorially particularistic. By repudiating identity as a form of self-interest, then, Gandhi sought to redefine it politically without lapsing into the false choice between what was universal and what was particular.

It was sacrifice, he argued, rather than interest that should constitute what it meant to be Indian. Just as humanitarianism meant going beyond the human, in other words, so, too, did all the lesser and greater

---

[16]   Gandhi, *Hind Swaraj*, 35.
[17]   Gandhi, *Autobiography*, 179.

forms of Indian identity acquire moral and political meaning by opening themselves to a world outside their confines in gestures of self-abnegating duty. Since the capitalist conception of property that made interest possible had not yet come to define the entirety of Indian social relations, thought Gandhi, such acts of sacrifice remained relatively commonplace and invariably characterized familial and other intimate relations. They were, in other words, not part of any utopian vision but eminently real, and so capable of being expanded politically as much as socially.

Parting the Waters

By the time Gandhi returned to India in 1914, he had learnt how to dismantle the universalistic pretentions of imperialism, in the form of 'modern civilization', without adopting the status of Indian particularity either. We might say that he refused to take his position either on land or sea and thus undid the relationship between them that defined colonialism. This frequently meant occupying no specific place and simply interrupting the expansive narratives of universality by breaking the links of causality on which they tended to depend. It was, of course, a lesson he had learnt from the *Gita*, which counselled separating means from ends and therefore causes from effects so as to snap the chain of karma that bound individuals to an endless cycle of rebirth. What Gandhi did was to build an entirely novel politics out of this moral insight.

Gandhi often interrupted the apparently inexorable and expansive causal links of his own narratives by introducing different kinds of trajectories within them. We can see this happening in the account of his near lynching in Durban that I described above. Surrounded by a crowd, Gandhi and his friend Mr Laughton initially thought to escape in a hand-pulled rickshaw, until its owner ran off and, in doing so, we are told, saved the future Mahatma from the sin of riding on such a dehumanizing form of conveyance. While it might sound like sanctimony, this little interruption of a violent narrative suddenly introduces a quite different moral consideration into it, one that is deliberately out of place. Shortly afterwards, when recounting the crowd's attack on him, Gandhi interrupts the narrative again:

They first caught hold of Mr. Laughton and separated us. Then they pelted me with stones, brickbats and rotten eggs. Someone snatched away my turban, whilst others began to batter and kick me. I fainted and caught hold of the front railings of a house and stood there to get my breath. They came upon me boxing and battering. The wife of the Police Superintendent, who knew me, happened to be passing by. The brave lady came up, opened her parasol though there was no sun then, and stood between the crowd and me.[18]

Why mention the fact that the police superintendent's wife opened her umbrella to protect him even though there was no sun to warrant it? Surely, the context in both the Gujarati and English text is clear, but what the interruption effects is a breach in the narrative's causal sequence by intruding an apparently bizarre new element into it. Evident throughout his career as a Mahatma, this logic of interruption characterized many of Gandhi's political experiments as well. This is especially evident in Gandhi's much-derided efforts to demonstrate his loyalty to the empire in the first half of his career. For these expressions of loyalty followed a logic entirely separate from that enjoined by the British, seeking to interrupt and so transform it from the inside.

From his South African activism starting late in the nineteenth century until the end of the First World War and even beyond, Gandhi had worked to radicalize loyalty to the British Empire in order to transform the vast concourse of humanity it represented from within and for the benefit of its subjects. He could do this because sovereignty (*swaraj* or self-rule) was understood not merely in collective or institutional terms but as a quality dispersed among individuals whose nonviolent practices were meant to revolutionize social relations and therefore political ones by default. It didn't much matter, therefore, what kind of political regime existed, with empires and nation states being seen as equally violent but also superficial and so amenable to internal transformation.

Gandhi's loyalty to the empire was independent as well as radical because it was detached from the aims and propaganda of the colonial state. His acts of organizing an Indian ambulance corps during the Boer and Zulu Wars in the first years of the twentieth century, as well as in England

---

[18] Gandhi, *Autobiography*, 160–1.

at the First World War's commencement, were all marked by an unconcern with which side was right or wrong in each conflict. In fact, his own sympathies were with the Boers and Zulus in the first two wars, and he insisted on serving their wounded as well as those of the British. Indian participation in these South African events was meant to return the humanitarian 'gift' of imperialism. Instead, Gandhi offered Britain a gift of loyalty that was meant to force the recognition of Indians as citizens of the empire.

With the Great War this reasoning changed slightly, as Gandhi, who reached London in 1914, grappled with the problem of abstaining from the conflict while yet living under the protection of the Royal Navy.[19] Since he thought this amounted to benefiting from violence, Gandhi decided that volunteering for ambulance service on the Western Front would at least cancel out the sin of such vicarious participation in war by deliberately putting oneself at risk. The ambulance corps was meant to break the chain of karma that linked its members to violence. The closer Gandhi approached the war as a loyal subject, in other words, the more distant he was from its aims and ethos, having turned it into the scene for a quite different moral trial.

In 1918, Gandhi also embarked upon a largely unsuccessful mission to recruit soldiers in India. As with the ambulance corps, Gandhi's arguments for recruitment were independent. On the one hand, India's participation in the war was meant to achieve home rule for her and equality within the empire. On the other hand, Gandhi offered far more intriguing reasons than home rule to his allies, not all of whom shared his belief in nonviolence. By making themselves responsible for recruitment, Gandhi contended, Indians would automatically switch the allegiance of soldiers to their own countrymen and civilians outside government. In the process they would also allay the risk of military rule at the end of the war, when large numbers of soldiers returned and were used against the nationalists.

But he also thought that, in order to claim their freedom, Indians should learn to risk their lives, which made the war into an arena for another kind of political morality. Indeed, recruits might even be able

---

[19] For Gandhi's views on the war, see Faisal Devji, 'Gandhi's Great War', in *India and the Great War I*, ed. I. Talbot and R. Long (London: Routledge, 2018), 191–206.

to demonstrate the power of nonviolence on the battlefields of Europe. However serious, disingenuous, or bizarre these ideas, it should be clear that Gandhi's loyalty was detached from the expansive colonial logic of cause and effect and at least intellectually free. He had already disengaged from the war and even British rule while still participating in both, having made it the site for an entirely different moral experiment. This practice of interruption, however, was not confined to imperialism, and Gandhi deployed it even against his own party and people when necessary.

Conclusion

Having struggled for much of his career to dismantle the relationship between land and sea that defined imperialism as much as 'modern civilization' with its narrative of universal and particular, Gandhi ended up erasing the dividing line that both joined and separated the two. In the Salt March of 1930, for example, he returned to the Gujarati coast on which he had been born and brought up to focus the attention of Indians upon the very edge of the territory they wanted to make their own. By retrieving salt from the sea, he not only broke the law that made its manufacture a colonial monopoly but in doing so also decentred the territorial imagination of Indian nationalism by including the sea within it.

With the Quit India movement of 1942, the Mahatma invoked India's maritime borders again, asking the British to leave the country in the same manner they had arrived in it—by way of the sea. India, of course, was a major source of labour, fighting men, raw materials, and food grains for the empire during the Second World War, all of which were procured in the name of collective security, necessity, and obligation. Gandhi was not against India's participation in the war effort but argued that it would be most effective when freely made. If Britain was fighting for freedom against fascist dictatorship, in other words, it would have to demonstrate it by freeing India for a relationship based on trust rather than force.

Instead of defending India against the sea and its logic of universality, in other words, in his last great mobilizations the Mahatma seemed to be pushing towards it in different ways. And I can do no better than end with a remarkable illustration of this movement from an article he wrote in *Harijan* towards the end of July 1946. Contrasting the hierarchical structure of the pyramid, itself a symbol of territorial empire, with the freedom of the ocean, Gandhi imagines India's future on the eve of its independence as one defined by the centripetal movement of democratic decision-making, beginning with individuals and villages and expanding outwards in a kind of wave, without any one site of democracy commanding another:

> In this structure composed of innumerable villages, there will be ever-widening, never-ascending circles. Life will not be a pyramid with the apex sustained by the bottom. But it will be an oceanic circle whose centre will be the individual always ready to perish for the village, the latter ready to perish for the circle of villages, till at last the whole becomes one life composed of individuals, never aggressive in their arrogance, but ever humble, sharing the majesty of the oceanic circle of which they are integral units.[20]

At the end of his life, then, the Mahatma joined land to sea by refusing any distinction between them. No longer was the universality of one to be defined by the particularity of the other in a relationship of forced dependency that was as much epistemological as it was economic and political. Instead, territorial hierarchies were literally to be washed out to sea in a tide of freedom where no border existed.

---

[20] M. K. Gandhi. 'Independence', *Harijan*, 28 July 1946, in the *Collected Works of Mahatma Gandhi* (New Delhi: Publications Division, Ministry of Information and Broadcasting, 1984), vol. 85, 32–4.

2

A Different Vision

Gandhi's Critique of Political Rationality

Uday Singh Mehta

Towards the beginning of his *Autobiography*, Gandhi says, 'what I have been striving and pining for these thirty years – is self-realization, to see God face to face, to attain **Moksha.** I live and move and have my being in pursuit of this goal. All that I do by way of speaking and writing, and all my ventures in the political field, are directed at this same end.'[1] The reason I start with this passage is because Gandhi explicitly links his political works to a spiritual goal. If one asks what makes the goal spiritual, the answer is that it is spurred by the desire for self-realization, which Gandhi elaborates in terms of wishing to 'see God face to face, to attain **Moksha**'. The passage goes on to claim that some things we do are known only to 'oneself and one's Maker. These are clearly incommunicable.' In contrast, the experiments that his *Autobiography* deals with are 'spiritual or moral'. And then he concludes the paragraph with the injunction 'for the essence of religion is morality'.[2]

Gandhi has been associated with the major political events of the twentieth century—decolonization, the fight against racial apartheid, the critique of war and violence, a critique of consumerism, a scepticism regarding the role of technology, and, more generally, bringing the common man and woman into the fold of public life. These associations have naturally engendered the view that he was in the main a political thinker, not simply that his views had political implications but that he thought in political terms; that his ideal was somehow itself political.

[1] M. K. Gandhi, *An Autobiography* (Ahmedabad: Navajivan Publishing Trust, 1940), xii.
[2] Ibid.

Uday Singh Mehta, *A Different Vision* In: *Gandhi, Truth, and Nonviolence*. Edited by: Vinay Lal, Oxford University Press. © Oxford University Press 2025. DOI: 10.1093/9780198936657.003.0003

The defining feature of modern politics is that it gives priority to self-preservation, sovereignty, order, power, and, in its liberal variant, to chastening of power, through the state and constitutional constraints. It does this because it is responding to a distinctly modern detritus, in which all these things are threatened. And, moreover, the claim is that in face of these threats there is a unique solution, which is politics power. They take the context as defined and constrained by an underlying fact expressed in the Latin maxim *salus populi suprema lex esto* ('safety of the people is the supreme law'), where *salus* no longer referred to salvation but to safety.

Gandhi does something altogether different. His radical idealism stems from the connection that he establishes between self-knowledge, seeing God face to face, *Moksha*, and his public endeavours, all of which he identifies with the spiritual. It is telling that he makes no reference to the narrative and the grammar of modern power and politics. He does so at least in part because he did not share the trauma that underlies modern politics. That trauma acquired its salience—at least in the English tradition—because it was seen as having a deep link with the English Civil War (1642–51), which was paradigmatic of anarchy. It has had this association over the next three and a half centuries, including in contemporary politics. Hobbes was the originator of this emphasis in which safety was the condition for society, rather than the reverse, the complex weave of society, the condition of security.

The point is that in the rationality of modern political thought, and to a substantial extent in modern political practice, conflict and even uncertainty precipitate an image falling off a precipice that culminates in anarchy and death. The social is defunct, having lost its historical capacity to offer any resistance and an alternative model to the political. The family, religious community, friendships, the conventions and practices of social clubs, individual self-discipline—in brief, the conviviality and conflict that are the marks of everyday practices with their ethical density—cannot retard, let alone obviate, the fall into desolation and anarchy. The political power is always responding, typically as an anxious anticipation, to a kind of brutality with its limiting case being death.

The hegemony of politics is now complete. In fact, it has been implicit ever since Hobbes declared that the central fact that was implicit in modern life was insecurity and the fear of death. Hobbes's response to this predicament was to make clear the conditions for security, articulated through the leviathan, and more generally, through the redemptive power of politics. Security is the central catechism of our contemporary secular lives. It is not merely that a concern with security has been the authorizing warrant for the perpetual motion of recent foreign wars, or that security, and not ideology in its traditional sense, now underwrites a global vision that needs the buttress of far-flung garrisons.

At one level, this capacious agenda of action testifies to the new ways in which everything is connected, and to the fact that the designation of 'separate spheres', on which modern liberalism relied and on whose denial totalitarianism prospered, are increasingly tenuous distinctions. It is now a familiar fact that officials routinely justify even the most mundane aspects of public policies by invoking the idea of security.

Implicit in this conception of political rationality is a normalization of a heightened regard for security, both individual and collective; a concern with unity, because it increases the prospect of clear identities and, hence, security; an emphasis on norms such as toleration, because they are deemed to be essential to coexistence, especially under conditions characterized by diversity; a devaluation of individual courage, because it almost always puts at risk self-preservation; a high valuation of technology, because it is typically tied to corporeal needs, such as health and corporeal well-being; finally, and in general, the progressive energy of state, because it alone has the power to secure many of the things mentioned above.

This political rationality finds expression in many things that characterize modern civilization; most conspicuously in the idea that the state is the ultimate guarantor of order, because it alone is, and can claim to be, sovereign. All the other forms of order are reliant on this guarantee. This is another way of saying that the social is defunct; that whatever order it does supply is illusory, and that ultimately it cannot be relied upon without an implicit or sometimes explicit reliance on the guarantees offered by the state. Through a chain of nested dependencies, the state underwrote all relations of power and authority; nothing could be wholly independent of what it offers. It is like a building in which all the floors, despite their apparent solidity, are in fact dependent on the solidity of the foundations of the building.

This vision is in sharp contrast with that of Gandhi. He did not give security, either individual or collective, any priority; he did not privilege borders, identity, unity, or the nation for that matter; rather, he thought in civilizational terms. Gandhi did not think that toleration had to be valued as an independent thing, which required the vigilance and mediation of the state; he did place a high value on individual courage, because it indicated a readiness for freedom and maturity; he was suspicious of technology, because it facilitated a kind of vicarious existence, that is, it gave an inducement to be and to live 'other than who one really was'; in brief, he was opposed to and suspicious of the sort of mediation and reliance on the power, especially reliance on the power of the state and its institutions.

Gandhi valued the social in its various forms—the family, religion, the 'face-to-face' practices, depth, slowness, and patience—because in his view these were the grounds through which self-realization was achieved. In brief, these were the constituent part of his spiritual vision. This had profound and significant implications, because if one embeds the familiar pieces of his thought and practice, they assume a wholly different meaning in this frame, with the spiritual and not the political at its centre. He did not rely on a rationality that put 'the political' at the centre because he was not drawn to its motivating assumption, namely that in absence of the power of the state we would have a condition of utter desolation and anarchy. Even anarchy did not, in the end, trouble him so much. When Gandhi was desperate to avoid partition, and the British were claiming that their imperial presence alone was the condition for retaining the unity of India, he said, 'leave us to our anarchy'.[3]

I will draw out some of these implications of the constituent parts of this alternative framing. It is an alternative because it puts the social and not the political at the centre of his thought, which in turn is deeply attentive to the needs of the self. I will focus on the ideas of toleration, courage, patience, and finally religion. I should say at the outset that because in my view all these are parts of the general claim of achieving self-realization, seeing God face to face, and *moksha*—in brief, of achieving a spiritual goal—they each make basically the same general point and therefore there is considerable repetition.

---

[3] Faisal Devji gives an extremely interesting account of British imperial thinking on the prospect of anarchy in the early 1940s and Gandhi's heretical embrace of that prospect. See Faisal Devji, *The Impossible Indian* (London: Hurst, 2012), ch. 6, 'Leaving India to Anarchy'.

Toleration

Gandhi was not opposed to toleration. He just did not think it had to be underwritten by the institutions of the state, which ultimately relied on its overwhelming power. In fact, he thought toleration was a part of the long-established civilizational inheritance of south Asia. Toleration therefore did not require the special support or protection of doctrines and institutions associated with secularism. For Gandhi religious diversity and a basic unity of coexistence, underwritten by civilization's rhythms and not unitary power, are simply facts. They are part of the warp and weft of an ancient land, and for him they provoked none of the anxiety that they do in the political tradition, or as in *Hind Swaraj*, his nationalist interlocutor. They are merely facts, banal and scattered in their obvious familiarity. Hindus and Muslims, Gandhi points out, have survived and prospered under rulers of each other's faith. They are part of a syncretistic way of life that has points of mutual contact and divergence. What matters is simply that those who are conscious of the spirit of civilizational coherence do not interfere with one another's religion. The unity Gandhi vouches for is a shared 'mode of life' and not a shared national form, because it—that is, the nation—required a superintending form of political governance.[4]

It is a unity tethered to civilizational routines of common and conflicting interests and social norms. It does not have, and does not need, in the manner of the typical nationalist and imperialist, clearly defined political boundaries or a clear font of power and obligation.

When in *Hind Swaraj* his interlocutor asks about the deep enmity between Hindus and Muslims, Gandhi is almost cavalier in his denial of such enmity. Instead, he thinks of the enmity (and conviviality) as occasioned by contingent circumstances that almost always admit of indifference, negotiation, and persuasion. Even on the loaded matter of the killing of cows by Muslims he says he would 'only plead' with Muslims. For Gandhi, the issue surrounding the cow was not a political matter which required the mediation of the blunt power of the state. Notwithstanding the reverence which he, as a Hindu, felt towards cows, he said, 'If he [the Muslim] would not listen to me, I should let the cow go

---

[4] Autobiography, 48.

for the simple reason that the matter is beyond my ability.[5] In some other context, one can well imagine Gandhi being willing to die for those convictions. But his point here is that he does not take the difference between the Muslim attitude towards the cow and his own Hindu reverence for it as sanctioning an escalation. Gandhi knows and accepts the fact of the occasional conflict between Hindus and Muslims. But what is striking is the degree to which he views such conflict as having no necessary or deep escalatory potential.

> I do not suggest that the Hindu and the Mahomedans will never fight. When people are in a rage, they do many foolish things. These we have to put with. But, when we do quarrel, we certainly do not want to engage counsel and to resort to English or any law courts. *Two men fight; both have their heads broken, or one only. How shall a third party distribute justice amongst them? Those who fight may expect to be injured.*[6]

What is striking in this and many similar passages is Gandhi's casual equanimity. There is no suggestion that the conflict stems from a deep friend/enemy animus in which the depth of the antagonism can be, or should be, the foundational ground of a political construct. Gandhi never gives an account of such conflict in which it arises from the essential nature of the two religions, or indeed from anything that has a deeper motivational basis. His thought is strikingly free of such underlying mandates. Instead, in the examples he gives the conflict is almost always occasioned by, and limited by, a narrow set of contextual considerations. In Gandhi's rendering the conflict is merely a foolish act motivated by prosaic anger, a kind of schoolyard brawl that will run its course, without any implied or necessary escalation, and following which, one assumes, the patterns of social conviviality and distinction would reassert themselves. Even the possibility of heads being broken, and hence of violence, does not occasion any special concern. Neither does the possibility that perhaps only one party's head gets broken, and hence that the initial conflict may have been between unequally matched opponents. In Gandhi's

---

[5] Ibid., 54.
[6] Ibid., 57 (emphasis added).

view such things sometimes just happen, without being the precursors to anarchy.

But what did deeply trouble Gandhi, and which numerous times in *Hind Swaraj* and elsewhere he returns to, is the idea that conflict required the mediation of 'a third party'. Gandhi is insistent in his refusal to countenance such mediation, be it the law with its warrant of justice or the imperial state as the guarantor of peace, order, and a progressive historical alignment, or the national state as it vouches for equality and through representation acting on behalf of the public interest. Elsewhere Gandhi writes, 'We [Hindus and Muslims] should be ashamed to take our quarrels to the English', making it clear that for him the issue of seeking mediation, where the warrant for the mediator lay in its superior power and alleged objectivity, was fraught with both psychological and ethical considerations.[7] They all interject a dependence, which Gandhi thinks is the hidden essence of modern civilization, in which the security and deepest values of the self become reliant on abstracted projections of power. Hence, they obviate the conditions required for self-knowledge.

Courage

Let me now move on to say something about courage. On the morning of 24 February 1919, in a context vitiated by the recent introduction of the Rowlatt Bills, which proposed to all but explicitly suspend the individual rights of Indians, along with their rights of association and assembly, Gandhi along with others issued the Satyagraha Pledge—that is, the call for civil disobedience. It was an act which he called the 'most momentous in the history of India'.[8] The pledge stated that 'in the event of these Bills becoming law and until they are withdrawn, we shall refuse civilly to obey the laws ... and we further affirm that in this struggle we will faithfully follow truth and refrain from violence to life, person or property'.[9] In a telegram sent on the same day to the Viceroy's private secretary, Gandhi again emphasized that the proposed national satyagraha was to be a civil

---

[7] Ibid.
[8] https://www.gandhiheritageportal.org/the-collected-works-of-mahatma-gandhi, 17: 318.
[9] Ibid., 17: 297.

form of action, as he said it was 'much better that people say openly what they have in their hearts . . . without fear of consequences [and] enforce the dictates of their own conscience'.[10]

Why did civility on his understanding turn on notions such as conscience, truth, suffering, the dictates of the heart, the ability to be steadfast, the practice of fasting, the injunction to refrain from designating an enemy, the courage of being prepared to stand alone, and, of course, abjuring from all forms of violence? Why did it ultimately rest on the willingness to be prepared to sacrifice one's life? In brief, what was the civil component of such action, which in its rigours was so starkly internal, relying as it did, above all else, on the internal resoluteness of the individual?

For Gandhi, civility was a mode of individual comportment, which had the crucial feature of tying ethics to politics. Civility referred to that kernel of what it meant to be human, that ember in the midst of social and political life that had the potential of constantly unsettling or enflaming those contexts with demands that invariably exceeded the contours of the social and the political by pointing to something beyond them. It referred to a metaphysical core of what it meant to be human, and because of that it could not be abstracted from the issue of death, self-sacrifice, and courage. Ultimately for Gandhi civility represented the ineradicable presence and challenge of the absolute in the midst of the everyday routines of life and struggle. As Gandhi said in a speech on 7 March 1919,

> Satyagraha was a harmless, but unfailing remedy. It presupposes a superior sort of courage in those who adopted it – not the courage of the fighter. The soldier was undoubtedly ever ready to die, but he also wanted to kill the enemy. A satyagrahi was ever ready to endure suffering and even lays down his life to demonstrate to the world the integrity of his purpose and the justice of his demands. His weapon was faith in God, and he lived and worked in faith. In his faith, there was no room for killing or violence and none for untruth.

Gandhi's emphasis was on individual courage and integrity, which he identified as anchored in faith. Gandhi was clearly resistant to linking

---

[10] Ibid., 17: 298.

civility solely with the claims of justice, thus giving them an independent normative credence such that their gravity alone would be the basis of behaviour.

Even though satyagraha was projected as a national response to the bills, it was clear from all the conditions and constraints that Gandhi placed on its public forms and the demanding personal conditions that had to be met, that it was hardly designed to give a fillip to mass action. In a speech given in Madras he explicitly stated that it was not the number of signatories but, rather, the purity and willingness of their sacrifice that mattered. As he said of the satyagrahi,

> He must make a continuous effort to love his opponent. He must be prepared to go through every form of suffering, whether imposed upon him by the government, which he is civilly resisting . . . or by those who may differ from him. This movement is thus a process of purification and penance. Believe me, if we go through it in the right spirit . . . the Rowlatt Bills will be withdrawn, and the country will recognize in sat-yagraha a powerful religious weapon.[11]

Gandhi's comments recall what he says in *Hind Swaraj*, where he asserted that swaraj (self-rule) itself did not require a mass movement but could be had 'in an instant' by the genuine courage and fortitude of a few people. If one views such comments as empirical predictions, their warrant seems implausible and unduly optimistic. But such a perspective misses the point. These comments suggest how on Gandhi's reckoning the logic of political transformation was itself susceptible to civil and ethical practices, which were pegged to self-suffering and indifferent to familiar political and social categories, and which therefore defied the very terms in which politics understood itself.

Patience

The theme of not wanting to be rushed, of slowing down, and of emphasizing patience as a capacious virtue runs through *Hind Swaraj* and

---

[11]   Ibid., 17: 341.

Gandhi's other writings with undeniable constancy. There is an explicit appeal to the importance of patience regarding just about all the substantive issues discussed by Gandhi throughout his long career and in all of his writings. As he said towards the conclusion of *Hind Swaraj*, 'There is need for patience.... It is difficult for me to understand the true nature of Swaraj as it seems to you [the reader] to be easy.'[12] Gandhi was pointing to a double contrast, not merely between his views and those of his interlocutor but also in the ease and rapidity with which they each arrived at and held their respective views. For Gandhi the comportment appropriate to *swaraj* (self-rule) in its many forms involved a difficult challenge, which not merely ultimately but, rather, from the very outset drew on the complex interiority of the self. That claim distinguished him from the typical nationalist, for whom national self-rule bore the imprimatur of moral and political self-evidence.

There is something puzzling about the claim that *swaraj* is difficult, just as there is something strange in Gandhi's demurring to answer the question what *swaraj* is. In *Hind Swaraj*, as elsewhere, Gandhi was hesitant in announcing his views in a declarative manner; instead, he emphasized the difficulties in the way of *swaraj* and the quality of patience that was requisite for coming to his views. What is the importance of patience in achieving the comportment appropriate to *swaraj*? Were those difficulties epistemic and cognitive, matters of knowledge and understanding, or did Gandhi in flagging them have something else in mind? Were Gandhi's disagreements with his interlocutor merely matters of opinion, knowledge, or tactics, or did they, perhaps more importantly, refer to ways in which one comes to 'hold' and embody opinions and thus to the quality of being and the patterns of life that opinions exemplify? Did opinions arrived at with patience hold us steady, or indicate a steadiness in us, as the Sanskrit and Hindi word *theeraj* suggests? Was patience a kind of moral and psychological adhesive that embedded values into the self, thereby not allowing moral abstractions to serve as surrogates for the moral self? Patience was a lure against living a vicarious life—the secret condition that made modern existence so appealing.

Such questions gather in their implications many of the reasons that make Gandhi not just a profound thinker with acute judgment and

---

[12] M. K. Gandhi, *Hind Swaraj*, 29.

analysis but also a penetrating and acute moral psychologist. For Gandhi moral and political matters always required more than epistemic and normative clarity.

Patience for Gandhi refers to an essential and underlying condition for crafting a way of being or a state of inwardness that stresses the importance of self-knowledge as a condition of moral and politically salutary action. It has as its antonym moral and political abstraction, and vicarious forms of existence. For Gandhi, patience sediments opinions, beliefs, and values. It gives them a mould. Modern civilization gave people inducements to live life as though it were someone else's life, freed of its prejudices and often arbitrary constraints. It was pegged on an imaginative fantasy. It invited people to be different than who they were on the shallow assumption that such transference was without costs to the self and to others. Patience for Gandhi was the redress to a similar worry. In the Indian context it was a worry about the empire and nationalists, the inducements of progress such as modern forms of life and living, all of which were indifferent to the real needs of the self. To add to this there were the emerging social conditions, which increasingly recessed those needs and offered instead the seductive emollient of politics, material well-being, power, and violence.

Gandhi's view of time and duration is ultimately psychological. It is directed at the individual and at the conditions through which individuals can secure a mature and self-confident selfhood. It abjures the abstraction implicit in moral principles. Gandhi expresses none of the urgency of a typical nationalist, precisely because he is not that. He interjects time and duration at every possible juncture. Modern civilization works by a kind of subterfuge. According to Gandhi it makes the body a stand-in for the whole self. In doing so it gives us an investment in the surface of things.

In contrast, practices such as spinning, celibacy, fasting, and silence, which Gandhi in his later years came to endorse, all have the effect of amplifying the internal domain of the self. These practices have no real external product and hence cannot and do not encourage an investment in something external. They are in a manner wholly contained by the act itself. They are forms of *gymnasia*, that is, exercises done when naked.

Religion

In the final chapter of *Hind Swaraj* Gandhi makes the following observations and claims:

> You English who have come to India are not a good specimen of the English nation, nor can we, almost half-Anglicized Indians, be considered a good specimen of the real Indian nation. If the English nation were to know all you have done, it would oppose many of your actions. The mass of the Indians have had few dealings with you. If you will abandon your so-called civilization, and search into your own scriptures, you will find that our demands are just. Only on condition of our demands being fully satisfied may you remain in India, and if you remain under those conditions, we shall learn several things from you, and you will learn many things from us. So doing, we shall benefit from each other and the world. But that will happen only when the root of our relationship is sunk in a religious soil.[13]

Gandhi was concerned with three issues in this passage. The first is the fact that the English in India, and the half-anglicized Indians, betray their real and best national traditions and inheritances. They are quite literally poor moral specimens of the genus of which, in the present, they are taken to be representatives. Regarding the former group, Gandhi believes that their actions would be disapproved of by the English nation, were it to become fully aware of them. The English in India operate in a moral penumbra and perpetrate a kind of moral subterfuge against the English people. It is a subterfuge that is not fully evident to Indians because few of them have any dealings with the English. The theme is one of self-betrayal and moral occlusion, by both the English and the Indians.

The second issue relates to the conditions that distort the mutual understanding between the two groups. The reason for this distortion is the extant context of their interaction, the imperial context; but Gandhi does not name it as such, with its conspicuous association with a regime of unequal power and racialized differentiation. As a general matter in his more reflective writings Gandhi avoids the term

[13] Gandhi, *Hind Swaraj*, 115.

imperialism. Gandhi's purposes exceed the political relationship by pointing to something deeper that underlies and disfigures it. Instead, he identifies the context through a broader reference. It is modern civilization that confines and distorts the relations between the English and the Indians. What Gandhi has in mind are the grand historical narratives that are wedded to a conception of progress and a corresponding belief in differential civilizational elevations. Gandhi is contending that such narratives make mutual learning impossible because they are premised on the immaturity of one group and the temporal assurance of a particular outcome. Even if a conversation between the English and the Indians were to occur, it would be premised on one of them being superior and the other inferior. This imbalance makes it difficult for the English to appreciate the justice of the demands being made by the Indians, because a particular conception of justice has already been written into those historical narratives. Instead, Gandhi suggests that mutual learning and the claims of justice would only become clear if the English sought guidance in their 'own scriptures', rather than in the warrant of history.

And third, in a more prescriptive voice, Gandhi writes of the conditions that could rectify both the hindrances in the way of mutual understanding and the self-betrayal within each group. Regarding these conditions Gandhi speaks of the essential need to return to scriptures and of rooting the relationship between the English and the Indians 'in a religious soil'. Gandhi's primary concern is with the need for self-searching. On Gandhi's view a return to scripture is essential to this self-searching. He is insistent that only a relationship anchored in a religious seedbed holds the potential for both groups. Moreover, in this repositioned relationship between the English and the Indians, he says that the broader world would learn from their interaction and suggestively, that there would also be the possibility—to which in this passage, as elsewhere, Gandhi makes explicit reference—that there might be no reason for the English to decamp from India.

The themes of self-betrayal, the distortion brought about by modern civilization, and the need to anchor mutual relations in the language of scripture and religiosity are a digest of the broader issues that matter deeply to Gandhi. They suggest both a positive purpose and a refusal to think in familiar terms.

Gandhi is refusing the categories which by the early twentieth century, and with redoubled zeal in the decades that followed, had come to suffuse the discourse of imperial relations from both sides. He does not, for example, speak of exploitation, inequality, racism, differentials of power, absence of political representation, economic immiseration, quotidian forms of violence, or the warrant and urgency of national independence—even though, in different degrees, all these mattered to him. Similarly, from a positive perspective, he does not engage with the idea of progress, the integration of India and the world, a modernity that moved India away from feudal and obscurantist norms and that carried the imprimatur of science, the prospect of democratic self-governance, and other mandates of a progressive future. As he comes to conclude his discourse on home and self-rule, all these categories seem at best secondary to Gandhi's ultimate purposes. Instead, his summation, both critically and positively, points to the importance of scriptures and the language of religion. It is the muffling and displacement of this language that obscure what for Gandhi is the most basic and essential fact of the empire and of modern civilization—namely, that it imperils the moral hygiene of both the English and the Indians. Why is Gandhi so insistent that a relationship fraught with so many vexations should be thought through the language of scripture and religion?

Gandhi's views on religion and his own religiosity are highly complex. This is not the context to propose even a cursory summary of their complexity.[14] What is relevant is that he associates religion in its diverse forms as something given, into which one is, as it were, arbitrarily cast. Gandhi's main preoccupation is with infusing the mundane aspects of life with meaning and moral depth, which for him turns ultimately on religious considerations that have to do with submission, where submission itself is not understood in terms of a willed act or a choice but, rather, as something which 'seizes' the person, and which therefore suggests a form of surrender. This is a thought familiar to many religious traditions regarding how faith is understood. Faith is not chosen but is constitutive of believers. They give themselves up to it. The view that faith is simply

---

[14] Akeel Bilgrami, 'Gandhi's religion and its relation to his politics', in *The Cambridge Companion to Gandhi,* ed. Judith M. Brown and Anthony Parel (Cambridge: Cambridge University Press, 2011), 93–116.

the language through which we pursue self-knowledge captures Gandhi's own understanding of religion and faith. It is linked with Gandhi's idea that the social is a prevenient mesh of interconnections. This is what allows Gandhi to affirm different religions as being of equal sanctity, while always claiming to be a devout Hindu himself, and it also explains his resistance to missionary attempts to change people's religion.

Religion, with a special poignancy, constitutes the language through which a bounded horizon is navigated and made meaningful to individuals and communities. It limits choice but also deepens its potential application. Gandhi never identifies religion as the basis for forging a homogeneous unity that could serve as a buttress to the nation or to any broad collective identity. He does not think of religion in terms of faith but, rather, as modes of living, which makes possible coexistence without having to lean on shared identities that must almost of necessity be secured and invigilated by a third party. It is, instead, a diverse inheritance, the grammar and the minutia through which the pursuit of self-knowledge is carried out in the practice of everyday life. That practice because it involves a deep and constant attunement to the question of who am I? Which, for Gandhi, is ultimately a spiritual pursuit.

Gandhi's passions found their clearest focus in the myriad, often apparently trivial, details that make up the texture of everyday life. He wanted to infuse that life with the spirit of civility, as he understood it. The courage of being willing to die was deeply intertwined with the essential question of the human, which for Gandhi was always conditioned by the transcendent and the utterly mundane. In a sense, for Gandhi courage and fearlessness were portals for a sort of spiritual truancy, which he sought to plant in the very midst of the mundane patterns of everyday life.

3

Along the Way to Gandhi's Neighbour

Ajay Skaria

In Fyodor Dostoevsky's *The Brothers Karamazov*, Ivan Karamazov remarks: 'I must make an admission. . . . I never could understand how it's possible to love one's neighbors. In my opinion it's precisely one's neighbors that one cannot possibly love. Perhaps if they weren't so nigh . . . If we're to come to love a man, the man himself should stay hidden, because as soon as he shows his face—love vanishes.'[1]

And Karamazov is hardly alone in his scepticism about the injunction. Half a century later, in *Civilization and Its Discontents,* Freud launches a swingeing attack on it.

> Let us adopt a naive attitude towards it, as though we were hearing it for the first time; we shall be unable then to suppress a feeling of surprise and bewilderment. Why should we do it? What good will it do us? But, above all, how shall we achieve it? How can it be possible?

Freud goes on to systematically eviscerate the injunction and closes his observations by describing it as a manifestation of the cultural superego:

> The commandment 'Love thy neighbour as thyself' is the strongest defence against human aggression and an excellent example of the unpsychological manner in which the cultural super-ego proceeds. It is impossible to keep this commandment; such a huge inflation of love can only lower its value, not remove the problem.[2]

---

[1] Fyodor Dostoevsky, *The Brothers Karamazov*, trans. Richard Pevear and Larissa Volokhonsky (New York: Vintage, 1992). I was reminded of this passage by the reference to it in Andrew Israelsen, 'And Who Is my Neighbour: Kant on Misanthropy and Christian Love', *The Heythrop Journal* LX (2019), 219–32.

[2] Sigmund Freud, *Civilization and Its Discontents*, trans. James Strachey (New York: W.W. Norton & Co., 1961).

Ajay Skaria, *Along the Way to Gandhi's Neighbour* In: *Gandhi, Truth, and Nonviolence*. Edited by: Vinay Lal, Oxford University Press. © Oxford University Press 2025. DOI: 10.1093/9780198936657.003.0004

Ivan Karamazov's and Freud's scepticism about the biblical injunction is quite symptomatic of the way the injunction has often been regarded with the consolidation of modernity—as a deeply inadequate and flawed demand, impossible to follow and irrelevant for our modernity.

But there has also been another tendency. This one, while not as influential, has turned to the neighbour and the friend to envision a democratic society and politics. For example, when describing satyagraha, Gandhi draws interchangeably on the figures of the friend and neighbour. During the Khilafat Movement, he writes: 'The Mussulman is my neighbour. He is in distress. His grievance is legitimate and it is my bounden duty to help him to secure redress by every legitimate means in my power even to the extent of losing my life and property. That is the way I can win permanent friendship with Mussulmans.'[3]

And sometime after the failure of the Khilafat agitation, in 1925, he still writes:

> This talk, therefore, of justice and nothing but justice is a thoughtless, angry and ignorant outburst, whether it comes from Hindus or Muslims. So long as Hindus and Mussalmans continue to prate about justice, they will never come together. 'Might is right' is the last word of 'justice and nothing but justice'. after we have sufficiently broken one another's heads. . . . we shall recognize that vengeance was not the law [kimmat] of friendship; not justice but surrender [tyaag] and nothing but surrender was the law of friendship.[4]

Gandhi is hardly alone in this emphasis on neighbour and friend. In India, Gandhi's most astute critic, Dr Babasaheb Ambedkar, centres his posthumously published *Buddha and His Dhamma* around the theme of *maitri,* friendship. In Europe, even though her writings remained uninfluential for long, Simone Weil turns to the figures of the neighbour and

---

[3] 'Cow Protection', 4 August 1920. Gandhi, Mohandas, *The Collected Works of Mahatma Gandhi (Electronic Book)* (New Delhi, Publications Division Government of India, 1999), 98. Available online at https://www.gandhiashramsevagram.org/gandhi-literature/collected-works-of-mahatma-gandhi-volume-1-to-98.php.

[4] 'The Science of Surrender', 9 July 1925, Gandhi, *Collected Works,* 32: 106. No strict equivalent to the term 'law' occurs in the Gujarati version, which goes: *mitratani kimmat pratikaar—badlo—nathi, nyaya nathi pan tyaga aj chhe em aapne samajhtha thayishu* ('We will come to understand that the value/criterion of friendship is not opposition—vengeance—not justice, but sacrifice').

friend. And in the United States, of course, Martin Luther King famously invokes the neighbour.

* * *

On the one hand flat-out dismissal, and on the other side a full-throated endorsement. Or so it appears. But things are rarely so simple. Both responses misrecognize the biblical injunction in different ways and so end up talking past each other. Karamazov and Freud conceive the self in terms of self-love and self-interest, and so cannot quite understand the premises of the injunction. Gandhi, Ambedkar, Weil, and King conceive of love in terms of equality and, moreover, put this love in conversation with nationalism, and so end up articulating a new neighbourliness.

Two agonisms shape this new neighbourliness. On the one hand, it has an agonistic relation with the citizenship involved in democratic nation states. The violence of that citizenship is now well recognized: how it excludes non-humans and non-citizens, how for it some humans are always unequal, how it kindles rampant inequality even amongst those whom it deems equal, and so on. But their relation with democracy is agonistic, not antagonistic. They cherish the slogan 'liberty, equality, fraternity', and want to rescue it from the nation state.

On the other hand, this new neighbourliness also has an agonistic relation with the classical figure of the neighbour. Unlike the agonism with democratic citizenship, this one is not intentional. But the very commitment of the thinkers of this new neighborliness to liberty, equality, and friendship means that they must rework the biblical injunction to love one's neighbour as oneself, or what for Gandhi is the Hindu injunction to love all life. They seek to infuse love of neighbour with a distinctive equality and freedom—one only intimated in the classical injunctions.

In this twofold agonism, we also see why the new neighbourliness matters: it is at the heart of the striving for a radical democracy. I use that latter phrase in a very specific way: to describe the striving for socialities that seek an equality of the minor. The minor, as I have argued elsewhere, 'embodies practices, actions, or even ways of being that are inassimilable to the norms of the majority' and, more broadly, of sovereignty.[5] So a

[5] Ajay Skaria, 'The Subaltern and the Minor: For Qadri Ismail', *Critical Times* 5, no. 2 (2022), 275–309.

radical democracy strives for a liberty, equality, and togetherness outside sovereignty-centred forms of democracy—the forms that we sometimes describe as republican or liberal democracy. Enacting an equality of the minor entails cultivating a certain sociality—that of democratic neighbourliness or political friendship, to use two terms to describe the same sociality from different angles. So we can ignore the new neighbourliness only at the risk of being grievously blind to what is most new about the political and our politics from the twentieth century to our present, even if what is most new is in this case also what is most fragile.

* * *

Elsewhere, I have also explored the difference between intimate friendship and political friendship, and the very different strategies or comportments of political friendship or democratic neighbourliness. Here, through a focus primarily on Gandhi, I would like to take up the prehistory of the neighbour as a modern and democratic figure. By prehistory I do not mean only premodern history. Though I will briefly and occasionally engage with premodern history, I wish to dwell most of all on the questions that must be implicitly or explicitly worked through along the way to thinking modern neighbourliness and the radical democracy it envisages.

I shall be concerned with two clusters of questions in particular. The first cluster is around the injunction to love one's neighbour. What makes a relation into one of neighbourliness? How does the injunction to love transform the neighbour? How does Gandhi encounter the emphasis on loving the neighbour or loving all life? The second cluster concerns Gandhi's assertion about the equality of the neighbour, and indeed his broader assertion that all religions are centred around the 'doctrine of equality'. In what ways can this assertion be made of the premodern neighbour or the premodern religions? How does the emergence of the modern vision of equality obscure the biblical injunction and its equivalents, leading to remarks such as Karamazov's and Freud's? How does the new neighbourliness return to the concept of equality?

Gandhi seems to think he is only reiterating the Christian injunction to love your neighbour as yourself and the analogous traditions he espies in Hinduism stressing the equality of all life. Certainly, he never thematizes or writes explicitly about how the figure of neighbour has been transformed in his writings and actions, or how his interventions are transforming the concept of religion itself—just as Ambedkar never quite dwells on how the figure of the friend is transformed in his writing. But regardless of what they intend or what they think they are doing, Gandhi and Ambedkar bring into being something radically new, and this newness emerges especially forcefully when we are attentive to the theme of equality.

In exploring this new neighbourliness, I shall be working between three modalities of doing history—the historical on the one side, and the genealogical and the historial on the other. To reprise what I argue elsewhere, the historical register involves making the past into a 'what', an object we are sovereign over, even if there are protocols that govern our exercise of sovereignty. At their most basic, these protocols insist that even if the questions that we ask of the past are drawn from our present, even if we recognize that the past influences the present, we focus on contextualizing and understanding the past in its own time. In other words, the relation between the past and our times is to be an orderly and regulated one where we have mastered the past in accordance with the protocols of disciplinary history.

By contrast, the genealogical and historial registers are at work wherever and whenever we construe the past through a relation of democratic neighbourliness, wherever and whenever we seek to practise an equality of the minor with the past. In these two registers we ourselves in our freedom and responsibility are the beings to be analysed, and we are in our very being complicitous with what we ask about. As such, the past grips us in our very being; we are not sovereign over it. At the same time, we strive to be not subordinate to it either. Rather, we seek an equal relation with it. The genealogical and the historial are the two complementary registers of this equality. The genealogical register seeks to annihilate both our sovereignty over the past and the past's sovereignty over us; the historial nourishes those aspects of it that envision another equality. This essay is an effort to be faithful to the genealogical and the historial, and to relinquish the historical.

The Who and the What

Why should the figures of the neighbour and friend matter so much? A first clue is provided by the etymology in both English and Gujarati. The Old English has 'neah' or 'nigh', and 'gebur' or 'inhabitant'. As for the

Gujarati phrase in *Hind Swaraj* that in 1909 Gandhi translates as 'neighbour' it is *aaspaas vasta manaso*, or 'people residing nearby'. So phenomenologically, neighbours are those who are nearby.

But nearby how? Here the word 'who' itself provides a clue. Neighbours are constituted by relations of 'who'—relations which have a bearing on us in our singularity as subjects, and so become near us. Relations of 'who' are quite different from those of 'what'. In the latter our singularity as subjects is attenuated, and we encounter entities either as objects or as autonomous subjects not essentially related to who we are. If a pure relation of 'what' were possible, such objects and subjects would be neither near nor far; they would be distanceless.

And if we are to be more precise still about this 'who' that constitutes the neighbour, then we should add: somebody or something is a neighbour because of their relation to who I am more than who or what they are. Somebody or something does not of themselves have to be a 'who', but if they become related to who I am, then they become neighbourly. For example, a table that is merely an object cannot be my neighbour, nor for that matter can a fellow citizen with whom I have no other relation. The table and fellow citizen can, however, become neighbours if I develop a singular relation with them, at which point I can still describe them in terms of what they are, but I will now be describing them in terms of what they are for me, or in terms of who I am.

And because neighbourliness is about who we are, the neighbour has no clear boundaries. My neighbour could be an ant or a cow or a god or an advertisement or a pair of shoes; all that is required for an entity to become a neighbour is that I do not experience it abstractly or, more precisely, distancelessly. In other words, we cannot define the neighbour in terms of the criteria of 'what'. (This is why the neighbour is not a concept but a quasi-concept or a concept-metaphor.)

So the question 'who is the neighbour?' is so preliminary as to be misleading. The article 'the' changes the question itself, transforms it into the quite different question 'what is the neighbour?'. But the neighbour is not, or at least not primarily, a what; the neighbour can become a what only when viewed from outside the problematic of neighbourliness. Within the problematic of the neighbour, one can ask only about the neighbour in a way that implicates a 'who': who is my, our, your, their neighbour? So too of friend and guest—all three figures are inseparable from the 'who' question, which is always addressed to one in the singular, whether that singular be individual or collective.

Of course, there is nothing necessarily at all democratic or empowering or nonviolent about relations of 'who'. Friendship is violent because of the way it authorizes the exclusion of all those who are not my friends. As for neighbourly relations, some of the most massive violence has been directed against neighbours, or against those identified as 'who' in a monstrous way—Jews under Nazism, or Muslims and Dalits in India today, to give just two of countless possible examples.

Indeed, part of the allure of modern citizenship for many of the most marginalized is that it enables an exit from the violence of unequal relations of 'who' and seems to affirm instead of an equality of 'what'. About that exit, more soon. But for now all I wish to stress is that if those who are critical of the equality of 'what' turn to the neighbour and friend, perhaps this is in part because of the very promiscuity of these figures—anybody and anything can be my neighbour and friend. If only these figures can be imbued with equality and freedom, then the inherent plurality of the neighbour seems to promise a far more democratic politics. And it is the questions that arise on the path to this more democratic politics that I would here like to dwell on.

The Quasi-universality of the Neighbour

Precisely because there is nothing necessarily at all democratic or empowering or nonviolent about relations of 'who', the transformation of the neighbour into a moral or religious figure must be located elsewhere—in the injunction to love one's neighbour as oneself. Gandhi likely seriously encounters this injunction for the first time when he reads the Bible while a student in England in the early 1890s. This is amongst his earliest systematic efforts to engage with religious texts, for it is around the same time that he reads the *Gita* in English translation. Of that first reading of the Bible, he writes that the Old Testament 'sent me to sleep'. 'But the New Testament produced a different impression, especially the Sermon on the Mount which went straight to my heart.'[6] And

---

[6] M. K. Gandhi, *An Autobiography, or the Story of my Experiments with Truth*. In his *Collected Works*, 44: 143.

in later years, he often invokes the New Testament when talking of the neighbour—specifically referring to the injunction 'love your neighbour as yourself'.

The biblical injunctions on the neighbour have been the subject of copious commentaries and analyses, but we may perhaps still glean something from them by attending to the question of the who and the what. If Gandhi was sent to sleep by the Old Testament, then this might well be because of the way the neighbour is construed there. In the King James Version of the Old Testament that Gandhi likely had at hand, the famous passage from Leviticus (19:15–17) enjoins love for the neighbour, but does so by constricting that figure. Neighbours are no longer every relation of 'who', as they are phenomenologically, but one sort of 'who'. They are thus contrasted with other relations of 'who'— for example, enemies and strangers. There are injunctions against vexing strangers (Leviticus 19:33); as for the enemies, hating them and wreaking destruction on them is quite acceptable, even desirable. By contrast, neighbours in this rendering are those who, even if not intimate, are one's own people.

Derrida notes that the 'who' and the 'what' are 'terribly reversible'. The Levitical injunction works this reversibility in both directions. Sometimes, all that matters is who the other is—the neighbour as an affine or intimate, the enemy or stranger as potentially monstrous, and so on. At other times, it accentuates reversibility in the direction of 'what'— separating neighbour, enemy, and stranger from each other in terms of what they are rather than only who they are. At work in this emphasis on 'what' is the universalism of the concept, which works by trying to come up with criteria so general as to include everybody or everything in its class. But whether it accentuates the 'who' or the 'what', the Levitical injunction works through a sovereign knowledge—one must know, individually or collectively, whether those whom one encounters are neighbours, strangers, or enemies.

If, by contrast, Gandhi was shaken to his heart by the New Testament, then this might be because of the way it construes the neighbour. The Sermon on the Mount famously declares: 'Ye have heard that it hath been said, Thou shalt love thy neighbour, and hate thine enemy. But I say unto you, Love your enemies, bless them that curse you, do good to them that hate you, and pray for them which despitefully use you, and persecute you' (Matthew 5:43–4; see also Matthew 5:46–7). And then there is the Pauline injunction about neighbour love as the fulfilling of the law:

> Owe no one anything except to love one another, for he who loves another has fulfilled the law. For the commandments, 'you shall not commit adultery,' 'You shall not murder,' 'You shall not steal' 'You shall not bear false witness,' 'You shall not covet,' and if *there is* any other commandment, are *all* summed up in this saying, namely, 'You shall love your neighbour as yourself.' Love does no harm to a neighbour; therefore love *is* the fulfilment of the law.

Four cascading implications of this should be noted. First, the New Testament's swerve away from the Levitical constriction of the neighbour, from the latter's contrasts between neighbour and stranger and enemy, is impelled by a concern for the relation between who and what. The New Testament refuses to operationalize a miscibility and reversibility between the who and the what. When the lawyer in the Book of Luke asks Jesus 'who is my neighbour?', the undertow of that question is: by what criteria shall I recognize who the neighbour is as distinct from enemy and stranger? In other words, here the 'who' is to be determined on the basis of 'what'.

By answering in the way he does, Jesus refuses to apply criteria of 'what' to sort neighbours. The 'who' at work here is very much the who that one oneself is: as Kierkegaard notes in his incomparable essay *Works of Love* (a work from which we will eventually have to step back quite considerably), 'Christ does not speak about knowing the neighbor but about becoming a neighbor oneself, about showing oneself to be a neighbor just as the Samaritan showed it by his mercy. By this he did not show that the assaulted man was his neighbor but that he was a neighbor of the one assaulted.'[7] Through his answer, Jesus radicalizes the notion of 'neighbour': now the neighbour is no longer merely the one who is in geographical proximity or the one to whom one has community obligations. Rather, the neighbour is the one who is in need and who calls forth one's

---

[7] Søren Kierkegaard, *Works of Love*, trans. and ed. Howard Hong and Edna Hong (Princeton, NJ: Princeton University Press, 1995).

compassion and mercy; the neighbour is now defined by the I–thou sacrament of encounter.[8]

Second, what potentially breaks down here also is the economic logic of the Old Testament—the logic where there is reciprocal and balanced relation between what is received and what is given. This economic logic is what Jesus ascribes to publicans. His exhortation to treat strangers and enemies as neighbours abandons the economic relation where we would treat others as they treat us; he introduces instead an aneconomic relation with the neighbour—a relation of giving without anticipation of return (such aneconomy is very evident in the emphasis on loving the enemy).

Third, because of this aneconomy, the Pauline neighbour becomes a mystical figure. I am drawing here on the distinction between the theological and mystical. A comportment is theological when it ascribes sovereignty to the sacred. This sovereign sacrality could be centred around a transcendent being, such as God, who may offer a sovereign love to all his devotees, or to all; it could also be centred around an immanent criterion, as with the various humanisms.

Contrast this with the neighbour, especially the neighbour of the Pauline formulation. Jacob Taubes notes of this formulation: 'No dual commandment, but rather one commandment. I regard this as an absolutely revolutionary act.'[9] What makes it revolutionary, one might add, is not just that the neighbour now becomes a purely immanent figure, with no necessary relation to a transcendent God. It is also that, to make explicit what remains implicit in Taubes, now the neighbour is sacred without being sovereign.

This sacrality without sovereignty is the crux of mystical traditions, whose most striking characteristic is the refusal or inability to conceive of the sacred as sovereign. (I say inability because often it is not so much that mystical traditions actively refuse to conceive the divine as sovereign as that they push their devotion to the point where it becomes impossible, most often despite their intentions, to so conceive the sacred.) With the Pauline injunction, as with so many other moments in the history of what we have retrospectively come to call 'religions', the neighbour

---

[8]   I thank an anonymous reviewer for this observation.
[9]   Jacob Taubes, *The Political Theology of Paul*, trans. Dana Hollander (Stanford: Stanford University Press, 2003), 53.

becomes a mystical figure. What this means, amongst other things, is that there is a breakdown of the economy which characterizes sovereign relations, where I give in expectation of return. Now, the relation with the neighbour must be aneconomic, a giving without expectation of return.

Fourth, leading most directly onto the rest of the argument here, this Pauline neighbour intimates a quasi-universalism. In our usual understanding, a subject is universal when it is both sovereign and all-inclusive. The Pauline neighbour, we saw already, is not sovereign. Now we might add that the neighbour is all-inclusive in a very distinctive way. The neighbour is all-inclusive in the sense that with the Pauline injunction everybody can and must be my neighbour. Usually, the universal is all-inclusive because of its infinitude. It is this infinitude that we ascribe to God in transcendent traditions, or to the human in immanent traditions. The all-inclusiveness of the Pauline neighbour does not belong to this order of infinitude. The all-inclusiveness of the neighbour works through innumerability, moving from one singularity to another. This innumerability or innumeracy is still a finitude, or it is what Hegel would dismiss as a bad infinity. Here, the figure of the neighbour negatively mirrors the logic of universality—it affirms the sacred through the mystical rather than the theological, and becomes all-inclusive through innumeracy rather than infinitude. This is why the neighbour intimates a quasi-universality, is a quasi-universal figure.

* * *

Maybe Gandhi's admiration for the quasi-universal neighbourliness he may have perceived in the New Testament is responsible for at least some of the anxiety that he voices in his letters to Shrimad Rajchandra around 1894—the anxiety about whether the religious resources of Hindu traditions are capacious enough to address his questions about right conduct. But, partially on Rajchandra's advice, he takes to reading the *Gita* carefully; around this time, he also finds his way to the *Ramcharitmanas* and perhaps reflects afresh on his experience of growing up with his Pranami mother. In these traditions, he came to discern arguments very similar to those he had encountered in the Bible. (These resonances are unsurprising: with somewhat different but nevertheless comparable inflections, the emphasis on universal love, rather than love for specific objects and relatedly on a critical relation with self-love, runs through all the post-axial religions.)

The text he turned to most often from the 1890s, the *Bhagavad Gita*, begins with Arjuna anguished by the fact that those he is to pick up arms against are not *parjanam,* another people, but *swajanam,* his own people. And the answer that Krishna gives in the *Gita* dismisses this distinction. That there is no distinction between neighbour and enemy, and that a love for the neighbour flows from the very formlessness of the divine—this is what Gandhi takes from the *Gita*, however tendentious his reading may be.

The association of love and a promiscuous rejection of conventional boundaries Gandhi could arguably also have read into the Pranami bhakti tradition in which he was brought up by his mother. The founder of that tradition, Mahamat Prannath (1618–94), was notable for his 'eclectic engagement with religious traditions, his critique of caste, and his condemnation Pranami of ritualistic orthodoxy'. In his own lifetime, Prannath faced considerable opposition for his insistence that 'both widows and lower castes (*nich jat*) be allowed to take initiation into the order'. His writings and life were marked by 'a particular combination of Vaishnavite belief with Sufi mysticism and Shia millenarianism'; all of this led, indeed, by the late twentieth century to charges that Prannath had been 'a Muslim who tricked Hindus into becoming Muslims'.[10]

Equally importantly, perhaps, Gandhi would have found an analogue to the quasi-universality of the neighbour in the ubiquitous figure of the guest in many Hindu traditions, as celebrated in the injunction *athithi devo bhavo,* 'guest is as god'. As Simona Sawhney points out, the etymology of *athithi* is especially suggestive here—the one who comes in an untimely way. So the guest is not just the one to whom reciprocal and timely obligations are owed; the guest is precisely the one who arrives outside the webs of reciprocity. Given all this, Gandhi arguably finds analogues enough to treat the injunction 'Love thy neighbour as thyself' as something that he can assert also as a Hindu.

Beyond a point (that point being the degree to which Eurocentrism must be contested), the question of whether Gandhi comes to the quasi-universal through the Bible or through Hindu texts is a historical one, not

---

[10] Brendan LaRocque, 'Maḥamat Prannath and the Pranami Movement', in Vasudha Dalmia and Munis D. Faruqui, *Religious Interactions in Mughal India* (New Delhi: Oxford University Press, 2014).

a genealogical or historial one. Symptomatically, Gandhi himself is quite uninterested in it. On one occasion, he remarks:

> I have nothing to be ashamed of if my views on ahimsa are the result of my Western education. I have never tabooed all Western ideas, nor am I prepared to anathematize everything that comes from the West as inherently evil. I have learnt much from the West and I should not be surprised to find that I had learnt something about ahimsa too from the West. I am not concerned what ideas of mine are the result of my foreign contacts. It is enough for me to know that my views on ahimsa have now become a part and parcel of my being.[11]

Part and parcel of my own being: involved here is a very powerful way of disinterring oneself, ourselves, from history framed primarily in terms of context. In this formulation, it is not the past that matters—not, at least, the past as a concept produced through the historical practice of context-ualization. What matters is whether it has become part and parcel of one's own being in the present. For Gandhi, recall, the question of being is inseparable from the question of satya or the truth that is the horizon of sat-yagraha. To make something part of one's own being is to be concerned with being rather than origins, with the historial rather than the histor-ical; it is to disinter oneself from the question of the origins, though by no means to be disinterested in the latter question. In this disinterring, Gandhi folds both the Gita and the New Testament injunction into the emphasis on a certain love as the crux of both nonviolence and religion.[12]

The Equality of the Neighbour?

Beginning in the nineteenth century the quasi-universal neighbour is cast into a new visibility and a new obscurity. Kierkegaard's *Works of Love* provides a fascinating point of entry into this phenomenon. Kierkegaard picks on equality as the key feature of neighbourliness. Where ordinary love is premised on preferences for some over others, love for the

---

[11] 'The Tangle of Ahimsa', 11 November 1928, in Gandhi, *Collected Works*, 43: 84.
[12] See, for instance, 'Love a universal virtue', 20 January 1939, in Gandhi, *Collected Works*, 74: 424.

neighbour is to refuse to make distinction between neighbours, as be-tween neighbours and self. 'The neighbour is one who is equal'; indeed, 'to love the neighbour is equality'. 'He is your neighbour by being your equal before God, but this equality is due unconditionally to every man, and everybody has it unconditionally.'[13]

Gandhi does something similar. For him, it is not just the figure of the neighbour but religion itself that is marked by what he describes, as early as 1899, as the 'doctrine of equality'. That phrase, doctrine of equality, becomes, along with other equivalents, quite pervasive in his writings. In 1899, he describes Christianity as characterized by this doctrine; in 1905, he remarks that Islam is marked by the 'doctrine of equality':

> It [Islam] offered equality to all that came within its pale, in the manner that no other religion in the world did. When, therefore, about 900 years after Christ, his followers descended upon India, Hinduism stood dazed. It seemed to carry everything before it. The doctrine of equality could not but appeal to the masses, who were caste-ridden.[14]

Soon afterwards, Gandhi begins considering the 'doctrine of equality' a key feature of many Hindu texts too, and makes explicit declarations to this effect on several occasions—remarking, for example, at a con-ference against untouchability in 1924 that he believes in the 'doctrine of equality as taught by Lord Krishna in the *Gita*'. Some years later, in 1937, he derives from the first verse of the *Ishopanishad* 'the doctrine of equality of all creatures on earth', a doctrine which he adds 'should satisfy the cravings of all philosophical communists'. In 1927, he also insists on the presence of that doctrine in Buddhism, declaring in Sri Lanka that 'the Buddha preached the doctrine of equality among persons', that 'one's neighbour was as good as oneself', and that Buddhists should therefore 'abolish caste distinctions'.[15]

* * *

[13] I have depended here on Theodor Adorno's translation from the Danish, which seems clearer than the official translation by Howard and Edna Hong. The latter goes: "He is your neighbour on the basis of equality with you before God, but unconditionally every person has this equality and has it unconditionally."

[14] 'The Indian Question in South Africa', 12 July 1899, in Gandhi, *Collected Works*, 2: 281; 'Hinduism', 11 March 1905, in Gandhi, *Collected Works*, 4: 208.

[15] Speech at Untouchability Conference, Belgaum, 27 December 1924, in Gandhi, *Collected Works*, 30: 15; Speech at a Public Meeting, Kottayam, in Gandhi, *Collected Works*, 70: 327.

But was equality the key motif of Christianity (Kierkegaard) or religion (Gandhi) before the nineteenth century? That seems unlikely. In fact, Kierkegaard and Gandhi are revolutionizing the figure of the neighbour by infusing it with equality; they are creating a new immanent figure of the neighbour, displacing the older figure of the neighbour.

Perhaps we can get to the figure of the neighbour before this transformation by reading more critically than Kierkegaard a moment he draws attention to—the tension between the way God and neighbour are to be loved (a tension, incidentally, that Taubes fails to pick up on, thus limiting the relevance of his analysis for our concerns). When Jesus is asked for 'the great commandment in the law', he replies: 'Thou shalt love the Lord thy God with all thy heart, and with all thy soul, and with all thy mind. This is the first and great commandment. And the second is like unto it, Thou shalt love thy neighbour as thyself. On these two commandments hang all the law and the prophets' (Matthew 22:36–40). In another account, Jesus again describes them as like, and adds, 'There is none other commandment greater than these' (Mark 12:31).

As this doubled commandment suggests, God and neighbour are not to be loved the same way. The devout are to love God with all their soul, mind, and strength, so much so that God must be loved more than one's dearest ones, more than oneself. In other words, God is to be loved not as an equal but as an absolute sovereign, sovereign over the devotee's entire being, calling forth adoration and obedience, in Kierkegaard's words. In turn, God loves his devotees not as a sovereign, not as an equal.

And this love of a sovereign God potentially destabilizes any claim to equality. This is all the more so since the divine in the post-axial religions is no longer so clearly a discrete and embodied being; now God is often infinite and all-pervasive. Because of this, a self-subordinating love for a sovereign God must be inscribed in oneself. So one can love God in obedience and adoration only by having a sovereign relation with oneself, or a relation in which one is not equal to that part of oneself which partakes of the divine.

In the Christian tradition, the acceptance of inequality with the self and neighbour is well thematized by the Augustinian moment, as Arendt's

Speech at a Girls' Weaving Institute, Akimama, 24 November 1927, in Gandhi, *Collected Works,* 40: 431.

classic study helps us recognize.[16] Augustine's intervention consolidates the conceptual grounding for a Bible that divides sovereign power into two—on the one hand, the sovereignty of the divine exercised over that part of oneself which is eternal, and, on the other, sovereignty of mortal rulers over that part of oneself. 'Love thy neighbour as thyself' is about loving the eternal part of the neighbour, even as one may remain in an inimical relation with the mortal or concrete part of the neighbour. With this, the quasi-universality and aneconomy that the neighbour intimated is reined in, contained within the reciprocal relation with the transcendent universality of God and the divine.[17]

And despite Kierkegaard's observation in the 1840s that the neighbour is the one who is equal, this thought remains radical in Christian traditions. A decade and a half after Kierkegaard, in her famous 1861 narrative, Harriet Jacobs, who had escaped from slavery in North Carolina, retells a story from her early childhood about her mistress, one described by Jacobs's editor (a white abolitionist, Lydia Maria Child) as 'kind, considerate':

> After a brief period of suspense, the will of my mistress was read, and we learned that she had bequeathed me to her sister's daughter, a child

---

[16] As Arendt points out in her classic study of Augustine, 'And just as I do not love the self I made in belonging to the world, I also do not love my neighbour in the concrete and worldly encounter with him. Rather, I love him in his createdness. I love something in him, that is, the very thing which, of himself, he is not: "For you love in him not what he is, but what you wish that he may be."' Moreover, 'In the equality of all people before God, which love of neighbour makes thematic', the concretely temporal question of whether my neighbour is my friend or foe, or how my neighbour regards me, becomes a matter of indifference. What matters, rather, is that 'in the being before God all people are equal, that is, equally sinful'.

[17] As we might infer from this, Carl Schmitt's observation about the related injunction 'Love your enemies' is quite misplaced. He observes that this injunction is not about the 'political enemy. Never in the thousand-year struggle between Christians and Moslems did it occur to a Christian to surrender rather than defend Europe out of love toward the Saracens or Turks. The enemy in the political sense need not be hated personally, and in the private sphere only does it make sense to love one's enemy, i.e., one's adversary. The Bible quotation touches the political antithesis even less than it intends to dissolve, for example, the antithesis of good and evil or beautiful and ugly. It certainly does not mean that one should love and support the enemies of one's own people.' But from the perspective consolidated after Augustine, Christians love both the political enemy and the private enemy. Only, they love the eternal aspect of both, not the mortal aspect. If they do regard the Saracens or Turks with greater antipathy, this has to do not so much with the public–private distinction as with the assumption that since the Church embodies also the eternal aspect, and its enemies are also theological enemies, or enemies of the eternal aspect. When Schmitt substitutes the political enemy for the theological enemy, he also substitutes one ontotheology for another—the public–private distinction for the very different eternal–mortal distinction.

of five years old. So vanished our hopes. My mistress had taught me the precepts of God's Word: 'Thou shalt love thy neighbour as thyself.' 'Whatsoever ye would that men should do unto you, do ye even so unto them.' But I was her slave, and I supposed she did not recognize me as her neighbour.[18]

Harriet Jacobs, like the disprivileged in many places and times, is drawn to the quasi-universalism that the injunction intimates. But Jacob's enslaver worked with the transcendentalized figure of the neighbour that had been consolidated in the post-Augustinian moment. So her enslaver likely did recognize her as a neighbour, and even an equal, but only a spiritual equal. Just as mastery of the self is itself part of obedience and adoration of the divine, so too mastery of the neighbour becomes quite compatible with love of them. Relatedly, demanding subordination could also be part of neighbour love.

* * *

A similar obscuring of equality is visible in the Hindu traditions that Gandhi draws on. In the *Gita,* if all are equal for the devotee, this is because the devotee is ready for absorption in Brahman, which is infinite just as the God of Christian traditions is (XIV:26). In other words, the equality of all life is mediated by the divine.

And even the bhakti traditions, famous for what is taken to be their emphasis on equality, are marked at best by an ambiguous relation between spiritual and immanent equality. This is brought out decisively in Jon Keune's path-breaking study of the Vārkarī bhakti traditions in western India, which begins with the question: 'can the idea that people are equal before God inspire them to treat each other as equals? Can theological egalitarianism lead to social equality?' The very idea of social equality, Keune stresses, is anachronistic for an earlier period. True, 'a strong socially inclusive ethos pervades the Vārkarī tradition, even as it preserves caste markers in its classic texts and hagiographies. To call attention to the double motion of including yet differentiating, I refer to this as [an] ideology of inclusive difference.' While the Varkaris included many from different

---

[18] Cited in Emerson Powery, 'Under the Gaze of the Empire: Who is My Neighbour?', *Interpretation: A Journal of Bible and Theology* 62, no. 2 (April 2008), 135.

castes, they also preserved caste differences. This was sustained in part by distinguishing between *sadharan dharma*, or the duties of all people, and *varnashramdharma*, or the duties specific to particular castes and stages of life. Thus, in the hagiography of the saint Eknath, his 'bringing an emaciated Dalit thief into his home, preparing food for him, and nursing him back to health' is justified by stressing the primacy of *daya* (compassion), part of *sadharan dharma*, over *varnashramdharma*. But a more systematic and sustained challenge to *varnashramdharma* could not be envisioned.[19]

In sum, the good slave owner, the kind Brahmin—these figures, whose violence is so evident to us, are also instantiations of the New Testament injunction to 'love thy neighbour as thyself' or comparable bhakti exhortations. Especially in its dominant historical manifestations, the injunction to love both neighbour and enemy is not about doing away with domination and the inequality it involves. Rather, paradoxical though this observation will sound, it is about generously inhabiting profoundly unequal relations of 'who', such as those involved in slavery or caste.

* * *

To say that equality could not have been thematized before the nineteenth century in the way that Kierkegaard and Gandhi thematize it is not at all to say that they were wrong in ascribing equality to the Bible and the *Gita*. In *Capital,* Marx famously notes that Aristotle falters in his analysis of the 'form of value'. And he falters, Marx goes on, because the circumstances were not ripe:

> The secret of the expression of value, namely the equality and equivalence of all kinds of labour because and in so far as they are human labour in general, could not be deciphered until the concept of human equality had already acquired the permanence of a fixed popular opinion. This however becomes possible only in a society where the commodity-form is the universal form of the product of labour, hence the dominant social relation is the relation between men as possessors of commodities.[20]

---

[19] Jon Keune, *Shared Devotion, Shared Food: Equality and the Bhakti-Caste Question in Western India* (New York: Oxford University Press, 2021), 198, 200.

[20] Karl Marx, *Capital: A Critique of Political Economy,* vol. 1, trans. Ben Fowkes (London: Penguin, 1976), 152. Both Marx and Engels are famously dismissive of equality as a criterion for a socialist politics, taking particular aim at Eugen Dühring's assertion that 'the

Marx's argument, in other words, is that the secret of the expression of value exists in the peculiar limbo of being intimated and yet not being knowable because the conditions for recognizing it do not exist.

Something not just analogous but related needs be said of the equality of the neighbour. Where the neighbour is taken up into a theological universalism, there the thought of any equality with the neighbour becomes difficult, maybe impossible. And while the quasi-universal tradition of the neighbour is inevitably drawn to equality, this is an equality that does not yet know its name. While it finds itself unable to accept either domination or subordination, it does not have the vocabulary to articulate this inability affirmatively.

Indeed, because the equality of the neighbour was organized around mystical love, it remained so untimely as to be unthinkable till the consolidation of the very different modern concept of equality, which could be called the equality of sovereignty, the equality of what, or the equality of the major. Only after this modern concept acquired 'the permanence of a fixed popular opinion' could its undertow, the equality of love, or what could also be called the equality of the minor, be thought.

A New Equality

In a way, as with the biblical injunction, we are very familiar, even over-familiar, with the new equality that acquires the permanence of a fixed moral opinion: it is constitutive of 'man' as an 'empirico-transcendental

---

touchstone of all social theory is the notion that "two human wills are as such entirely equal to each other"'. Marx expresses his ire not only with 'Dühring and his "admirers," but also with a whole gang of half-mature students and super-wise doctors who want to give socialism a "higher ideal" orientation, that is to say, to replace its materialistic basis (which demands serious objective study from anyone who tries to use it) by modern mythology with its goddesses of Justice, Freedom, Equality and Fraternity.' Engels is even more critical, remarking that the 'notion of socialist society as the realm of equality . . . is a superficial French idea resting upon the old "liberty, equality, fraternity"—an idea which was justified as a stage of development in its own time and place but which like all superficial ideas of the earlier socialist schools, should now be overcome, for they only produce confusion in people's heads and more precise forms of description have been found.' Marx and Engels's criticism of the abstract and bourgeois concept of equality is, of course, spot on. And yet, as in the formulation above, it turns out a certain equality is necessary even to arrive at Marx's central concepts of value. That equality is the 'equality and equivalence of all kinds of labour because and in so far as they are human labour in general'. And that equivalence in turn rests on 'the concept of human equality' acquiring 'the permanence of a fixed popular opinion'.

doublet', to recall Foucault's description.[21] But as with the biblical injunction again, overfamiliarity sometimes obscures things from us, and
we might be able to glean some additional insights about the empirico-
transcendental doublet by placing its new equality in relation to the figure
of the neighbour, and to the question of the 'who' and the 'what'. For the
crux of this new equality is that it puts in place a new sovereign subject: a
subject whose universality works through a distinctive doublet: an incommensurability built on commensurability, a 'who' built on a 'what'.

'Equality of What?' is, of course, the title of a famous essay by Amartya
Sen. The unspoken assumption of that essay—an assumption so commonsensical to Sen that he does not bother to thematize it—is that
equality is always in terms of some criteria; hence the 'what' of the title.
This 'what' is the crux of the new concept of equality, for it makes equality
abstract and commensurable. The emphasis on 'what' is exemplified
in the 'natural equality' ascribed to humans, for that natural equality is
understood in terms of 'what': qualities that separate humans from all
other forms of life; qualities such as the capacity to reason, to possess
property in their own person, or, by an even more general criterion, to
will. In specifying such a 'what', humans render themselves into finite
and empirically knowable beings. Such a commensurable and abstract
equality of 'what' is fundamentally different from the equality of, say,
warriors who are equal to each other in their fearlessness in relation to
death.[22] This commensurable and abstract equality arguably forms the
'empirico' part of Kant's doublet.

At the same time, this new equality also brings into being a distinctive
'who' the 'transcendental' part of Foucault's doublet. Towards the closing
pages of *Civilization and Its Discontents,* Freud observes that 'the commandment to love one's neighbour as oneself [is] probably the most recent of the cultural super-ego's demands'.[23] Saving for another occasion
the elemental question about whether the quasi-universal articulation of
this injunction is part of the cultural superego (I would argue not), let
us ask here a preliminary one: is the Augustinian iteration of the biblical

[21] Michel Foucault, *The Order of Things: An Archaeology of the Human Sciences*
(London: Routledge, 1989), 347.
[22] Ajay Skaria, 'Living by Dying', in *Ethical Life in South Asia,* ed. Anand Pandian and Daud
Ali (Bloomington: Indiana University Press, 2010).
[23] Freud, *Civilization and Its Discontents,* 89.

injunction the *most recent* of the cultural superego's demands? Surely not: by the time Freud was writing, a shift was taking place, and the Augustinian injunction was being displaced—had been displaced—by a new superego centred around the distinctive new 'who' constituted by an incommensurable and abstract equality.

This new superego is instantiated perhaps most clearly in the Kantian categorical imperative, or the injunction to treat humanity, whether in oneself or another, as never merely a means to an end but also an end in itself, and the injunction also, by extension, to act according to the maxims of a universally legislating member of a kingdom of ends. It is this injunction which anchors the emphasis in liberal traditions on dignity, the incommensurable equality attributed in these traditions to all humans.

And arguably this new superego is also manifest in the nation state. Precisely because the equality of nationalism is centred around the fiction that all citizens participate in the sovereignty of an existing or prospective nation state, here equality takes a distinct form—that of being an immeasurable subject, a 'who'. This 'who' is again very different from the neighbour: it is premised on the 'what' involved in shared citizenship.

So both the Kantian and the nationalist equality of 'who', because of their incommensurability and immeasurability, are more expansive than, and build on, the equality of 'what' exemplified by Locke and, more broadly, by the working of generalized commodity production, or capital. Where the latter centres only on a 'what', the equality of man and citizen centres on a similarity which allows for a 'who'. In other words, the Kantian and nationalist visions are premised on something paradoxical—a commensurable incommensurability. (Arguably, part of the distinctiveness of the communicative capitalism dominant since the 1980s is precisely that, like nationalism and the categorical imperative, it too harnesses incommensurability or the 'who': it generates value from incommensurable labour, rather than seeking to abolish incommensurability as industrial capitalism often seemed to.)

And while this new equality is organized around the sacralization of immanent rather than transcendent entities, it is still theological in that it treats these entities as sovereign. If Carl Schmitt could declare that 'all significant concepts of the modern theory of the state are secularized theological concepts', this is most of all because modern nation states have now usurped the sacred sovereignty of the transcendent, have in their immanence become the principal loci of theological love—the principal recipients and bestowers of this love. And not only the nation state. This theological universalism is articulated also by the 'rights of man and citizen' and its modern reworkings, all of which presume the equal sovereignty of citizens, usually conceived in terms of either Lockean self-ownership or Kantian autonomy. And again, this theological universalism is articulated in speciesism and Eurocentrism.

Describing in *Hind Swaraj* the general contours of this transformation, Gandhi writes of the emergence of *aadhunik sudhaaro*, or 'modern civility', and notes that the votaries of modern civility 'usurp the function of the godhead' (*ishwari daavo karta chalya chhe*).[24] For him, the defining feature of 'modern civility' is the pursuit of infinitude, or the installation of a sovereign subject, divine or human, who is limitless or infinite in the sense of constantly seeking mastery. It is clear that for Gandhi modern civility predates what we usually call the modern age, even if he recognizes that it becomes especially dominant with the latter.

* * *

Three aspects of this abstract equality, simultaneously commensurable and incommensurable, are especially worth noting. First, precisely because it works with abstract criteria, the inclusions within and exclusions from this equality are categorical and universal. For example, humans share a natural equality here by definition, and conversely there is no possibility of equality between humans and non-human animals or things.

Second, precisely because it is abstract, even where this equality acquires the permanence of a fixed popular opinion, it is quite compatible with actual exclusion of concrete individuals and groups. Thus, even as dominant groups acknowledge the abstract equality of humans, they have consistently found ways to exclude entire classes and communities of concrete humans—women, the colonized, the enslaved, terrorists, criminals—from this equality, usually on the grounds that they lack the capacity for reasoning or willing.

---

[24] His own translation of the phrase is 'modern civilization'. But I prefer the phrase 'modern civility', which is more faithful to the gap between the Gujarati phrase and Gandhi's own translation of it into English in key texts like *Hind Swaraj*. He describes 'modern civility' as *kudharo*, the opposite of *sudharo*, and contrasts it to 'true civility'.

Third, again precisely because this equality is abstract, inclusion within it is quite compatible with actual and concrete inequalities. Thus it is that in the era where the abstract equality of humans has been most emphatically affirmed, actual inequalities between humans have grown to unprecedented levels, so that the social, economic, and political inequalities today between the most powerful and the least powerful humans are far greater than before the affirmation of the 'natural equality' of all humans.

In other words, once modern civility and its abstract and sovereigntycentred concept of equality acquire the permanence of a fixed popular opinion, actual inequality becomes ever more rampant, and the wholly enlightened earth becomes radiant with calamity.

The Obscuring of the Neighbour

With the emergence of this new immanent equality, the figure of the neighbour, whether theological or quasi-universal, is obscured in new ways. First, because of the increasing separation of the transcendent and the immanent, it is no longer possible to hold together the two versions of the commandment in the Sermon on the Mount that are 'like unto each other'—the injunction, on the one hand, to love God with all one's soul and mind and, on the other hand, to love one's neighbour as oneself. Now, each of these goes their own way, and love of neighbour bereft of love of God (for let us not forget that even the mystical tradition is marked by love of God, even if this is a God that cannot be found) seems a rather sorry affair.

Second, there is also the wilting of the self that had anchored love of neighbour. In *Works of Love,* Kierkegaard stresses that much turns on the phrase 'as oneself'. 'Is it possible for anyone to misunderstand this, as if it were Christianity's intention to proclaim self-love as a prescriptive right? Indeed, on the contrary, it is Christianity's intention to wrest self-love away from us human beings. . . . [I]f the commandment is properly understood it also says the opposite: You shall love yourself in the right way'; it leads to 'proper self-love'.

That Kierkegaard had to declare this is itself a symptom of how the times had changed. From the perspective of the New Testament, and we might add more broadly from the perspective of all the post-axial religions, it would have been self-evident that to love oneself with all one's soul, mind, and strength would be plain wrong. It would install precisely the self-love that the post-axial religions uniformly rail against. But by the time Kierkegaard wrote, and arguably much earlier, this background common sense had become so unfamiliar that it needed to be explicitly asserted.

What had come to be commonsensical instead was the self-organized around self-interest and self-love. The increasing primacy accorded to the economic logic of self-interest is very explicit in Lockean traditions, where 'man', having been given reason by God, becomes a godly figure himself. And as a being who possesses property in himself, when man exercises this reason, he appropriates external things as private property by depositing his labour—that is to say, himself—in them. The *Two Treatises on Government,* especially the second, is about instituting forms of governance that build on this reciprocity. Even his 'duty of toleration', and the neighbourliness it introduces, are premised on the 'good fences' introduced by property in the person and things.[25]

And it is from within a field where self-love and self-interest have come to be synonymous that both Freud and Dostoevsky write. Indeed, Freud's remarks exemplify how difficult it had become to comprehend or even perceive the New Testament injunction. Recall Freud's questions: 'What good will it do us? But, above all, how shall we achieve it? How can it be possible?' And he goes on:

> My love is something valuable to me which I ought not to throw away without reflection. It imposes duties on me for whose fulfilment I must be ready to make sacrifices. If I love. someone, he must deserve it in some way. . . . He deserves it if he is so like me in important ways that I can love myself in him; and he deserves it if he is so much more perfect than myself that I can love my ideal of my own self in him. Again, I have to love him if he is my friend's son, since the pain my friend would feel if any harm came to him would be my pain too—I should have to share it. But if he is a stranger to me and if he cannot attract me by any worth of his own or any significance that he may already have acquired for my

---

[25] Anthony G. Wilhelm, 'Good Fences and Good Neighbours: John Locke's Positive Doctrine of Toleration', *Political Research Quarterly* 52, no. 1 (March 1999), 145–66. What I suggest above is not, of course, Wilhelm's argument. But I believe the material Wilhelm presents is amenable to being read in a manner that stresses the primacy of 'good fences'.

emotional life, it will be hard for me to love him. Indeed, I should be wrong to do so, for my love is valued by all my own people as a sign of my preferring them, and it is an injustice to them if I put a stranger on par with them. But if I am to love him (with this universal love) merely because he, too, is an inhabitant of this earth, like an insect, an earth-worm or a grass-snake, then I fear that only a small modicum of my love will fall to his share—not by any possibility as much as, by the judge-ment of my reason, I am entitled to retain for myself. What is the point of a precept enunciated with so much solemnity if its fulfilment cannot be recommended as reasonable?

On closer inspection, I find still further difficulties. Not merely is this stranger in general unworthy of my love; I must honestly confess that he has more claim to my hostility and even my hatred. He seems not to have the least trace of love for me and shows me not the slightest consid-eration. . . . Indeed, if this grandiose commandment were to read: 'Love thy neighbour as thy neighbour loves thee', I should have no quarrel with it . . .

The reality behind all this, which many would deny, is that human beings are not gentle creatures in need of love, at most able to defend themselves if attacked; on the contrary, they can count a powerful share of aggression among their instinctual endowments. Hence, their neigh-bour is not only a potential helper or sexual object, but also someone who tempts them to take out their aggression on him, to exploit his la-bour without recompense, to use him sexually without his consent, to take possession of his goods, to humiliate him and cause him pain, to torture and kill him. *Homo homini lupus* [Man is a wolf to man]. Who, after all that he has learnt from life and history, would be so bold as to dispute this proposition? . . .

These remarks spring from a logic that privileges self-love as self-interest, and the economic logic that flows from this. Freud's questions would not have arisen in the same way for either theological or quasi-universal versions of the biblical injunctions, both of which have an antagonistic or agonistic relation with self-love as self-interest. The theological injunction would have resolved these questions by bringing together God and neighbour, insisting that love here is not for the neigh-bour in their singularity but of God in the neighbour, and that this love is reciprocated by God even if not by the neighbour; the quasi-universal injunction would have sidestepped these questions by saying that they are the wrong ones to ask.

* * *

Third, as I noted earlier, the neighbour is displaced by a new injunction—the categorical imperative. Indeed, while Freud's objections are powerful, it would not be unfair to say that many—most—of his criticisms have been anticipated and deflected by Kant, who is quite inclined to draw a line of descent from the New Testament injunction to the categorical imperative.[26] Like Freud, Kant begins with the assumption that man is wolf to man. Like Freud again, Kant is sceptical of extending a singular love (Freud: 'something valuable to me', 'my preferring them') to neighbours. But unlike Freud, Kant gets around this by distinguishing between a singular love that is 'pathological' and a neighbourly love that is 'practical' and 'benevolent'.

And then, the categorical imperative folds into itself some of the aneconomy of the neighbour. Within its own terms (the terms of 'humanity') there is nothing economic about the injunction to treat humanity, whether in one's person or in another, as never merely a means to an end but an end in itself. And yet, sharing as he does with Freud the assumption that man is evil, Kant emphatically stresses that he does not seek the 'moral reformation of mankind'. Instead, even though he never quite puts it this way, it turns out that the categorical imperative can be secured only through the hypothetical imperative involved in the economic pursuit of self-interest. Thus, in the first supplement to 'Towards Perpetual Peace', he remarks:

> The problem of establishing a state, no matter how hard it may sound, is soluble even for a nation of devils (if only they have understanding) and goes like this: 'Given a multitude of rational beings all of whom need universal laws for their preservation but each of whom is inclined covertly to exempt himself from them, so to order this multitude and establish their constitution that, although in their private dispositions they strive against one another, these yet so check one another that in their public conduct the result is the same as if they had no such evil

---

[26] Kenneth Reinhard, 'Neighbour', in *Dictionary of Untranslatables*, ed. Barbara Cassin (Princeton, NJ: Princeton University Press, 2014).

dispositions.' Such a problem must be soluble. For the problem is not the moral improvement of human beings but only the mechanism of nature, and what the task requires one to know is how this can be put to use in human beings in order so to arrange the conflict of their unpeaceable dispositions within a people that they themselves have to constrain one another to submit to coercive law and so bring about a condition of peace in which laws have force. It can be seen even in actually existing states, still very imperfectly organized, that they are already closely approaching in external conduct what the idea of right prescribes, though the cause of this is surely not inner morality . . . .[27]

What Kant envisages here is precisely the kind of social order that is put in place in republican and liberal democracies, both of which are distinctive ways of inflecting the 'rights of man and citizen'. (Notably, Kant broadly endorses Locke's formulation about man possessing property in him; he sees it as folded into his own reformulation.)

If we are to return to Freud's remarks cited at the beginning of this essay about the New Testament injunction as 'an excellent example of the unpsychological manner in which the cultural super-ego proceeds', then perhaps the categorical imperative could be described as the cultural superego proceeding inversely—in a psychological manner. And where this psychological manner of instituting the cultural superego becomes commonsensical, then the unpsychological manner seems increasingly ludicrous. Ironically, it may have been partially from within the fold of the psychological manner of the categorical imperative that the unpsychological nature of the biblical injunction may have seemed self-evident to Freud.[28]

---

[27] Immanuel Kant, 'Toward Perpetual Peace', in his *Practical Philosophy,* trans. and ed. Mary Gregor (Cambridge: Cambridge University Press, 1996), 335.

[28] In his 1924 essay 'The Economic Problem of Masochism', Freud remarks that the categorical imperative is 'the direct heir of the Oedipus complex' (167). That remark occurs after a discussion where he remarks that the superego 'came into being through the introjection into the ego of the first objects of the id's libidinal impulses—namely, the two parents. . . . Only in this way was it possible for the Oedipus complex to be surmounted'; it is followed by a description of the superego as a 'substitute for the Oedipus complex'. On the other hand, the essay also distinguishes between the superego and a 'moral masochism', which occurs when morality becomes sexualized once more, the Oedipus complex is revived, and the way is opened for a regression from morality to the Oedipus complex. Does Freud view the categorical imperative the direct heir of the Oedipus complex as a superego, or a moral masochism, or a coming together of both? The answer to this question is not clear from Freud's own pronouncements. But given the centrality of the hypothetical imperative to the categorical imperative, given also Kant's insistence

Towards a New Neighbourliness

And yet, this psychological manner of instituting a cultural superego has proved to be violent in new ways. (Let us not get too hung up on the question of whether it is less, as, or more violent than the older superego of the theologized neighbour—that is the wrong question to ask.) On the one hand, the categorical imperative includes within its aneconomy only humans or rational beings. So its aneconomy excludes by definition most of the living world and all of the non-living world. The enormous consequences of this exclusion, of which the Kantian injunction is only one manifestation, are arguably the single largest factor in the climate change that our world faces today.

On the other hand, even for those included within the aneconomy, the fact that the categorical imperative can only be realized through the hypothetical imperative ends up ruining the categorical imperative itself. To treat others as ends in themselves is to sacralize their self even where this self is constituted by self-interest and self-love. And in this dependence the hypothetical imperative comes to dominate and suffuse the categorical imperative, even speak the language of the latter.

Even though he does not explicitly target Kant, the young Marx teases out the mechanism of this domination very forcefully in 'On the Jewish Question'. As Marx notes there, the words 'man' and 'citizen' in Declaration seek to institutionalize nothing less than the way humanity was to be equally treated as an end: in the private sphere, 'man' as a monadic being pursuing his own desires and goals was treated as an end, and in the public sphere, the citizen as a being pursuing the collective good was treated as an end. Marx also points to the inevitable outcome: 'man' comes to dominate and spectralize the citizen.

* * *

It is at the devastation that accompanies the world of the categorical imperative that Gandhi too takes aim when he attacks 'modern

---

that he does not seek the 'moral reformation of mankind', it seems appropriate to suggest that while the categorical imperative is indeed the modern form of the a cultural superego, it is not a moral masochism.

civility' and its manifestation in 'parliamentary swaraj'. And yet, those who questioned the categorical imperative, or 'modern civility' more broadly, could not simply return to the old figure of the neighbour. Most of all, the democratic spirit had transformed their horizon. So even as they question modern civility's conceptions of a democratic society, they do so in the spirit of the trinity of liberty, equality, and fraternity.

To conceive of the neighbour in terms of the immanent trinity of liberty, equality, and fraternity is to transform that figure. Now love of neighbour can no longer be articulated in the terms that Kierkegaard still resorts to—equality in the eyes of God. Now love of neighbour becomes about an immanent equality. And at the same time this immanent equality is very different from the immanent equality involved in capitalism or nationalism. Unlike the latter, this reformulation of neighbourly love tries to envision an immanent equality that does not have inequality as its undertow, an equality that is unconditionally opposed to inequality.

This is not just a more intense version of the same equality as that organized around commensurable incommensurability, as with liberal traditions or democratic forms of the nation state. Nor even is it premised on the immeasurability or incommensurability that is involved in embracing the possibility of one's own death, as arms-bearing warriors do in their heroic moments. Far from any of these, equality here begins from an incommensurability without ground, an incommensurability all the way through.

And precisely because it does not require any commensurability or abstract criterion as its cut-off, neighbourly equality when it turns immanent is open to a promiscuous inclusion.[29] In other words, here equality is not only with other humans. It must be with animals and things, with any and every entity. This promiscuous equality is implicit already in the

---

[29] It could perhaps be argued that such a promiscuous inclusion is Marx's horizon too. But if we go by the 'Critique of the Gotha Program', the only occasion where he articulates a positive communist vision at any length, then that inclusion is only in the remote future, not in the now. By contrast, what is striking about the immanent equality of the neighbour is that it seeks an equality in the here and now.

injunction to love the neighbour as oneself, but it is rarely thematized. How to think and enact this other equality, this equality of the minor— that is the challenge that Gandhi is brought to in the wake of the ruination of both premodern traditions of the neighbour and modern sovereignty-centred visions of equality.[30]

[30] For conversations about this essay and its arguments, I would like to especially thank Vinay Gidwani, Vinay Lal, Karuna Mantena, Chakravarthi Ram Prasad, Simona Sawhney, Tridip Suhrud, Shiney Varghese, and the participants in the workshop on Gandhi in January 2020 at the University of California, Los Angeles, and the 2022 Winter School, University of Western Cape.

4

Historical Memory and American Nonviolence

Recovering the Radical Roots and Vision of

the 'American Gandhi' A. J. Muste

Leilah Danielson

Today few Americans, much less South Asians, have heard of A. J. Muste, the radical Protestant minister who was second only to Martin Luther King in making nonviolence a central feature of American social movement culture.[1] In this context, it is important to recognize that nonviolence was a tactic not only of the African American civil rights movement but also in campaigns against American imperialism, conscription, and war that predated and then burgeoned in the 1960s.[2] By focusing on Muste, this essay will demonstrate that adapting Gandhian nonviolence to American political culture was a theoretical and—probably most importantly—an organizational project. Virtually none of M. K. Gandhi's

[1] There have been only three biographies of Muste: Leilah Danielson, *American Gandhi: A. J. Muste and the History of American Radicalism in the Twentieth Century* (Philadelphia: University of Pennsylvania Press, 2014); Jo Ann Ooiman Robinson, *Abraham Went Out: A Biography of A. J. Muste* (Philadelphia: Temple University Press, 1981); and Nat Hentoff, *Peace Agitator: The Story of A. J. Muste* (New York: Macmillan, 1963). In-depth treatments of him can also be found in Vaneesa Cook, *Spiritual Socialists: Religion and the American Left* (Philadelphia: University of Pennsylvania Press, 2019), and Kip Kosek, *Acts of Conscience: Christian Nonviolence and Modern American Democracy* (New York: Columbia University Press, 2007).

[2] For the use of Gandhian nonviolence in movements against US empire, nuclear weapons, and war, see, for example, Danielson, *American Gandhi*; Marian Mollin, *Radical Pacifism in Modern America: Egalitarianism and Protest* (Philadelphia: University of Pennsylvania Press, 2008); Kosek, *Acts of Conscience*; Scott Bennett, *Radical Pacifism: The War Resisters League and Gandhian Nonviolence in America, 1915–1963* (Syracuse, NY: Syracuse University Press, 2003); and Lawrence Wittner, *Rebels Against War: The American Peace Movement, 1933–1983*, rev. ed. (Philadelphia: Temple University Press, 1984).

Leilah Danielson, *Historical Memory and American Nonviolence* In: *Gandhi, Truth, and Nonviolence*. Edited by: Vinay Lal, Oxford University Press. © Oxford University Press 2025.
DOI: 10.1093/9780198936657.003.0005

American admirers, white or black, actually tried nonviolent direct action until the 1940s, and this was largely due to the efforts of A. J. Muste.[3] Attention to Muste also highlights the hybrid roots of American nonviolence and allows us to identify some of the similarities and differences between American nonviolence and Gandhian nonviolence, as well as recurrent tensions within the tradition of nonviolence itself over its relationship to the nation state.[4]

These differences and tensions played out in the late 1950s and early 1960s when Muste collaborated with Indian Gandhians like J. P. Narayan, Vinoba Bhave, and Devi Prasad in a transnational organization called the World Peace Brigade, which sought to combine nonviolence, anti-colonialism, and nonalignment in the Cold War. Their efforts raised the question: What is the role of nonviolence in a postcolonial context? Should it be used to consolidate the power of the new nation state or was it to continue to struggle for a more expansive vision of human liberation? A similar question confronted civil rights activists with the passage of civil rights legislation in 1964 and 1965. Should they work within the Democratic Party to move it to the left or continue to work outside of the system through mobilizing poor and exploited peoples in solidarity with the 'Third World'? Muste's mentee Bayard Rustin famously—or

[3] Recent scholarship highlighting black American solidarity with Indian *swaraj* in the 1920s through the 1940s has tended to obscure the fact that most African Americans, radical and liberal alike, viewed *satyagraha* as impractical or as culturally unassimilable. Those African Americans who did apply M.K. Gandhi's methods to American race relations, such as Bayard Rustin, James Farmer, and Pauli Murphy, did so as part of interracial and Christian contexts and organizations, such as the Fellowship of Reconciliation, which was led by A.J. Muste. White Americans who admired Gandhi were also deeply ambivalent about nonviolence and did not adapt it for American conditions until the 1940s, again under the leadership of Muste. See discussion below and Leilah Danielson, "In My Extremity I Turned to Gandhi': American Pacifists, Christianity, and Gandhian Nonviolence, 1915–1941', *Church History: Studies in Christianity and Culture* 72, no. 2 (June 2003): 361–88.

[4] See, for example, Karuna Mantena, 'On Gandhi's Critique of the State: Sources, Contexts, Conjunctures', *Modern Intellectual History* 9, no. 3 (2012): 535–63; Sandipto Dasgupta, 'Gandhi's Failure: Anticolonial Movements and Postcolonial Futures', *Perspectives on Politics* 15, no. 3 (September 2017): 647–62; and Bhikhu Parekh, *Gandhi's Political Philosophy: A Critical Examination* (London: Macmillan, 1989), esp. ch. 5. American nonviolence grew partly out of the tradition of nonresistance which had strong anti-statist tendencies. See Charles DeBenedetti, *The Peace Reform in American History* (Bloomington: Indiana University Press, 1980), esp. 41–4, 70–1. Significantly, and in some ways similarly to the differences between M. K. Gandhi and B. R. Ambedkar, white pacifists tended to be more libertarian than African Americans, who sought justice through the federal government over and against local social structures. For a discussion of these tensions, see Danielson, *American Gandhi*, 296–315.

infamously—chose politics over protest. Muste, like his comrade J. P. Narayan, argued that nonviolence had no place within the world of power politics and chose to work outside of—and indeed against—the state in his efforts to build the 'beloved community'.[5]

Despite Muste's centrality to the history of nonviolence and indeed to the history of the left, he has been virtually erased from American historical memory. For if Gandhi and King are perhaps remembered too much, Muste is remembered hardly at all. One reason for this may be that he is unassimilable within the language of American nationalism; as a revolutionary socialist, a Christian pacifist, and an internationalist, he hardly fits within narratives of exceptionalism, progress, opportunity, and martial prowess. But this does not explain why historians have failed to give him the historical and critical attention he deserves. I will suggest that even as historians express concern about living in a post-truth, post-facts world, they have been complicit in distorting the historical record to fit present-day political sensibilities. Here I want to be careful to draw a distinction between, on the one hand, the inevitable and productive ways in which the present shapes the questions we ask of the past and, on the other hand, cherry-picking the past to affirm contemporary political projects and identities.[6] Among these are a contempt of nonviolence, which is associated with weakness and gradualism, and of religion, which is

[5] See Bayard Rustin, 'From Protest to Politics: The Future of the Civil Rights Movement' [1964], reprinted in Devon W. Carbado and Donald Weise, eds., *Time on Two Crosses: The Collected Writings of Bayard Rustin* (San Francisco: Cleis Press, 2003): 116–29; Muste, 'The Civil Rights Movement and the American Establishment' [1965], reprinted in Nat Hentoff, ed., *The Essays of A. J. Muste* (New York: Simon & Schuster, 1967): 451–61; and Muste, 'Rifle Squads or the Beloved Community' [1964], reprinted in Hentoff, ed., *The Essays of A. J. Muste*, 426–37. There are numerous accounts of civil rights activists' disillusionment with liberalism and their debates about their relationship to the state. See, for example, Daniel Lucks, *Selma to Saigon: The Civil Rights Movement and the Vietnam War* (Lexington: University of Kentucky Press, 2017), and Peniel Joseph, *Waiting 'Til the Midnight Hour: A Narrative History of Black Power* (New York: Holt, 2006). My (limited) understanding of Narayan comes from the research I conducted on the World Peace Brigade and Lydia Walker, 'Jayaprakash Narayan and the Politics of Reconciliation for the Postcolonial State and its Imperial Fragments', *India Economic and Social History Review* 56, no. 2 (2019): 147–69; Eva-Marie Nag, 'Marxism and Beyond in Indian Political Thought: J. P. Narayan and M. N. Roy's Concepts of Radical Democracy', PhD diss., London School of Economics and Political Science, 2003; and Thomas H. Keene, 'From Marxism to Gandhianism', *Journal of Third World Studies* 7, no. 2 (Fall 1990): 116–29.

[6] For a nuanced discussion of presentism, see David Armitage, 'In Defense of Presentism', in *History and Human Flourishing*, ed. Darrin M. McMahon (Oxford: Oxford University Press, 2020).

associated with fundamentalism and political conservatism. As a result, the historiography of the civil rights movement and of the American left more broadly has been overwhelmingly secular, neglecting the reality of more diverse genealogies, including those rooted in nonviolence, spirituality, and interracial solidarity.[7]

The centrality of religion to Muste's worldview and politics was rooted in his upbringing. He immigrated from the Netherlands to the United States in 1891 when he was 6 years old. His parents were strict Calvinists and members of the Reformed Church of America, which held to doctrines like predestination that had long been abandoned by most American Protestants. They were also working class; his father worked for decades as an unskilled labourer in Grand Rapids furniture factories. A precocious child with exceptional intellectual abilities and a deeply spiritual nature, Muste earned a scholarship to a Reformed Church's preparatory high school and college and in 1907 went on to pursue his divinity degree at New Brunswick Theological Seminary in New Jersey.

Muste later recalled that the seminary was a hotbed of reaction and orthodoxy, but it gave him access to the great metropolis of New York City, where he took classes at Columbia University, New York University, and Union Theological Seminary. There he was introduced to biblical criticism, social gospel theology, Christian mysticism, and the pragmatic philosophy of William James and John Dewey. These were radical ideas at the time: the social gospel suggested that the roots of sin were social, not individual, and that Christians had a moral obligation to work for social and economic justice. As for pragmatism, it was a distinctly modern philosophy which held that 'truth' emerges out of the dynamic interaction

---

[7]   The post-1954 era of civil rights used to give Christian nonviolence pride of place, but this has receded in recent decades. Indeed, the literature has become strikingly materialist, suggesting that religion was something the movement had to overcome. See Jacquelyn Dowd Hall, 'The Long Civil Rights Movement and the Political Uses of the Past', *Journal of American History* 91, no. 4 (March 2005): 1233–63; Timothy Tyson, *Radio Free Dixie: Robert E. Williams and the Roots of Black Power* (Chapel Hill: University of North Carolina Press, 1999); Martha Biondi, *To Stand and Fight: The Struggle for Civil Rights in Postwar New York City* (Cambridge: Harvard University Press, 2003); Joseph, *Waiting 'Til the Midnight Hour*; and Charles E. Cobb, *This Nonviolence Stuff 'll Get you Killed* (New York: Basic Books, 2014). The marginalization of religion in the history of the left can be seen in two recent otherwise outstanding syntheses: Michael Kazin, *American Dreamers: How the Left Changed a Nation* (New York: Alfred A. Knopf, 2011), and Howard Brick and Christopher Phelps, *Radicals in America: The U.S. Left since the Second World War* (Cambridge: Cambridge University Press, 2015).

between the individual and the environment, theory and practice, and thus is always subject to change and revision.[8] As we shall see, a commitment to the pragmatic method—to grounding theory in practice and the individual in community—would shape Muste's long career as a political activist; he was, we might say, a flexible revolutionary, able to adapt and change his position in light of new evidence and experience. This would also make him a skilled organizer and shrewd political strategist. As the recently deceased Socialist Party leader David McReynolds said of his mentor, Muste was both 'a saint' and as 'sly as a fox'.[9]

Muste's move toward a more modern religiosity and sensibility can be seen in his 1914 decision to leave his Reformed pulpit in Manhattan for a more liberal church outside of Boston. His new pastorate placed him at the centre of the Anglo-American tradition of nonconformity. Nearby Concord was the place where Henry David Thoreau went to jail rather than pay taxes to support the US–Mexican War, and Muste's parishioners felt a deep sense of identification and connection with the tradition of nonresistance and abolitionism that had played such a prominent role in the region. Liberated from the theological and political constraints of his former pastorate, Muste drew deeper into Christian mysticism and left politics.[10] He joined the Socialist Party and the Fellowship of Reconciliation (FOR), an international organization founded in 1916 that would become the largest peace organization in the United States.

The FOR was something new in the history of Western pacifism. Prior to World War I, pacifism (also known as nonresistance) was associated with the Historic Peace Churches—the Quakers, Brethren, and Mennonites—and conscientious objection to war. Aside from Quaker involvement in abolitionism and women's rights, it was a largely apolitical and individualistic tradition. By contrast, FOR members were mostly from mainline Protestant churches, and they saw themselves not

---

[8] On pragmatism and modernism, see James Livingston, *Pragmatism and the Political Economy of Cultural Revolution, 1850–1940* (Chapel Hill: University of North Carolina Press, 1994). For a recent account of the social gospel, see Christopher Evans, *The Social Gospel in American Religion* (New York: New York University Press, 2017). For the links between mysticism, Social Christianity, and cosmopolitanism, see Leigh Eric Schmidt, *Restless Souls: The Making of American Spirituality* (San Francisco: HarperCollins, 2005).

[9] David McReynolds, interview with author, 16 June 2006, New York City.

[10] See Muste, 'Sketches for an Autobiography', in Hentoff, ed., *Essays of A. J. Muste*, 45; Muste, Oral Memoir, Reminiscences of Abraham John Muste (1954), Oral History Collection of Columbia University, 264 (hereafter COHC).

only as witnesses for Christ but as political beings committed to using 'the method of Jesus' to resolve vexing industrial, racial, and international problems. As we shall see, what that would exactly mean in practice would turn out to be quite contentious, but for the duration of World War I the FOR provided community and support for those persecuted for their anti-war views.[11]

Indeed, the decision to join the FOR would turn out to have momentous consequences both for Muste and the American left. Before the war, socialism and anti-militarism were not necessarily seen as 'un-American', but this would change over the course of the war and into the post-war era. President Woodrow Wilson demanded conformity in his crusade to 'save democracy' and supported the passage of the Sedition Act and the Espionage Act, which essentially made it a crime to criticize the government or the war. A repressive atmosphere quickly enveloped the country as socialists and other opponents of the war found themselves hounded, jailed, and even deported.[12] Muste was among the persecuted; he lost his pulpit and became a sort of freelance minister and organizer for the nascent American Civil Liberties Union, which had organized to protect dissenters and conscientious objectors.

Although impoverished and harassed by patriotic mobs and the Bureau of Investigation (the precursor of the FBI), Muste was eager to put his twin ideals of labour's emancipation and Christian 'brotherhood' into practice, and he travelled to nearby Lawrence, Massachusetts, to see if he might be of service to the 30,000 textile workers on strike. An inspiring and charismatic speaker with a remarkable ability to reconcile different points of view and construct a cohesive vision out of the strike's kaleidoscopic ideological and ethnic diversity (with a largely immigrant workforce, strike pamphlets had to be posted in twelve different languages), he was quickly elected executive secretary of the general strike committee. Reflecting his

---

[11] See Patricia Appelbaum, *Kingdom to Commune: Protestant Pacifist Culture between World War I and the Vietnam Era* (Chapel Hill: University of North Carolina Press, 2009); Kosek, *Acts of Conscience*; Wittner, *Rebels against War*; and Charles Chatfield, *For Peace and Justice: Pacifism in America, 1914–1941* (Knoxville: University of Tennessee Press, 1971).

[12] See Nick Salvatore, *Eugene V. Debs: Citizen and Socialist* (Urbana: University of Illinois Press, 1984); Christopher Capozzola, *Uncle Sam Wants You: World War I and the Making of the Modern American Citizen* (New York: Oxford University Press, 2010); Kosek, *Acts of Conscience*, 16–48; Thomas J. Knock, *To End All Wars: Woodrow Wilson and the Quest for a New World Order* (New York: Oxford University Press, 1992); and DeBenedetti, *The Peace Reform in American History*, 96–107.

pragmatism, Muste had also 'demonstrated an ability to learn on the job' and to adapt his principles to fit the situation. As he explained at the time, 'there are no absolute roles, formulas . . . You have, on the one hand, a 'social situation'; and, on the other, an individual. But neither of these terms is set and static; they are fluid and dynamic.' Ultimately, the 'rebel must submit himself to the test of results' and 'the test of group discussion . . . in spite of all the risks of compromise involved.'[13]

At the time, Muste identified as a pacifist, eschewing the use of violence and war, but he had no theory of nonviolent resistance. Still, his response to the violence that characterized the strike foreshadows his interest in Gandhian nonviolence. As he later recalled, this was the 'jungle era' of industrial warfare; police were deliberately provocative with daily attacks on the picket line and, at one point, even pointed machine guns at the striking workers. As the strike dragged on, pessimism set in and fights broke out between strikers and scabs. The policy was for strike leaders to avoid the picket line because they would be 'picked off' by the police. But, to boost morale, Muste decided to lead the picket line. No sooner had he begun than police on horseback immediately swarmed into the crowd, beat him savagely, and then carted him away in the police wagon. Bailed out later that evening, Muste returned the next morning to head up the picket line. The tactic proved a tremendous success. It lifted sagging spirits and turned liberal opinion toward the strikers. After four turbulent and violent months, it finally ended in victory with Muste elected head of the newly formed union, the Amalgamated Textile Workers of America.[14]

The Amalgamated Textile Workers would ultimately be defeated in the Red Scare that swept the United States in the years after World War I, but Muste had found his cause. He became a major figure in the era's dynamic workers' education movement and many of the dramatic labour struggles

[13] Muste, quoted in George Soule, *The Intellectual and the Labor Movement* (New York: League for Industrial Democracy, 1923): 21; Muste, 'Contradictions the Rebel Faces', *The World Tomorrow* 7, no. 5 (May 1924): 141–4. For the history of the 1919 Lawrence Strike and the Amalgamated Textile Workers of America, see David Goldberg, *A Tale of Three Cities: Labor Organization and Protest in Passaic, Paterson, and Lawrence, 1916–1921* (New Brunswick: Rutgers University Press, 1989). There is no evidence that Muste was aware of Gandhi's engagement with the Ahmedabad textile workers' strike of 1919.

[14] Muste, COHC, 367–75, 402–5; Muste, 'Sketches', 62–3, 75–7; 'Muste and Long on Trial in District Court', *Lawrence Daily Eagle* (13 March 1919), copy in Anthony Capraro Papers, 1891–1975, Immigration History Research Center, College of Arts and Letters, University of Minnesota, Box 8. See also Muste, 'Lawrence Strike Ended after Mills Grant 15 Percent Wage Increase', *The New Textile Worker* 1, no. 3 (24 May 1919), 1.

of the 1920s and 1930s. As he put it, the labour movement became his 'messiah', destined by history to usher in the Kingdom of God on earth where 'every man would sit under his own vine and fig tree, and none should make them afraid.'[15]

Muste's involvement in the labour movement put him in conflict with his fellow pacifists. Although most members of the FOR identified as socialists, they generally opposed labour strikes and boycotts, viewing them as coercive and therefore violent. According to FOR policy, 'true reconciliation' came from identifying with 'both sides of the quarrel' and then drafting a solution 'in which the true interest of every party can be satisfied'. In the case that one party to a dispute was unwilling to 'be converted', they suggested that it was better to let evil triumph than to violate their principles of nonviolence and love.[16] The FOR's insistence on this point led to Muste's disenchantment with pacifism. As he explained in a 1928 article, such thinking ignored the fact that the 'economic, social, political order in which we live was built up largely by violence, is now being extended by violence, and is maintained only by violence. . . . In a world built on violence, one must be a revolutionary before one can be a pacifist; in such a world a non-revolutionary pacifist is a contradiction in terms, a monstrosity.'[17]

Here we can see some of the parallels between Muste's thinking and Gandhi's. Muste's pragmatism—his commitment to grounding his ideals in experience—has obvious parallels with Gandhi's experiments with truth, and his insistence that being a revolutionary was ultimately more important than being a pacifist is reminiscent of Gandhi's dictum that 'where there is only a choice between cowardice and violence, I would advise violence'.[18] Gandhi felt he found the solution to this dilemma with *satyagraha*, but as much as American pacifists admired the Mahatma, they were deeply uncomfortable with the militant and confrontational nature of tactics like boycotts and collective civil disobedience. For example, the

---

[15]   Muste, 'Sketches', 85.

[16]   'FOR: A Constructive Policy', *c.*1915, Fellowship of Reconciliation Records, 1915–current, Swarthmore College Peace Collection, Box 1, folder 3 (hereafter FOR Records). See also John Haynes Holmes's editorial criticizing labour strikes in *The World Tomorrow* 10, no. 3 (March 1927), 41–2, and Henry Cadbury, 'The Strike: An Unethical Means of Coercion', *The World Tomorrow* 3, no. 5 (May 1920), 131–2.

[17]   Muste, 'Pacifism and Class War' [1928], reprinted in Hentoff, ed., *The Essays of A.J. Muste*, 179–85.

[18]   M. K. Gandhi, *The Power of Nonviolent Resistance: Selected Writings*, ed. Tridip Suhrud (Penguin Books, 2019): 114.

prominent peace activist Emily Greene Balch criticized the *satyagraha* campaigns Gandhi led in 1930 because they appeared to lack the spirit of goodwill that made repentance possible: 'An ultimatum is in essence a war method and issues from a war mentality. One never presents an ultimatum to a friend and if Gandhi does not consider the British as friends – however wrong and however wicked – then he has surrendered something more precious than the non-violence principle – the good will principle.'[19]

For his part, Muste did not take up serious study of Gandhi until the late 1930s; disillusioned with pacifism and caught up in the massive industrial unrest that accompanied the early years of the Great Depression, he had become a Marxist and a Leninist. Indeed, he had developed quite a following of working-class militants and radical intellectuals with his uniquely pragmatic understanding of Marxist theory. The 'Musteites', as they were known, differed from other Old Left groups in their emphasis on praxis as a means of building working-class consciousness. By the early 1930s, they could boast of having hundreds of thousands of workers organized in their Unemployed Leagues and of having played a leadership role in the movement for industrial unionism. But in 1935 their party—called the American Workers Party—was undermined by the decision to merge with the Trotskyists and form the Workers Party, USA, with Muste as national secretary. The Trotskyists did not conduct the merger in good faith, reneging on its conditions of the merger and working behind the scenes to undermine Muste's leadership.[20] Broken in body and spirit by the tactics his opponents had used against him, in the summer of 1936 he travelled to Europe, where he met with 'the old man', as Trotsky was known by his followers. Despite Trotsky's assurance of support, Muste found himself inexorably drawn back into Christianity. While sightseeing in France, he entered a Paris church, where he was 'saved', as it were, by a mystical experience, which reignited his religious faith and his commitment to nonviolence.[21]

---

[19] Emily Greene Balch to Mrs Cousins, 31 July 1930, quoted in Linda Schott, *Reconstructing Women's Thoughts: The Women's International League for Peace and Freedom Before 1941* (Stanford: Stanford University Press, 1997), 102. Emphasis in original. Even John Haynes Holmes, the Unitarian minister who helped to popularize Gandhian nonviolence, opposed its use by US pacifists. See his editorial, *Fellowship* 10, no. 7 (July 1944), 118.

[20] See Danielson, *American Gandhi*, chs 6 and 7, for a fuller discussion of Muste's time as a Marxist–Leninist.

[21] For his meeting with Trotsky, see Muste, 'My Experience in Labor and Radical Struggles', in *As We Saw the Thirties: Essays on Social and Political Movements of a Decade*, ed. Rita Simon

After his reconversion to Christianity, Muste came to see his experiences on the secular left as a parable for the limitations of Marxism and, to some degree, the Enlightenment as a whole. As he would argue in his 1940 book *Nonviolence in an Aggressive World* as well as in countless articles and speeches, the Enlightenment's emphasis on reason and progress marginalized the values of love, empathy, and cooperation that revolutionaries claimed would predominate in a socialist society. The 'proletarian movement' had been 'right in prophesying that men cannot live the good life under a 'bad system', but they had erred in assuming that a 'good system' would automatically create 'good men'. Questions of ethics and morality, of the relationship between means and ends, had to be faced if radicals hoped to build a just and peaceful world. 'If we are to have a new world,' Muste asserted, 'we must have new men; if you want a revolution, you must be revolutionized.'[22]

This was when Muste took up serious study of Gandhian nonviolence and began to theorize it for American conditions. Like Gandhi, Muste believed that suffering love was transformative. Also like Gandhi, who saw no contradiction between struggling for Indian freedom and regarding the British as friends, Muste believed that siding with workers and oppressed minorities was not an expression of hatred but rather of a love for justice and reconciliation. Just as Gandhi argued that there were limits to moral appeals and reason, Muste insisted that direct action was not incompatible with nonviolence but, rather, brought tension out into the open where it could be resolved.[23] Muste also, as we have seen, shared much of Gandhi's critique of materialist philosophy and held that social action had to be rooted in spiritual and moral values.

Indeed, Muste's understanding of nonviolent resistance was as expansive as Gandhi's. He frequently asserted that it was not exclusively direct action against injustice but a way of life that required a

(Urbana: University of Illinois Press, 1967), 146. For his 'reconversion' experience, see Muste, 'Return to Pacifism' [1936], and Muste, 'The True International' [1939], both reprinted in Hentoff, ed., *The Essays of A.J. Muste*, 195–202 and 207–14, respectively.

[22] Muste, 'Return to Pacifism', 199–201, and Muste, *Nonviolence in an Aggressive World* (New York: Harper & Bros, 1940), 3–5, 174–5.
[23] See Muste's notes on William Lovell's paper, FOR Study Conference on Revolutionary Pacifism, 1 February 1945, series A-1, box 5, folder 11, FOR Records; Muste, *Non-violence in an Aggressive World*, 125–6.

radical transformation of self as well as society. He called upon his fellow Christians and pacifists to model themselves on Gandhi's followers and subject themselves to training and discipline designed to cleanse themselves of self-righteousness and fear.[24] Though he was 'dubious' about what he saw as Gandhi's pre-industrial nostalgia, he also believed that there were 'elements implied or suggested by Gandhi's emphasis on spinning [that are] essential to an adequate non-violence movement'. Those elements included clarifying precisely what 'kind of economic order to strive for', the need to take action 'now' as opposed to waiting for some day in the future, and the importance of manual work for lifting 'the individual spirit' and for 'unifying' pacifists and their non-pacifist neighbors.[25]

Muste further shared Gandhi's distrust of the modern state and its centralizing, bureaucratic character for undermining genuine democracy and personal responsibility. Muste often warned that until people recognized that 'systems and institutions exist for man, not man for institutions', the trend toward 'totalitarianism' in modern life would continue.[26] Most of all, Muste wanted American pacifists to recognize that Gandhi's movement was a political movement. Like Gandhi, they had to build a mass movement, one that reached out to 'oppressed and minority groups such as Negroes, share-croppers, industrial workers, and help them to develop a nonviolent technique, as Gandhi did in the India National Congress'.[27]

The similarities between Muste and Gandhi should not, however, obscure the indigenous roots of many of Muste's ideas, as well as differences in form and substance. As we have seen, Muste's faith in the power of love drew from liberal Protestant theology and his mystical encounters with the divine. Indeed, part of his reworking of Gandhian nonviolence involved developing a theological basis for pacifism that would serve as a counterpoint to the rise of realism—also known as neo-orthodoxy—in

---

[24] See, for example, *Nonviolence in an Aggressive World*, 174–5, 181–2; Muste to James Farmer and George Houser, 4 June 1943, FOR Records, box 2, folder 1.

[25] Muste, 'The World Task of Pacifism' [1941], reprinted in Hentoff, ed., *The Essays of A.J. Muste*, 223–5.

[26] See, for example, Muste typescript, 'The Foundations of Democracy', c.1938, Abraham Johannes (A. J.) Muste Papers, 1920–67 (microfilm), Swarthmore College Peace Collection, reel 4 (hereafter Muste Papers).

[27] Muste, 'The World Task of Pacifism', 225.

liberal Protestantism during World War II and into the Cold War era. 'Realist' theologians like Reinhold Niebuhr—who, it should be noted, had been a member of the pacifist FOR in the 1920s and early 1930s— chastised liberals and pacifists for being naïve about the 'realities' of sin and power, and called for compromise with the coercion and violence that characterized relations between social classes and nation states. He did not, however, condone this reality but, rather, hoped that prophets (such as himself) would act as society's conscience and curb its excesses.[28] Muste sharply disagreed. Christianity was not an unrealizable ideal or individual ethic but a 'social concept' that offered a blueprint for social transformation. He argued that Jesus modelled himself on the Hebrew prophets, who held that righteousness was more important than power and saw defeat as a sign not of God's injustice but, rather, of one's own failure to be righteous and just. Just as the prophets emphasized the importance of repentance, Christ suffering on the cross was an essentially repentant act; it suggested that taking responsibility for one's own sins would liberate others to do the same. Thus, Muste concluded, if Christians expressed love for their enemies and accepted that they might be killed, they would fundamentally transform human society and perhaps even usher in the Kingdom of God.[29]

Muste's politics were also more socialist and his sensibility more modern than the Mahatma's. In 1937, *Time* magazine observed perceptively that although he had 'recanted the barricades, he is still vaguely Marxian'.[30] Unlike Gandhi, his goal was less decentralism per se than to democratize and demilitarize a left that he believed had been corrupted by Stalinism and scientism. He had little interest in rural life,

---

[28]   See, for example, Reinhold Niebuhr, *Moral Man and Immoral Society* (New York: Charles Scribner's & Sons, 1932; repr. 1948), and Reinhold Niebuhr, *The Children of Light and the Children of Darkness* (1944; Chicago: University of Chicago Press, 2011). There is a vast literature on Niebuhr, the Christian realists, and their criticism of pacifists, including Heather A. Warren, *Theologians of a New World Order: Reinhold Niebuhr and the Christian Realists, 1920–1948* (New York: Oxford University Press, 1997); Richard Fox, *Reinhold Niebuhr: A Biography* (Ithaca, NY: Cornell University Press, 1985; repr. 1996); and Donald Meyer, *The Protestant Search for Political Realism, 1919–1941* (Connecticut: Wesleyan University Press, 1989).

[29]   Muste made this argument in many forums, including *Nonviolence in an Aggressive World*, esp. 21–5, 33–4; Muste, *Not By Might, Christianity: The Way to Human Decency* (New York: Harper & Bros, 1947; Garland Library repr. ed., New York, 1971), esp. 56, 106–7; Muste, 'Theology of Despair' [1948] and 'Pacifism and Perfectionism' [1948], both reprinted in Hentoff, ed., *The Essays of A. J. Muste*, 302–7 and 308–21, respectively.

[30]   'Muste to Temple', *Time*, 10 May 1937, https://time.com/archive/6757046/religion-muste-to-temple/.

preferring the diversity, commotion, and cultural life of urban environments. Indeed, despite his Calvinist heritage, there was a 'sensuality' about him; he smoked 'innumerable cigarettes', ate meat, loved living in New York City, enjoyed baseball and poetry alike. 'I believe men are meant to lead the "abundant life", and this means physically, aesthetically, intellectually, spiritually', he explained to comrades interested in forming 'intentional communities' in rural settings. 'This involves variety, nonconformity, experimentation.'[31]

Notably, Martin Luther King would similarly interpret Gandhi through his own cultural and religious lens. King rarely used tactics like fasting as part of his nonviolent campaign for freedom and equality. He also had a stronger conviction of human sinfulness than Gandhi, frequently urging his fellow activists against 'superficial optimism'. There were, indeed, varieties of what we might call 'American-Gandhian nonviolence'; whether white, African American, or Mexican American, all reflected a process of synthesis and adaptation.[32]

In 1940, Muste was given the opportunity to realize his vision when the FOR hired him as national secretary. The organization had been in an ongoing crisis over the meaning and ethics of pacifism in the context of the class struggle and the rise of fascism in Europe. Keen to maintain its cultural and political relevance in the face of dwindling membership and prestige, the national committee had decided that it was finally time to overcome their apprehensions and experiment with Gandhian nonviolence. Muste was the ideal figure for moving the peace movement in this

---

[31] Muste to Committee on Nonviolent Action, 26 March 1963, Barbara Deming Papers, 1908–85, Schlesinger Library, Radcliffe Institute for Advanced Study of Women, Harvard University, Box 9, folder 151. See also Muste, 'Sketches', 90; Muste, COHC, 176–84, 353, 412–13.

[32] Martin Luther King Jr., *Stride Toward Freedom: The Montgomery Story* (New York: Harper & Row, 1958): 99. See also Bhikhu Parekh's brief discussion in his *Gandhi: A Very Short Introduction* (New York: Oxford University Press, 1997), 75–7, and Taylor Branch, *Parting the Waters: America in the King Years, 1954–1963* (New York: Simon & Schuster, 1988): 259. Still, some Americans who practised nonviolence did engage in fasting and other practices designed to self-purify and prepare for nonviolent struggle, including, at times, Muste. This was particularly true of pacifist 'actions' against nuclear weapons since they were eager to repent for their country's 'sin' of dropping the atomic bomb. See Danielson, *American Gandhi*, 243, 258–9. Catholic practitioners of nonviolence were more inclined to fast than Protestants, and fasting was central to the nonviolent approach of Cesar Chavez of the United Farmworkers. See Mel Piehl, *Breaking Bread: The Catholic Worker and the Origin of Catholic Radicalism in America* (Philadelphia: Temple University Press, 1982), and Matt Garcia, *From the Jaws of Victory: The Triumph and Tragedy of Cesar Chavez and the Farm Worker Movement* (Berkeley: University of California Press, 2014).

new direction. Not only did he have impeccable radical connections, but he had begun to attract a following among younger pacifists who were eager for action.[33]

Upon assuming office, Muste immediately appointed a committee on nonviolent resistance headed by J. Holmes Smith, a missionary who had just returned from India a committed Gandhian.[34] He also hired a slew of young organizers. These included James Farmer, a young African American who would later become one of the leading lights of the civil rights movement; Bayard Rustin, an African American Quaker with whom Muste was exceptionally close and who would organize the famous 1963 March on Washington Movement; George Houser, a white minister who later became prominent in the anti-apartheid movement; and Glenn Smiley, another white minister who would lead dozens of workshops on nonviolence from the 1940s through the 1980s (there is a well-known image of him sitting next to King on a bus after the famous Montgomery bus boycott came to a successful end). Muste directed them to organize 'cells'—a term clearly borrowed from his time as a Leninist—in which members would study nonviolence, develop a common discipline, and put their ideas into action. Some of these cells involved communal living, such as one in Ohio called Ahisma Farm and another in New Jersey called the Newark Christian Colony (later known as the Newark Ashram), but most were less formal.[35]

The main target of these early experiments with nonviolence was racial discrimination and segregation. Long before the civil rights movement of the late 1950s and 1960s, tiny FOR cells desegregated

---

[33] For details, see Danielson, *American Gandhi*, ch. 8. In December 1936, Muste organized the first use of Gandhian-style nonviolent resistance in the US. when he helped the American Federation of Full-Fashioned Hosiery Workers organize a 'lie-in'. See Muste, 'Sit Downs and Lie Downs', *Fellowship* 3, no. 3 (March 1937), 5–6; Herbert Bohn, 'We Tried Non-Violence', *Fellowship* 3, no. 1 (January 1937), 7–8. The industrial labour movement of the 1930s used the 'sit down' technique, but it was not nonviolent in the Gandhian sense.

[34] In a recent book, Michael Thompson charts the rise of anti-colonialism among Christian missionaries in the 1920s and 1930s, arguing that it drew from their experiences in the field and the agency of Christian converts, particularly in China but also India. See Thompson, *For God and Globe: Christian Internationalism between the Great War and the Cold War* (Ithaca: Cornell University Press, 2015).

[35] Muste was a member of the Mt. Morris cell in which members committed themselves to a common discipline of 'personal devotions' and vowed to practise humility, speak truth, live joyously, fearlessly, and simply, and refuse 'to earn my livelihood by any form of exploitation'. See 'Common Discipline of the Mt. Morris Cell', 1950, Peacemakers Movement Collected Records, 1948–80, Swarthmore College Peace Collection [hereafter PMR].

restaurants, swimming pools, and roller rinks throughout the Midwest and Northeast. In an effort to attract non-pacifists to their cause, they formed the Congress of Racial Equality (CORE) in 1942, which would become one of the most important civil rights organizations of the post-war era. They also provided critical support for A. Philip Randolph's 1943 March on Washington Movement, which threatened massive civil dis-obedience by African Americans to demand fair labour practices and the desegregation of the military. Probably most famous during this period was their 1947 Journey of Reconciliation, in which an interracial group travelled throughout the Upper South to test compliance with a recent Supreme Court decision declaring segregation in interstate travel illegal. The Journey would serve as the model for the more famous Freedom Rides in 1961, which would be led, not coincidentally, by CORE.[36]

Here it is important to note that during the 1940s few African Americans—much less whites—supported the use of Gandhian nonvi-olence to oppose racial discrimination and segregation. Although well connected, these self-identified 'radical pacifists' (a.k.a. 'nonviolent revo-lutionaries') in the FOR and CORE were an extreme minority; many of them had been conscientious objectors during World War II, an exceed-ingly unpopular position across the political spectrum, and their counter-cultural practices of interracial living put them well outside the American mainstream. Indeed, historians interested in documenting transnational links between African Americans and Indian nationalists in the 1930s and 1940s have exaggerated the degree to which these collaborations translated into practice. They have also distorted the historical record by depicting them as exclusively between people of colour; in fact, they took place within interracial contexts and within organizations com-mitted to interracial solidarity.[37] Muste, of course, is a prime example, as

---

[36] For details on CORE's organizational history and evidence that the organization would not have survived without Muste's support at the FOR, see August Meier and Elliot Rudwick, *CORE: A Study in the Civil Rights Movement* (Urbana: University of Illinois Press, 1975). See also Kosek, *Acts of Conscience*, 203–23.

[37] Scholarship in this vein includes Nico Slate, *Colored Cosmopolitanism: The Shared Struggle for Freedom in India and the United States* (Cambridge: Harvard University Press, 2012), and Sarah Azaransky, *This Worldwide Struggle: Religion and the International Roots of the Civil Rights Movement* (New York: Oxford University Press, 2017). For the movement's commit-ment to inter-racialism, see, for example, Meier and Rudwick, *CORE*, 34–9, 81; Erna Harris, 'It's Time We Outgrew "Race" Relations', *Fellowship* 11, no. 10 (October 1945); and James Farmer, *Lay Bare the Heart: An Autobiography of the Civil Rights Movement* (New York: Arbor House, 1985), 168–84. The rise of Black Power in the mid-1960s led many to rethink these ideas. See

he was the central figure in promoting nonviolence as an 'answer' to Jim Crow, whether by penning theological tracts or by providing critical institutional funding and support to activists on the ground. Yet despite his best efforts, most sympathetic whites and blacks alike responded by asserting that what worked in India certainly wouldn't work in the United States because of vast cultural differences and because African Americans were in the minority.[38]

King was typical. He read Muste in divinity school and attended one of his lectures, but thought his ideas were impractical, so much so that the two men 'got into a pretty heated argument'.[39] He changed his mind in 1955 during the Montgomery Bus Boycott when he observed the tremendous power and potential of a grassroots movement rooted in nonviolence and love. He found an indispensable ally in Muste, who helped to provide publicity through outlets like *Fellowship* magazine and *Liberation* magazine (an important organ of the emerging New Left edited by Muste, Rustin, and Dave Dellinger). He also provided financial support and human resources; he was the one largely responsible for deploying and funding figures like Rustin, Smiley, and James Lawson to the south, where they trained activists in nonviolent tactics. This explains King's 1963 statement that 'the current emphasis on nonviolent direct action in the race relations field is due more to A.J. than anyone else in the country'.[40]

Even as radical pacifists provided crucial support for the civil rights movement, there were tensions between the two movements. Many

---

Leilah Danielson, 'The 'Two-ness' of the Movement: James Farmer, Nonviolence, and Black Nationalism', *Peace and Change: A Journal of Peace Research* 29, no. 3 & 4 (July 2004): 430–53.

[38] See, for example, Muste et al., 'Civil Disobedience, is it the Answer to Jim Crow? A Symposium with Reinhold Niebuhr and Others' (New York: Nonviolent Action News Bulletin, 1943); Muste, 'What the Bible Teaches about Freedom' [1943], in Hentoff, ed., *The Essays of A. J. Muste*, 279–95.

[39] Francis Stewart, quoted in David Garrow, *Bearing the Cross: Martin Luther King, Jr. and the Southern Christian Leadership Conference* (New York: HarperCollins, 1986), 41. See also Branch, *Parting the Waters*: 73–4, 86–7. By contrast, James Lawson became a convert to nonviolence after hearing Muste speak at his alma mater in the autumn of 1947. He spent the next ten years exploring nonviolence in India and South Africa. When he returned to the US, Muste found the funds to deploy him to Nashville, where he became a major figure in the movement. James Lawson comments, Los Angeles, CA, 30 January 2020; Jo Ann Robinson notes from interview with James Lawson, 11 May 1979, Muste Papers, Later Accession, Box 2, Swarthmore College Peace Collection (hereafter Muste Papers-LA).

[40] Martin Luther King, Jr., quoted in Hentoff, *Peace Agitator*, 18.

African Americans feared that association with peace activists during the 'McCarthy era' (the 1950s witnessed the second Red Scare in US history) would undermine the legitimacy of black calls for equality. There has been a substantial literature on civil rights and the Cold War, which has shown the tremendous pressure placed on black activists to toe the line on US foreign policy and to adopt a narrow, nationalist approach to the freedom struggle.[41]

What this meant in practice was that during the height of the Cold War—the years 1948 through 1963—peace activism and civil rights activism developed along separate yet intersecting lines. Pacifists who embraced nonviolence in the 1940s, after all, were concerned about not only white supremacy but also American nationalism, militarism, and imperialism. Their concerns had magnified with the dropping of the atomic bomb and the emerging Cold War with the Soviet Union. As Muste asserted in numerous forums, including a 1947 book entitled *Not by Might: Christianity, The Way to Human Decency*, the bomb 'was the end-product of an age of mechanism, of power, of mass action, of totalitarianism, an age which looked down upon the individual and placed its faith in systems'.[42] To persuade his fellow Americans to repent for the 'sin' of atomic warfare and renounce their power, he and other radical pacifists engaged in civil disobedience 'against the war-making and conscripting State' by refusing to register for the draft or pay taxes for war.[43]

Not surprisingly, pacifist resistance failed to inspire other Americans to do the same. These were the early years of the Cold War in which there was widespread anti-communist consensus and a high degree of political conformity. Starting in the mid-1950s, however, Muste began to argue that a political and ideological space had opened for building 'what some call a Third Camp, others, perhaps, democratic socialism, others the Gandhian revolution'. Pointing to the Montgomery Bus Boycott, rising concerns about nuclear fallout, Soviet premier Nikita Khrushchev's

---

[41] See Mary Dudziak, *Cold War Civil Rights: Race and the Image of American Democracy* (Princeton: Princeton University Press, 2000); Penny Von Eschen, *Race against Empire: Black Americans and Anti-Colonialism* (Ithaca: Cornell University Press, 1997); and Brenda Gayle Plummer, *Rising Wind: Black Americans and U.S. Foreign Affairs, 1935–1960* (Chapel Hill: University of North Carolina Press, 1996).

[42] Muste editorial, *Fellowship* 11, no. 12 (December 1945), 1–2; Muste, *Not By Might*, 42–3.

[43] Muste, 'Of Holy Disobedience' [1952], reprinted in Hentoff, ed., *The Essays of A. J. Muste*, 355. See also Muste, *Not by Might*, 106–7.

denunciation of Stalin, and the emergence of a non-aligned movement in the decolonizing world, he called upon his perfectionist comrades to build alliances across the ideological spectrum of the American left and build a transnational movement against nuclear proliferation and empire. 'The American government and the American economic and cultural regime will not do this job', he stated unequivocally.[44] A flurry of organizing activity followed, including the formation of a new group called the Committee for Nonviolent Action (CNVA) to coordinate civil disobedience campaigns against nuclear weapons testing and proliferation—such as a 1959 protest at the Mead Missile Base in Omaha, Nebraska, which featured the 74-year-old Muste climbing over the fence and being arrested by the authorities. Radical pacifists also collaborated with Britain's Campaign for Nuclear Disarmament on a number of projects such as the San Francisco to Moscow March for Peace in 1961 to popularize disarmament and to advocate for nonalignment in the Cold War.

Starting around 1959–60, Muste's efforts to internationalize the peace movement increasingly focused on involving nationalist leaders and movements in the decolonizing world. He had long harboured hopes that anti-colonial movements might serve as the fulcrum for building a 'third camp' in opposition to the foreign policies of both the United States and the Soviet Union.[45] In 1949, he and Rustin had attended a meeting in New Delhi to discuss the idea of forming a transnational 'nonviolent army' that would oppose war and oppression. He also explored ways of supporting the anti-apartheid movement, meeting with African nationalists in London and supporting efforts by activists to set up training centres for nonviolence (a.k.a. 'positive action') on the continent.[46]

But even as Muste developed relationships and alliances with activists in India and Africa, he doubted the feasibility of this vision. He feared that the Cold War rivalry was so powerful that the emerging nations

[44] Muste, 'Proposal for a Bi-Monthly [Bi-Weekly?] Magazine', PMR, 21 February 1955. See also Muste, 'The Camp of Liberation', pamphlet published by *Peace News* (London, 1954).

[45] See, for example, Muste, typescript, 'Neutralism or Third Force', April 1955, Muste Papers, Reel 4.

[46] See D'Emilio, *Lost Prophet*, 187–9; Muste to the IFOR Council, 'World Trends and Pacifist Policy', FOR Records, Box 2, folder 1; FOR National Council Meeting Minutes, 3–4 December 1953, FOR Records, Box 4, folder 7; Bill Sutherland, interview with author, 1 April 2000, Austin, Texas; and George Houser, interview with author, 7 May 2000, Nyack, New York. Muste served on the board of the anti-apartheid American Committee on Africa, which had been organized by Houser and Sutherland.

would be unable to escape the ideological tug of war between the United States and the Soviet Union. He was also uncertain about the relationship between nonviolence and nationalism, and whether the place of pacifists was within a nation-building paradigm. Finally, he believed that it was desperately important for nonviolence and anti-nuclearism in the Global South to develop organically without the interference of 'outsiders', particularly those from the West, given the legacy of colonialism, white supremacy, and American responsibility for instigating the nuclear arms race.[47]

Still, he had reason to feel encouraged. In 1959, he participated in the Sahara Protest, a peaceful protest involving Americans, Europeans, and Ghanaians against French plans to test a nuclear bomb in the Sahara Desert. The interest aroused by the project encouraged Ghanaian President Kwame Nkrumah to call the All-African Conference on Positive Action for the Peace and Security of Africa in April 1960, which Muste attended with Ralph Abernathy of the Southern Christian Leadership Conference. Although the delegates refused to unequivocally endorse nonviolence, they drew up a manifesto stating that the larger struggle against the nuclear arms race was 'an integral part of the African liberation struggle' and expressed support for 'positive action' against white supremacy and colonialism.[48]

As it turns out, plans for setting up centres for positive action never really got off the ground (only one was ever established). Nevertheless, Muste continued to hope that stronger linkages might be made between Western pacifists and those struggling against colonialism. In December 1961, he joined approximately sixty other nonviolent activists in Beirut, Lebanon, to revive the idea, first proposed at the 1949 meeting in New Delhi, of an international 'peace army' that would oppose war preparations and assist anti-colonial struggles through nonviolent protest. The meeting concluded with the unanimous decision to form the World

---

[47] See, for example, Muste to J. P. Narayan, 25 January 1963, Muste Papers, Reel 36; Muste, 'Report on the Indian Crisis, 1962–63', 8 February 1963, typescript of article for *Peace News*, Muste Papers, Reel 5; and Muste, 'Peace and the Power States', *Liberation* 7, no. 8 (October 1962), 16–19, 23.

[48] Kwame Nkrumah, 'Against Nuclear Imperialism', *Liberation* 5, no. 3 (May 1960), 16–18. See also 'Some Notes on the Positive Action Conference to be Held in Accra April 7 to 9' [probably authored by Sutherland], 20 March 1960, and Muste to Harrison Butterworth, 15 April 1960, both in Muste Papers, Reel 7.

Peace Brigade (WPB); Muste, Michael Scott of England, and J. P. Narayan served as co-chairmen and respective heads of the organization's three regional councils (North American, European, and Asian).[49] Ultimately, it was short-lived; Western pacifists were uncomfortable in the world of high politics and power, while anti-colonial nationalists tended to privilege national liberation and state formation over nonviolence and antinuclear activism.

This paradox can be seen in the WPB's first major project, a demonstration to express solidarity with the Northern Rhodesia Independence Movement, led by Kenneth Kaunda, a proponent of nonviolence who had endorsed the WPB. With Muste heading up operations, the plan was to have an international team march across the border from Tanganyika (which became Tanzania in 1964) into Northern Rhodesia (now Zambia) in support of Kaunda's calls for free elections. Although Muste raised the necessary funds and recruited local, regional, and international volunteers, Kaunda ultimately called off the march because the British agreed to hold elections. As the African leader explained to Brigade member Bill Sutherland, 'it's quite clear now that we're going to have an election which will provide for majority rule, and the end of British control. I have been with you all this time. I have been nonviolent in principle . . . . But I have decided that I am going to be a politician and go into government.'[50] Kaunda's decision to forgo the protest in the interest of consolidating the new Zambian state foreshadowed the fate of other WPB initiatives, which tended to collapse within the context of state-centred politics. Sutherland, who was African American and who had decided to stay in Africa as an advisor to Kaunda and other African leaders, expressed his frustrations in a letter to Muste: 'I just can't find room within modern statehood for basic nonviolence.'[51]

---

[49]   The idea of an international peace army had been discussed at the 1949 World Pacifist Meeting at Sevagram, which Muste attended, but only Belgians and Indians followed through and created 'satyagraha units'. See Barbara Deming, 'International Peace Brigade', The Nation, 7 April 1962; Muste, typescript, 'Some Meanings of the Beirut Conference' c.1960], Muste Papers, Reel 5; and Muste, 'Nonviolence – A World Movement', Liberation (February 1962), 10–16.

[50]   Bill Sutherland and Matt Meyer, Guns and Gandhi in Africa: Pan African Insights on Nonviolence, Armed Struggle and Liberation in Africa (Trenton, NJ, and Asmara: Africa World Press, 2001), 96.

[51]   Bill Sutherland, quoted in Robinson, Abraham Went Out, 180.

The WPB's response to Chinese aggression on India's northern border in the early 1960s is further illustrative. The Gandhi Peace Foundation had invited Muste—whom they had dubbed the 'American Gandhi'—to an Anti-Nuclear Arms Convention in New Delhi in June 1962.[52] There he witnessed debates between former President Rajendra Prasad, who seemed to favour the idea of Indian disarmament, and Prime Minister Jawaharlal Nehru, who suggested that the masses would view it as an act of cowardice and fear, an offence to national pride, and a violation of the democratic process.[53] The patriotic reaction of the Indian people to Chinese excursions in the Himalayas several months later placed these tensions between nonviolence and nationalism in stark relief. As the government moved to defend its borders, Narayan asked Muste to return to New Delhi to participate in discussions about how Gandhians should respond to the national crisis. There, Muste showed that he recognized the complexity of the situation. On the one hand, he viewed China as the primary aggressor and maintained that the Indian reaction was understandable in the context of their recent struggle for independence. Yet he remained firm in his stance that self-proclaimed Gandhians should refuse to support the war, asserting that it would be impossible for those 'who sit in on the game of nationalism and power' to avoid becoming compromised by supporting military defence and national unity.[54]

Together, he and other WPB activists conceived of a project that they hoped would ease the tension between India and China, an 'International Friendship March from New Delhi to Peking' that would express 'the friendship and unity of peoples, irrespective of the policies pursued by their governments' and call upon the two countries to resolve their dispute without violence. Yet the international team, which began its trek in March 1963, faced criticism from Indian nationalists who saw them as apologists for Chinese aggression and resolute opposition from the Chinese who refused to let them cross through the border area. Internal

---

[52] Indian satyagrahis were the first to refer to him as 'the American Gandhi', a term that was picked up by the press at the time of his death in 1967. See clippings of appreciations, telegrams, and obituaries in the Muste Papers, Reels 1, 36, and 37. See also *WIN Special Supplement on A.J. Muste, 1885–1967*, copy in Muste Papers-LA, Box 2, and *Liberation* 12, nos. 6 and 7 (September and October 1967), a special issue on A. J. Muste.

[53] Muste, 'Prasad's Unique Challenge', *Liberation* 7, nos. 5–6 (July–August 1962), 16–17, 36.

[54] Muste, 'Report on the Indian Crisis, 1962–63'; Muste, 'Tiger at the Gates', *Liberation* 7, no. 12 (February 1963), 4–11.

debates further complicated matters; as Muste commented, Indian Gandhians had 'a much greater sense of identification with the nation-state than most Western pacifists do', refusing to publicly condemn the Indian state's use of force.[55] In fact, Indians themselves were divided over the question of Gandhi's legacy for national defence. Vinoba Bhave, for example, maintained that Gandhians should provide nonviolent assistance for national defence, while Narayan joined with Muste in arguing that India should resist militarism and strengthen its commitment to nonviolence.[56] These questions played themselves out every time the marchers arrived in a new village, as public meetings became scenes of passionate debate about the role of nonviolence in national defence, the future and nature of the nonaligned movement, and the implications of a nuclear-armed China.

In the end, the March ended in failure; in October, the team was stopped at the Burmese border by officials fearful of alienating China. Muste spent weeks trying to negotiate with the Chinese, but they remained unmoved. At the same time, the WPB faced a dearth of funds, as its financial sponsors in the United States prioritized aiding the African American civil rights movement. Regional concerns also drew attention away from transnational projects. The question of Kashmir's status and relations between India and Pakistan absorbed Narayan, while the conflict between the Cuban revolution and the American government preoccupied Muste. The WPB soon thereafter fell into disuse.[57]

---

[55] Muste, typescript, 23 April 1963; Muste 'Our Responsibility to the Friendship March', World Peace Brigade Reports, July 1963; Shri Siddharaj Dhadda, Statement, 16 April 1963; and Devi Prasad, 'Friendship Marchers in Difficulties', clipping from Peace News [c. March 1963]. All in Muste Papers, Reel 23.

[56] On these differences between Indian nationalists, see, for example, World Peace Brigade, Minutes of Meeting, 2 December 1962; 'In Orbit' (regarding Muste's interview with Vinoba Bhave on 'the Indian's pacifist's dilemma'), Arunodayam (June 1963), 6–8; J. P. Narayan, 'Delhi-Peking Friendship March: A Bridge of Friendship and Understanding', Arunodayam (June 1963), 9–11; Muste, 'India Yet Must Show the Way', Arunodayam (April 1963), 92–8. All in Muste Papers, Reel 23. My interpretation here is slightly different from Lydia Walker's, who paints a starker divide between Indian Gandhians and Western pacifists. See Walker, 'Jayaprakash Narayan and the Politics of Reconciliation', 157–9.

[57] Narayan to Muste, 22 September 1964; Narayan to Donald Groom, 4 April 1965; Muste, Memorandum on the Peace Brigade [1965]; Devi Prasad to Muste, 10 June 1965. All in Muste Papers, Reel 23. See also Robinson, Abraham Went Out, 182–3. The organizations that helped to sponsor the Friendship March were CNVA, FOR, the War Resisters International, and the American Friends Service Committee.

Muste was not unduly distressed by the failure of the WPB; rather, it reinforced his long-standing conviction that American activists had to primarily focus on building opposition to US foreign policy and the nuclear arms race, which he viewed as the biggest 'obstacle' to world peace.[58] As he pointed out, these positions were not mutually exclusive, since the Cold War rivalry placed a stranglehold on 'Third World' revolution and struggles for self-determination. Moreover, he strongly believed that the task of the peace movement was not to criticize or blame others but to 'concentrate on truly liberating itself and in so doing liberate its adversary'. These views would shape his response to the political developments of the 1960s and positioned him to take the lead in the movement against the Vietnam War.[59]

Notably, the challenges Muste faced in building an anti-war coalition were like those he had confronted in the WPB. American socialists and liberals alike were profoundly anti-communist and worried that activism against the war would alienate President Lyndon B. Johnson and the Democratic Party, which had just passed critical civil rights legislation and had an ambitious anti-poverty agenda. Bayard Rustin, for example, refused to break with the Johnson administration over the Vietnam War, arguing that the civil rights movement needed to consolidate its gains through institutionalization.[60] Yet Muste was adamant that this made the movement complicit with American militarism and empire. The movement for 'Freedom Now has to be for *liberation* of subjugated and humiliated people everywhere, or carry a cancer on its own body', he proclaimed in a famous essay chastising civil rights leaders for their reluctance to come out publicly against the war in Vietnam.[61] Through arguments like these, Muste would manage to pull together a diverse group of liberals and leftists, pacifists and Black Power militants, religious leaders and counter-culturalists, veterans and women peace activists, into the influential anti-war coalition, the Spring Mobilization Committee Against

[58] Muste, 'Who Has the Spiritual Atom Bomb?' [1965], reprinted in Hentoff, ed., *The Essays of A. J. Muste*, 500.
[59] Muste, 'Peace and the Power States', 16–19, 23.
[60] Rustin, 'From Protest to Politics'. John D'Emilio discusses the rift between Rustin and peace activists, as well as the anti-communist culture of the liberal left in *Lost Prophet*, 407–16. See also Doug Rossinow, *Visions of Progress: The Left-Liberal Tradition in America* (Philadelphia: University of Pennsylvania Press, 2008), ch. 5.
[61] Muste, 'The Civil Rights Movement and the American Establishment', 458–60.

the War in Vietnam (known by the acronym MOBE), with himself as executive secretary and civil rights leader James Bevel as national director. On 15 April 1967, MOBE led a massive, nationwide coordinated protest against the war that culminated in King's famous sermon at the Riverside condemning the war. Muste had died two months earlier, just days after returning from a meeting with Ho Chi Minh in North Vietnam.[62]

With Muste's death, newspapers in the United States, India, and throughout the world proclaimed that the world had lost 'the American Gandhi'.[63] This begs the question of why he has been largely invisible in the historiography of the civil rights movement, of transnationalism, of the American left, and of American religion. Undoubtedly, King's martyrdom a year later played some role in overshadowing Muste's contributions. But it also had to do with an increasingly pessimistic assessment of nonviolence by the American left, one that historians have to a large degree shared. The Johnson administration's refusal to end the war in Vietnam, along with the persistence of black inequality and white supremacy, convinced many activists that Gandhian nonviolence lent itself more toward reformism than revolution. Black, white, and brown activists thus increasingly distanced themselves from the Christian and interracial origins of the movement and identified with the guerrilla tactics of 'Third World' revolutionaries in such places as Vietnam and Latin America. This politics of identity and spectacle led to cultural revolution with a celebration of difference and diversity that continues through to the present, embedded as it has become in American institutions of higher education and power bases inside American cities.[64] Yet it has ultimately proven as ineffective as American Gandhianism in revolutionizing US

---

[62] For Muste's Herculean efforts to pull together this coalition, see Danielson, *American Gandhi*, 305–28. Muste made two visits to Vietnam, one to Saigon in the spring of 1966 and the other to North Vietnam in January 1967. For the internal debates within the civil rights movement about the Vietnam War, see Lucks, *Selma to Saigon*.

[63] See clippings of appreciations, telegrams, and obituaries in the Muste Papers, Reels 1, 36, and 37.

[64] Historians and critics continue to debate the consequences of this shift in left politics and even the extent to which it took place. My point is less to pass judgment than to point out that it led to a devaluation of the philosophy and tactics of the earlier movement and that it has proved to be reformist, not revolutionary. For the debate, see, for example, Todd Gitlin, *The Twilight of Common Dreams: Why America is Wracked by Culture Wars* (New York: Metropolitan Books, 1995); Michael Tomasky, *Left for Dead: The Life, Death, and Possible Resurrection of Progressive Politics in America* (New York: The Free Press, 1996); Martin Duberman, 'Bring Back the Enlightenment', *Nation* 263, no. 1 (1 July 1996); and Robin D. G. Kelley, 'Identity Politics and Class Struggle', *New Politics* 6, no. 2 (Winter 1997).

society, and in preventing the resurgence of a powerful New Right, which has largely dominated American politics since the 1980s.

Recovering Muste's story allows us to appreciate the intellectual and organizational achievements and radical vision of the earlier movement. As we have seen, American nonviolence involved a critical engagement with Marxism and Gandhianism, transnational collaboration, a reworking of Christian faith and practice, and a profound critique of Western materialism, militarism, and empire. It allowed American activists to transcend—however imperfectly—the boundaries of race, religion, and nation, and fostered interracial and international collaborations that helped to end Jim Crow and put limits on the arms race and American imperialism in East Asia. As with nonviolence globally, it existed uneasily within the paradigm of the nation state, which limited its effectiveness in state-building projects. For Muste, at least, this was not cause for despair but, rather, a source of creative tension, a dialectic to be worked out through experience and human action; as he often said, paraphrasing Proverbs 29:18, 'without a vision, the people perish'.

5

On the Exchanges between
Gandhi and Tagore

Sudipta Kaviraj

Can We Be Prepared for the Surprises
History Throws at Us?

In living inside history, we are often told, we need to prepare ourselves for surprises. There is a paradox at the heart of this idea. A surprise is the unexpected, different from what we thought would come: how can you prepare for something that is unexpected and unpredictable? The discipline of political theory has been unprepared for a surprise that recent history has presented. Since the end of the Second World War, political theory has been suffused with the idea that as time passed the world would become more uniform in terms of the basic shape of political communities. The common sense of the social sciences assumed that the world would become, as political modernity evolved, increasingly similar to the modern West: all states will become 'nation' states. But on the question of the nature of the *political community*—the central concern for political theory—the opposite process is on display. Other parts of the world are not becoming increasingly like the West; rather, the West is becoming increasingly like the rest of the world. Other societies are not becoming more homogeneous; Western societies, through vast processes of migration, are becoming more diverse— making some of the deep background assumptions of conventional political theory questionable. If we accept this as a plausible hypothesis, political theory thinking needs some revision. The conventional one-way traffic of political thought—other cultures learning from Western

Sudipta Kaviraj, *On the Exchanges between Gandhi and Tagore* In: *Gandhi, Truth, and Nonviolence*. Edited by: Vinay Lal, Oxford University Press. © Oxford University Press 2025.
DOI: 10.1093/9780198936657.003.0006

political theory—needs to be supplemented by a process in which Western theory should evince more curiosity about the way in which other cultures have thought about the question of diversity inside the political community. Such change, if it happens, would involve greater attention to the thought of Tagore and Gandhi, who were both sceptical about the ethical justifiability and universal imitation of the form of the European 'nation state'.[1]

Clearly, the world produced by modernity has a contradictory structure. It has two sides, and what is true of its metropolitan side is not true of the colonial or postcolonial one. Since in societies like India there is a long history of reflecting on the problem of producing democratic government in a society of deep diversity, Western political theory ought to take more interest in these traditions of thinking. Now, these questions are no longer questions of *comparative* political theory but political theory *in general*. History is always a history of surprises.

This proposal faces a preliminary objection. Should we take the thinking of authors like Gandhi and Tagore as serious political *theory*? James Tully has analysed this objection closely and offered a deeply persuasive affirmative answer.[2] I want to supplement that answering argument with a further extension—by suggesting a distinction between two kinds of political theory. After accepting Tully's distinction between theory as a *form* and theory as a *function*, we can take a further step to suggest that the function of political-theoretical analysis can be performed by political theory presented in two subforms. Gandhi and Tagore have produced a kind of thinking that I would like to characterize as 'critical' theory. The sense in which I want to present them as critical does not use the term critical in the Kantian sense or in Horkheimer's.[3] Neither attempted to build up a comprehensive structure of theoretical thinking about political life. But some questions of political life were highly significant to them, and they thought rigorously and consistently about those issues. If translated into more theoretical

---

[1] On this question, the American case has been a major counterexample. The US has not been subjected to the vast processes of religious homogenization and its theoretical reflection on 'peoplehood'—what makes Americans one people - has also embraced considerable diversity.

[2] 'De-parochializing political theory', in *De-parochializing Political Theory*, ed. Melissa Williams (Cambridge: Cambridge University Press, 2021).

[3] Max Horkheimer, 'Traditional and critical theory', in *Critical Theory: Selected Essays* (Continuum, New York, 1972), 188–243.

language, these ideas can become significant additions to the available range of ideas and arguments on modern politics. They agreed on their scepticism about the ethical acceptability of the 'nation state' as a universal ideal for political community. Leaving that aside, I shall focus in this essay on questions on which they displayed disagreements. On some of these, their differences are clear and profound—for example, about the dangers implicit in mass movements; on others, their conclusions are similar, but they are derived from distinct arguments and starting points. These narrower differences are sometimes the most instructive. I shall argue that although on many important political questions they agreed, their thought constructed two separate ideals of life—one ethical, the other aesthetic. Serious reflection on these arguments does not help us decide to side with one or the other; rather, it expands and diversifies the argumentative resources through which we can try to resolve similar questions.

Comportment and Conversation

It is common to characterize the exchanges between Gandhi and Tagore as 'debates'—which I find misleading. In each case of difference, they state their positions with utmost clarity—in order to make sure they did not answer to a distortion. There is a remarkable feature in the intellectual comportment of their exchanges.[4] In the case of the Bihar earthquake, Tagore read newspaper reports of Gandhi's remarks—which he found unacceptable. He sought to make sure, as a first step, that reports accurately presented Gandhi's views. Once confirmed, he conveys his deep disagreement to Gandhi, but seeks Gandhi's permission before stating his differences in public. Remarkably, Tagore drafted a rejoinder but, instead of publishing it, sent it to Gandhi, who printed it in his journal—quite an extraordinary way of quarrelling. But Gandhi does not allow the argument to rest: he publishes a strong reply, stating his beliefs unchanged. Neither alters his opinion but insists that the other's view must be stated publicly. There is a sense that both believed that they could have settled the disagreement in

---

[4] This question of 'comportment' was raised in Uday Mehta's presentation in our discussions.

private correspondence, but precisely because this was a question of public importance, their arguments must be conducted in public.

It is best to characterize these exchanges as true *conversations*. Conversations, Gadamer suggested, require an initial disposition of openness on both sides—where the interlocutors state their opinions about a subject, but in principle hold themselves open to the other and to possible change.[5] This possible change might not take the form of a conversion—which means that A comes to accept the position of B. Rarely, if ever, is the conversational process so comprehensively and one-sidedly successful. Commonly, conversation produces change—though the change might consist in not a change in the opinion but, through the interlocution, a different way of grounding it. I wish to add another dimension to that Gadamerian conception of conversation. Conversations are rarely, at least when they are about large issues of political life, confined to the paradoxical privacy of two interlocutors. Evidently, the principals would draw upon and use not private languages of political discussion but a necessarily public language of an ongoing wider discussion: their positions would define themselves in an intricate geometry of discursive positions on a particular political issue. So, although conversations would always possess this paradoxical privacy of two agents, there is always a penumbra of agents who are shadow participants in the exchange. This is a matter of comportment, but clearly this is different from the external demands of mutual civility—this is constitutive of their thinking. Their divergent positions need to be stated with clarity, without compromise—but not in the spirit of one cancelling out what the other says but a subtler process of suggesting that if another view is not placed next to it, we cannot have a clear or comprehensive understanding of truth. Despite the seriousness of the difference, they acknowledge that the cause of truth is advanced precisely by this contestation.

Gandhi's differences with Tagore are quite distinct from disagreements he had with others. In the case of some of his most important interlocutors—Nehru, Ambedkar, Iqbal, Savarkar, the communists—the disagreements were much wider and deeper. Probably the strongest disagreements, paradoxically, were with Nehru, though those with Ambedkar were no less profound. No less profound were his evident

---

[5] Hans Georg Gadamer, *Truth and Method* (London: Sheed & Ward, 1969).

disagreements on interpretation of Hindu doctrine with Hindu nationalists like Savarkar. Thus, in one sense, the disagreements between Gandhi and Tagore were much smaller; and, at times, it appears that their differences are not about a position but about how each justifies a conclusion that is identical. Yet sometimes such narrower arguments are also the most illuminating, because they allow us—concentrating on fine differences—to grasp the accurate outline of the grounding of their thoughts. I shall suggest that despite the narrowness of their differences, they display two strikingly different ideals of what a good or fulfilled human life means.

Disagreements on Political Movements

Several features are notable in the disagreement Gandhi and Tagore had on the nature and limits of mass movements. I have argued elsewhere that Tagore had a highly insightful critical intuition about the modern state—strikingly similar to Tocqueville's misgivings about its unanswerable power in modern societies. Weber's theoretical characterization of the modern arrangement of sovereignty conferring on the state a monopoly of legitimate violence captures an essential, but primarily benign, aspect of this vast, undeniable historical fact. A decisive and irreversible redistribution of the capacity for violence in society drained violent power from all competing actors and concentrated it in a single agent—the state. Evidently, this meant that any rational actor would be dissuaded from contesting the power of the state violently. In a great paradox, the modern state can deliver peace precisely because its own capacity for violence is unanswerable. By rendering everybody helpless in face of the state, a modern social order creates a much greater and more reliable background condition for peace. This is the great Hobbesian moment that is latent in every modern state. Tocqueville, more sensitive to contradiction than Weber, discerned a more threatening, contradictory potential. In effect, the actual modern state realizes the equilibrium that Hobbes's model rendered in a stylized form: modern society was characterized by a relation between two entirely unequal sides—an all-powerful state with entirely unanswerable force and individualized singular agents separated by their constant jostling of self-interest into monadic, discordant billiard balls. Sociologically astute observers must be aware of the possibility that this state may turn against some individuals or groups, or perpetrate some gross injustice. If this state became unjust—either generally or selectively against some groups—what, sociologically, could be its remedy or an efficacious answer?

This argument is sociological, not legal. It is not concerned with the restraining effects of a Lockean constitution or a Montesquieuian separation of powers.[6] Those are legal arrangements, but to take effect, they presuppose an obedience to law on the state's part. This, by contrast, is a sociological examination of possibilities. This is a diagnosis of a problem shared between European thinkers like Tocqueville and Indians like Tagore and Gandhi. What can be a device that can be effective against an unjust state? But there the similarity ends. For Tocqueville, the answer to this overwhelming preponderance of state power is the growth of an active associational life—his theory of a vibrant, active intermediate sphere of a 'civil society'—which he thought he saw working in the municipal life of American towns.[7] I need not repeat the details of that well-known argument. Somewhat like Marx, Tagore conceives of a possibility that a state could be systematically unjust to a large segment of its subjects.[8] In fact, the imperial state was the classic instance of a state of persistent injustice, because of its irremediably alien relation with its colonial subjects. The historical setting of colonial sovereignty was the most obvious instance of a state that was unjust and invincible. Theorists eventually concluded that the only possible answer to the overwhelming power of the state was the mass popular movement. European socialists thinking about systematic class injustice felt that its only answer was a mass movement of the workers. Sociological theory also evinced some alarm in thinking through this problem. Some thought that organization of the proletariat in the vast socialist movements of nineteenth-century Europe mimicked the disciplinary power of the state—by mobilizing the immense numbers of the working class organized by bureaucratic

---

[6] Because these were the two major contrivances modern liberal theory devised against the power of the state: either a state restrained by a set of rules contained in a constitution; or a state kept in check by one part of government restraining the power of another.

[7] Alexis de Tocqueville, *Democracy in America* [1835], trans. Henry Reeve, 2 vols. (Ann Arbor: University of Michigan Scholarly Reprints, 2005), Vol. II.

[8] Marx thought of the unjust power of the capitalist state against the proletariat, Tagore of the imperial state against its colonial subjects.

disciplines of their own. Works like Robert Michels's graphic analysis of Socialist Party bureaucracy laid bare this process of mimicking: the power of the socialist movement was based on sociological devices that mirrored the disciplinary mechanisms of the state. The Socialist Party was an apparatus which could hope to resist the state's bureaucratic apparatus by being equally bureaucratic.

A similar argument is developed in Tagore's fictional work. Of course, there is a change of genre: instead of detailed sociological analysis he deploys the imaginative power of fictional construction. But fiction can generate a kind of shadow sociology: it portrays interactions between spectral people in real situations. Consequently, fiction can produce analyses and prognostications that are as real as sociology or, as some Indian theorists would claim, analyses that are 'more than real'[9]. In narratives of several novels, Tagore explores the inner logic of the mass political movement—in a polyphonic diegetic structure that reveals the perspectives of individual politicians, of ordinary individuals entangled in social relations with them, of other, antagonistic political agents, from the point of view of bystanders, and of women who cannot influence the events but bear the consequences.[10] Tagore's great masterpiece on nationalism, *Gora*, examines some of these dilemmas regarding nationalism.[11] A shorter novella, *Car Adhyay* ('Four Chapters'),[12] explores both the external trajectory and inner lives of political actors involved in the vortex of violence of revolutionary terrorism—who are also primary argumentative antagonists addressed in Gandhi's *Hind Swaraj*.[13] I shall focus instead on the more complex tapestry of fictional action depicting a real mass movement in *Ghare Baire*.[14] This work was written in the shadow of the Swadeshi movement of 1905–8 in Bengal: an unprecedented political eruption involving widespread mass mobilization that Tagore initially endorsed but later subjected to increasingly intense criticism.[15]

---

[9] David Shulman, *More Than Real* (Cambridge, MA: Harvard University Press, 2008).
[10] This is most clearly portrayed in the early novel, *Ghare Baire* (1915), trans. by Surendranath Tagore as *The Home and the World* (New York: Penguin Books, 2005).
[11] Rabindranath Tagore, *Gora* [English trans. *Gora* (London: Macmillan, 1924)].
[12] Rabindranath Tagore, *Car Adhyay*, RR, Vol. [English trans. *Four Chapters*].
[13] Gandhi, *Hind Swaraj* [1909], various editions.
[14] Rabindranath Tagore, *Ghare Baire*, [English trans. *Home and the World*].
[15] For an excellent historical analysis of the movement, see Sumit Sarkar, *The Swadeshi Movement in Bengal 1903–1908* (New Delhi: People's Publishing House, 1973), which also has an analysis of Tagore's changing evaluation.

The colonial state was based on a most direct form of injustice —the rule of exclusion of native subjects from political power. Was there a recourse against the irresistible, unanswerable power of an unjust modern state? Evidently, both Tagore and Gandhi believed that the only political instrumentality that could effectively contest the power of the modern colonial state was the mass political movement. Gandhi's *Hind Swaraj* presented a concise but very powerful argument that the only instrumentality Indians could deploy to fight against and dislodge that state was a mass political movement based on nonviolence (ahimsa). A nonviolent movement sought to paralyse and overcome the potential violence of the state by drawing it on to the unfamiliar terrain of nonviolent disobedience. On this question, Tagore was entirely in agreement with Gandhi—that the only means that could realize the objective of freedom from British colonial rule was the answering power of the mass movement. When the Swadeshi movement broke out in Bengal in 1905, Tagore had given it an ecstatic reception and regarded it as a transcendence of a politics of mendicancy by a politics of self-assertion.[16] As the movement spread and gathered strength, however, it revealed features of organization and mobilization which made him increasingly hesitant in his support. Tagore found a logic of organization based on a total surrender of followers to the leaders' orders, intolerance of any independent, critical questioning of the leadership, and a tendency to coerce people into joining its ranks. But what appalled him was a clear inclination in some leaders to enlist supporters by appealing to their religious identity. Often the movement mobilized Hindu supporters against their Muslim neighbours, who were either indifferent or opposed to it. As the movement subsided in half-success, Tagore used his imaginative sovereignty as a fiction writer to explore the intricacies of the movement's complex history. As the novel was his main technique for this exploration, it presented in vivid detail the grain of individual destinies to reveal the vast narratives of history.

Ghare Baire runs two political subjectivities parallel to each other— those of Nikhilesh and Sandeep, friends who interpret the political moment in different ways. Sandeep's character is that of a quintessential mass leader—drawn from the lower middle class, endowed with political

---

[16] Sarkar, *The Swadeshi Movement.*

talents of oratory and personal magnetism, and genuinely propelled
by a fiery defiance of injustice, his character lit up by political idealism.
All these are Sandeep's genuine personal qualities, which, as the narrative unfolds, push him into a leadership role as a fiery orator and political leader, and which, at the personal level, more ambiguously, win
his friend's wife's, Bimala's, admiration. She finds her more circumspect
and introspective husband pale in comparison to Sandeep's flaming enthusiasm, and the emotional centre of the novel is the development of a
tense and ambiguous attraction between the two. Sandeep demands personal sacrifice from his supporters, and correspondingly from Bimala—
initially as the surrender of her jewellery and later her admiration. But
his mass following, mirroring the occurrences in the Swadeshi movement, is roused by appeals to their communal belonging, inflaming the
border between the two neighbourly communities of the village. Equally,
it causes Nikhilesh's paternalistic concern as their zamindar. When the
conflict between the two communities flares up into rioting, and their
lives are in danger, Sandeep flees from the scene of conflict. He is armed
with an incontestable politicians' argument—that his life, as the leader,
is more precious than those of dispensable ordinary followers. Tagore
nurses our suspicion that he would emerge somewhere else at some other
time again as a 'leader of the masses'—to serve the great cause. He has
'vowed to preserve his life at all costs to serve the nation'.[17] Feeling his
obligation as a landlord that he must enter the rioting mob and end the
killing amongst his tenants, Nikhilesh rides his horse into the night and is
brought back grievously injured, probably dying, in the end. Bimala, who
is given the right of the last scene in the novel, looks out of the window
and finds a large mass of people—whose bodies have been fused by fury
into a mammoth serpent—advancing towards the gates of her residence.

All the major reservations Tagore had developed in his continuing ru-
mination on the Swadeshi movement find their fictional expression in
the narrative movements. The figure of Sandeep shows the demand for a
peremptory submission to the judgment and decision of a leader. Idealists
who can disregard the disapproval of society, ironically, accept servility to

---

[17] To quote an immortal line of contempt from a contemporary comic poem by Dwijendralal
Ray, 'Nanadalal': 'Nandalal to ekada ekta karila bhisan pan; / Deser lagiya ja kariei hok, rakhibei
se jiban ('Once Nandalal took this terrifying vow: / That for the sake of the nation, / by whatever
means, / he must always preserve his life').

a charismatic leader. Getting used to his own power slowly but irreversibly alters Sandeep's character—and strengthens a belief that ends justify the means. An originally genuinely idealistic character is slowly transformed into a manipulative political puppeteer who becomes skilled in using others not as ends but as means for his own purposes. When associates and friends seek to appeal to his 'real' self—what he was before—they realize that politics has not covered up his earlier personality but transformed and obliterated it. The older self no longer exists—to be appealed to. Nikhilesh obviously symbolizes the type of political rationality Tagore prefers. He does not submerge his initial critical capacity, which first drew him to the dissenting movement, and is not afraid to use it against the internal suppression inside the dissenting movement itself. Consequently, his personality is less decisive in political action; but he is precisely the kind of individual who can practise Gandhi's satyagraha, because he cannot surrender his own understanding of the *satya*—a sense of truth of the world, and the moral truth because of which he entered politics.

The Wrath of God: on the Bihar Earthquake

Differences between Tagore and Gandhi are also shown in the remarkable exchange after the Bihar earthquake in 1934. This exchange is interesting for several reasons and on many distinct levels. First, we need to look at the way the conversation proceeded. After the disaster, Gandhi gave a public statement claiming that he felt deeply that this was a punishment from God for the sin of practising untouchability.[18] Tagore expressed shock and disbelief at the statement,[19] and began a correspondence whose comportment was truly remarkable. There are two distinct levels at which their statements are being made. The first, more explicit, level comprises the statements themselves and their strictly semantic content. But clearly there is another, less explicit but if anything even more important, level at which they are making statements about

---

[18] Gandhi's statement: 'I want you to be superstitious enough to believe with me that the earthquake is a divine chastisement for the great sin we have committed against those we describe as Harijans'. See *The Mahatma and the Poet*, ed. Sabyasachi Bhattacharya (New Delhi: National Book Trust, New Delhi, 1997, 156).

[19] 'I find it difficult to believe it': ibid., 156.

how debates on serious issues ought to be conducted between interlocutors who disagree but display mutual respect.

The difference on interpreting the Bihar earthquake is not a small matter of emphasis or inflection. Despite the sharp difference, there is a profound shared belief working in the background: both of them believe in an incontrovertible incessant 'presence' of God in the world. Reflected in their arguments are two entirely different philosophical readings about what this 'presence' means. To understand this enormous difference clearly, we need a detour through some philosophic doctrines. These philosophic differences are coded into the locutions of their 'correspondence'.

Interestingly, Tagore does not present Gandhi's statement in *indirect* reporting. He keeps Gandhi's own wording—which could be for two reasons. The first is for simple accuracy; he wanted to make sure that what he found objectionable were really the true sentiments of Gandhi, not ideas already bent by interpretative slide. But there could be a second reason—seeking a deeper and more unusual kind of accuracy that was demanded by the strange locution of Gandhi's actual invitation to that belief. 'I want you', Gandhi says, 'to be *superstitious enough to believe with me* that the earthquake is a divine chastisement for the great sin we have committed against those whom we describe as Harijans.'[20] This is hardly a standard move of Hindu bigotry: the superstitious do not call themselves superstitious. By using the phrase 'to be superstitious enough' Gandhi makes a distinction between two possible positions on interpreting God's intentions—the rationalist and the non-rationalist, playfully termed 'superstitious'.[21] Though he realizes that a larger number of people among his readers would subscribe to the rationalist position, he invites them to *temporarily* place themselves in the position of the 'superstitious' and interpret the event through that altered interpretative optic. Appeals for deep perspectival change of this kind are not uncommon in Gandhi. When he explains what 'respect for another religion' means to him, he offers a similar—much deeper, more complex—reading than the usual associations of that phrase. To him, it does not mean allowing others to honour God in a different way to which they remain indifferent; but to

---

[20]   Ibid., 156, emphasis mine.
[21]   This is a clearly self-ironical move, which is capable of many distinct semantic functions.

ignite a curiosity in them to find out what it means to inhabit their perspective. The task of the Hindu is not to leave the Muslim to honour God in his way but to be curious and try to understand what it means for a Muslim to honour God, to honour God in the Muslim way. It is not a re-enactment, or, if it is, this implies that re-enactment cannot succeed without a re-embodiment. However, this is not a conversion: the Hindu can return to being a Hindu, but his understanding of Muslims would be enriched. He will be able to share a world with them.

To anyone familiar with theological controversies it is clear that the two positions illustrate two classic dispositions towards God's relation to the world—particularly the meaning of God's defining quality of 'omnipotence'. Gandhi illustrates a reading of the meaning of omnipotence that sees the active intent of God in every single occurrence. Omni—infinitude—means a spread of God's intentional-causational capacity to an exhaustive notion of infinity over everything that exists or happens—because, in God's case, these two have no distinction.[22] Creation is an act indivisible and instantaneous with his intention, rather than a process similar to the creative process in a human actor, where intention and action are logically and temporally distinct, which then allows for the possibility of slips or failure. For Gandhi, 'he rules me in the tiniest detail of my life. . . . Not a leaf moves without his will, every breath I take depends on his sufferance.'[23] Serious difference from such a doctrine is also common in most theological traditions. Islamic thought was split between this meaning of omnipotence and a more rationalist view that God's language consisted only of universals.[24] Tagore is clearly stating a position that Taylor calls 'providential deism'—centred on the notion of a prior, omnipotent, but hidden and absent God. In Bengal, even before Tagore, this form of deism was highly influential. God does not, Bankimchandra said in his typical sardonic style, run the universe the way a coachman runs his coach through Calcutta streets. Nor does he revise his opinion about the immutable fixity of nature's laws. Common to some strands of

---

[22] That is, for God intending is the same as causing to exist. Many Indian religious doctrines emphasize this idea—that for God intending is creating, causing to exist. God is sometimes designated 'icchamaya' or, in case of a feminine form, 'icchamayi'—constituted of intention.

[23] Bhattacharya, *The Mahatma and the Poet*, 160.

[24] For instance, the idea in Ibn Sina and Islamic philosophers that God's language consists only of universals.

providential deism is a related idea that the absent God has left a constant reminder of benign presence in the aesthetic beauty of the universe. God's created universe is imposing in two different ways: in its immensity and infinity, and in its beauty. Two wholly distinct faculties are required to respond to these two attributes of creation. Science seeks to know nature's laws and art its beauty. For Tagore, therefore, there could not be a contradiction between the purposes of two human creations—science and aesthetics—and artists could be content to accept the view of the universe science revealed.

Gandhi's response to Tagore does not take the easy solution of a perspectival relativism between these two notions of God's presence in the universe. Gandhi begins with the interesting remark, 'Gurudev and I early discovered certain differences'.[25] Since both felt the presence of God deeply, these were, in one sense, not differences of principle. To others these may appear minor differences of inflection, but in fact, for people as deeply thoughtful as these two, they were still quite fundamental. Yet these differences were such that any observer or interlocutor in this debate would not be forced to choose between them, because of the broader overlap of their positions. If these readers were more exacting, it might matter a great deal whether they believed that God's presence in the world is primarily *ethical* and that he speaks to us through an inner sense that we must strive to constantly refine, so as not to miss a single whisper of this inner voice; or we think God's presence in the world is *aesthetic*, and we must ask, 'Why can I see you at times, but not always?'[26]

Gandhi's answer to Tagore, however, is not the expected one that he felt that the voice of God spoke through the event. It is more interesting. There is a slight tension between the statements that he 'spoke with greatest deliberation' and 'out of the fullness of my heart'. Did this conviction arise out of rational deliberation, or strike him as a moral revelation? But this tension can be straightened out by saying that he felt the presence of God's chastisement in his heart, and he deliberated seriously before making that known to the world. The primary argument is forceful: he had always believed in a cosmic order in which physical phenomena

---

[25] 'Superstition vs faith', in *The Mahatma and the Poet*, 159.
[26] 'majhe majhe taba dekha pai, ciradin kena pai na? Kena megh ase hrdaya-akase, tomare dekhite dey na?' See Rabindranath Thakur, *Puja, Gitabitan* (Kolkata: Visvabharati, 1970) 162.

were connected to the spiritual: 'physical phenomena produce results both physical and spiritual. The converse I hold to be equally true.'[27] The earthquake was no caprice of God, nor the result of a meeting of 'blind' forces. Humans do not know all the laws of God and the modes of their working. Neither science nor spiritualism can make the claim of exhaustive knowledge of God's creation. Using this qualification—that we do not know the laws of God fully or the finitude of human knowledge—Gandhi seeks to validate his 'spiritual' belief that the earthquake was a sign of God's wrath. Natural events like floods, earthquakes, and famines appear to him to be somehow connected to man's morals. But he concedes Tagore's point that conservative Hindus might, on the contrary, consider it to be punishment for preaching against untouchability. Gandhi admits that he 'cannot prove' this connection, though he instinctively felt it. The following remark is interesting: If my belief turns out to be ill-founded—that is, it was not God's intended punishment—still it would perform a useful and beneficial purpose: 'it would have done good to me and those who believed with me'. Because they would have been spurred to greater effort in a just cause. It also puts pressure on people to feel the sin of untouchability and to seek ways of repentance.

Both Tagore and Gandhi believe/feel with uncommon intensity God's presence in the world; but these are two very different ways of perceiving it. Gandhi feels the presence of God at every moment in every movement of every leaf. For Tagore there is a dual quality to God's presence in the world. In one sense, God is present in everything and in every instant of time—but that is the presence of a hidden God, who has bound the world of his creation in a constantly sounding *dhruvapada* (dhrupad).[28] It is an effort for human beings to tune their own lives to that engulfing melody which resounds constantly and which, like the sound of the sea, can go unheard. That tune, which is Tagore's preferred version of the aesthetic (because he could have likened it to a painting, a sculpture, or a poem, but he sees the aesthetic nature of nature itself as *musical*—which can sound while remaining silent—that is, wordless), constitutes the presence of God. Music alone can sound and mean wordlessly. But that song

[27] Bhattacharya, *The Mahatma and the Poet*, 159.
[28] A form of classical music. In one song, he writes, 'je dhruvapada diyecho bandhi visvatane, milaba ta jibanagane' ('the dhrupad that you have set to the taan of the universe, I shall try to tune my own life's song to that melody').

demonstrates something else central to Tagore's understanding of this aesthetic quality. Aesthetics exists in many forms—painting, sculpture, poem, story, music—but they are permeable. This is shown in a remarkable feature of his writing: the application of verbs to strange objects. A reader passes through two stages of reception in such a line—an initial sense of misplacement, but becoming aware slowly about its character as deliberate displacement to turn its meaning in a surprising, unexpected direction. *Phuler mata sahaja sure prabhata mama uthibe pure, Sandhya mama se sure jena marite jane*[29] ('My morning will be filled with tunes that will bloom naturally like a flower. / Let my sunset too know how to die to that tune'). God is present in everything taken together—the world—as its aesthetic quality. And it is the aesthetic perception of humans which can capture that quality. The perfection of an ethical act makes it, or simply is, beautiful.

This reveals the peculiar proximity of their thinking about God. Their thinking is very similar, because they both feel God's presence, but also irreducibly dissimilar, because of the intrinsic distance between the right and the beautiful.

Ethical and Aesthetic Ideals: *Aparigraha* in Gandhi and Tagore

Gandhi was a great admirer of the *Gita*—for him, the finest among Hinduism's diverse texts. But the *Gita* itself in its resplendent second chapter on the *sthitaprajna* places two somewhat different ideals of life of undesire next to each other—probably deliberately for purposes of surprise, in the same section.[30] Krishna, in his omniscience, is finding for

---

[29] ('The great music to which you have tuned the universe / To that I shall try to merge the song of my life. / Your sky is a stainless blue—I shall try to make my heart mirror that, The deep language of that stillness will come into my silent heart. / The language of music that the dawn plays when it reaches the shores of the night, will raise my new hopes. / My morning will be filled with tunes that will bloom naturally like a flower. / Let my sunset too know how to die to that tune').See *Gitabitan, Puja*, (Kolkata: Visvabharati, 1970), 140.

[30] Slokas from the start of the *sthiprajna* section build up this conception. Slokas 58—quoted here—to 68 consistently expand on this ideal of *indriyanigraha*. In sloka 70, the ideal presented seems somewhat different—what is condemned is not *kama* (desire) in itself, but the *kamakami* (the agent who desires desires).

Arjuna a description of a difficult ideal—the life of the *sthitaprajna*, the man whose mind is stilled, is at rest. The two slokas are placed close to each other. The first sloka states:

> *Yada samharate cayam kurmangani iva sarvasah*
> *Indriyani indriyarthebhyah tasya prajna pratisthita.* (II: 58)
> (As the tortoise withdraws its limbs inside itself, just like that, the man who withdraws his senses from the objects of the senses, his mind can be said to be at rest [placed on a firm ground—*pratisthita*].)

This is clearly similar to what Gandhi believes about calming the mind—it is the ascetic ideal best expressed in *brahmacarya*.

Yet in composing the second verse God seems to have second thoughts. Remarkably, a few verses later there is a second statement of the ideal—in a different chanda *upajati*, not in standard *anustup*. It says:

> *Apuryamanam acalapratistham*
> *Samudram apah pravisanti yadvat*
> *Tadvat kama jam pravisanti sarve*
> *Sa santim apnoti na kamakami.*

Not surprisingly, this is one of the Gita's most memorable verses because of the surprise, semantic force, and beauty of the final word—*kamakami*. This verse translates as:

> As the river waters constantly enter the sea/ocean
> Which is being constantly filled up, yet always calm (unagitated)
> Like that, he whom all desires enter
> That person achieves calm, not him who desires desires (*kamakami*).

Despite the common divine provenance, the two verses outline two distinct attitudes towards desire and its place in human life. In the first, the senses are shut down and withdrawn, literally retracted from things that are desirable.[31] In the second, the senses are not closed down but

---

[31] *Gita*, ch. 2, sloka 58.

remain open towards the desirable. But there is no relentless seeking of an endless series of desires which produces agitation and unfulfilment. Clearly, an idea of *aparigraha* is presented in the second verse, where the desires are fulfilled but do not perturb or agitate the mind. The word *apuryamana* should be read in both its senses—of filling in and being fulfilled or completed. In the second model a full human life requires desires. *Purna*—fulfilment—is an important concept for Tagore.

Aparigraha is an important and polysemic concept in Hindu thought, usually associated with yoga texts and the *Gita*. I want to note its religious meaning but suggest that Tagore uses a more expansive connotation which can encompass entirely secular purposes as well. A major difficulty with ideals of religious ethics is that usually these presuppose a pre-existing social world that is not available in modern times. Ideals of religious ethics are not usable as rules of practical reason if they are not taken through a process of thoughtful adaptation. In the *Gita*, the concept is meant to help us grasp the elaborated meanings of the ideals of *ahimsa*. *Aparigraha* is also related to ideals of Hindu askesis and its techniques. Ascetics are meant to follow a life ideal of minimization of needs, so that the hermit takes as little as possible from the bounties of the earth, which becomes his gift to the rest of humanity. Gandhi clearly fashioned and followed such a model of minimality of needs—both physical and material.[32] Interpreted in this fashion, *aparigraha* requires a repression of *srngara* in every form—not just the manifest *srngara* as sexuality but also a turning away from the wider *srngara* with creation—because it suspects a subtle connection between *srngara's* two forms.[33] The two forms of *srngara* are distinct, because they bear different implications. Erotic love is enjoyment—*bhoga* or *sambhoga*—but it is linked to senses in a restrictive way, because it is personal. Sex or food are tactile, and they appropriate things in the world. But the passage about the flowers refers to a different sense—sight—which also enjoys visual things in the world without appropriating them.[34] The activity of gathering, accumulating

---

[32] Common symbolic representations of Gandhi capture this by a metonymic mention of his spectacles and chappals.

[33] In Vaishnava texts in Sanskrit, the verb *ram* is often used in puns drawing on both meanings.

[34] *Kata phul niye ase basanta age padita na nayane / takhan kebal byasta chilam cayane/ madhukar sama chinu sancaya-prayasi / kusumkanti dekhi nai madhupiyasi* ('Never did I see

(*cayana*) is restrictive; that of seeing is not. Enjoying the world must consist of both kinds of acts. Or the creation is wasted. Remember Jayadeva's witty invitation in the *Gitagovinda* to his readers linking the alternative paths of *harismarana* or *vilasakalasu kutuhala*.[35] For a thoughtful person, one would lead to the other.

Buddhist doctrines rejected and strenuously argued against an ascetic model of life: they enjoin only the rejection of excessive desire, not desire itself.[36] Clearly, these two ideals persist indistinctly side by side in the *Gita* itself. Tagore presented a poetic account of this anti-ascetic ideal of *aparigraha*[37] in a poem, *Udasin*.[38] What is remarkable about the ideal presented in this poem is that its antithesis is not the status of the householder (*grhastha*) in the style of the older opposition between the householder and the renunciant.[39] If we observe it closely, this, by contrast, is directed against, and set in opposition to, a distinctively modern ideal of maximization of desirable things as the enhancement of life. 'I have come to a rest in my life,' the poem says; 'I am not running after anything. I ignore opportunities and dangers', which appear economic or professional. 'If I don't find an opportunity to rise, I lie happily below. I wander around creation/the earth, and what I get, I do not renounce (*chadi ne ko bhai chadi ne*) (*chadi* can mean leaving or letting go, which have slightly different inflections of meaning). *Tai bole kichu kadakadi kore kadi ne*: 'But that does not mean that I get into a scramble to get anything.' The third stanza of the poem reveals how there is a connection between the two meanings of *srngara*; it talks humorously about the life of romantic love:

how many flowers spring brings in its train. I was busy plucking them. I was intent on collecting like the bee, in my thirst for honey, never saw the beauty of the bloom').

[35] *Yadi harismarane sarasam mano/yadi vilasakalasu kutuhalam / Madhurakomalakanta padavalim/srnu tada jayadevasarasvatim* (*Gitagovinda,* verse 3).

[36] The *Kamagita*—the brief but powerful reflection on the impossibility of renouncing desire, because that itself is driven by a desire—is a cryptic and acerbic comment on the hubris of renunciants.

[37] My decision to use this term for Tagore's ideal is not that he draws upon the strict meaning of the theological concept. But this appears to be the perfect word to capture the meaning of his ideal of non-aggressive, non-competitive living.

[38] *Sancayita* (Kolkata: Visvabharati, 1972), 423.

[39] Use of the term *udasin/udasina* in Sanskrit is interesting: in some contexts, the term can mean someone who has renounced the world.

I have given my heart to many, have tinkled like an anklet on many
dainty feet. I have threaded drops of tears into garlands, and stained
them red with my blood. After a long time, I am on leave/ holiday;
I have left my heart/mind behind, and joined in the room for play.[40]
Returning the broken shackles to Him who forged them, I have raised
my head at last. I never had eyes to see how many flowers the spring
brought with itself. I was absorbed in plucking/hoarding them. Like
the bee, I was after the honey, never saw the splendor of the bloom.

The final passage is worth quoting in full:

Now I roam the far world, my mind is not after anything. (Perhaps)
that is why the whole world now runs after me. I don't clasp anything in
the fist of my desire [basana-muthite]. I allow everyone to bloom—on
a bud of their own. When I gave up my ambition of rising high, everything came down within my grasp. Now I roam the far world, my mind
is not after anything. That is why now the world runs after me.

Here too a strategy of life is at work that could be called minimalizing,
but it is strikingly different from the ascetic ideal of renunciation. It is a
strategy that renounces only the endless possessiveness that a modern
acquisitive society imposes on its inhabitants. In the case of Gandhi, the
social ethic renounced is the ethic of the householder, which only the ascetic can do. The ethic that Tagore deplores is a recognizable form of the
ethic of modern acquisitiveness. But it is totally different from the ideal
of renunciation. In a very long historical arc, this could be seen as an
adaptation of the Buddhist ideal of non-ascetic modesty, acceptance of
an abundant life within limits and finiteness. Readings of other poetic
writings clarify what this ideal means more fully. A life of this kind of
minimalization also requires a high cultivation and refinement of sensibilities. A mind that is refined, which has a finer attunement to the
smallest presences of beauty, would find the world populated by many
more beautiful things. To see the beauty of nature, people travel to high

---

[40] It is hard to capture the meaning of the phrase 'man phele aj chutechi'—'I have left my
mind behind/I have run away from my own mind'—probably meaning that I have left all that
can bind my heart.

mountains or the limitless expanses of the ocean; but there is waiting to be seen, just two steps outside my door, a dewdrop trembling on a blade of grass.[41] This is also a life of 'descent', of a different meaning of decency, of being content with whatever comes one's way, but without contestation and competitiveness—the great drivers of modern life.

This is why studying the difference between the two figures is so profoundly instructive. It is a short distance, but the gulf is philosophically very deep. This can be explicated by drawing on Neelima Shukla-Bhatt's discussion on rasas.[42] Clearly, if we think of the nine rasas, there is one that Gandhi fears—the *adi* (original, first, or primary) rasa of *srngara*—which he wants to overcome, not just suppress; and conceptual ideals like *brahmacarya* capture what Gandhi is trying to achieve. For Tagore, the absence of *srngara* in its most expanded sense would leave the world bereft of meaning; God created a world of infinite beauty and instilled a sense in human beings to capture it, and reason to think about its significance. Gandhi also honoured a love of humanity, though there was a vast hole in the middle: he did not include erotic love within its meaning. For Tagore, erotic love is just an intimation for *srngara* about the world—what gave the world its meaning. What makes a human life meaningful for Gandhi is ethical; for Tagore, aesthetic.

The Ethical and the Aesthetic

What is remarkable in the exchanges between Gandhi and Tagore is the subtlety with which both turn their differences to account. They disagree but do not dispute. A rare gentleness and civility in the choreography of this discussion stops it from becoming a debate—where the ultimate objective turns into an intellectual victory, rather than seeking the truth. Differences of opinion—on vastly significant questions—are not erased,

---

[41]   *Bahudin dhare bahu krosh dure/bahu byay kari, bahu desh ghure / dekhite giyachhi parbatmala, dekhite giyachhi sindhu / dekha hoy nai caksu meliya, ghar hate shudhu dui pa pheliya / ekti dhaner shisher upar ekti shishirbindu* (*Sancayita*, 757). This may be translated as, 'On long journeys, with enormous expense, traveling through many lands, I went to see the mountains and the sea. But I have not seen, simply opening my eyes, two steps from my door, a drop of dew trembling on a blade of grass (literally, on a sprig of rice paddy).' *Sphulinga* ('Sparks') is a collection of Tagore's haiku-style compositions.

[42]   @@@Chapter 7 in this volume.

elided, but turned into resources for thinking about one's own position and exploring its possible inadequacies. Uday Mehta's emphasis on 'comportment' in thinking is crucial. The two positions are presented to us in a way that we are not asked to decide which one is right, because there is an acknowledgement in the use of words—and in the gestures before words are uttered—that choosing is not the right thing to do. If we choose one, we must regret the loss of the other. Ultimately, the exchange is governed by two gestures—of parrhesia (not -failing to speak the truth) but also of *vinaya* towards each other, which binds each to the peculiar truth of his experience but also accepts the finiteness of that truth. But whichever we choose—a life of striving towards ethical perfection or a life of a search for aesthetic rapture—they urge us to act in ways which leave the world better than we found it.

For both these thinkers, interestingly, 'truth' is a profound problem. Neither accepts a predominantly cognitive factual notion of what is true. Truth is not exhausted in factuality. It could be said that both 'experimented' with truth—Gandhi ethically, Tagore in an aesthetic mode. For Gandhi truth is hard to attain because it is linked to inwardness, the certainty of deep inner conviction. For Tagore, truth is distinct from mere accurate information, occasionally captured only in the 'more than real' truth of art. Their encounter is so powerful because they present two differently attractive views of what is ultimately fulfilling in human life— an ethical and an aesthetic ideal. Any thoughtful person who is forced to choose will also regret the act of choice.[43]

---

[43] Although this is not the place for an expanded discussion on this subject, this is a subject on which we—as intellectual historians—can have some fun at the ignorance of these two great thinkers. Gandhi obviously believed—mainly correctly—that his thinking was deeply influenced by Vaishnavism. This is broadly true, but Vaishnavism has numerous strands, and the Gaudiya strand precisely develops the figure of Krishna as a God of love, utterly different from the Krishna of the *Gita*, whom Gandhi admired so greatly. Tagore, on his side, evidently believed that his own conception of God and of his presence in the world was derived from the Upanishads. Again, this is only broadly true. A sense of the infinite presence of God in nature in his thought is certainly derived from the Upanishads, and in his opinion this view is confirmed by modern science. But equally clearly there is a strand of his thinking that seeks God as a *priya* (beloved)—which is certainly not the address appropriate to the Upanishads. It clearly owes much to Gaudiya Vaishnava thinking, which does the most in Indian philosophy to establish and refine an ultimate aesthetic ideal of human life. True, the exact valence of the relation in his use of *priya* is different from the primarily erotic form of Vaishnava bhakti, precisely because it is overlaid by other powerful ideas. But that line of thinking about the presence of God in a flowering nature enveloping human existence, and the dominance of the trope of *viraha* (separation) in human relation to God despite his infinite presence is not thinkable without the Vaishnava element.

6

The Unbearable Lightness of Being Mahatma

Sumathi Ramaswamy

Greatness lies in becoming small and smallness in assuming greatness. We should therefore only serve by becoming as small as dust particles.[1]

How strange, I think, that, of all people, Gandhi, who lived in such starkly simple circumstances, should be so encumbered after death.[2]

Some Things about Nothing

Is it possible to lead an engaged social and political life in our times and yet yearn to be immaterial and to pass on without a trace? This is the question that this essay addresses by considering—yet again—the career and aspirations of Mohandas K. Gandhi (a.k.a. 'the Mahatma') but from the largely understudied perspective of the material lifeworld with which he was entangled.[3] This might well be a paradoxical angle from which to consider this much-written-about man, given his famed minimalist penchants and proclivities. As we are learning, however, from material culture studies, the objects whose company we keep reveal a lot about us,

---

[1] *Collected Works of Mahatma Gandhi* (New Delhi: Publications Division, Government of India, 1969–94), 82: 176 (henceforward, *CWMG*).
[2] Ved Mehta, *Mahatma Gandhi and His Apostles* (New York: Viking, 1976), 46.
[3] For an important beginning in this regard, see Ritu Khanduri, 'Some Things About Gandhi', *Contemporary South Asia* 20, no. 3 (2012), 303–25.

Sumathi Ramaswamy, *The Unbearable Lightness of Being Mahatma* In: *Gandhi, Truth, and Nonviolence*. Edited by: Vinay Lal, Oxford University Press. © Oxford University Press 2025.
DOI: 10.1093/9780198936657.003.0007

offering perspectives otherwise occluded. Such objects are, in the words of philosopher of science David Baird, 'bearers of knowledge'.[4] An object-driven exploration of M. K. Gandhi's words allows me to critically (re-) evaluate his oft-expressed desire to reduce himself to zero, and to ask if the pursuit of such a goal led him into a life of plenitude, spiritually and ethically for sure, but also trapped him, ironically, in materiality.

Reducing himself to zero was not a passing fancy but a much-expressed sentiment in Gandhi's writings and speeches. To invoke a few revealing instances from among many, in 1927, in response to a request for an up-lifting message to the youth of the world who had recently declared him to be 'the greatest man living', Gandhi wrote to Basil Matthews, editor of Geneva-based *World's Youth,* with this homily to pass on to them:

> TRUTH and LOVE have been jointly the guiding principle of my life . . .
> LOVE can only be expressed fully when man reduces himself to a cipher.
> This process of reduction to cipher is the highest effort man or woman
> is capable of making. It is the only effort worth making, and it is pos-
> sible only through ever-increasing self-restraint.[5]

Or consider his advice to Mary Osborn (a devout Christian and paci-fist) in November 1931 that a life dedicated to the service of others was only possible 'if we reduce ourselves to zero'.[6] Not least, in January 1947—about a year before his violent assassination—he confessed to his devoted follower Mirabehn, 'If I succeed in emptying myself utterly, God will pos-sess me. Then I know that everything will come true, but it is a serious question when I shall have reduced myself to zero'.[7]

Occasionally, Gandhi appears to suggest that he had no 'choice' but to empty himself utterly to zero, for it was only then that God would 'possess' him. It is in this sense that he concludes his autobiography (written serially

---

[4]   David Baird, *Thing Knowledge: A Philosophy of Scientific Instruments* (Berkeley: University of California Press, 2004). I have also been inspired by Sigfried Giedion's statement that 'for the historian there are no banal things', and by Marc Bloch's exhortation, 'Everything that a man writes or says, or everything that he makes, everything he touches can and ought to teach us about him'. See Sigfried Giedion, *Mechanization Takes Command: A Contribution to Anonymous History* (New York: Oxford University Press, 1948), 3, and Marc Bloch, *The Historian's Craft* (New York: Knopf, 1953), 66.

[5]   *CWMG* 33: 452.

[6]   *CWMG* 48: 302.

[7]   *CWMG* 86: 314.

in Gujarati and published between November 1925 and February 1929, at the near peak of his political career), suggesting that his personal salvation lay in 'reduc[ing] myself to zero'.[8] Or, as in a November 1928 letter to Kusum Desai, 'Anyone who wants to do all work in love has no choice but to reduce himself or herself to zero'.[9] But more often than not, as in the many ancestral religious traditions from which he derived his understanding, the pursuit of zero was an *active* yearning that shored up his other aspirations, including control over the palate, the overcoming of anger and lust, greed and attachment, pride and fear, and a life of 'service to all that lives' (*sarvodaya*). So, as he declared to a workers' meeting in Rajkot in his native Gujarat in 1939, 'It was only when I had learnt to reduce myself to a zero [*sic*] that I was able to evolve the power of satyagraha in South Africa'.[10] The quest for zero status not only gave him a sense of 'power' but was also 'the only *real freedom worth having*'.[11] Rather than being nothing, zero was everything. Its pursuit may well have been his most consuming 'experiment'.

The principal technology of the self that Gandhi appears to have deployed in this consuming experiment is what he named *aparigraha*, literally non-possession, a condition that he recognized was a near-impossible 'ideal' but also a 'cardinal virtue'.[12] Aparigraha, or 'the vow of non-possession', was a requisite for all those who chose to reside in his ashrams, and was an ideal that Gandhi even sought for all Indians.[13] As

---

[8] Mohandas K. Gandhi, *An Autobiography, or the Story of My Experiments with Truth, translated from the Original in Gujarati by Mahadev Desai*, Introduced with Notes by Tridip Suhrud (Gurgaon: Penguin Random House, 2018), 770. The Gujarati word that Gandhi used (which he subsequently co-translated into English as zero) is *shunyavat*, cognate with the Sanskrit *shunyata* ('emptiness'), a complex concept ascribed to the Buddhist thinker Nagarjuna (*c.*150–250 CE), with a substantive mathematical, grammatical, and philosophical development over subsequent centuries of Indian thought. Among others, *shunyata* carries a sense of purity and plenitude, even bliss.

[9] *CWMG* 38: 103.

[10] *CWMG* 69: 166.

[11] *CWMG* 38: 248.

[12] *CWMG* 30: 387; 14: 134, and 39: 221. I use the concept of technology of the self in the sense developed by Michel Foucault of 'knowing oneself' through 'taking care of oneself' (Luther H. Martin et al., eds., *Technologies of the Self: A Seminar with Michel Foucault* (Amherst: University of Massachusetts Press, 1988).

[13] In a speech he gave in Madras in February 1916 a few months after establishing his first ashram in Ahmedabad, Gandhi observed, revealingly, 'I am no socialist and I do not want to dispossess those who have got possessions; but I do say that, personally, those of us who want to see light out of darkness have to follow the rule' (*CWMG* 13: 231). For a recent analysis that explores how Gandhi's quest for 'nothingness' translated itself into the built environments of the various ashrams he inhabited, see Venugopal Maddipati, 'Architecture as Weak Thought: Gandhi Inhabits Nothingness', *Marg* 71, no. 2 (2019), 44–51

he asked rhetorically in 1924 (revealing as well the local roots of many of his 'global' ideas), 'Every good Hindu is expected, after having lived the household life for a certain period, to enter upon a life of non-possession of property. Why may we not revive the noble tradition?'[14] He insisted that 'civilization'—a much-loaded term that he sought to redefine over the course of his career, as we well know—consisted 'not in the multiplication, but in the deliberate and voluntary reduction of wants'.[15] In his September 1931 speech at Guildhouse Church in London (in what was likely his longest systematic exposition of his idea(l) of voluntary poverty), he insisted, 'The only thing that can be possessed by all is non-possession, not to have anything whatsoever. In other words, a willing surrender.'[16] If non-possession is a virtue, 'possession seems to me to be a crime'.[17] In such an understanding, much of bourgeois humanity with its penchant for (industrial-scale) accumulation stands indicted as criminal.

In a provocative essay, literary scholar Rajeswari Sunder Rajan has persuasively suggested that voluntary poverty for Gandhi was 'less an act of *giving* than of *ridding oneself of things*. When he came to write at length about it, it is in terms of self-dispossession that he primarily described it: "I must *discard* all wealth, all possessions." He goes on to use other terms similar to "discard"—"give up . . . things" (note: not "give away",) "things slipped away from me," "I threw overboard things which I used to consider as mine," "a great burden off my shoulders".'[18] It was, in other words, a matter of shedding and jettisoning 'things' in order to become 'nothing', his life and career becoming a long experiment in doing so.

It all began for Gandhi in real seriousness around 1904, after having spent the previous two decades or so accumulating things that would allow him to both 'play the English gentleman' in London,[19] and become a successful barrister in Johannesburg—everything from Western-style furnishings and crockery to a vast library of books across a range

---

[14]   *CWMG* 24: 345.
[15]   *CWMG* 44: 103.
[16]   *CWMG* 48: 52.
[17]   Ibid.
[18]   Rajeswari Sunder Rajan, 'Refusing Benevolence: Gandhi, Nehru, and the Ethics of Postcolonial Relations', in *Burden or Benefit? Imperial Benevolence and Its Benefits*, ed. Helen Gilbert and Chris Tiffin (Bloomington: Indiana University Press, 2008), 139, emphases in original.
[19]   For things Gandhi thought essential for other Indians like him aspiring to play the English gentleman in Victorian England (especially on a shoestring budget), see his handbook titled *Guide to London* (c.1893–4), *CWMG* 1: 66–120.

of subjects (some of which stayed with him till the very end of his life). Urges he experienced to 'simplify' in this period were, however, sparked more by a sense of thrift and the ethic of self-reliance than a yearning for achieving zero status per se. In a revealing chapter of his memoir titled 'Simple Life', Gandhi recalled in words that echo Sunder Rajan's argument, 'I had started on a life of ease and comfort but the experiment was short-lived. Although I had furnished the house with care, *yet it failed to have any hold on me.* So, no sooner had I launched forth on that life, than I began to cut down expenses.'[20] After recollecting with a mix of self-deprecating humour, but also pride, the steps he took in this regard, including doing his own laundry and cutting his own hair, this chapter ends: 'The extreme forms in which my passion for self-help and simplicity ultimately expressed itself will be described in their proper place. The seed had been long sown. It only needed watering to take root, to flower and to fructify, and the watering came in due course.'[21]

The 'watering' came in 1904 in the form of a book, John Ruskin's *Unto the Last*, under whose 'magic spell', as is well known, Gandhi began a conscientious transition towards shedding the material stuff that a life of bourgeois consumption had gathered around him. It is clear—as he also confesses—that it was easier said than done:

> How was one to divest oneself of all possessions? Was not the body itself possession enough? Were not wife and children possessions? Was I to destroy all the cupboards of books I had? Was I to give up all I had and follow Him? Straight came the answer: I could not follow Him unless I gave up all I had.[22]

And yet, despite the apparent 'straightness' of the answer, he did not surrender everything he possessed, and this distinguishes Gandhi's career as a worldly Mahatma from the well-worn model offered by asceticism, *sanyasa*, across many of India's religious traditions. As he perceptively observed,

---

[20] Gandhi, *An Autobiography*, 349, emphasis in original. An alternative translation for the phrase in emphasis is 'I failed to cultivate any attraction for it'.

[21] Gandhi, *An Autobiography*, 353.

[22] Gandhi, *An Autobiography*, 422. See also *CWMG* 48: 51.

Such *sanyasa* may be necessary for some rare spirit who has the power of conferring benefits upon the world by only thinking good thoughts in a cave. But the world would be ruined if everyone became a cave-dweller. Ordinary men and women can only cultivate mental detachment. *Whoever lives in the world, and lives in it only for serving it, is a sanyasi. We of the Ashram hope to become sanyasis in this sense.* We may keep necessary things but should be ready to give up everything including our bodies.[23]

His rejection of what he called cave dwelling, and the embrace instead of what Lloyd and Susanne Rudolph have called 'this-worldly asceticism', meant that Gandhi continued to be entangled in the world of things and encumbered by materiality, as we will see shortly, even as he cultivated in himself and enjoined upon his followers 'mental detachment' towards even one's few necessary possessions.[24] It also meant that, rather than an act of unilateral (especially violent) dispossession of all stuff that accumulates, Gandhian aparigraha turns around an ethic of each according to their want or need. There is a certain degree of flexibility built into the ethic which emerged from a candid realization that as long as one desired to live in the world, if only in order to do good in the world by serving others, the conditions of that living meant that stuff would accumulate. As Gandhi repeatedly noted, 'Aparigraha is an ideal condition. It can be said that an ideal is never realized perfectly. But we should not lower our ideal on this account.'[25] Voluntary poverty was one of the compromises that he worked out in response to the pursuit of this elusive ideal.

The voluntary cultivation of poverty did bring him into conflict with close kin: among the more unsavoury moments of his life his struggles with wife Kasturba over gold jewellery and other trinkets she had been saving up on for her (future) daughters-in-law,[26] and a bitter estrangement from his elder brother Lakshmidas after he stopped sending home

---

[23] *CWMG* 50: 213–14, emphasis added.
[24] Lloyd I. Rudolph and Susanne Hoeber Rudolph, *The Modernity of Tradition: Political Development in India* (Chicago: University of Chicago Press, 1967), 216–40.
[25] *CWMG* 30: 387.
[26] Gandhi, *An Autobiography*, 358–62

much-needed remittances in 1906.[27] In both instances, in his own recollection, Gandhi prevailed, ethically but also pragmatically making
his argument to those who resisted his desires by redefining the very
concept of 'family', and also underscoring his commitment to serving
others rather than aggrandizing his own. On another memorable
occasion—which he also recalled later in his memoir—he threw away a
pair of expensive binoculars belonging to his intimate friend Hermann
Kallenbach, but not before an argument that he claimed brought them
even closer. As he asked rhetorically in *Young India,* 'Experience shows
that the richest gifts must be destroyed without compensation and
hesitation if they hinder one's moral progress. Will it not be held a sacred duty to consign to the flames most precious heirlooms, if they are
plague-infected?'[28]

Not least, as he 'experimented' with practising the ideal of aparigraha
in the cause of sarvodaya, Gandhi also arrived at his concept of 'trusteeship', perhaps the last 'weapon' to be fashioned in his arsenal of 'disobedient' practices—and the only core Gandhian concept that found
primary expression as an English word. As he wrote in his memoir, an-
choring his ideas in his reading of his favourite text, the *Bhagavad Gita,*
'I understood the Gita teaching of non-possession to mean that those
who desired salvation should act like the trustee who, though having
control over great possessions, regards not an iota of them as his own.'[29]
This also meant that one could continue to hold on to stuff, but not in a
proprietary manner or with greed and desire. 'Anyone who has taken the
vow of aparigraha may not keep anything for himself, but he can keep
crores in his custody while acting as a trustee.'[30] Such an understanding
enabled Gandhi to become the Congress Party's most successful fund-
raiser and money manager, and, in fact, the emergent nation's most
'trusted' trustee, even as he diligently threw himself into reducing himself to zero.

---

[27] *CWMG* 5: 334–5 and 6: 430–5. See also ibid., 39: 211–13.
[28] *CWMG* 21: 42. For a different argument that he did what he did to wean Kallenbach from
his 'infatuation' with this expensive object, see Gandhi, *An Autobiography,* 536–7.
[29] *CWMG* 39: 211–13. See also 49: 132–46. The germ of this idea was espoused as early as
1909 in *Hind Swaraj* (*CWMG* X, 52; 63).
[30] *CWMG* 42: 142.

The Material Mahatma

The result of such experiments over time, and such accommodations and amendments, is that stuff did accumulate around Gandhi, his efforts at shedding and self-dispossession notwithstanding, possibly even as a consequence of his insistence that he was a sanyasi 'who lives in the world, and lives in it only by serving it'. For instance, at the crack of dawn on 12 March 1930, when he set out from Sabarmati Ashram on his 220-mile march to the Dandi seashore with the resolve not to return to Ahmedabad until India won freedom, all his worldly possessions reportedly went into two shoulder bags that photographs of that famous moment capture for us. About seventeen years later when he embarked as 'a lone pilgrim' on foot on what was his last heroic march through riot-ravaged Noakhali in late 1946 and early 1947, clearly his wants had multiplied—and along with that, his possessions:

> [His] kit included practically everything he required from pen, pencil, and paper to needle and sewing thread for mending clothes; a few cooking pots, an earthen bowl and a wooden spoon, a galvanized iron bucket for bath, a commode, a hand-basin and soap; and last but not least, his spinning wheel and its accessories. There were, besides, files, papers and a few books. A portable typewriter completed the office equipment.

His kit also included at least twenty-one books that his devoted secretary Pyarelal lists, including Bengali and Urdu readers. It appears that Gandhi's grand-niece Manu and two other travelling companions hauled all this stuff, the Mahatma at 78 being too frail to do so himself.[31]

Similarly, despite practising what another of his followers called 'the art of thrift',[32] his bare and spare ashram in Sevagram—which astonished foreign visitors in the 1930s and 1940s with its sparseness—was filled

---

[31] Pyarelal, *Mahatma Gandhi: The Last Phase* (Ahmedabad: Navajivan, 1956), I: 494–5. For other items that he carried on his trip, including a pumice stone gifted to him by Mirabehn which was a 'cherished companion' for twenty-five years, see Manu Gandhi, *Bapu: My Mother* (Ahmedabad: Navajivan, 1949), 23–5, 32.

[32] Appasaheb Patwardhan, 'The Art of Thrift', in *Gandhiji: His Life and Work*, ed. D. G. Tendulkar et al. (Bombay: Keshav Bhikaji Dhawale, 1944), 227–9.

with things that a female devotee recalled with great attention to detail to writer and critic Ved Mehta some years later: spectacles 'with their cheap wire frames', leather sandals, wooden clogs, a clock in the dining hall, lanterns, iron and brass bowls and tumblers, a bed made of hard board, a couple of pillows and woollen shawls, wooden spoons, a Lifebuoy-soap crate turned upside down and spread with a khadi cloth that served as a desk, a makeshift clipboard and a pad of paper, handmade wooden penholder with three or four old pens, a few loose nibs, an ink bottle, three or four shiny polished stones used as paperweights, the *Bhagavad Gita*, the Quran, the Bible, an English dictionary, a red khadi satchel of manila files containing papers, his pocket watch, 'a fat cheap old Ingersoll ... [t]urnip watches, I think they are called—the kind that Englishmen in Victorian novels wear at the end of chains in their waistcoat pockets', a safety pin and bamboo staff, tin tub, spittoon, straight razor, a wooden rack, a commode, and 'false teeth'.[33] Clearly this was an unusual amount of material to attach themselves to a man who yearned for zero status.[34]

Some of the stuff that accumulated was a consequence of the fact that the body too is 'a possession, and so long as it is there, it calls for other possessions in its train'.[35] As he aged, Gandhi needed dentures (of which he owned several sets, reportedly),[36] a spittoon (on account of suffering from catarrh), and, of course, spectacles (although he fretted over his dependence on these).[37] Until the very end of his life, he continued to sport

[33] Mehta, *Gandhi*, 3–16. The devotee also concluded with the observation, 'What a Banya he was! He didn't believe in wasting anything; he once scolded his son Devdas for losing a pencil stub. Now and again, when he didn't like what he'd written and the paper he was writing on was completely used up, he dropped it into an embroidered woollen wastepaper basket—a present someone had brought him from Kashmir, and probably the most expensive thing in the ashram' (ibid., 11).

[34] As he complained in 1942 when he was incarcerated yet another time, but in the luxurious rooms of the Aga Khan Palace in Poona, he complained, 'Many households are so packed with all sorts of unnecessary decoration and furniture which can very well do without, that a simple living man will feel suffocated in those surroundings. They are nothing but means of harbouring dust, bacteria, and insects. Here in the house where I am under detention, I feel quite lost. The heavy furniture, chairs, tables, sofas, bedsteads, innumerable looking glasses, all get on my nerves' (*CWMG* 77: 36).

[35] *CWMG* 50: 213.

[36] On Gandhi's dentures, see also Louis Fischer, *A Week with Gandhi* (New York: Duell, Sloan & Pearce, 1942), 6, and Devendra N. Dixit, 'Gandhiji's Personal Effects', *Illustrated Weekly of India* (25 January 1970), 8–9.

[37] Many members of Gandhi's inner circle also wore spectacles, Kasturba and loyal aide Mahadev Desai even apparently owning several pairs. Since his death, Gandhi's spectacles (or 'copies' of them) have had a fascinating afterlife, worth exploring in and of itself, including being auctioned off in distant global venues at most un-Gandhian prices, and serving as the logo for Narendra Modi's Swachh Bharat Abhiyan (Clean India Mission), launched in 2014.

a moustache but no other facial hair, which in turn necessitated periodic shaving. The artist Mukul Dey recalls seeing him using a Gillette razor (an imported object though it was) when he visited him at his ashram on the Sabarmati in 1928, and the Swiss German photographer Walter Bosshard captured him on camera shaving the day after the historic breaking of the colonial salt laws, captioning his effort, 'Gandhi shaving with a Gillette, Dandi, April 7, 1930'.[38]

Possibly out of deference to his middle-class followers, and partly because of his own ambivalence about nudity, Gandhi did not discard all his clothing (despite a yearning to go completely naked, especially in the eyes of God). He owned several lengths of the dhoti, his trademark waist cloth (frequently mistranslated, including by the man himself, as 'loin cloth'), although he was not above being mischievous about his dependence on the garment. The pacifist Maude Royden—who chaired the meeting at Guildhouse Church in London on 23 September 1931 when he spoke to 'a huge crowd' about his evolving theories on non-possession—wrote to a friend on the following day thus:

> Gandhi noted that even though he believed in voluntary poverty he still had his loincloth, and while he had a body, he had to wrap it in something. However, he added with a beaming smile that 'if anyone wants to take it off me, he can have it. I shan't call the police.' The eighteen police that the government had provided to guard him burst into a roar of laughter as he turned to look at them, and the whole audience followed suit.[39]

Gandhi being Gandhi, he used objects that adhered to him to deliver object lessons. Thus, on his way to London in 1931, where among

---

For thoughtful reflections on the place of spectacles—at once common but not necessarily easy to procure—in the Victorian world (of which Gandhi was a critical inheritor), see Asa Briggs, *Victorian Things* (Chicago: University of Chicago Press, 1989), 104–21.

[38] Sumathi Ramaswamy, *Gandhi in the Gallery: The Art of Disobedience* (New Delhi: Roli Books, 2020), 16. For a reproduction of the Bosshard photograph, see Barbara Mittler and Sumathi Ramaswamy, eds., *Envisioning Asia: Gandhi and Mao in the Photographs of Walter Bosshard* (Heidelberg: Centre for Asian and Transcultural Studies, 2019), 32. Bosshard's caption notwithstanding, Gandhi reportedly started to use a 'cut-throat' razor belonging to his nephew Maganlal (who had died recently) on 11 April 1929 (email communication, Tridip Suhrud, 31 July 2021, to whom many thanks for this detail).

[39] Quoted in Thomas Weber, *Going Native: Gandhi's Relationship with Western Women* (New Delhi: Lotus, 2011), 102. See also *CWMG* 48: 52–3.

other events he delivered his speech on voluntary poverty to 'a huge crowd', he reportedly declared to a customs official in Marseilles where he first disembarked, 'I am a poor mendicant; my earthly possessions consist of 6 spinning wheels, prison dishes, a can of goat's milk, six homespun loin cloths and towels, and my reputation.'[40] Repeatedly, as we know, the spinning wheel (charkha) became the principal object with and around which he delivered lessons on a whole host of pet Gandhian issues ranging from cultivating self-sufficiency to a critique of industrial capitalism. On this most important of Gandhian objects, much has been written, including in a fine monograph by art historian Rebecca Brown.[41] I will therefore consider an object on which there has been less commentary, but which was essential to Gandhi's persona as an inveterate, some might even say compulsive, writer—namely, the pen. In fact, it is ironical that his travelling kit in Noakhali included a typewriter, given his dislike of the machine, which he dismissed as a cover for indifference and laziness, lamenting as well that it had 'all but destroyed the magnificent art of calligraphy'. Gandhi conceded that reading typed materials was easier, and also acknowledged that he 'knew very few whose writing is worse' than his own. Nonetheless, 'I will inflict that illegible hand in preference to having my letters typed or typing them myself.'[42]

And 'inflict' himself he did, as we know from thousands of pages of handwritten letters and missives, some also displayed in various Gandhi museums after his death. He wrote most of those with a fountain pen—ironically, an instrument finessed during the industrial age that he much bemoaned[43]—and appears to have been particularly attached to some that were gifted to him over the years by friends and associates, including one by Kallenbach, despite his expressed 'dislike' for the object. In a discussion in 1937 with Maurice Frydman, he confessed, 'Every time, I use the fountain pen it hurts me ... Compromise comes in at every step, but one must realize that it is a compromise and keep the final goal constantly

---

[40] Quoted in D. G. Tendulkar, *Mahatma: Life of Mohandas Karamchand Gandhi*, Volume 3: 1930–1934 (Bombay: Vithalbhai K. Jhaveri and D. G. Tendulkar, 1952), 142.

[41] Rebecca Brown, *Gandhi's Spinning Wheel and the Making of India* (London: Routledge, 2010).

[42] *CWMG* 33, 396–7. On the typewriter as a Victorian-era object, see Briggs, *Victorian Things*, 410–14.

[43] For the development of steel and fountain pens in nineteenth-century England, see Briggs, *Victorian Things*, 182–7

in front of the mind's eye.'[44] Even as he settled for the fountain pen as a 'compromise' in the interest both of efficiency and because it enabled him to write more legibly, there were two Gandhian projects he conducted around it. With the help of K. V. Ratnam, pen-maker of Rajahmundry, he promoted the use of swadeshi pens and swadeshi ink, as a 'substitute for the foreign pens one sees in the bazaars'.[45] And he also learned the 'art' of using a reed pen, and particularly encouraged its use among children, especially as part of his *nayi taleem* (new learning) pedagogy. One obvious reason for so doing was because he considered the reed pen as indigenous, and hence swadeshi, but he also promoted its use on account of its affordability.

'Aparigraha is an attitude of the mind. If we regard a thing like a pen as belonging to us, we commit *parigraha*.'[46] He expressed a similar sentiment about his pocket watch (for affixing which to his dhoti he also needed safety pins, turning it into a waist watch). Gandhi's obsession with (clock) time is well known: he prided himself on punctuality, and in fact his last moments on earth were spent fretting over the fact that he was running late for his prayer meeting. From his youthful days in London, he seems to have had a fondness for watches and had to find ways to accommodate this fondness within his 'vow of non-possession'. When specifically questioned about this apparent contradiction in London in 1931 by an interviewer (after Gandhi had looked at his watch just as the meeting was commencing!), he responded,

I must know what time it is, consequently, I must use a watch. Moreover, I am doing nothing against my principles. I am an enemy not of mechanism but of organized mechanism. I consider this system, which has become the basis of your civilization, as the greatest danger which could menace man. If I use a watch, that does not mean that I am its slave. But when it is a question of the machine organized, man

[44]   *CWMG* 68: 266. See also Manu Gandhi, *My Memorable Moments with Gandhi* (Ahmedabad: Navajivan, 1960), 10–11.

[45]   *CWMG* 61: 358 See also Taran Deol, 'Ratnam Pens: The 'Swadeshi' Pens that were Made on Mahatma Gandhi's Demand', *The Print* (29 December 2019), https://theprint.in/features/brandma/ratnam-pens-the-swadeshi-pens-that-were-made-on-mahatma-gandhis-demand/341501/ [accessed 18 July 2021].

[46]   *CWMG* 41: 190–1.

becomes its slave and loses all of the values with which the Lord endowed him.[47]

In an earlier letter to one of his grand-nephews (and followers), Prabhudas, who must have also been troubled by the contradiction, he wrote,

> What you write about my vow regarding a watch is embarrassing not because of the vow but because the mind is not yet trained in aparigraha. But I know no other way of training the mind against possessiveness. If a person having any number of watches is indifferent over one of them, that certainly is no great merit in him. His indifference might be at the cost of some other person. If one is not worried about one's watch in spite of such a vow, and in spite of knowing that another cannot be had if this is lost, one has at least a remote chance of attaining aparigraha.[48]

Despite offering such object lessons on aparigraha, he was clearly attached to a watch gifted to him by industrialist and patron Narottam Morarjee, and also one given to him by young Indira, daughter of his political heir, Jawaharlal Nehru, which he used for some twenty years before it was stolen. He appears to have made an exception even for British-made watches (and the British typewriter), despite his commitment to swadeshi, and 'even though I had to pay a little more'.[49]

If the watch as material object came early into his life, a statuette of three monkeys arrived late, gifted to him sometime around 1940. One of the few artworks in his possession, it also became the basis on which new lessons were delivered or, rather, old ideas presented succinctly in a formula that we now indelibly associate with Gandhi: 'Hear no evil, see no evil, speak no evil.' As he recalled in a letter to a follower dated 8 September 1941,

> I have a beautiful figure of three monkeys, which I always keep in front of me. They are three representations of the same monkey. His ears,

[47]   CWMG 48: 386.
[48]   CWMG 30: 149.
[49]   CWMG 48: 61.

mouth and eyes are closed. The lesson the figure teaches is that one should not listen to criticism of or see or speak of anybody's defects. The original of this figure is found on a tall pillar in Japan, and was carved thousands of years ago. We should engrave this lesson in our hearts.[50]

When he was imprisoned in the Aga Khan Palace in 1943, the object occupied a prominent place on his desk in his room, 'so it faced' him, the anointed 'guru' for the man who prided himself on being a guru to and in the modern world.[51]

The Art of Becoming Immaterial

Anthropologist Kenneth George has written with great delicacy and nuance about 'companionable objects', which he defines as 'those things with which we have ethical and affective ties'. As we dwell together with such things, 'we become vulnerable to them, and they to us. In that mutuality of influence between people and things, there is both care and violence. An ethical realm stretches between human actors and things, and palpably so in our contemporary art worlds.'[52] Building on George's insight, I now consider the aesthetic aspects of the Gandhian aspiration for 'possessing non-possession', and explore how some visual artists of India, in his time and since, respond to a range of companionable objects that adhere to the Mahatma even as he pursued his quest for zero status. In fact, a veritable, even sumptuous, body of work in all sorts of media ranging from paper and canvas to stone and metal has emerged to charge such quotidian objects with an aura that only modern art can arguably confer in our secular times, even as they 'rematerialize' the Mahatma in intriguing new ways.[53]

---

[50] *CWMG* 74: 304.

[51] *The Diary of Manu Gandhi, 1943-1944, Edited and Translated by Tridip Suhrud* (New Delhi: Oxford University Press, 2019), 157. See also the floor plan of Bapu Kuti, Gandhi's residence in his ashram at Segaon (Sevagram), where we see it placed centrally (Madipatti, 'Architecture as Weak Thought', Fig. 4).

[52] Kenneth George, 'Lifewriting and the Making of Companionable Objects: Reflections on Sunaryo's Titik Nadir', in *Locating Life Stories: Beyond East-West Binaries in (Auto)Biographical Studies*, ed. Maureen Perkins (Honolulu: University of Hawaii Press, 2012), 35–6.

[53] Sumathi Ramaswamy, '"Reducing Myself to Zero": The Art of Aparigraha', *Marg: A Magazine of the Arts*, 71, no. 2 (2019), 68–79.

For one, Gandhi's chosen objects themselves have become works of art, as in the Gandhian artist Haku Shah's *Gandhi and His Things* (2014), which renders for aesthetic contemplation his spectacles and his waist watch, his staff and his sandals, in the belief that 'Simply because an object is common in the social sense, it does not mean that it is ordinary, not worth placing in an exhibition or museum.'[54] Noted New Delhi-based painter Krishen Khanna's untitled sketch (1995) also throws in for good measure his pen, inkpot, and hymn book, not to mention the ubiquitous charkha (Figure 6.1). The words inscribed in English around the margins of Khanna's sketch—Ahimsa, Truth, Simplicity, Love, Tollerance [*sic*], Self-reliance—signal the artist's sense that these lofty Gandhian ideals are pegged to these paltry possessions. In Baroda-based Gulammohammed Sheikh's stunning large canvas *Ahmedabad: The City Gandhi Left Behind* (2015–16), the viewer is invited—as if on a treasure hunt—to search for the objects that he held close: his watch (stopped at 5.10 p.m., the near time of his murder), his eating bowl and plate, his spectacles (and their case), and his sandals, all scattered around his modest home in Sabarmati Ashram. Sheikh was compelled to make this painting as he was working on another project related to Ahmedabad. As he did so,

I chanced upon the news of an auction with photographs of Gandhiji's prized possessions published in the Sunday magazine section of *The Hindu*. The spectacles, slippers, a watch, a metal bowl and a plate of this faqir who did not possess a penny sold at phenomenal prices. The images of these objects inserted in the ashen grey map of Ahmedabad continue to float before my eyes: a bodiless being with spectacles [without] the face, slippers without a foot, clutching a watch and holding an empty bowl and plate, staggers to soothe the sighs of souls gone to bed hungry.[55]

As art historian Chaitanya Sambrani observes of this luminous work, 'In this city of 2016, the ashen expanse is only relieved by the burning

---

[54] Quoted in Rebecca Brown, 'Haku Shah: The Handcrafted Art of the Curator', in *Nitya Gandhi: Living Reliving Gandhi* (New Delhi: Centre for Media and Alternative Communication, 2014), n.p.

[55] Gulammohammed Sheikh, 'Reading Gandhi in Our Time', *Social Scientist* 47 (2019), 3–7, quote on 6–7.

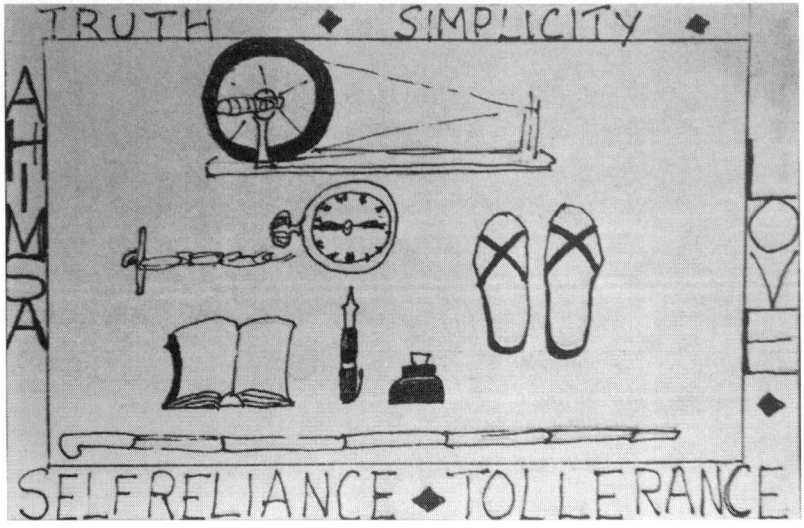

Fig. 6.1 Krishen Khanna, Untitled (from *Postcards for Gandhi* project), 1995. Pen on paper, 14.6 x 8.9 cm. Courtesy Sahmat, New Delhi.

rickshaw and silenced laneway of forsaken dwellings in the center of the painting, and the museumized personal effects of the Mahatma along the banks of the Sabarmati.'[56] The Mahatma as embodied figure, however, is strikingly absent. The very emptying of his physical presence, the work seems to suggest, leads to riots and death, casting a ghostly pall over the city. Gandhi is also corporeally missing in Kolkata-based Debanjan Roy's *Absence of Bapu* (2007/2010), but he is at the same time summoned back through his few possessions—his spectacles, a book, his leather sandals and wooden clogs, and a statuette of the three monkeys—carefully arranged on a fibreglass white mattress, guarded over by an armed soldier in fatigues. The Mahatma's personal possessions are now the nation's patrimony, and as such, need the state's armed protection, it seems.

In evacuating the embodied figure of Gandhi thus, such works appear to be true to his aspiration to become immaterial and shed his own body—which he once lamented was his last possession but on account

---

[56] Chaitanya Sambrani, 'At Home in the World', in *At Home in the World: The Art and Life of Gulammohammed Sheikh*, ed. Chaitanya Sambrani, 94–157 (New Delhi: Tulika Books in association with Vadehra Art Gallery, 2019), 149.

of whose needs, as I have already noted, stuff accrued around him. The artist emerges as a critical collaborator in this regard by disappearing his corporeal presence from their canvases or installations, and turning instead to his paltry possessions to stand in for him as proxy. His spectacles and staff, his spinning wheel and waist watch had in Gandhi's own lifetime been critical to his distinctive look and may even have been put to use thus by this master choreographer of his own image. Since the turn of this century, however, these companionable objects have become disassociated from the Mahatma's person and body and have taken on an aesthetic life of their own within this complex that I call the art of aparigraha.

Such a disassociation is especially striking in a landmark project titled *Postcards for Gandhi* undertaken in 1995 by the New Delhi-based activist and left-oriented organization Sahmat. The conceit of the project was to draw upon another quotidian object that Gandhi relied on extensively, namely, the humble postcard, one of his favoured means of communication. Of interest to me is the extent to which the artists who participated in the process—many among India's most famous—turned to a handful of his possessions to underscore his 'political leadership, philosophy, and relevance to contemporary India'.[57] Repeatedly, across close to 600 postcard-size works, the artists turned to the most companionable of these possessions: his watch, his footwear, his statuette of the three monkeys, his walking stick, and, not least, his spinning wheel. What might Gandhi have made of the fact that his paltry possessions resurface as proxies for his presence? And what should we make of the fact that these objects have taken on aesthetic afterlives of their own, certainly far in excess of what was intended for them in Gandhi's lifetime?

For instance, consider the humble bamboo staff (*danda*) that we so associate with Gandhian iconography: the statue of the striding Mahatma, staff in hand, is ubiquitous in the Indian urban landscape and abroad to the point of having become a visual cliché. Gandhi likely took up a staff as part of his new look for the first time in December 1913 in Durban, when he shed, in an act of mourning, his bourgeois sartorial wardrobe of the past twenty years to don the clothing of the abject indentured labourer. Yet it was not until over fifteen years later from the time of the Salt March that the staff became a regular accessory. On the morning

[57] Ramaswamy, *Gandhi in the Gallery*, 177–9.

of 12 March 1930 as he was about to set out on his historic march to Dandi—with all his worldly possessions packed in two shoulder bags, as I noted—Kaka Kalelkar reportedly presented him with one such staff, 54 inches long and 1 inch wide, made from lacquered bamboo and iron-tipped. In artworks from the time of Nandalal Bose's iconic images of the Salt March—while his two shoulder bags with all his worldly possessions disappear—Gandhi is routinely painted with a staff in hand. In some cases, as in Amit Ambalal's beautiful watercolour for the Sahmat project (1995), Gandhi is only partially present, but no visually literate viewer in India would be confused about the owner of the bony hand wrapped around the staff. Vadodara-based Balaji Ponna's *He Relaxed it and It Upturned* (2007) celebrates the labour of walking performed by Gandhi over his political lifetime, literally moving with his body across the map of British India which he traversed from one end to the other on his bony legs and sandal-clad feet (Figure 6.2). The Mahatma is absent in the work, but his staff, converted into an elegant walking stick, makes a neat appearance.

In the enigmatic *Eraser Pro* (2012), while the rest of Gandhi's body is sculpted in a state of disintegration, the staff, sheathed in (faux) bronze, stands whole and unbroken. Tallur L. N., an artist who spends his time between his native Mangalore and adopted city Seoul, 'created' the fabulous sculpture by 'erasing' life-size statues of Gandhi that are routinely mass-produced across India. Preoccupied as he is with image construction and destruction, Tallur's goal might well have been to reflect on the process by which Gandhi has been systematically transformed from embodied substance into a bio-icon, making visible in the process the hollowness of what lies beneath the surface. That he leaves the staff intact in doing so is a revealing reminder of the importance of this accessory for rendering Gandhi visually and iconographically recognizable, even while paying homage to the Mahatma's aspiration for zero status. In the hands of one of India's most expensive artists, Subodh Gupta, Gandhi's humble bamboo reed has even become a stand-alone bronze artefact, a high-end art object—and collector's item! Gupta has also famously scaled up and repurposed the humble figurine of the three monkeys in an arresting installation piece (completed between 2006 and 2009) on display in Doha, Qatar. Similarly, Ahmedabad artist Ratilal Kansodaria's evocative sculpture which celebrates the Mahatma's spectacles (by also tethering them to

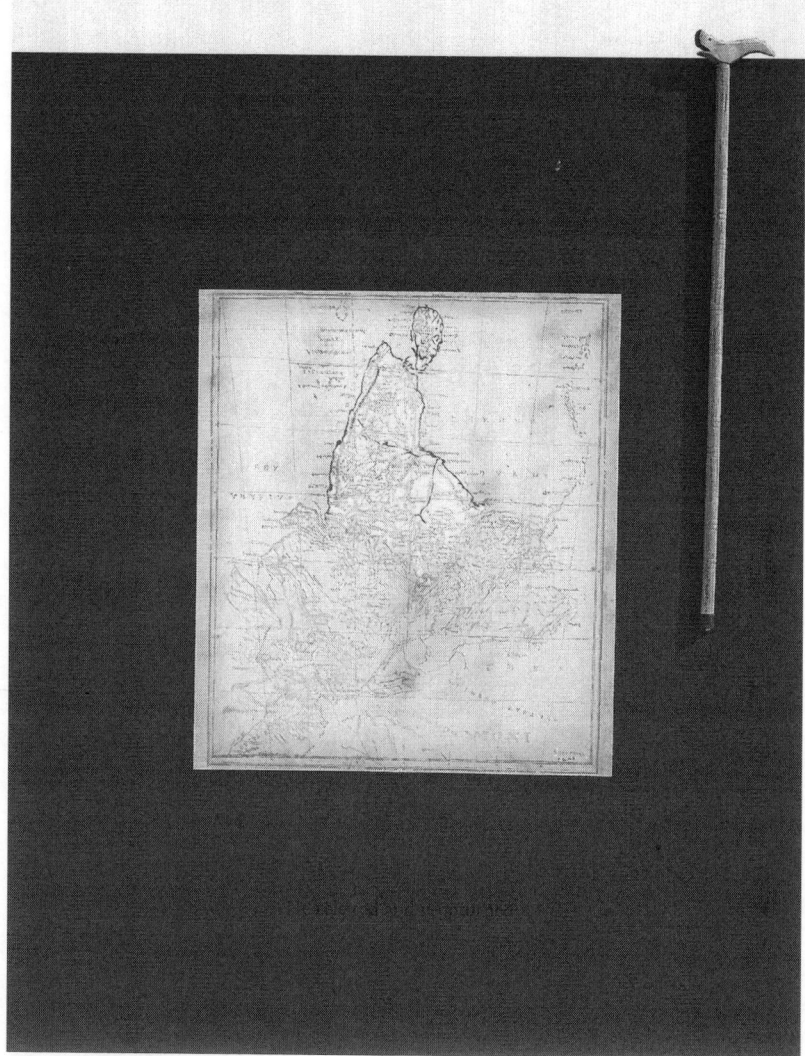

Fig. 6.2 Balaji Ponna, *He 'Relaxed' It and It 'Upturned'*, 2007. Oil on canvas, hand stick, 152 × 122 cm. Courtesy the artist.

a famed marble screen in the city's Siddi Saiyyed Mosque) now resides in a private art collection in Spain.

Arguably the most unexpected aesthetic journeys within this complex of the art of aparigraha are undertaken by Gandhi's footwear. Although he frequently took trains, buses, cars, and ships to get his message out and his work done (and has been photographed and painted doing so), walking remained Gandhi's favoured mode of transportation. A daily regimen, sometimes solitarily, at other times with his followers or with family, was critical to the production of his disobedient body, enabling a lifetime of frugality and fitness as well as a retort to what he famously described as 'the organized violence of the British empire'. As he observed in 1909 in *Hind Swaraj*, 'God set a limit to man's locomotive ambitions in the construction of his body.'[58] Years later in the course of the momentous march of 1930 that made him globally famous, he insisted to his followers, 'The rule is, do not ride if you can walk.'[59] Although he is shown walking on bare feet in the most iconic of images by Nandalal Bose from that momentous march, Gandhi mostly appeared in public in handmade sandals, often made for himself and for others, writing in 1911, for example, to his nephew Maganlal,

> I am mostly busy making sandals these days. I like the work and it is essential too. I have already made about fifteen pairs. When you need new ones now, please send me the measurements. And when you do so, mark the places where the strap is to be fixed—that is, on the outer side of the big toe and the little one.

A drawing, the earliest we know of in the adult Gandhi's hands—which unfortunately appears to not have survived in the archives—accompanied these instructions.[60]

Gandhi also possessed wooden footwear (*chakdi* in Gujarati, *kadau* in Hindi), in the style habitually favoured by subcontinental mendicants; eyewitness reports suggest that he wore these typically in domestic contexts. A grainy photograph, taken soon after he formally adopted his famed 'loin cloth' in Madurai in September 1921, in which he appears wearing a pair, survives in the archives.[61] In some artworks, these wooden clogs have been placed in his presence (rather than on his feet, per se): a

---

[58] *CWMG* 10: 28.
[59] *CWMG* 43: 148
[60] *CWMG* 10: 407.
[61] For a reproduction, see D. G. Tendulkar, *Mahatma: Life of Mohandas Karamchand Gandhi*, Volume 2: 1920–1929 (Bombay: Vithalbhai K. Jhaveri and D. G. Tendulkar, 1951), 89.

pair is visible in Frieda Hauswirth's sketch from 1927, perhaps the earliest instance of their appearance in an artwork. A pair of clogs is also painted delicately on the mat next to the Mahatma's prone figure on the cot in Vinayak Masoji's *The Midnight Arrest*. Over the years, though, as with so many of the other paltry possessions of the Mahatma, these wooden clogs also take on an aesthetic afterlife in which they come to be disassociated from Gandhi's body and presence and assume a trajectory of independence, as in Surendran Nair's untitled work for the Postcards for Gandhi project in which they are pierced with nails, hinting at the martyrdom of his body (Figure 6.3). Most strikingly, for example in New Delhi-based G. R. Iranna's *Cuffed Object* (2009), a single pair of *kadau* is bolted down with a pair of handcuffs, likely the artist's tribute to the Mahatma as India's most famous nonviolent 'lawbreaker', a man who was willing, even cheerfully, to be incarcerated for standing up for his principles. In *Naavu* (2019), showcased in the India Pavilion at the 2019 Venice Biennial, the artist assembles a throng of these wooden footwear, close to 700 of them, many artfully embellished, bringing back to memory the multitude in the constitution of the Mahatma. In Arpana Caur's terracotta relief, a single pair of *kadau* stands in for the absent Mahatma, a barbed wire stretched across them invoking the bloody Radcliffe Line that divided up British India even as it provides a melancholic rejoinder to Gandhi's statement that Partition would only happen over his dead body. Although the photographic evidence confirms that most often Gandhi wore handmade sandals in public, his saintly status, especially in the aftermath of his assassination, has made the *kadau* ubiquitous in the visual culture that has emerged around the Mahatma, even while providing material and visual sustenance to Nehru's much-quoted words, 'Where he sat was a temple, where he walked was hallowed ground.'[62]

In his own lifetime when his follower Prema Kantak sought his permission to hold on to a precious pair of *kadau* worn by her Bapu, Gandhi wrote a chastising letter, condemning her action as 'smacking of idolatry.'[63] Such an admonition has not stopped their enshrinement, or the display of his handmade leather sandals, in the regimes of memorializing

---

[62] S. Gopal, ed., *Selected Works of Jawaharlal Nehru* (New Delhi: Oxford University Press, 1987), 5: 48–9. For several of the art works referred to in these pages, see Ramaswamy, *Gandhi in the Gallery*.

[63] *CWMG* 44: 192

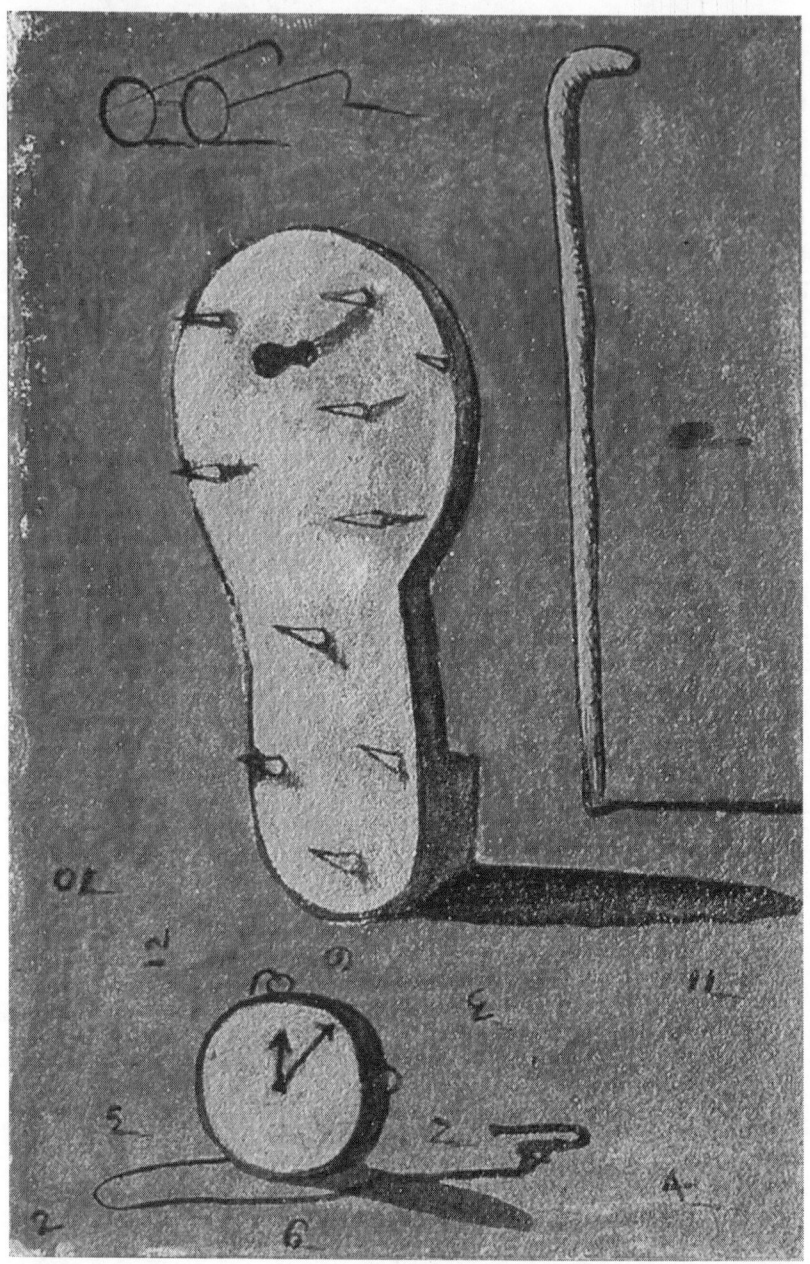

Fig. 6.3 Surendran Nair, Untitled. Acrylic on paper, 8.9 x 14.6 cm. Courtesy Sahmat, New Delhi.

the Mahatma since 1948, beginning with a much-circulated photograph published a few months after his assassination, likely taken by his grand-nephew Kanu under the supervision of his youngest son, Devdas.[64] There is the paradoxical fact of the hyper-vegetarian Gandhi working with dead animal hide, and his almost obsessive desire to become an ex-pert tanner; tannery itself was critical to Gandhi's Constructive Work agenda that he carried out across India's villages, and, at his ashrams in Sabarmati and Sevagram, he opened tannery workshops. On the other hand, of course, such work being habitually confined to the lowest of low 'untouchables',—indeed even indelibly defining their subjectivity in the eyes of the so-called touchables, as Gopal Guru powerfully notes—this gave the Mahatma one more opportunity to disobey some norms of the caste system in his project of getting his fellow caste Hindus to overcome 'the sin' of untouchability.[65] No wonder, then, that the humble sandal has attracted the eye of the artist and become an object of aesthetic contem-plation in numerous works across many media. By virtue of the fact that they had touched his feet and protected them as he performed his labour of walking on behalf of self and nation, Gandhi's sandal is transformed within the art of aparigraha into an artefact that invites melancholic marvel.

'Everything He Touched'

The roots of what I have characterized as the art of aparigraha—in which his paltry possessions assume a powerful aesthetic afterlife, even as they are disassociated from the Mahatma's body and also become proxy for his physical presence—can be traced back to his own lifetime.[66] This is

---

[64] Devdas Gandhi, ed., *Memories of Bapu* (New Delhi: Hindustan Times Press, 1948), n.p. See also Figure 6.6.

[65] Guru Guru, 'Aesthetic of Touch and the Skin: An Essay in Contemporary Indian Political Phenomenology', in *The Bloomsbury Research Handbook of Indian Aesthetics and the Philosophy of Art*, ed. Arindam Chakrabarti (London: Bloomsbury, 2016), 297–316.

[66] I derive this title of this section from Ravikumar Kashi's artwork (2011–12), which I dis-cuss later in the section. My reflections are also inspired by anthropologist Ritu Khanduri's ob-servation, 'Located in secret closets, bank vaults, and auction houses; sipped as holy water; and marketed as a brand, Gandhi's things constitute a story about circuits of access to a "sensory reality". Gandhi's touch through his pre-ownership of things, his ashes, and his hand writing made ordinary things extraordinary ... We need an anthropology of the touch, and how people learnt to fragment this basic human experience' (Khanduri, 'Some Things About Gandhi', 320).

evidenced in a collage taken by the Gandhian photographer and memor-
ialist Vithalbhai Jhaveri and published in a volume presented to Gandhi
on the occasion of his seventy-fifth birthday in 1944 with the caption
'Bapu's Few Possessions' (Figure 6.4). The collage assembles photographs
of a hank of khadi, a rosary, a fountain pen, some cutlery, a thermos, and
a pair of handmade sandals, some of these a surprising choice given, for
example, Gandhi's caustic comments about the fountain pen that I noted
earlier.[67] The next step on the road to memorialization was in the immediate aftermath of Gandhi's assassination and cremation in early 1948,
when objects from the last moments of the Mahatma's life on earth were
carefully assembled on the grounds of Birla House in New Delhi where
he was murdered, and lovingly photographed by his grand-nephew
Kanu (Figures 6.5 and 6.6). Even his (considerable) ashes, deposited in
ceremonial urns, did not escape the entanglement of memorialization,
despite his yearning for reaching zero.[68]

Soon after, most likely under the supervision of his youngest son,
Devdas, Gandhi's 'last' possessions were formally rearranged on a
stepped display stand and photographed, likely by a photographer associated with the *Hindustan Times*, and published in April 1948. Over
the years, this particular photograph has been multiply reproduced, but
it is worth noting that at the very moment of its first public appearance
it was accompanied by these curious words: 'His "property": The bowls
and wooden spoons he used for his meals; by the side of the black bowl
the three wise monkeys nicknamed by him "Guru" Teacher. The Gita,
rosary, watch, spectacles, receptacle, ink-stand, and book of hymns. His
footwear.' The image, capturing the most intimate among the Mahatma's
companionable objects, is captioned (perhaps by Devdas himself)
'These too are bereft', suggesting that by virtue of having been once
touched by the Mahatma, these objects are in mourning after his final departure, never to be touched by him again.[69] In January 1949, on the first
anniversary of his death titled Sarvodaya Divas, a major exhibition was
held in New Delhi, the first of its kind featuring artworks, photographs,

---

[67]   Tendulkar et al., *Gandhiji: His Life and Work*, 201.

[68]   Yasmin Khan, 'Performing Peace: Gandhi's Assassination at a Critical Moment in the
Consolidation of the Nehruvian State', *Modern Asian Studies* 45, no. 01 (2011), 57–80; and
Khanduri, 'Some Things About Gandhi', 309–14.

[69]   Gandhi, ed. *Memories of Bapu*, n.p.

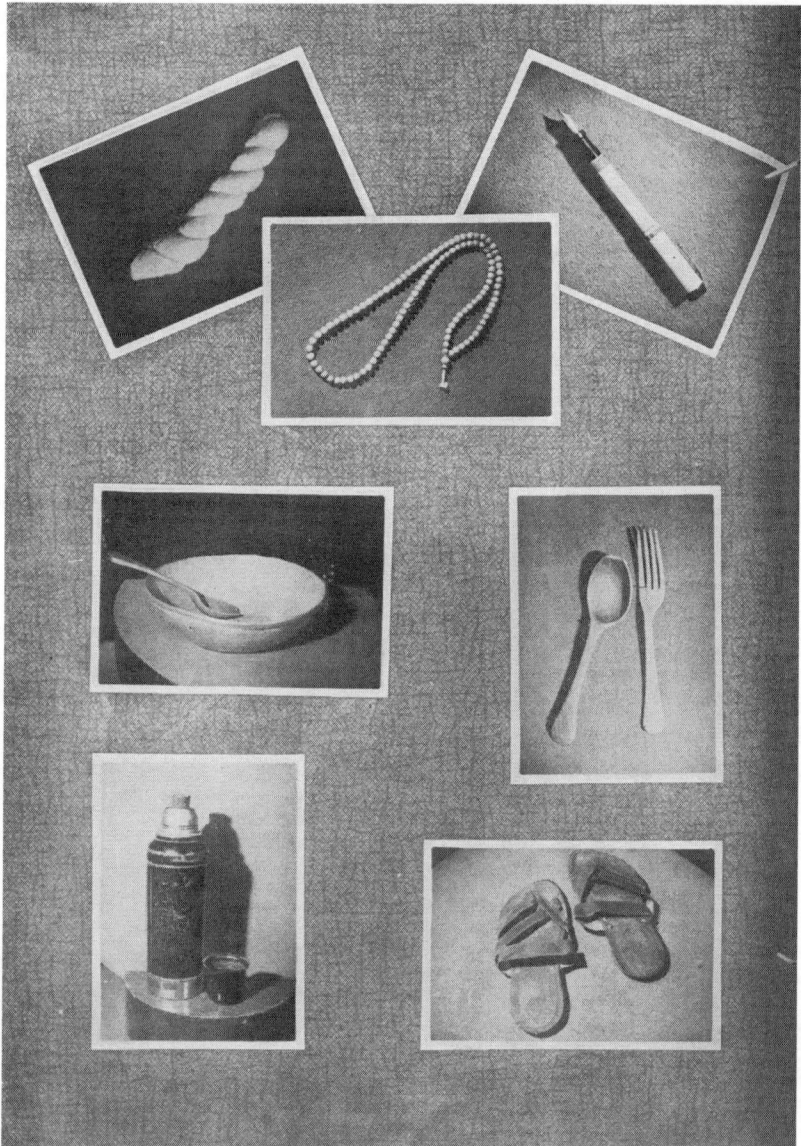

Fig. 6.4 *Bapu's Few Possessions*, 1944. Photograph by Vithalbhai K. Jhaveri,
published in D. G. Tendulkar et al., eds., *Gandhiji: His Life and Work
(Published on His 75th Birthday)* (Bombay: Keshav Bhikaji Dhawale, 1944).

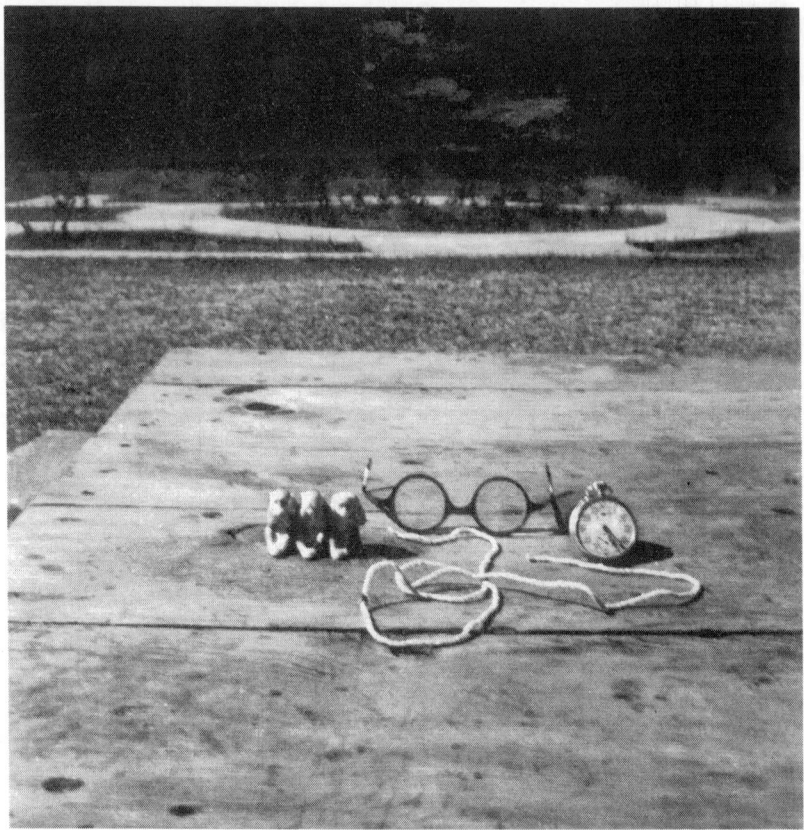

Fig. 6.5 Untitled photograph by Kanu Gandhi, February 1948. Birla House, New Delhi. Courtesy National Gandhi Museum, New Delhi.

letters written by Gandhi, and so on; these very objects were placed on display for citizen-viewers to recall and remember their beloved Bapu, and mourn his passing through a sensory and material encounter with things that he had once touched and used.[70]

In the aftermath of Gandhi's death, the custodians of Gandhi's memory—men like Devdas Gandhi, Vithalbhai Jhaveri, and others associated with the Gandhi Smarak Nidhi (The Gandhi Memorial

---

[70] The Films Division of India released a short documentary titled *Glimpses of Gandhiji* in 1949, in which one can glimpse these objects on display (https://www.youtube.com/watch?v=1PC0Unzierc [accessed 21 July 2021]).

Fig. 6.6 Untitled photograph by Kanu Gandhi, February 1948. Birla House, New Delhi. Courtesy National Gandhi Museum, New Delhi.

Fund)—salvaged a few things from all such stuff and granted them a hal-lowed status as 'relics' and 'remains' that are subsequently replicated for display in various Gandhi museums. Even in his own lifetime, Gandhi issued periodic warnings directed 'to all those who want to honour me—I heartily dislike any exhibition or memorials in my name'.[71] He also in-sisted, 'The only praise I would like and treasure is promotion of the ac-tivities to which my life is dedicated'.[72] Despite such admonitions, which clearly fell on deaf ears, memorials to Gandhi abound across the length

[71] *CWMG* 68: 386
[72] *CWMG* 70: 221–2

and breadth of India in which his paltry possessions have been subjected to what has been called the museum effect. Indeed, a mini cottage industry has emerged around these, with every museum claiming it has the original spectacles, or the authentic watch, notwithstanding the fact that many such 'original' objects ended up elsewhere at some point and come up for auction in distant global venues.[73]

And so it is that a modern life dedicated towards passing on without a material trace yields in the aftermath to the production of so much material paraphernalia, precisely in order to remember that life, recall it, and keep it relevant. The desire for becoming immaterial is overlaid by a vast material trace. The 'trash' of a Gandhian past, to use a Benjaminian term, become necessary aide-memoires in the debris of a present that we will agree is most non-Gandhian. It is almost as if we can no longer remember Gandhi if we did not have around material reminders of these objects that he had once touched and used. The scholarly literature on memory underscores that 'remembering is entangled with things'.[74] Materiality is essential, we have been told, to memory making. As the much-discussed arguments of Marcel Proust in this regard make clear, 'It is the feel, smell and touch of things that trigger memory; it is the encounter between the embodied human being and the inanimate thing that occasions the act of remembrance, not some 'exercise of the will'. Proust also observed:

> But when from a long-distant past nothing subsists, after the people are dead, after the things are broken and scattered, still, alone, more fragile, but with more vitality, more unsubstantial, more persistent, more faithful, the smell and taste of things remain poised a long time, like souls, ready to remind us, waiting and hoping for the moment, amid the

---

[73] A systematic account of the memorialization of Gandhi is much needed, but for some valuable beginnings, see Kshits Roy, 'Gandhi Sangrahalayas', *Cultural Forum* VIII (January 1966): 109–14; Claude Markovits, 'Representing Gandhi in Independent India', in *Thinking Social Science in India: Essays in Honour of Alice Thorner*, ed. Sujata Patel, Jaosdhara Bagchi, and Krishna Raj (New Delhi: Sage, 2002), 367–79; William Mazzarella, 'Branding the Mahatma: The Untimely Provocation of Gandhian Publicity', *Cultural Anthropology* 25, no. 1 (2010), 1–25; Santosh Desai, 'The Meaning of Rajghat', *India International Centre Quarterly* 38, no. 2 (2011), 16–23; Makarand Paranjape, *The Death and Afterlife of Mahatma Gandhi* (Abingdon: Routledge, 2014); and Khanduri, 'Some Things about Gandhi'.

[74] Laszlo Muntean, Liedeke Plate, and Anneke Smelik, 'Things to Remember: Introduction to Materializing Memory in Art and Popular Culture', in *Materializing Memory in Art and Popular Culture*, ed. Laszlo Muntean et al, 1–25 (New York: Routledge, 2017), 1.

ruins of all the rest; and bear unfaltering, in the tiny and almost impalp-
able drop of their essence, the vast structure of recollection.[75]

In the inimitable words of material culture anthropologist Daniel Miller,
stuff matters.[76]

The trouble with such assertions for my argument is that a particular
soul, also recalled by his followers as the Great Soul, consciously and con-
scientiously aspired to an immaterial life, to disappear without a trace,
having reduced himself to a cipher or zero. And yet the paltry possessions
that clung to him—and that he undoubtedly also needed, and to which
he even seemed attached—outlived him and return to materially haunt
his memory in the aftermath. In the process, these humble everyday
things have been rendered sacred and beloved: the ordinary has become
extraordinary.[77]

I have sought to track the role of the contemporary artist in the passage of these objects from the ordinary towards the extraordinary, even
the enchanted thing imbued with magical potency, as Ritu Khanduri has
suggested. On the one hand, the contemporary artist appears to have
been wilfully disobedient to the Mahatma's own wishes in producing
what I have referred to as the art of aparigraha that is at once as marvel-
lously melancholic as it is melancholically marvellous. This body of work
has emerged from the aesthetic imperative to visualize Gandhi's desire
for 'possessing non-possession', but it also follows from the artist's desire
to 'to retrieve him', in the words of Gulammohammed Sheikh, 'from his
busts and statuary at roadside corners, city squares, from postage stamps
and rupee notes'.[78] Such an act of rescue and retrieval from a life of visual
banality is one of the driving impulses of the artist of aparigraha, undoubtedly Gandhi's conscience keeper in our illiberal times.

But what then do we do with the fact that rather than freeing him up
from things, the artist once again entangles the Mahatma, or at least
our memory of him and our ongoing visual sense of him, with his stuff
which in turn takes on a new life, indeed an autonomous trajectory? To
work towards an answer, I turn to two interesting recent projects, both

---

[75] Quoted in Muntean et al., 'Things to Remember', 1
[76] Ibid.
[77] Khanduri, 'Some Things about Gandhi', 304.
[78] Sheikh, 'Reading Gandhi', 5.

undertaken by relatively young artists, that deepen our sense of the ethical imperatives of the art of aparigraha, but also the contradictions that underpin in. The first of these is a photographic project titled *In Search of...Bapu* (2017), undertaken in Ahmedabad by Anuj Ambalal, the son of renowned artist and collector Amit Ambalal, who produced some luminous works for the Postcards for Gandhi project in 1995. As the younger Ambalal sets out 'in search' of Bapu—and also invites his viewers to 'search' for the father of the nation—it leads him into the museumized space of the ashram at Sabarmati in his own native city, only to find that the man who yearned to become immaterial (in the spiritual sense of that word) is completely swathed in materiality, which the artist with humour, sarcasm, *and* reverence restages in his resonant photo-book, with playful and ironical titles. Thus, a photograph of Gandhi's bust in the museum shop is titled 'Sold'. Another covered in plastic is captioned 'Preserved' (Figure 6.7). A photograph of a modern office space complete with a desk, empty chairs, and a large portrait of Gandhi on the wall is titled 'Absent', while a terracotta statue of Gandhi enclosed in glass is captioned, poignantly, 'Bulletproof' (Figure 6.8). The entire project shows an intelligent awareness of what has been done to the Mahatma in the name of memorializing him by the custodians of the Gandhi memory machine in what is perhaps the most iconic of Gandhian museums, created out of the first ashram that he established in 1915 on his return to India (albeit at first in a different location). The conscientious artist's role, then, becomes one of revealing a life reaching for immateriality circulating now in the form of the most trivial—and frequently dusty, often forlorn—of material objects.

A different take on the irony of a life yearning for immateriality circulating in the form of material traces is offered by Bangalore-based Ravikumar Kashi's exquisite artist book titled *Everything He Touched* (2011–12). Kashi's work was provoked by a visit to Gandhi museums in Ahmedabad, New Delhi, and Mumbai, where an absent Mahatma is summoned back to the present through his material possessions (and grainy photographic reproductions of these): 'Everything he touched was memorialized, museumized, and frozen in time.' In particular, the core of Kashi's sketches is based on what he saw in a museum installation at Mani Bhavan Sangrahalaya, a stately two-storey mansion in south Mumbai that served as Gandhi's Bombay headquarters for many

Fig. 6.7 *Preserved*. Photograph by Anuj Ambalal, 2017. Courtesy the artist.

Fig. 6.8 *Bulletproof*. Photograph by Anuj Ambalal, 2017. Courtesy the artist.

Fig. 6.9 Ravikumar Kashi, *Everything He Touched...Artist Book* (detail), 2011. Conté, ink, and photocopy transfer on Japanese Raka-stained Hanji paper. Courtesy the artist.

years, and which was converted in 1955 to a museum. Titled 'Earthly Possessions', the installation is a photograph of objects that once belonged to Gandhi but were subsequently presented by him to wealthy devotee Sumati Morarjee, after he had stayed in her residence in Juhu in 1944, and which she in turn donated to the Sangrahalaya of which she was a patron. The objects include a statuette of the three monkeys; a book (presumably a printed edition of the *Gita*), a charkha, a hank of khadi, a thermos, a handkerchief, a lantern, a wooden spoon and fork, a bowl with a spoon, a fountain pen, a spittoon (Figure 6.9), a safety pin (Figure 6.10), some pieces of cloth (dhoti and shawl), a rosary, and a pair of handmade sandals. Kashi recasts these photographed objects in exquisite detail in his artist book, the very colours of the work casting a melancholic glow over them, transforming the mundane into the magical.

In another related installation titled *Ideas for Preserving Bapu* (2011), Kashi assembles miniature Gandhi sculptures in a collage which he describes thus on his website (Figure 6.11):

Fig. 6.10 Ravikumar Kashi, *Everything He Touched…Artist Book* (detail), 2011. Conté, ink, and photocopy transfer on Japanese Raka-stained Hanji paper. Courtesy the artist.

Fig. 6.11 Ravikumar Kashi, *Ideas for Preserving Bapu*, 2011. Mixed media. Courtesy the artist.

These works are inspired by the question as to how do we preserve/protect the legacy of Bapu. Protecting him a like a light with a glass casing, like a tender sapling with a fence, with bubble sheet so that he is not damaged, or an aluminium foil so that heat remains or mummify him so that he lives on etc. Again, it suggests that we as a society have made a ritual out of him rather than following him in deed. (Artist's website (http://www.ravikashi.com/RavikashiWorks.aspx)

Kashi is deeply aware of the ethics and politics of such preservation and freezing of the Mahatma's possessions, now recycled as the nation's patrimony:

For my generation, who are far away from him in time, he is an idea. A remnant. He lives through memory. Memory captured in words, images, objects . . . They are at once a reminder of a great life lived and a marker of an alienating process by which Gandhi is kept away neatly in boxes. Sealed forever . . . The range of objects kept in these museums range from his books to cups and utensils he used to his denture, objects he touched when he visited some place like microscope or lab equipments [sic] to pens to piece of cloth. While it reveals the great respect the nation placed on him, it also reveals a trend to capture him in objects and forget the spirit of his life and words. A fetish for objects substituting the actual person. But in the way he is reinvented and re-engaged by successive generations, it is amply clear that he touched our lives in more ways than one can imagine.

Thus, even as the artist book reveals Kashi's own fascination with such objects, which become the focus of such exquisite aesthetic contemplation, it is accompanied by rebuke and reprimand. Rather than making a 'fetish' of the objects Gandhi had touched, the artist proposes, let us all reflect on the ways his life 'touched' us: there is a call implicitly embedded in these cryptic words of moving from the material to the immaterial. I imagine Gandhi would have liked that.

Kashi's work can also be drawn upon to reflect upon the sensory experience provoked by 'touch', as Ritu Khanduri proposes, and Gandhi's own complex (and not uncontroversial) experiments with repudiating 'untouchability', as well as the critiques that have also followed in their wake. There is also the fact that these quotidian objects that he once used are imagined to bear the imprint of his touch, but once they enter the museum space and get sealed off in glass vitrines or placed behind showcases, they become 'untouchable': they are to be seen rather than held and felt. Hence also the longing of the artist for the Mahatma's 'touch', and his call for liberating us from the fetish of the objects through which Gandhi as figure and person had been 'captured' and 'sealed' up, out of reach, out of sight, but hence also out of touch.

'So Many Busts'

If beauty consisted in shape or colour, we would have gratified our sight by looking at statues. Beauty lies in virtue and this is not a thing which can be perceived by the senses.[79]

For a man who sought to leave the world having reduced himself to zero, the most tangible snub to this expressed aspiration came in the form of what was intended as tribute, namely, the repeated attempt by his devotees and admirers to summon him back as statue (in cement, metal, stone, and other durable materials). As I bring to a close this essay on the Mahatma and materiality, I reflect on the penchant for setting up statues of the man, the most among India's political leaders to be so 'honoured' both at home and abroad to this day, notwithstanding some other rivals (like B. R. Ambedkar) who are also emerging on the scene. It is worth reflecting on this penchant at a time when, across the world, as a result of varying projects for reckoning with difficult inherited pasts, statues of (big) men are being defaced, destroyed, or displaced.[80] Gandhi's statue too has not escaped a similar fate in India and elsewhere, as Rahul Rao has documented in a recent essay.[81] I underscore, though, a critical difference: the Mahatma, one suspects, would not disagree with his detractors who do him the greater honour by taking down his statue(s).

---

[79] *CWMG* 21: 417.
[80] For a wide-ranging recent analysis, see especially Alex von Tunzelmann, *Fallen Idols: Twelve Statues that Made History* (London: Headline, 2021).
[81] Rahul Rao, 'Gandhi Falling… and Rising', *Journal of Historical Geography* 82 (2023), 1–10.

In February 1939, on hearing that some well-wishers sought to install his statue, he commented on the futility of erecting 'a clay or metallic statue of the figure of a man who is himself made of clay and is more fragile than a bangle which can keep by preservation for a thousand years, whereas the human body disintegrates daily and undergoes final disintegration after the usual span of life.'[82] But he was not content with offering a philosophical critique of statue making that turned around the recognition of the impermanence of the body. Taking his cue as well from his mentor Gopalkrishna Gokhale, on other occasions he scolded statue-installing enthusiasts thus: 'I attach no importance to these things, for I dislike such things intensely. They are a sheer waste of money... I would rather wish that instead of setting up my statues or unveiling my photographs, people opened spinning and weaving schools or did something else which would benefit the country socially, spiritually, economically or politically.'[83]

Such admonitions notwithstanding, the building of Gandhi statues across the nation proceeded apace, especially in the two decades or so after his violent assassination. Over the years, some of India's best sculptors—artists of the stature of Devi Prasad Roy Chowdhury and Sankho Chaudhuri—were drafted into projects that yielded some landmark art. Most Gandhi statues dotting the national landscape are, however, the work of indifferent, even hack, artists.[84] As early as February 1948, Jawaharlal Nehru lamented, 'The standard in India of such statuary has been low and most people are satisfied with anything that bears a remote resemblance to the person concerned.'[85] Similarly, in November 1965, in the run-up to the Gandhi centenary celebrations in 1969, a Member of Parliament complained in that august assembly that these installations 'had become so ugly and ridiculous that they have become

[82]   CWMG 68: 386.
[83]   CWMG 88: 347. See also ibid., 70: 221–2. For Gandhi's invocation of Gokhale's views on the futility of the statue form as a commemoration, see CWMG 13: 27, 13: 202, and 14: 28. Despite his own protestations in this regard, Gandhi participated in the inauguration ceremonies of the statues of other national leaders over the course of his long political career (for example, CWMG 40: 53. See also ibid., 42: 527).
[84]   For a touching defence of these 'humble' efforts offered by no less than one of the Mahatma's grandsons, see Gopalkrishna Gandhi, 'More Than Clay', The Telegraph Online, 20 October 2018.
[85]   Prime Minister's Secretariat: Funds Section/Branch, File No. 2 (76)/48-PMS–PMS, Vol. 1 (NAI, New Delhi).

a laughing stock and create improper feelings among the people for Gandhiji's statues'.[86]

B. C. Sanyal, a veteran artist who had captured Gandhi in a memorable sketch on the eve of the Mahatma's death, put it most acerbically in his memoirs: 'Donors and devotees were busy dotting the Indian landscape with three-legged—one stick and two stick legs—Gandhi statues which, I am sorry to say, were neither Gandhi nor art!'[87] Other artists have turned to image work to cast aspersions on what we might call Gandhi statue mania. Thus, in Jagannath Panda's ironically titled work *The Icon* (2008), the artist offers a visual commentary on the cruel fate visited upon the typical Gandhi statue in our time as it comes to be festooned in faded garlands or serves as a perch for birds and their droppings. Vivek Vilasini's *Vernacular Chants II* (2007) confirms that the endless reproduction of Gandhi's visage in street statuary can (and does) lead to distortion to the point of making the familiar face unrecognizable. Gigi Scaria's *Caution! Men at Work* (2015) visually underscores the public hollowing out of a haloed figure, the emptying of substance. Placed on a pedestal, the half-completed statue of the sandal-wearing, dhoti-clad Gandhi, his waist watch prominently on display, stands poised to go somewhere. However, he has nowhere to go in an India that has abandoned him.[88]

As I end this essay, I give the last word to Mumbai-based Atul Dodiya and his magnificent *Bako Exists. Imagine*, a series of twelve large mixed-media paintings that the influential artist completed in 2011. Based on the poetry of fellow Gujarati Labshankar Thakar, each painting in the series recasts a dream encounter between a young boy named Bako and his Bapu, their intimate exchanges recreated on faux blackboard canvases inscribed with faux chalk writing. Each painting captures mischievously but insightfully the dilemmas of being a sainted Mahatma alongside the tribulations of being a schoolchild growing up in the hustle and bustle of modern India. As they exchange their thoughts across the body of work, Bako and his Bapu turn out to be utterly in sync, the differences in their status and age vanishing. In *So Many Busts*, the child commiserates

---

[86] Ibid.

[87] B. C. Sanyal, *The Vertical Woman: Reminiscences of B. C. Sanyal, from 1947 to Present* (New Delhi: National Gallery of Modern Art, 1999), 2.

[88] For reproductions of these artworks, see Ramaswamy, *Gandhi in the Gallery*, 172–4.

with the Mahatma's exasperation over having been turned into a statue (Figure 6.12):

> Bakaa, in your sleep, even streams ask.
> In my sleep
> they've made so many busts of me
> and installed them everywhere without ever bothering to ask.
> Frozen. Petrified.

In a related work titled *Crow* (Figure 6.13), Bako informs his Bapu that he 'once saw a crow shitting on your bust'.

Fig. 6.12 Atul Dodiya, *So Many Busts*, 2011. From series *Bako Exists. Imagine.* Oil, acrylic, watercolour, oil bar, and marble dust on canvas, 198 × 198 cm. Courtesy the artist.

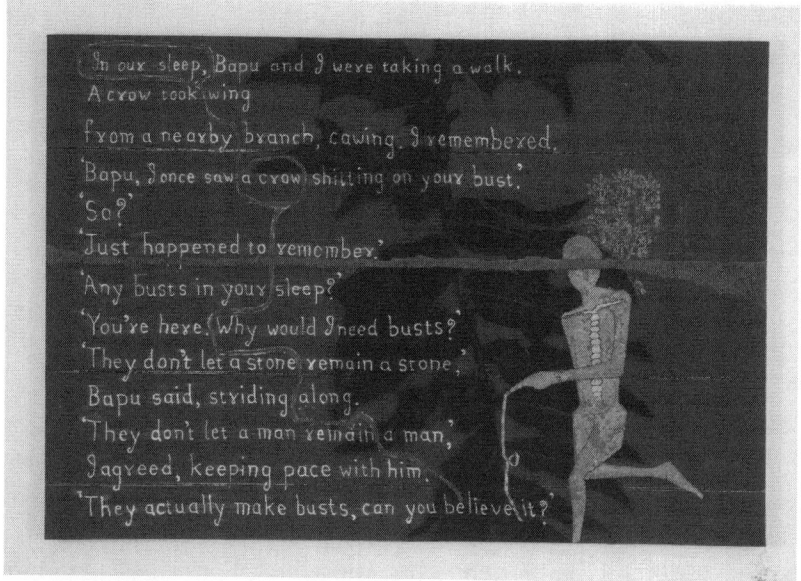

Fig. 6.13 Atul Dodiya, *A Crow*, 2011. From series *Bako Exists. Imagine.* Oil, acrylic, watercolour, oil bar, and marble dust on canvas, 137 × 198 cm. Courtesy the artist.

Gandhi's response? 'They don't let a stone remain a stone, . . . They don't let a man remain a man.'

Herein lay the dilemma of a man who aspired to become zero. He was, instead, transformed into a Mahatma, and frozen and petrified in and by objects that he spent a lifetime trying to jettison. These objects in turn have come to serve as proxy for his presence, in fact to the point of quite displacing him as a man and as the leader of a vast movement, as I have suggested. Ironically but inevitably, as an excess of memory and over-remembering set in around such objects, a veritable 'empire of forgetting' takes hold around the Mahatma's disobedient words and deeds, deemed too uncomfortable and inconvenient for moderns for whom life is anything but aspiring to become zero.[89]

[89] Paul Ricoeur, *Memory, History, Forgetting* (Chicago: University of Chicago Press, 2004).

7

A *Rasātmaka* Journey

Aesthetics and Moral Fervour in Gandhi's Quest

Neelima Shukla-Bhatt

This essay explores the relationship between the aesthetic and the moral in Gandhi's quest for inner transformation to reach one of his cherished goals—perfect selflessness. The exploration leads us to see that a vital component of Gandhi's moral quest was a relishing of aesthetic flavour—termed '*rasa*' in Indian aesthetic theories—which sustained him even during the most challenging moments of his life. Therefore, his moral quest can be termed a *rasātmaka*[1] (with *rasa* as its essence) journey, which was rich, complex, and marked with paradoxes. We get a peek into it in Pyarelal's portrayal of the last phase of Gandhi's life in Delhi, the capital of a newborn nation torn apart by violence and communal hatred. Pyarelal recalls Gandhi exclaiming on 29 January 1948: 'Where will this take us? Where do I stand? What must I do to realize unruffled calm and serenity in the midst of this disquiet?' And then, with what Pyarelal terms 'infinite sadness', he repeated a verse by Urdu poet Nazir:

> Short-lived is the splendour of spring
> in the garden of the world,
> Watch the brave show while it lasts.[2]

[1] As per Monier-Williams's Sanskrit dictionary, '*ātmaka*' in compound nouns means 'having or consisting of the nature or character of'. And two meanings of the compound noun '*rasātmaka*' are: a) having juice for its essence, and b) consisting of nectar. Following this, in this essay the term *rasātmaka* is used with the meaning 'having *rasa* as its essence'. See Monier Monier-Williams, *A Sanskrit–English Dictionary* (Delhi: Motilal Banarasidass, 1899), 136, 870.

[2] I have accessed Gandhi's writings and important writings about him from https://www.gandhiheritageportal.org/, created by Sabarmati Ashram Preservation and Memorial Trust, Ahmedabad. Pyarelal, *Mahatma Gandhi: The Last Phase, Volume II* (Ahmedabad: Navajivan Trust, 1958), 766.

Neelima Shukla-Bhatt, *A Rasātmaka Journey* In: *Gandhi, Truth, and Nonviolence.* Edited by: Vinay Lal, Oxford University Press. © Oxford University Press 2025. DOI: 10.1093/9780198936657.003.0008

In the original Urdu poem (in the *gazal* form), which was one of Gandhi's favourites and was included in the compilation of hymns for his communes, the verse reads:

> *hai bahār-e-bāgh-e-duniyā chand roz, chand roz*
> *dekh lo iskā tamāśā chand roz.*[3]

What Pyarelal translates as 'while it lasts' is the phrase '*chand roz*', literally meaning 'a few days'. When he recited this line, Gandhi did not have even a day left before the violent end of his life. Indeed, the last line of the *gazal*, which reads '*zindagī kā hai bharosā chand roz*' (life can be trusted only for a few days), came true the very next day. Yet as scholars point out, Gandhi had anticipated such an end rather willingly, in what James W. Douglass aptly calls his *Final Experiment with Truth*, almost as a culmination of an aspiration to meet a death like Jesus since his South Africa days.[4] Vinay Lal also reminds us that Gandhi had long prepared for such an end and had in fact declared that 'one must learn the art of dying in the training for nonviolence'. His assassination, the second and successful attempt to take his life in January 1948, brought fulfilment for himself and a relief in many ways for members of diverse sections of the Indian polity for different reasons.[5]

Gandhi's aspiration to meet his end on the path of nonviolence as an art is striking. In view of this aspiration, Pyarelal's poignant depiction of Gandhi's state on the eve of his death offers a rich locus to examine. It makes one wonder what could have been stirring in the deep recesses of his mind during the last phase of his life, spent in an increasingly disapproving public gaze. A few aspects of that scene draw attention. First, as Gandhi acknowledged, he was shaken and was unsure about where he stood. The search for a way to fruitfully serve people in a constantly shifting and violent context was a painful struggle, often without the

---

[3] See Narayan Vaman Khare, ed., *Ashrambhajanavali* (Ahmedabad: Navajivan Press, 1925), 69–70.

[4] James W. Douglass, *Gandhi and the Unspeakable: His Final Experiment with Truth* (Vadodara, India: Yagna Prakashan, 2019), ix.

[5] Vinay Lal, 'On the Art of Dying: Death and the Spector of Gandhi', in *Experiments with Truth: Gandhi and Images of Nonviolence*, ed. Josef Helfenstein and Joseph Newland (Houston: The Menil Collection, 2014), 329–36. On p. 332, Lal cites Gandhi's words from *Gandhi on Non-Violence*, ed. Thomas Merton (New York: New Directions, 1965), 68.

hope of finding an answer. Second, despite the acuteness of the struggle, he believed that there was an unruffled calm and serenity to be realized in the midst of the horrible chaos and violence around. And third, in that moment of intense turmoil, he found at least fleeting solace in the words of a poet, here an Urdu poet.

With Gandhi's life, his quest ended too. Had he reached his goal of finding 'an unruffled calm and serenity' in the midst of that disquiet? Perhaps; or perhaps not.

What the snapshot of the evening previous to his death brings into focus, however, is the nature of his quest. His larger concern was for the public good in two newborn countries. But looking for a pathway for that goal was also linked to an intensely personal search for inner peace that would give him the strength to address that concern. And he found a pointer to a possible direction for this in an aesthetic expression, a poet's words.

In what follows, this essay will explore how these three threads— dedication to public service, an aspiration for 'unruffled calm and se- renity' even in the midst of disquiet, and aesthetic sensitivity termed *rasavṛtti* (*vṛtti* [disposition] toward *rasa*)—were linked in Gandhi's life and works. Since we do not find an elaborate statement about such a link by Gandhi, this link can only be traced in brief records of his words preseved by others and a few focused comments scat- tered through the vast corpus of his writings and communications. Even though not explicitly stated, it is distinctly discernible in them. This essay suggests that tracing this link helps us to better understand not only Gandhi's view of art that has been widely characterized as utilitarian but also some unresolved paradoxes and pathos in his life, which often get overshadowed by a perception of glory bestowed on his life and legacy exclusively.

I was drawn to exploring the link between the moral and the aesthetic in Gandhi's life and work while writing my book on Narasinha Mehta, the fifteenth-century Gujarati *bhakti* poet who was a major source of moral inspiration for Gandhi since his youth. In order to understand his relationship with Narasinha, it was important to read his autobiography *Satya nā Prayogo* (*Experiments with Truth*) in its Gujarati original. As I reached the end, I was struck by the beauty of the simple prose of the last paragraph, its intense sincerity, and, above all, the use of the term *rasa* specifically. Here it is in my translation, which, like all translations, is at best an approximation:

> I experience every moment that the path of self-purification is arduous. Attaining perfect purity demands becoming completely free of discord in mind, speech, and body; and getting rid of all attachments and envy. Despite ceaseless striving, I have not reached that state yet. That is why people's praise does not move me; in fact, it often pains me. Conquering my passions seems to me even more difficult than defeating the whole world in an armed conflict. Even after coming to India, I have been real-izing my hidden passions. I have felt embarrassed; but have not accepted defeat. I have enjoyed *rasa* in conducting my experiments with Truth, and I am enjoying it even today. But I know that I still have to tread a difficult path. For it, I have to become absolutely egoless [*śunyavat* lit. 'like zero']. Until a person willingly puts himself last, there is no lib-eration for him. *Ahimsa* is the furthermost limit of humility. And it is proven by experience that liberation can never be attained without that humility. Praying for such humility, and urging for the world's support in it, for now, I bring these chapters to a close.[6]

In this passage, written in the latter half of 1920s, Gandhi makes clear that for him experiments with truth were an experience of enjoying *rasa*—aesthetic flavour. The paragraph highlights the significance of the experi-ments as sources of *rasa*. Thus, interestingly, both the subjective side (the enjoyer) and the objective side (the source) of *rasa* were closely linked to his inner world. And the goal of the experiments, still to be reached with a difficult journey, was to become completely egoless—*śunyavat*. The ul-timate goal of reaching that state is to both liberate the self and put it in the service of the world. What is the nature of that striving? How does a person, who is striving to completely dissolve his sense of self, enjoy aes-thetic delight? And how does a person without a strong sense of self also put himself/herself last?

---

[6] Mohandas K. Gandhi, *Satyanā Prayogo Athavā Ātmakathā* (Gujarati, *The Story of My Experiments with Truth*) (Ahmedabad: Navajivan, 1952), 492. Gandhi uses the term '*rasa*' spe-cifically in this paragraph, the source of which were his experiments.

The language in the passage is dense with vocabulary found in mystical writings and is similarly paradoxical. The aspiration to dissolve 'the self' in perfecting nonviolence and then putting it last is comparable to the Islamic Sufi concepts of *fanā* (annihilation of 'the self' and in uniting with the pure consciousness of God) and *baqā* (returning with the pure self to the world and infusing it with that purity), which are at once antithetical and complementary.[7] In Gandhi's use of the term *śunyavat*, the passage also reminds one of the Mahayana Buddhist concept of *śunyatā* (awareness of emptiness of any entity including the self) and the related ideal of Bodhisattva (an enlightened being who forgoes nirvana in order to serve beings in the world).[8] Yet, by conjoining the aesthetic concept of *rasa* with the path of getting rid of ego and perfecting nonviolence, Gandhi incorporates in his language an additional layer of meaning, making its connotations more complex. The richness of this section compelled me to look closely at how spiritual endeavour, moral action, and aesthetic joy became closely linked in Gandhi's view of a perfected life over the course of his own life beginning in late nineteenth-century Saurashtra.

Phases of the Journey

Gandhi's autobiography recounts several childhood experiences that had a profound impact on him and kindled in him a desire to lead a morally sound life. What was common in these experiences was that they all had an appeal to his emotions and imagination. Some were rooted in deep personal bonds—with his mother, father, and nurse. Others had aesthetic and performative aspects—reading a play about filial piety of Shravan (a mythological figure), watching a play about Harishchandra's (another mythological figure) dedication to truthfulness, listening to a melodious recitation of the *Rāmāyaṇa*, and learning by heart a poem about returning

[7] Kazuyo Murata, 'Fana and Baqa'. In *Oxford Bibliography Online* in Islamic Studies, https://www.oxfordbibliographies.com/view/document/obo-9780195390155/obo-9780195390155-0256.xml [accessed 6 September 2024].

[8] Merriam-Webster Dictionary. 'sunyata', https://www.merriam-webster.com/dictionary/sunyata 'Bodhisattva' https://www.merriam-webster.com/dictionary/bodhisattva [accessed 6 September 2024].

good for evil. Gandhi mentions playing the character of Harishchandra in his imagination innumerable times. These experiences, when compared with ones that stirred aversion in him—worship ceremonies in temples, reading the *Manusmṛti*, or listening to the Christian missionaries outside his school—highlight that from his early life what moved his moral sensitivity were things with aesthetic and emotional dimensions and not those with the dogmatic weight or power of authority. Gandhi writes in his autobiography that, by the end of this phase,

> ... one thing took deep root in me – the conviction that morality is the basis of things, and truth the substance of all morality. Truth became my sole objective. It began to grow in magnitude every day, and my definition of it also has been ever widening.[9]

The last sentence here indicates that, for Gandhi, 'truth' became a long journey for discovery, an ever-unfolding process rather than a fixed entity to be grasped. Even though the autobiography was written years after his childhood in Rajkot, he refers to it as a starting point of an exploration that continued.

During his time in London for legal studies, Gandhi's moral experiments focused greatly on simple living because of the promises he had made to his mother and the necessity to cut expenses. In the autobiography he mentions that when he adopted simplicity after a few months of trying to be a stylish gentleman against his grain, 'the change harmonized my inward and outward life ... [My life] was certainly more truthful and my soul knew no bounds of joy.'[10] For Gandhi, making his life austere was not dry discipline leading to a sense of deprivation but a source of joy and feeling of harmony. He also became acquainted with important religious texts including his own, but this exercise does not seem to have engaged him very deeply. Gandhi admits that even after his return to India when he engaged in conversations with the Jain philosopher Shrimad Rajachandra, he was not seriously interested in religious issues.[11]

---

[9] M. K. Gandhi. *An Autobiography or the Story of my Experiments with Truth*, trans. Mahadev Desai (Ahmedabad: Navajivan Press, 1940), 16–17, 41, 47–51 (chs 2, 8, 10).
[10] Ibid. 75.
[11] Ibid. 113.

The next phase of an intense spiritual stirring in Gandhi's life is seen during his South Africa years. It was in South Africa that, with several interreligious encounters with devout Christians and Muslims as well as involvement in the public life of Indians, Gandhi began to think seriously in that direction. About his year in Pretoria (1893), he writes that it was 'a most valuable experience in life. Here it was that I had opportunities of learning public work and acquired some measure of my capacity for it. Here it was that the religious spirit in me became a living force.'[12] It is significant that his friend Shrimad Rajchandra, who had greatly impressed Gandhi earlier and helped him resolve his queries about Hinduism during the South Africa years—what he (Gandhi) calls 'religious ferment'—was a poet. In his letters of advice, Rajchandra extolled *bhakti* (devotion) as the best path for spiritual advancement and recurrently invoked medieval India's saint-poets, whose devotional lyrics in regional languages are immensely popular as songs.[13] References to verses of saint-poets like Kabir, Mira, and Narasinha Mehta as well as narratives about their lives, which are preserved through performance in the cultural memory of millions of Indians, are found in abundance in Gandhi's writings from this point on. His engagement with lyrics and lives of *bhakti* poets grew deeper over the years, since they also offered ideals for a just society in condemning caste and gender hierarchies. The spiritual is intrinsically ethical in the lyrics and sacred biographies of these saint-poets. As I have discussed in relation to the fifteenth-century Gujarati saint-poet Narasinha, in Gandhi's writings a large number of references to lyrics and biographies of saint-poets appear in support of his points about ethical action and social reconstruction; some also appear in letters of advice for inner search and peace. Gandhi made devotional songs of these saint-poets an integral part of daily life at the communes he established in South Africa and later in India as well as of his public meetings.[14] It was not a coincidence that a few months before his death, in the midst of intense turmoil following Partition, he asked the well-known musician of Carnatic music M. S. Subbulakshmi to send him a recording of a song of the woman saint-poet

---

[12]   Ibid. 165.

[13]   Shrimad Rajchandra, *Śrīmad Rājcandra* [Collected Works], ed. Ravjibhai C. Desai. (Agas: Srimad Rajchandra Ashram, 1976), 279, 733.

[14]   Neelima Shukla-Bhatt, *Narasinha Mehta of Gujarat: A Legacy of Bhakti in Songs and Stories* (New York: Oxford University Press, 2015), 181–95.

Mira, which was subsequently played along with the announcement of his assassination by All India Radio.[15] The song is in the form of praise for Krishna for compassionately rescuing his devotees in critical moments. The refrain of the song, *hari tum haro jan kī pīr* ('Krishna, you remove people's pain'), however, can also be interpreted as expressing an ardent plea— 'Krishna, please remove people's pain'. Seeing the request for this song in juxtaposition with Gandhi's reciting Nazir's couplet on the eve of his assassination, as discussed above, further illuminates how he sought solace in mystical poetry and devotional music throughout his life. This deep engagement had started while he was in South Africa.

During this period, Gandhi also began to link ethical action and beauty in his writings. It was not simply that he found aesthetically appealing forms such as poetry, songs, and narratives to be powerful sources for moral inspiration; he had also begun to see ethical action itself as a thing of beauty. From the early days of the satyagraha in South Africa, Gandhi recurrently referred to its 'beauty' in *Indian Opinion*. The word used in the original Gujarati is '*khūbī*', meaning 'beauty' or 'excellence', derived from Persian (etymologically related to *khūb* meaning 'beautiful', as in *khūbsūrat*— 'with beautiful face').[16] It is notable that in the Gujarati section of an issue of the *Indian Opinion* in 1908, in introducing the newly adopted term 'satyagraha' for what was earlier termed 'passive resistance', Gandhi first explains that 'resistance' means using '*jor*' (force) against something. He then discusses satyagraha and its *balihārī*, a synonym of *khūbī*, which also means 'magic' (translated in *CWMG* as 'miraculous power'), rather than *śakti*, which means 'power' or 'energy'.[17] The references suggest that Gandhi's moral and aesthetic sensitivities were getting more closely tied in his action-oriented public life. He even encouraged satyagraha participants to express their views and emotions about the movement in poems that were published in the *Indian Opinion*. A prominent voice among them was Sheikh Mehtab, Gandhi's childhood friend with whom he had a complex relationship. While the poems were not of

---

[15] Swati Thiyagarajan, 'Gandhiji's Request to My Grandmother, MS Subbulakshmi', NDTV (1 January 2016), https://www.ndtv.com/blog/gandhijis-request-to-my-grandmother-ms-subbulakshmi-1261287 [accessed 8 July 2021].
[16] *CWMG* Vol. 8: 71 and 368. For the Gujarati originals, see *Gandhiji no Akṣar Deh* (Ahmedabad: Navajivan, 1968), 67 and 347 (hereafter referred to as *GAD*). *Indian Opinion* (8 February and 18 July 1908).
[17] *CWMG* Vol. 8 (1962), 80–1; *GAD* Vol. 8, 22–3.

high literary quality, they allowed the participants to integrate creativity in a political movement and perform their identity.[18] During the same period, Gandhi's experiments in austere living were developing full speed in the communes he established—Phoenix Settlement and Tolstoy Farm. Here his associates and some participants in satyagraha lived following a strict discipline developed by Gandhi in relation to diet, material possessions, and community service. Communal living with farming, physical labour, and daily prayers was seen as a step toward building a spiritual basis for social change and political action.[19] On the one hand, Gandhi's view of satyagraha as a thing of beauty was enriching and sustaining his public life during the South Africa phase. On the other hand, his increasing focus on austerity and service was beginning to put strict boundaries on all aspects of his life including his view of art.

After Gandhi's return to India, with his growing fame and popularity as well as an influx of Indian and international visitors from diverse backgrounds to his communes, perhaps by necessity he began to express his views on art occasionally in brief statements in interviews, speeches, letters, and other writings. He maintained, however, that since he was not an artist or a student of art of any type, he was not qualified to make theoretical statements about it. His statements expressed only his personal convictions.[20] These convictions, expressed in his own words, give us a lens through which to see the direction of the journey in which his moral, spiritual, and aesthetic sensitivities were getting closely tied. An interview with G. Ramachandran in 1924, his remarks on Gujarati literature, his speech at the Akhil Bharatiya Sahitya Parishad (All India Literary Conference) in Nagpur in 1936, a few letters, and reflective personal conversations illuminate these convictions as well as the paradoxes contained within them.

In his interview, Ramachandran, a student of Gandhi's friend C. F. Andrews and the poet Rabindranath Tagore at Shantiniketan, asks direct and penetrating questions. The interview begins with a question about a

[18] See Surendra Bhana and Neelima Shukla-Bhatt, *A Fire that Blazed in the Ocean: Gandhi and the Poems of Satyagrah in South Africa 1909–1911* (Delhi: Promilla, 2011).

[19] For a succinct account of South Africa communes, see James D. Hunt, 'Gandhian Experiments in Communal Living – The Phoenix Community and the Tolstoy Farm in South Africa', in *Peace Research* 30, no.1 (February 1998), 83–95.

[20] *CWMG* Vol. 25 (1967), 248–50.

widely spread opinion at the time that Gandhi's programme for national reconstruction excluded art. Gandhi clarifies that he is not against art but values it only in as much as it helps inner development and is an expression of 'the inner spirit of man'. When Ramachandran counters that all artists—poets, painters, musicians—refer to their art as expression of their spirit, Gandhi responds that some artists also tend to beautify immorality. He further states that only truthful things can be beautiful and, rather than finding truth through beauty, he found beauty in and through truth. For this reason, he says, he considered Jesus Christ and the Prophet Mohammad as 'supreme artists' who 'strove for truth' for the sake of humanity. But he admits that in rare instances untruthful artists may also create truthful and beautiful art, since truth and untruth can coexist. The interview veers into a discussion about spinning, where Gandhi's concern for the starving poor of India is paramount and quite moving. Yet the tension between his emphatic statement that art must be at the service of humanity and Ramachandran's questions about artistic freedom is not fully resolved.[21]

A similar tension marks Gandhi's remarks in his foreword to K. M. Munshi's 'Gujarat and its Literature', his speech at the Akhil Bharatiya Sahitya Parishad, and his personal letters to relatives who sought his guidance about pursuing a career as an artist. In the foreword to Munshi's book, while appreciating the faithful survey of the region's literary works, he critiques it for focusing exclusively on what appeals to educated middle-class readers. Drawing attention to the 'gulf that exists between the language of people and ours', he is especially critical about not considering folk literature as well as Parsi and Muslim literary works that are enjoyed by large populations and influence their lives. His concern is that the elite Gujarati literature as surveyed in the work served to widen the gap between the educated privileged section of society and others, and not to educate the underprivileged.[22] Yet the issue that folk literature, which is neglected in Munshi's survey, may not align with Gandhi's own ideals of morality in its glorification of heroic deeds and portrayal of gender relations is not addressed.

---

[21]   Ibid., 247–56.
[22]   *CWMG*, Vol 61 (1975), 26–7.

In his speech at the Akhil Bharatiya Sahitya Parishad, he puts forward convincing arguments for the promotion of vernaculars, the wider circulation of literature in Indian languages across regions, and making Hindustani the link language among regions. However, in commenting on the proper moods to be conveyed in literature, he dismisses as unworthy the erotic, which is considered a core human experience in many Indian aesthetic theories. He presents as his ideal 'such literature as fosters unity, morality, valor and such other qualities, and science' and would be helpful in spreading modern useful ideas 'among villagers'.[23] Gandhi expresses such views in relation to other arts too. In a personal letter written in 1933, he advises a relative to support his son in his plans to join a painting school. 'Painting is silent music', he writes, and even goes to the extent of saying that even if the young man could not complete the training, it is worthy of pursuit. At the same time, he also stresses that he would expect the boy to emerge as a painter whose art 'would purify us of passions' and to dedicate his 'painting to service'.[24] Clearly, in Gandhi's view as expressed in his formal speeches or advisory roles, the measure of great art was how it serves people, especially the disadvantaged, and how it helps moral transformation. Gandhi recognized the transformative quality of art but stressed that great art had to be socially relevant. By this measure, even a political movement like satyagraha could be seen as a thing of beauty, but a highly appreciated poem like Jayadeva's Gītagovinda, which celebrates love between Krishna and the cowherd woman Radha, could not be.[25] Even in the earliest reference found in Gandhi's writings about Gujarati poems focusing on Krishna's circle dance (rās) with cowherd girls (gopīs)—in his diary entry for 29 July 1894—he clearly indicates that he did not like them. The numerous allusions to Krishna bhakti saint-poets like Mira and Narasinha in his writings also completely avoid references to their songs in the erotic mood. Gandhi only refers to their songs conveying messages about inner transformation, compassion, and resistance to oppressive social norms. In alluding to their lives, he praises them as moral exemplars and true satyagrahis who stood up for their convictions and served the

[23]   CWMG, Vol. 62 (1975), 346–7.
[24]   CWMG, Vol. 54 (1973), 243.
[25]   Gandhi had explicitly stated in an article in Navajivan (18 July 1926) that the reading of the Gītagovinda 'proved a torture' for him; CWMG Vol. 31 (1969), 158.

marginalized in their societies. In its exclusive stress on morally inspiring messages for public good, Gandhi's view expressed in the contexts discussed above is constrictive for artistic freedom, but paradoxically empowering for social activism.

During the same period when Gandhi was making remarks on the links between ethics and art, his reflective conversations with two artists, the musician Dilip Kumar Roy and the dramatist and writer Romain Rolland, throw light on quite a different and deeper current at work in his conception of art. These express his view that life is more sacred than art; and an ideal life in its totality is art. In an interview with Roy, who was happy to learn that Gandhi was not averse to art as he had heard, the latter explained that while he (Gandhi) was greatly moved by art, he held that 'Life is and must be greater than all arts put together.'[26] For this reason, 'value of art is in how it ennobles life. Life is art. The basic function of art is to serve life and I value it as such ... .Art should show great awareness about the world. It should be deeply aware of life.'[27] Here, Gandhi's concern is with life in its more fundamental sense. He speaks of life itself as art and social awareness as one aspect of it. Ethical action and beauty, which were linked in his writings since his first satyagraha, were also getting tied to a search for a deeper spiritual meaning of life.

Among Gandhi's extensive communications with Rolland, some were in-depth conversations about art. Both shared the view that art cannot be an end in itself but can serve the flow of life in all humans. Deeply devout, Rolland had once written to Madeleine Slade (Mirabehn), 'if I've devoted myself to art, it's because it keeps me in perpetual contact with the divinity. I try to pass on to other men that mysterious touch of the Eternal, which is just under the surface of all forms of life.'[28] Rolland however, had questions about Gandhi's definition of 'truth'. In explaining his reason for identifying truth as God in a 1931 conversation, Gandhi said that we can and do identify the divine with qualities such as love, majesty, and so on. But the fundamental attribute of that Being or Entity is that

[26] *CWMG*, Vol. 23 (1967), 193.

[27] *GAD*, Vol. 23 (1971), 188. This part is a continuation of the same remarks cited in the previous note; but the last two sentences are omitted in the English translation. Translation from Gujarati mine.

[28] *Romain Rolland and Gandhi Correspondence*, trans. R. A. Francis (New Delhi: Government of India, 1976), 80.

it is, what is termed '*sat*' in Sanskrit— 'that which exists'. Gandhi identified nonviolence as an infallible path to reach that entity, which requires
utmost humility or reducing oneself to '*zero*' (the same word he used in
the autobiography). A few days later, when Rolland pointed out that his
difficulty in identifying the divine as 'truth' was that it lacks the aspect of
joy, Gandhi responded by introducing the Vedantic concept of the all-
pervading Ultimate as *sat-cit-ānanda* ('existence', 'true knowledge' [lit.
'consciousness'], and 'ineffable joy'), where truth is inseparable from joy.
Therefore, he said, he did not see art as separate from truth. And he was
quick to add, 'Yet one must suffer in search for truth . . . despite everything [the suffering], you draw joy and felicity from it.' What one needs is
'a heart tender as lotus and hard as granite'—sensitive, but courageous to
accept truth in any form it is encountered. Even scientific discoveries that
shake dearly held sacred beliefs of people are blissful in the end because
they are about truth.[29] This is among the clearest statements one finds in
Gandhi's work about the relationship between the search for truth, nonviolence manifested in ethical action, and aesthetic joy—which were all
inextricably woven in his holistic view of life as art.

Pithy statements illuminating these views continued to appear in his
personal communications and other writings until the very end. In a
letter written in 1940, echoing John Keats's famous line, he referred to
firm faith as 'a thing of beauty and joy forever'.[30] A few months before
his death, he asked in a letter, 'Isn't truth also an art?'; and he continued,
'anybody who makes a distinction between truth and beauty knows neither'.[31] We also find references to the beauty associated with the search
for Truth in terms of *rasa*. In the Akhil Bharatiya Sahitya Parishad speech
discussed above, he states that the *rasa* emerging from a passionate search
for meaning is the sustaining force of life and, therefore, inseparable from
it.[32] These recurrent remarks suggest that Gandhi was convinced that the
human quest for meaning, whether directed inward or outward to social engagement, derives its force from aesthetic sensitivity. The nature
of joy one experiences in inner search or in ethical action is essentially
aesthetic.

[29]   Ibid., 189, 208–10.
[30]   *CWMG* Vol. 71 (1978), 138.
[31]   *CWMG* Vol. 88 (1983), 304. The letter is dated 9 July 1947.
[32]   *Harijan* (2 May 1936). *CWMG* Vol 62 (1975), 347.

How did these convictions about life as art with truth, and morality as its basis, and ethical action as an essential component of it, relate to Gandhi's personal journey after his return to India ? An important implication of viewing life as art is that it is not a finished product that can be beheld in its entirety. It remains essentially a process unfolding in time, which is generally filled with routine activities but has a few high points where artistry is discernible. In Gandhi's life after coming back to India, a major juncture was his visit to Champaran in Bihar, in early 1917, which he describes as 'unforgettable'. Here, in the warm welcome and love offered by the poorest and unlettered peasants who knew nothing about him or even Congress, Gandhi says, he came 'face to face with God, Ahimsa, and Truth'.[33] The instance of seeing and feeling connected with some of the most marginalized in India was a creative and sacred moment in Gandhi's life.

Yet, for the man who connected so deeply with the Champaran peasants, the relationship with his sons was challenging. In an insightful essay, C. N. Patel, a key editor of Gandhi's works in both English and Gujarati for many years, surveys several painful episodes that reflect Gandhi's strained relations with three of his sons. Patel describes them as part of an unfolding of a tragedy of epic proportions. Aspiring to attain selfless love for the multitude and to instil the same passion in his children, for a long time Gandhi engaged with them with strictness and an unbending attitude, which Patel terms a form of 'immature detachment'. The oldest son, Harilal, was lost forever as a result. But with two others and his nephews, Gandhi grew softer over time and eventually apologized. The pain of weakening emotional ties with his children led him to understand their point of view and led him to the deeper humility he aspired in his art of life. As Patel's essay further discusses, Gandhi met with similarly intense pathos in his public life in later years. His experiments in nonviolent resistance succeeded in galvanizing large masses into nationalist social reconstruction causes such as the opening of temples for Dalits in Travancore in 1936. But at several junctures—as in the police killings in 1922—they also failed terribly. Gandhi questioned his ability to lead at times. The violence in the communal conflicts following Partition, rather than Gandhi's actual death, was the climax of the unfolding tragedy in

---

[33] Gandhi, *The Story of My Experiments with Truth*, 504.

the devastating disillusionment it brought. Yet he strove tirelessly to turn the tide because his faith in truth and the art of life remained unshaken. His death, an appropriate end for a tragedy, was an offering into the fire of communal hatred and lulled it for a while.[34] Patel's consideration of Gandhi's life as an epic tragedy draws attention to the deep pathos that marked it. Yet through these challenging years pain led him to deeper humility, and the satisfaction derived from engaging it with moral creativity sustained him, allowing him to refine his art, which was life. How do we understand the aesthetics of a play spanning decades and performed on the immense stage of public life in colonial India?

Understanding Gandhi's Aesthetics of Truth and Nonviolence

Despite the widely held image of Gandhi as indifferent to beauty and art or at best holding a utilitarian view of them, several scholars have examined Gandhian aesthetics and its relationship to his ethics from different perspectives. An important work in this area is a long essay by C. N. Patel in *Gujarati Sāhitya no Itihās* ('History of Gujarati Literature'). Here, Patel draws attention to the qualities of Gandhi's prose that give a glimpse of his poetic sensibility (*kavicetanā*).[35] While Gandhi's close associate Dattatreya Kalelkar (popularly known as Kaka Kalelkar) had indeed recorded his (Gandhi's) statement that if he had sacrificed anything for the country, it was the leisure to read English poetry, Patel uses the term *kavicetanā* with more extensive connotations.[36] He suggests that Gandhi not only enjoyed poetry but also had a creative sensibility. In *Gandhiji nī Satyasādhana* ('Gandhi's pursuit of truth'), Patel cites Gandhi's descriptions of Zulu men and women in Africa as exemplifying human beauty in its pure and natural form.[37] The poetic sensibility reflected in passages such as these, Patel suggests, was the source of

---

[34] C. N. Patel. 'Gandhiji', in *Ṭrejaḍī Sāhitya māane jīvan mā* ('Tragedy, in Literature and in Life') (Ahmedabad: Gujarati Sahitya Parishad: 1978) 138–72.
[35] C. N. Patel, 'Gandhiji', in *Gujarati Sāhitya no Itihās*, Vol. 4, ed. Raman Soni (Ahmedabad: Gujarati Sahitya Parishad, 2005), 290.
[36] Dattatreya Kalelkar, *Stray Glimpses of Bapu* (Ahmedabad: Navajivan, 1960), 35.
[37] C. N. Patel, *Gandhiji nī Satyasādhana* (Ahmedabad: Patel, 1978), 122.

Gandhi's ability to enjoy all aspects of life (*jīvan-rasa*)—political action, mundane activities, and meditative prayers. Even Gandhi's reading of the *Bhagavad Gītā*, he stresses, is not that of a philosopher but that of a man who deeply appreciated poetry.[38] In the preface to his commentary on the *Gītā*, Gandhi indeed stresses that it is a poetic text and, for that reason alone, it has potential for innumerable interpretations and its meaning is immeasurable.[39] Gandhi's expressions such as the following in a letter to his son-like Mahadev Desai (who translated both his autobiography and his translation of the *Gītā* from Gujarati into English), written from Kausani when he first visited this Himalayan village resort in June 1929, illuminate Patel's point: 'I am nestling in the lap of the Himalayas. And this greatest of *rishi*s [sages] clad in white is bathing in sunrays and is absorbed in his bliss. His *samadhi* [meditative trance] is enviable.'[40]

If Patel considers Gandhi's writings in terms of their poetic quality, Anthony Parel focuses on his aesthetics in relation to action. Considering important influences on Gandhi and his conversations and debates, including one with Tagore, Parel discusses how the Gandhian approach to political action made him an artist in a Tolstoyan or Ruskinian sense. He points out that as a person who laid much greater importance on experience than theory, Gandhi embraced experiences that had a transformative effect and led to self-cultivation. Such experiences appealed to his aesthetic sense but also led him to action. The Tagore–Gandhi debates, he observes, were based on two very different views of art and political action—one poetic and the other propelled to ethical activity. Throughout their debates Gandhi acknowledged the poet's visionary insights. Tagore also acknowledged Gandhi's inspiring presence in India. Yet he was unsure of the implications of the Gandhian approach. Toward the end, however, Tagore recognized Gandhi as an artist 'who gives evidence to the uniqueness of his mind' through 'expression in his practice.'[41] Narayan Desai examines the Gandhi–Tagore debates through the lens of a Sanskrit expression. Gandhi and Tagore, he writes, worshipped

---

[38] Patel, 'Gandhiji', 324.

[39] M. K. Gandhi, *The Bhagavad Gita According to Gandhi*, ed. John Strohmeier (Berkeley, CA: North Atlantic Books, 2009), xxiv.

[40] *GAD*, Vol. 41 (1977), 66. Translation mine.

[41] Anthony Parel, 'Aesthetics and Action in Gandhi's Political Philosophy', in *Indian Horizons* Vol. 43, No. 3 (1994), 236–44.

a trinity: Gandhi *satyam śivam sundaram* (truth, auspiciousness or goodness, and beauty); and Tagore *sundaram śivam satyam*. For Gandhi, truth led to beauty; for Tagore beauty in all forms led to realization of truth. Their meeting point was *śivam*.[42]

Discussing Gandhi's remarks on literature and art, such as those discussed earlier, Avadhesh Kumar Singh suggests that if we do not take his views as expert opinion, which by his own admission they were not, we can see the contextual and larger relevance of his questions. Gandhi welcomed questioning in the public sphere and presumed his own right to ask questions. Therefore, his views on art and literature are best seen as an opening for debate regarding his broader concern for inclusivity. While the questions he asked seemed to encroach upon artistic freedom, they helped Gujarati and perhaps other literary figures to think in new directions. Singh suggests that Gandhi's uncompromising position that art should serve a larger good, rooted in his concern for the underprivileged, also raises fundamental questions about the notion that beauty and utility belong to different spheres.[43]

Some recent works have looked at the broader resonances of Gandhian aesthetics beyond the Indian context. Nicholas Gier discusses the Gandhian approach as the 'aesthetics of virtue' that he shared with Confucius. This approach makes it possible to develop virtue as a thing of beauty that gives joy. It engages imagination and is a process of self-discovery rather than a matter of following rules.[44] John Clammer discusses parallels between the stress on ethical action for larger good in Gandhian aesthetics and the thought of some important modern thinkers—Herbert Marcuse, Ludwig Wittgenstein, and Elaine Scarry. Using the four *puruṣārthas* or aims—*dharma* (duty), *artha* (worldly gains), *kāma* (desire), and *mokṣa* (liberation)—for good life in Hindu thought as a frame, Clammer suggests that Gandhi's concern for larger good and *mokṣa* subordinated *kāma* but did not dismiss imaginative engagement with the world. Gandhi, Clammer suggests, imagined and

[42] Narayan Desai, *Maru Jivan Eja Mari Vani* ('My Life is my Message'), Vol. 2 (Ahmedabad: Navajivan, 2003) 240–57.
[43] Avdhesh Kumar Singh, 'Critiquing Mahatma Gandhi's Views on Art and Literature', in *Indian Literature* 53, no. 3 (2009), 147–62.
[44] Nicholas Gier, 'Confucius, Gandhi, and the Aesthetics of Virtue', *Asian Philosophy* 11, no. 1 (2001), 41–54.

sought to create an ideal society through his holistic approach in which beauty and ethical action were tied.[45]

Stephanie Chadwick offers an art-historical perspective, pointing out the resonance of Gandhian aesthetics more broadly beyond India. In 2014 the Menil Foundation in Houston held an exhibition titled 'Experiments with Truth: Gandhi and Image of Non-violence'. Among the wide array of art from diverse cultures around the world featured at the exhibition was a painting by American artist Barnett Newman, *Be I* (1949). Newman had never met Gandhi and did not even refer to him in his writing, but he did share with Gandhi a concern for equality and inclusivity. Newman's imposing non-figural painting with only one line dividing the red rectangular background in two equal parts, Chadwick suggests, resonated with Gandhian ideals in inviting the viewer to engage temporally, visually, and spatially to experience the self. In its visual economy, it also resonated with key pieces in the exhibit related to Gandhi, including a photograph of his simple belongings and him spinning the *charkha*, an iconic image of his ascetic life. Chadwick suggests that in its minimal aesthetics based in the ethics of inclusivity, Newman's *Be I* offered an American counterpart to Gandhi's ascetic approach.[46]

Even though scholars exploring Gandhian aesthetics agree on Gandhi's insistence that art should be directed to ethical ends for larger good, their foci differ. Gandhi's deceptively simple statements containing complex thought do need a multiplicity of approaches to parse. Drawing on Gandhi's use of the term *rasa* to describe his quest for truth and perfect humility and building on Patel's use of the terms *kavicetanā* and *jīvan-rasa*, the following sections of this essay look at the link between Gandhi's inner search, ethical orientation of his life, and aesthetic sensitivity through the lens of *śāntarasa*, a concept developed by the eleventh-century mystic and aesthetician Abhinavagupta of Kashmir.

---

[45] John Clammer, 'Can Art Embody Truth? Ethics, Aesthetics, and Gandhi', *Social Change* 51, no. 1 (2021), 92–103, DOI: 10.1177/0049085721996859.

[46] Stephanie Chadwick, 'Barnett Newman, Gandhi, and the Aesthetics of Nonviolence', *Rupkatha Journal on Interdisciplinary Studies in Humanities,* VIII, no. 4 (2017), 1–12.

Śāntarasa—Abhinavagupta

Abhinavagupta was a great thinker in the tradition of Kashmir Shaivism and Indian poetics. It is unlikely that Gandhi was familiar with Abhinavagupta's mystical insights or theoretical contributions to aesthetics. He had perhaps not even heard of Abhinavagupta. Yet the resonances between Abhinava's concept of *śāntarasa* and Gandhi's use of the term *rasa* as joy in his experiments with truth are striking. They both refer to a deep joy experienced in tranquillity and rooted in spiritual transformation.

Abhinava's concept of *śāntarasa* is a major milestone in the long history of Indian aesthetics, where the term *rasa* has meant 'aesthetic relishing'. The use of this term, which literally means 'nectar' or 'juice', can be traced back to the *Taittiriya* Upanishad (2.7.1), composed a few centuries before the Common Era. Here, the Ultimate principle is identified with it as the source of bliss. In the area of aesthetics, it was first introduced by the legendary sage Bharata in his treatise on dramaturgy, *Nāṭyaśāstra*, composed in the early centuries of the Common Era. In *Nāṭyaśāstra,* a major focus is evocation of sentiments in drama. Bharata lists eight human emotions (*bhāvas*) as durable and dominant (*sthāyī-bhāvas*): passion, humour, anger, sadness, effort, wonder, disgust, and fear. These *bhāvas,* when evoked in a dramatic setting, lead a qualified spectator to enjoy their aesthetic flavours—*rasas*, likened to the relishing of a meal that consists of dishes having different flavours. Bharata explains that even though the relishing is derived from the flavours of the dishes, it is different from their direct experience. The factors leading to the experience of *rasa* in a dramatic performance are emotions expressed in the play, the ability of the performer, and the sensitivity of the spectator. A *bhāva* is transformed into *rasa* in an aesthetic experience. Following this line of thought, Bharata lists eight *rasas* corresponding to the eight *sthāyī-bhāvas* listed above: (1) the erotic (*śṛngāra*), (2) the humorous (*hāsya*), (3) the furious (*raudra*), (4) the pathetic (*karuṇa*), (5) the heroic (*vīra*), (6) the amazing (*adbhuta*), (7) the repulsive (*bibhatsa*), and (8) the terrible (*bhayānak*).[47] Being primarily concerned with the elements of performance, Bharata

---

[47] Bharat Muni, *Nāṭyaśāstra, English Translation with Critical Notes,* trans. Adya Rangacharya (Bangalore: IBH Prakashana, 1986), 38.

does not elaborate in the *Nāṭyaśāstra* on *how* a *sthāyī-bhāva* evoked in a drama is transformed into *rasa* for a spectator. He, however, makes an important distinction between the emotions a person experiences in her/his own life and the ones that she/he experiences in a play. He states that the emotions aroused in a play are purged of the 'egoistic' basis of everyday emotions where the subject's self is directly involved.

In the centuries following Bharata, the concept of *rasa* continued to be developed further. In the ninth century, Anandavardhana of Kashmir introduced the concepts of *dhvani* (suggested meaning) and *pratibhā* (imaginative insight) that greatly expanded the understanding of the nature of aesthetic relishing. Anandavardhana proposed that with his imaginative insight a poet has a deeper understanding of human emotions, which he conveys in his poem through the skilful structuring of poetic elements. When a sensitive enjoyer (*sahṛdaya*) reads or listens to a poem, she/he grasps this suggested meaning because she/he shares the imaginative insight of the poet. In the tenth century Bhatta Nayaka put forward the idea that the emotion presented in a poem or work of art is not a raw personal emotion but distilled to purity by the artist. Building on the thought of these earlier thinkers, Abhinavagupta explored the subjective side of the experience of *rasa* much further. He suggested that a *sthāāyī-bhāva* is present in the consciousness of the enjoyer of a play or a poem in a latent form. When suggested in a play or poem, due to her/his imaginative insight a good enjoyer first gets attuned to the *bhāva* conveyed in its idealized form and then gets absorbed in it. In this state of absorption, she/he is freed from her/his ego and experiences joy that is the nature of her/his own self (*ātman*). The joy does not emerge because of getting attuned to the emotion but from being freed from the narrow world of personal ego and encountering one's deeper self in connection to others. This is the experience of *rasa*. Abhinava's theory suggests that *rasa* is intrinsic to the enjoyer's self. Its experience is the discovery of that aspect of the intrinsic self.

In Kashmir Shaivism, as in all non-dualistic (*advaita*) and theistic schools of *Vedānta* (interpretation of Upanishadic thought), freedom from ego is the basic condition for the experience of pure joy, which is an aspect of Brahman, the Ultimate spiritual reality. It is the basis of the bliss experienced by a mystic in meditation. According to Abhinava, in leading the enjoyer to freedom from ego, aesthetic experience closely parallels mystical bliss. Elaborating on Bharata's notion of uplifting of emotions from their egoistic basis in the dramatic context, Abhinava linked aesthetic experience with the highest spiritual experience. He held that detachment from one's personal emotions allows the emotion as conveyed in poetry or drama to be experienced in its pure form, leading to a joyous experience similar to yogic meditation. But it can only be experienced by an enjoyer who has imaginative insight like the poet or the artist.

In Abhinava's explication of purity of sentiment in the aesthetic context, he added a *sthāyī-bhāva* to the Bharata's list of eight—termed '*sama*' (tranquillity). This *sthāyī-bhāva* leads to *śāntarasa*. It is not associated with the emotions of the phenomenal world but with consciousness or awareness that allows a deeper understanding of a human emotion. Because of aesthetic distance or detachment, the enjoyer gets absorbed in an emotion in its pure form, leading to *sama*. This aestheticized emotion forms the basis of the experience of *śāntarasa*, which is *similar* to yogic bliss and *alaukika* (not this-worldly). In Abhinava's view, it is the ultimate *rasa*. All other *rasa*s are subordinate to it. The *rasa* experienced by an enjoyer of a play or a poem, however, is *not identical* to the bliss experienced by a yogi in the highest meditative state (when his personal self merges into the Ultimate Reality), because it takes place in the phenomenal world and does not have a permanent impact on the personality of the spectator. It gives the spectator only 'a foretaste of the bliss of *mokṣa* (liberation)'.[48] Even though in Abhinava's view the experience of *śāntarasa* as an aesthetic mood is impermanent, in his conceptualization of it as intrinsic to the self of the enjoyer he brings out the implications of the Upanishadic aphorism *raso vai sah* ('He verily is *rasa*') to a great degree. What one deeply enjoys even in a fleeting manner is the discovery of the self as identical to the Ultimate, Brahman. In dance performances, *śāntarasa* is often portrayed with half-closed or closed eyes, subtle movement of the body, and peaceful expression, signifying *nirveda* or indifference to the world, not as its rejection but as detachment. The colour associated with *śānta* is white, which, instead of exuberance of life, signifies tranquillity. The concept of *śāntarasa* as developed by Abhinava,

---

[48] For an accessible introduction, see T. P. Ramachandran, *The Indian Philosophy of Beauty, Part II, Special Concepts* (Madras: University of Madras, 1980), 107–12.

and its representation in art, offer helpful lenses through which to understand Gandhi's use of the term *rasa* in relation to his quest for truth.

Before we look at Gandhi's quest, however, it is helpful to look briefly at another important school of thought that linked the aesthetic and the spiritual, which developed greatly in the centuries following Abhinava and reached immense sophistication in the works of theologians Jiva and Rupa Goswami of the Gaudiya tradition of Krishna devotion. This school identified *bhakti*, or devotion, as *rasa*. As per this theory, even though the several characters found in Krishna narratives experience different *bhāvas*—parental love, friendship, erotic sentiment, and so on—in relation to him their deeper joyful emotion is *bhakti* to the Lord. By imaginatively developing a particular *bhāva* (including *madhura* or erotic) in relation to Krishna, a *bhakta* (devotee) gradually develops deeper *bhakti* for him. In this theory too, various *bhāvas* lead to a single ultimate *rasa*— *bhakti*. But unlike Abhinava's *śāntarasa*, it is relational and not purely oriented to knowledge. It relies on directing emotions toward the divine rather than developing detachment. Another important way in which *bhakti-rasa* as proposed by this school differs from Abhinava's conception of *śāntarasa* is that it is conceived not as temporary but as gradually becoming a permanent part of a devotee's self.[49]

Rasa in Gandhi's Quest

How does Gandhi's quest relate to the concept of *śāntarasa*? As seen above, Gandhi did not see art as separate from life and truth. For him, life in its totality was a work of art. It presented to Gandhi continued opportunities to perfect *ahiṃsa* and conduct experiments with truth. This journey, with the dual foci of inward transformation and ethical action in the world, was his source of *rasa*. He also identified Truth, which he saw as both the source and destination of moral transformation, as the Lord of *rasa*.[50] With such stress on inner transformation, Gandhi appreciated fine and performing arts only in so far as they had an ennobling

[49] For a detailed discussion of *rasa* in Bharata's, Abhinava's, and Vaishnava theories see Neelima Shukla-Bhatt, *Nectar of Devotion: Bhakti-rasa in the Tradition of Gujarati Saint-Poet Narasinha Mehta* (unpublished dissertation, Harvard University, 2003).
[50] *CWMG*, Vol. 31 (1969), 159.

effect on people and did not stir 'passions'. Taking an austere lifestyle as an essential component of the search for truth, Gandhi adopted a minimalist approach—restricting the needs to the minimum possible and shedding all that he found unhelpful in cultivating the self and society. Gandhi's writing style in both Gujarati and English, his residence and living spaces, his diet, and his simple white attire of dhoti and shawl—all give evidence of his increasingly minimalist approach linked to detachment. His expectation that his close followers also practise such minimalism can be and is often seen as a form of imposition. But for him this emphasis on minimalism was a part of his quest for a transformative *rasa*, which he wanted to experience himself and share with others. It was integral to his political and social activism rooted in nonviolence and identification with the most marginalized.

In its close link to the spiritual, the connotations of Gandhi's references to the *rasa* derived from experiments with truth come close to concepts of both *bhakti-rasa* and *śāntarasa*. In the expectation that the experience of *rasa* transforms one's inner being permanently, Gandhi's understanding comes close to the concept of *bhakti-rasa* in Vaishnava traditions. It does not align with that of Abhinava, who clearly wanted to distinguish between the aesthetic and the mystical in this regard. But Gandhi's references to *rasa* differ sharply from the connotations of *bhakti-rasa* in that they do not imply a deepening 'love for a divine being' like Krishna. Rather, they refer to a search for truth inwardly and in the world. Nor is there place for the erotic emotion in Gandhi's understanding of *rasa*. In its focus on detachment and 'unruffled calm', and with the ultimate goal of becoming zero-like (*śunyavat*), the *rasa* sought by Gandhi comes closest to Abhinava's concept of *śāntarasa*, a state similar to mystical bliss. There is, however, a key difference. Reaching mystical bliss is necessarily an individual journey, and its experience is limited to the person undertaking it. Abhinava's concept delineates the experience of an individual. Gandhi sought to share his experiments broadly with diverse people, which led to paradoxical outcomes.

In some ways, Gandhi's aesthetic journey with its stress on austerity opened new vistas for participation in social and political processes for India's poor and illiterate masses. His political acts like the Salt March, in which he walked on dusty roads with a walking stick, were marked by a minimalist aesthetics and allowed crowds to join in. His simple communes became centres of inclusive living where the elite and people from the margins of society could come together. These ashrams, now mainly memorial sites, continue to have an inviting aura in their austere aesthetics. Visitors to his ashram in Ahmedabad often report that even though the Ashram Road on which it is located is now terribly noisy, as soon as one enters the ashram premises, one experiences a peacefulness evoked by the simplicity of the ambiance. His call for spinning (half an hour a day) and the associated icon of the *charkha*, sharply critiqued from various angles, were meant as recognition of the dignity of labour of the poor, especially women, who spun every day, as he explained.[51] They can be compared to the *charkha* songs of the eighteenth-century Punjabi Sufi poet Bulleh Shah (1680–1757).[52] Gandhi's use of such symbols made room for people from diverse backgrounds in his projects for national causes.

In the area of literature, Gandhi's questions sharpened discourses of the time that helped chart a new direction of inclusivity and bring clarity in Gujarati prose. In what came to be known as *Gandhi Yug* in Gujarati literary history (roughly from the 1920s to 1950), socially relevant themes appeared profusely in fiction and poetry. Even though these specific themes lost contextual relevance in later periods, they helped Gujarati authors think about the lives of the marginalized as worthy of literary attention. Literature also became accessible to the masses. In the area of music, too, he encouraged, in fact promoted, the singing of *bhajan*s (devotional songs), lyrics of medieval saint-poets in India's regional languages. This choice of genre, often critiqued as emerging from narrow traditionalism, seems well considered for two reasons. First, most of the carefully selected *bhajan*s in the compilation for his commune, *Ashram-Bhajanavali*, are not about love for any specific deity but are songs of supplication to a higher power or are about inner search. They are songs of *śāntarasa* and were meant to appeal to the moral sensitivity of the singers and listeners. The second

---

[51] *CWMG*, Vol 21 (1966), 289.
[52] For accessible translations of two Bulleh Shah songs, see Shailendra Sharma, https://shaile ndrasharmahome.wordpress.com/2019/11/16/charkha-kalam-by-bulleh-shah-translation/ [accessed 25 July 2021].

reason, as I have discussed with regard to Gujarati *bhajan* by Narasinha Mehta, *Vaiṣṇava jana to*, was that popularity of these songs made them a ready platform to connect with the masses. While this traditional genre was especially useful in his efforts to mobilize the masses for national causes, Gandhi's use of *Vaiṣṇava jana to* and other *bhajan*s was hardly traditional. He pulled Hindu *bhajan*s and a few songs of other religious communities out of their traditional devotional contexts and introduced them to large masses as resources for moral reconstruction. For the purpose, he sought the expertise of the finest musicians of India at the time. Pandit Narayan Khare, the musician who composed the well-known tune of *Vaishnava jana to*, was a disciple of Pandit Vishnu Digambar Paluskar, one of the best-known musicians of modern times in India. Pandit Khare was the lead musical voice on the entire road of the Salt March in 1930 and contributed significantly to the appeal of the march. Gandhi also invited Nandalal Bose to contribute paintings for the 1938 Haripura congress.

Why did Gandhi want to bring art forms with the potential to evoke *śāntarasa* to the public platform? The answer may lie in his sense of self. Gandhi identified with the suffering multitudes of India and aspired to their transformation too. He hoped that they would also be touched by the transformative power of these art forms. But there lies the tragic paradox of his experiment. He sought to share with multitudes of people what is conceived as a deeply personal experience—*śāntarasa*. On some occasions, he thought his experiments were having an impact, and indeed they seemed to. But in the months following India's independence from the British, he must have realized that they had tragically failed, as the poet Tagore had warned years earlier in 1921. In his famous debate with Gandhi following his disenchantment with the burning of foreign cloth in the *swadeśī* movement, Tagore had spoken about the dangers of 'blind obedience' out of fear or hope, which 'makes everyone talk in the same voice and make the same gestures'. People giving up their own freedom of mind, he said, 'deprive others of their freedom'. Tagore had stressed that true swaraj can be built only by the mind 'within us', which the 'slavish mentality' is incapable of accomplishing. And while paying generous tribute to Gandhi for touching the hearts of the poor multitudes of India with true love, he had also expressed a grave concern that not everyone can 'grasp the meaning of the great love kindled in the people's heart by the Mahatma's love'.[53] Tagore's severe critique with use of words and phrases such as 'slavery' and 'falsehood passing as moral dictum' in some ways hinted at the limits or even failure of Gandhi's nonviolence. Was that the case? Gandhi, of course, defended his call for spinning as drawing attention to the need of the hungry millions for work and indicated that people were joining the movement voluntarily and not forcibly.[54] Yet as is well known, during the last few months of his life he had serious doubts about his attainment of *ahimsa*, leading him to take up a test of his celibacy. It was indeed a dark hour.

The question had arisen again for others and himself: had he failed in his experiments with truth and *ahiṃsa*? I propose that approaching the question in view of the paradox emerging from Gandhi's identification with the suffering millions and his striving to share with them a *rasa* that is in the domain of individual spirituality is helpful. Over many decades, even as he sustained his inner journey with the *rasa* he derived from his spiritual/ethical striving, he had advised Hindus, Jews, Muslims, and many other groups facing terrible violence to respond to it with nonviolence and have firm faith in it. But he had not communicated with them, as he had done in conversation with Romain Rolland, his view of the deeply nourishing aspect of his quest—*ānanda*—without which it would run dry. He had hoped, as his famous expression indicates, that his life would convey the message. But his appeal to embrace nonviolence met with a great deal of scepticism or outright rejection, as seen after India's partition because the people to whom he was appealing did not have the experience of the sustaining inner resources. The rejection of his appeals for peace and nonviolence during the last phase may be understood not as the failure of his *ahiṃsa* but, rather, as Tagore had perceptively hinted, as a result of the impossibility of drawing multitudes into the experiment of its perfection with the nourishing experience of ever deepening *śāntarasa*.

---

[53] Rabindranath Tagore, 'The Call of Truth' in *Sources of Indian Traditions: Modern India, Pakistan, Bangladesh,* ed. Rachel McDermott et al. (New York: Columbia University Press, 2014), 390–3.
[54] *CWMG*, Vol. 21, 287–91.

Conclusion

There can hardly be a definitive conclusion to such an exploration as undertaken in this essay. What the exploration has drawn attention to is that the spiritual, the ethical, and the aesthetic were integrally linked in Gandhi's search for truth and striving to perfect his practice of nonviolence. His writings and communications suggest that through various phases of his life he became increasingly more aware of this link. To a large degree, he was able to sustain his inner search and engagement with the world during an intense phase of India's independence movement because he found beauty in them and deeply relished the experience. He described this experience using the term *rasa*, aesthetic delight in Indian parlance, and linked it to *ānanda*—the blissful aspect of the divine. The *rasa* of Gandhi's experience was drawn from life in its totality and not only from artworks. As austerity and detachment became a part of his quest and became integrally linked with his dedication to service and identification with the poor, the *rasa* of his experience came close to *śāntarasa* or the tranquil mood as delineated by aesthetician Abhinavagupta. It offered him deep sustenance in its transformative power. Yet his attempts to share it with the multitudes and transform their lives were fraught with paradoxes. While the pathos of the last act of Gandhi's life as a tragedy of epic scale was overwhelming, as discussed by Patel, his experiments to turn life in its totality into a *rasātmaka* journey of self-discovery and ethical action were glorious. Even Abhinavagupta would have been amazed by the creativity with which Gandhi extended the limits of *śāntarasa* experientially (not theoretically) by conjoining it with ethical action in the world and striving to make it not a fleeting but a permanent experience.

8

On Sorcery of Peace and Nonviolence

A Note on Gandhi's Yogic Fearlessness and

Omnipotent *Yoga*

Yohanan Grinshpon

Suppose we compare moral energies and those of evil: which are more forceful? It is perhaps a question impossible to answer. History is an enormous reservoir of events and experience. Sometimes good has won; sometimes evil. However impossible to answer, Gandhi's life and thought provide an occasion for reflection on questions of good and evil, and the respective forces involved. For Gandhi was a staunch optimist, never tired of insisting on the superior force of *satyāgraha* and *ahiṃsā*, on true peace and nonviolence as the law of human existence. He invariably associated the force of morality with his successful application of *ahiṃsā* and *satyāgraha*. Indeed, he was, no one would deny, a self-confident person. However, his self-confidence, even as an old man in the face of harsh circumstances of violence and hostility, invites further thinking of its degree or the special quality and nature of it and Gandhi's optimism. Was it recognition of the undeniable (tautological) *moral* superiority of the good over evil which made him so courageous, unflinching in the face of cruelty? Or was it his share of yogic fearlessness and imagination which energized the great man's being to a degree unknown to ordinary people?

This paper addresses what seems to me a somewhat under interpreted dimension of Gandhi's experience and thought: his sense of omnipotence embedded in his unique fearlessness and self-confidence. That Gandhi did express such a sense is well known. *Ahiṃsā*, he said, was an invincible, never failing strategy in life (in the family, in the economy, in international relations, etc.). Indeed, he moved in the midst of half-crazed,

Yohanan Grinshpon, *On Sorcery of Peace and Nonviolence* In: *Gandhi, Truth, and Nonviolence.*
Edited by: Vinay Lal, Oxford University Press. © Oxford University Press 2025.
DOI: 10.1093/9780198936657.003.0009

hostile environments of Hindus and Muslims in the deeply rooted conviction that he could have done something to change the world around
him. Facing waves of horrible violence all around, he dared question himself: what shall I do, what shall I do? Suspecting failure in sexual continence (*brahmacarya*), he thought he could not exercise *ahiṃsā* to the rescue
of the Indian nation. If only he were fully accomplished in *brahmacarya*
in the midst of the 1946–7 horrors in the immense Indian subcontinent,
hundreds of thousands lives could be saved, Gandhi believed. And indeed, the man survived trials and challenges of enormous intensity. In
many respects, it seems Gandhi was amazingly successful. A certain sense
of 'ontological trust of reality', as it were, and unbelievable self-confidence
(on the verge of omnipotence) seem to accompany his long life and career.

Whence then Gandhi's sense of fearlessness and omnipotence? In what
follows, I propose that yogic discipline and sorcery, productive of so-called
supranormal experiences or 'achievements' (*siddhi*) are the coins applic-
able to the Mahātma's sense of power. Rather than exclusively grounded in
the superiority of good over evil, Gandhi's optimism of infinite proportion
also rests upon a sense of yogic omnipotence. In his peacemaking cap-
abilities, as well as in his own self-understanding (omnipotent by virtue
of *ahiṃsā* and *satyāgraha*), Gandhi inherits much of the spirit informing
the descriptions of the *siddhi*s in classical *yoga*. By implication, pending
Gandhi-like sorcerers of peace and nonviolence, the world is a place more
dangerous (or doomed) than most people realize.

Mysterious energies are in action in an accomplished *yogin*'s life.
According to Patañjali's *Yoga Sūtra* [hereafter *YS*], so-called supranormal
achievements (*siddhis*) are consequent of yogic practice. The larger part
of the third section of the *Yoga Sūtra* (the *Vibhūti-Pāda*) is devoted to
these attainments. Most of the supranormal powers described in this
section emerge as results of a meditation called *saṃyama*, defined in the
YS as a combination of the three techniques of meditation which are the
last members of the eightfold *yoga* (*aṣṭāṅga-yoga*).[1] Thus, for example,
saṃyama applied to bodily boundaries brings about disappearance (in-
visibility, *antar-dhāna*) (of the *yogin*'s presence in the eyes of others).[2]

---

[1]   The three types of meditative practices are *dhāraṇā* (*YS* 3.1), *dhyāna* (*YS* 3.2), and *samādhi*
(*YS* 3.3). The three, applied to one point, are called *saṃyama* (*trayam ekatra saṃyamaḥ*) (*YS*
3.4). Translations from the original in Sanskrit are mine. I use Hariharananda Aranya, *Yoga
Philosophy of Patanjali* (New York: State University of New York Press), 1983.
[2]   *YS* 3.21.

Saṃyama applied to a navel-centre (*nābhi-cakra*) produces knowledge of anatomy ('bodily order', *kāya-vyūha*).[3] *Saṃyama*-meditation on the subliminal impressions (*saṃskāra*) brings about knowledge of previous lives.[4] And so forth.

The second part of the *Yoga Sūtra* (*Sādhana-Pāda*) contains some of the *siddhi*s most pertinent to Gandhi's infinite trust in the power of *ahiṃsā* and *satyāgraha*. The ten 'prescriptions' which constitute the first two limbs of the eightfold *Yoga* (*yama*s and *niyama*s),[5] each one of them, are of innate transformational power to produce specific consequences of yogic sorcery and imagination. Patañjali devotes to each prescription a special *sūtra* which describes the effect of the respective prescription. Thus, for example, 'non-possessiveness' (*aparigraha*) produces know-ledge of previous births.[6] Yogic contentment (self-sufficiency) (*santoṣa*) is associated with supreme happiness.[7] A *yogin*'s unconditional commit-ment to truth (*satya*) results in the inherence of the result in the action itself. Thus *YS* 2.36: 'For the *yogin* well-grounded in 'truthfulness' the fruit resides in the action' (*satya-pratiṣṭhāyām kriyā-phalāśrayatvam*). 'Inherence of the fruit in the action itself' (*kriyā-phalāśrayatvam*) be-tokens a flavour of omnipotence. According to the traditional commenta-tors, the words of the powerful *yogin* are necessarily fruitful (not in vain) (*amoghāsya vāg bhavati*), as Vyāsa, the authoritative commentator of the *Yoga Sūtra* says. If the *yogin* says (to a person) 'go to heaven', that person does go to heaven (*svargaṃ prāpnuhīti svargaṃ prāpnoti*).

Most important for our concerns is, of course, the first (and, according to the traditional commentators, foremost), opening prescription of *ahiṃsā*, nonviolence, or better (more accurately) 'innate avoidance of any desire for violence'. Thus, *YS* 2.35 states: 'In the vicinity of the *yogin* accomplished in the avoidance for any desire of injury, there is cessation of every type of injury'; or, 'creatures in contact with a *yogin* capable of avoiding any aggression renounce their own (aggression)'

---

[3] *YS* 3.29.

[4] *YS* 3.18.

[5] These are non-injury, truthfulness, non-stealing, continence, non-possessiveness, cleanli-ness, contentment, heating practices (austerity), study of scripture, surrender unto God (*ahiṃsā*; *satya*; *asteya*; *brahmacarya*; *aparigraha*; *śauca*; *santoṣa*; *tapas*; *svādhyāya*; *īśvara-pranidhāna*).

[6] *YS* 2.39: *aparigraha-sthairye janma-kathantā-sambodhaḥ.*

[7] *YS* 2.42: By virtue of yogic self-sufficiency one attains unsurpassed pleasure (*santoṣād anuttamaḥ sukha-lābhaḥ*).

(*ahiṃsā-pratiṣṭhāyām tat-saṃnidhau vaira-tyāgaḥ*). Vyāsa says here: 'And (this cessation of injury) is true with respect to every creature' (*sarva-prāṇinām bhavati*).

Cessation of any trace of violence in the vicinity of the *yogin* who practises *ahiṃsā* is a *siddhi*, a supranormal consequence of the application of nonviolence. In this respect *ahiṃsā* is no different than other moments of discipline listed as *yama*s and *niyama*s. Thus, for example, being grounded in non-stealing (*asteya*) brings about jewels all around.[8] Was Gandhi a *Pātañjala-yogin* committed to the extraordinary force of non-violence? As suggested above, he used to refer to the force of *ahiṃsā* and *satyāgraha* in terms of morality, love, and hate rather than in terms of yogic omnipotence. 'Hate dissolves in the presence of love.' However, as we shall see below, A. J. Parel says:

> Patañjali Yoga-Sūtra was another important source. The thirty fifth aphorism of book ii of this work – 'When one is well grounded in non-violence, there is abandonment of violence in one's presence' – was a favorite of Gandhi. He used to repeat it like a mantra in times of personal crisis. He was convinced that perfect non violence was self acting. 'I literally believe in Patañjali's aphorism that violence ceases in the presence of non-violence.'[9]

Gandhi is perhaps the greatest commentator known to us on some of Patañjali's statements. He shares with traditional *yoga* the belief in the overall importance of *ahiṃsā*. Vyāsa makes explicit the dominance of *ahiṃsā* among Patañjali's prescriptions (*yama*s). In his *bhāṣya* on YS 2.30 he says:

> *Ahiṃsā* implies non-injury (*anabhirodha*) to every creature, always and by no means (*tatrāhiṃsa sarvathā sarvadā sarva-bhūtānām anabhirodhaḥ*). The other *yama*s and *niyama*s have their root in this (*ahiṃsā*) (or are the roots of *ahiṃsā*) (*uttare ca yama-niyamās tan-mūlās*). They (*yama*s and *niyama*s) are taught for its (*ahiṃsā*'s)

---

[8]   YS 2.37.
[9]   J. Anthony Parel, *Gandhi's Philosophy and the Quest for Harmony* (Cambridge: Cambridge University Press, 2006).

instruction and fulfilment (*tat-siddhi-paratāya tat-pratipādanāya pratipādyante*). They are also means for making *ahiṃsā* pure (*tad-avadāta-rūpa-karaṇāyaivopādīyante*). In this context (of what makes *ahiṃsā* pure) it is said: as this brahmin proceeds in the observance of many vows he moves on away from bad actions of violence perpetrated by careless obsession (*pramāda*); thus, he purifies non-violence (*tatha coktam sa khalv ayam brāhmaṇo yathā yathā vratāni bahūni samāditsate tathā tathā pramāda-kṛtebhyo himsā-nidānebhyo nivartamānas tām evāvadāta-rūpam ahiṃsām karotīti*).

Following the tradition of *Pātañjala-Yoga*, Gandhi gave explicit expression to the connection of the central concept of his self-understanding—*ahiṃsā*—with this tradition of classical yoga. In a discussion with Bharatanand (1940) he says:

> Well, well, no amount of argument can teach us *ahiṃsā*. And you must not forget that one cannot be sure of the purity of one's intention until one has gone through the whole course of spiritual training laid down by masters of *yoga* like Patañjali. Perfect *chittashuddhi* cannot be achieved in any other way.

The *yama*s are omnipresent in Gandhi's mind and self-understanding. Thus, for example, he writes:

> Truthfulness, Brahmacarya, non-violence, non-stealing and non-hoarding, these five rules of life are obligatory on all aspirants.[10]

Traditional commentators on the *Yoga Sūtra* see the *siddhi*s as 'signs' (*sūcaka, cihna*) of successful yogic practice. As Vācaspati says,

> Now, in the absence of obstacles due to the practice of *yama*s and *niyama*s, he (Vyāsa, the author of the *Yoga-sūtra-bhāṣya*) proceeds in pointing to the indicatory signs which are the *siddhi*-experiences. Upon

---

[10] *The Selected Works of Mahatma Gandhi* (Ahmedabad: Navajivan,1968), vol. 4, 360.

their discernment, the yogi who has accomplished his task proceeds to
what is yet to be accomplished.[11]

Thus, the implications of yogic discipline in terms of the *siddhi*s are at the
core of the classical commentators on the *Yoga Sūtra*. The result of yogic
practice is evidence of the correct use and process of yogic practice. It
is apparently a most esoteric dimension of the *yoga* universe. However,
it is definitely there, a part and parcel of the classical tradition. Can one
imagine that Gandhi—a most realistic man, sober, committed to experience and experiment—would ever consider cessation of violence in the
vicinity of an *ahiṃsā*-expert—the crux of the *siddhi*-theory (or reflection
on experience) of *Pātañjala-yoga*—as consequent of yogic practice? It is
unlikely, I think. As we shall see below, Gandhi was explicit in his denial
of any value to the so-called miraculous attainments (*siddhi*). However,
notwithstanding Gandhi's own self-understanding, his multidimen-
sional yoga-being (including practice of yogic postures and breathing exercises; see below) suggests experiential affinity of the twentieth-century
yogin with the scholarly *yogin*s of old. As seen above, the science of the
miraculous attainments consists of the alleged discovery of connections
between practice and consequences thereof. A sense of causal connectedness between one's being and one's environment nourishes Gandhi's
consciousness throughout his life. The power of never-failing *ahiṃsā* is
most conspicuous in Gandhi's reflection on the source of his own success. A report of a talk Gandhi gave to relief workers at Srirampur (on
27 December 1946), in the most difficult time of violence and atrocities,
a little more than a year before his death points to Gandhi's own association of the power of *ahiṃsā* and *Pātañjala-yoga*:

Gandhiji said that many years ago a friend of his used to carry Patañjali's
Yoga-sūtra constantly in his pocket. Although Gandhiji did not know
Sanskrit yet the friend would often come to him to consult about the
meaning of some of the *sūtra*s. In one of the *sūtra*s it was stated that
when *ahiṃsā* had been fully established it would completely liquidate
the forces of enmity and evil in the neighbourhood. Gandhiji felt that

[11] Tattvavaisaradi 2.35: *sampraty apratyūham yama-niyamabhyāsāt tat-siddhi-parijñāna-*
sūcakāni cuhnāny upanyasyati yat parijñānād yogī tatra tatra kṛta-kṛtyaḥ kartavyeṣu pravartate.

the stage had not been reached in the neighbourhood about him and this led him to infer that his *ahiṃsā* had not been succeeded in the present test. That was the reason why he was saying that there was still darkness all around him.[12]

The importance of *ahiṃsā* in the eyes of Patañjali the *sūtra-kāra* becomes obvious as he devotes three *sūtras* to the yogic procedure underlying the accomplishment of 'nonviolence' (YS 2.33; 2.34; 2.35). YS 2.33 asserts that visualization (*bhāvana*) of the severe consequences of improper thought (and motivation) restricts (violent) inner condition. YS 2.34 classifies the types of violent thought and behaviour to be opposed and eradicated by 'visualization of the opposite' (*pratipakṣa-bhāvana*). 'Cultivation of the opposite is as the following: 'violent thoughts are of infinite ignorance and painful results (*duhkhājñānānanta-phala*), produced by greed (*lobha*), anger, and delusion; such violent thoughts and behavior are done either by oneself (*kṛta*), compelled by another (*kārita*), or recommended by others (*anumodita*); they are of mild, medium, or great degree.'[13]

Vijñānabhikṣu of the sixteenth century connects the practice of 'opposite visualization' with the signs of success in the accomplishment (*niṣpatti*) of the prescriptions: 'The author introduces special statements which specify the observable signs (*sūcaka*) of successful use of opposite visualization.'[14]

Gandhi himself interpreted his successful life as a reformer, politician, and leader in terms of the superiority of good over evil. People are inherently good, he thought. Even butchers are not necessarily bad people:

> To take an extreme case, there can perhaps be no greater contradiction in terms than a compassionate butcher. And yet it is possible even for a butcher if he has any pity in him. In fact I have already known butchers with gentleness that one would hardly expect from them. The

---

[12] I am indebted to Shimon Lev, a scholar of Gandhi's and Kallenbach's lives, for his important references.

[13] YS 2.34: *vitarkā hiṃsādayaḥ kṛta-kāritānumoditā lobha-krodha-moha-pūrvakā mṛdu-madhyādhimātrā dūkhājñānānanta-phalā iti pratipakṣa-bhāvanam.*

[14] *yama-niyama-niṣpatti-sūcakānām siddhāntānām pratipādakāni sūtrāni avatārayati – pratipakṣeti.* See T. S. Rukmani, *The Yoga-vārttika of Vijñānabhikṣu* (New Delhi: Munshiram Manoharial, 1983), v. 2., p. 209.

celebrated episode of Kaushik the butcher in the Mahabharata is an instance in point.[15]

Understanding himself as a moral agent, Gandhi devoted much thought
on the nature of morality. Here is a typical example:

> So long as we act like machines, there can be no question of morality. If
> we want to call an action moral, it should have been done consciously
> and as a matter of duty. Any action that is dictated by fear, or by coer-
> cion of any kind, ceases to be moral. It also follows that all good deeds
> that are prompted by hope of happiness in the next world cease to be
> moral.[16]

It is indeed possible that doing the inherently good act even in the face
of improbable success generates a feeling of elation associated with a
unique sense of self-confidence.[17] However, resisting Gandhi's own self-
understanding at this point, we offer a somewhat different interpretation
of the man's unique sense of trust and confidence. As suggested above,
the science of the *siddhi*s grounded in the power of yogic imagination
is also a tangible source of Gandhi's experience. Still, we must note that
Gandhi himself, due perhaps to his profound exposure to Western ideals
and ideological commitments, sees in morality the feature exclusively
predominant in his interpretation of power (in particular the force of
ahiṃsā). See, for example, his use of the notion of (Christian) suffering
implied by the exercise of *tapas*:

---

[15] Raghavan N. Iyer, *The Moral and Political Thought of Mahatma Gandhi* (repr. ed., New
Delhi: Oxford University Press, 2007), 64. [Editor's note: The 'celebrated episode' in the
Mahabharata of which Gandhi speaks is found in the *Vana Parva* ['Forest Book'], chs. 27–33;
this particular portion is often referred to as the 'Vyadha Gita' (the teachings of the butcher), and
takes its name after Dharmavyadha (the 'righteous butcher'), who earns an honest living in the
city of Mithila as a butcher. It is from Dharmavyadha that the sage Kaushik learns the meaning
of *swadharma* or the importance of performing the duties that have been assigned to one; he
also comes to an awareness that even the slightest work, or work that is considered filthy, has
value if performed in the right spirit. This is clearly the episode that Gandhi had in mind, though
he misidentifies Kaushik as the butcher rather than the arrogant sage that he is before he is hum-
bled by a butcher. The story also appears in a slightly modified form in the *Bhagavata Purana*
(11.12.3–6).]

[16] Iyer, *The Moral and Political Thought of Mahātmā Gandhi*, 64 (citing Gandhi, *Ethical
Religion*, Ganesan, Madras: 1922: 40–43).

[17] D. Shulman associates such a feeling of elation generated by doing what is inherently good
in itself (not instrumental to anything else) with freedom (unpublished manuscript).

Real suffering bravely borne melts even the heart of a stone. Such is the potency of suffering or *tapas*. And there lies the key to *Satyāgraha*.[18]

Like Gandhi, writers on Gandhi's life and thought emphasize almost invariably his moral, even saintly, character as the key to the meaning of his life:

> Mahātmā Gandhi was no Christian, and the Christians were amazed that this should be so, for never in modern times had they seen any man tread more faithfully in the footsteps of Christ.[19]

Nevertheless, Gandhi, however absorbed in his self-understanding as a predominantly moral agent, was also conscious of his indebtedness to Patañjali's 'prescriptions' (*yama*s and *niyama*s): 'In my talks with hundreds of men here I place the various *yama*s above everything else.'[20] In a letter to Narandas Gandhi (May 1933) Gandhi says that '(Patañjali's) *Yoga-sūtras* seems wonderful to me. I do not understand its later portion. But it seems likely that every aphorism of his is based on long experience.' On another occasion he writes:

> Our seers and sages of old said that one must have an inner ear to hear the inner voice, that one must have the inner eye, and must cultivate self-control to acquire these. Hence in Patañjali's treatise on *yoga* the first step prescribed for the student of *yoga*, for one aspiring after self-realization is the observance of the disciplines of *yama-niyama*.[21]

Scholars who recognize Gandhi's obvious indebtedness to the discipline of *yoga* and its related forces tend to associate his *yoga*-being with morality:

---

[18] M. K. Gandhi, *Satyāgraha in South Africa* (Ahmedabad: Navajivan, 1928), 40.

[19] R. C. Zaehner, *Hinduism* (London: Oxford University Press, 1962), 170.

[20] Letter to Maganlal Gandhi [After March 14, 1915], *The Collected Works of Mahatma Gandhi* (Electronic Book) [hereafter *CWMG*], New Delhi: Publications Division Government of India, 1999, vol. 14: 383.

[21] Speech on Birth Centenary of Tolstoy [September 10, 1928], *CWMG*, vol. 43: 11.

As early as 1903 he studied Patañjali's Yoga-sūtra. No Indian before him had made this book the basis of the ethical discipline of people engaged in politics and social work as Gandhi did in the Satyāgrahāśram at Sabarmati.[22]

The majority of scholars identify Gandhi's yogic accomplishment with the *yoga* of the *Bhagavad-gītā*, essentially viewed as *yoga* of action. Thus, for example, one of Gandhi's most well-known biographers contemporary to him, Louis Fischer, writes:

> Gandhi did, however, achieve the status of yogi. A yogi may be a man of contemplation, or he may be a man of action. Both yogi and commissar may devote their lives to action. The difference between them is in the quality and purpose of their lives.[23]

However indebted to the spiritual yoga of the *Bhagavad-gītā*, Gandhi shared with the *yogin*s of old the most elementary experience, consequent upon the practice of yogic postures (*āsana*) of *Haṭha-yoga*. His correspondence with Swami Kuvalayānanda (1927) offers a glimpse into his thorough acquaintance with the practice and principles of classical *yoga*. See, for example, his letter of 8 June 1927:

> The *prāṇa-yama* causes no difficulty, and as a rule, I take all the deep breath without a break. I did not notice the effects you ascribed to *śavāsana*. May it not be that the prescribed period is too short, that is two minutes? I did feel refreshed when I used to lie flat on my back for nearly 15 minutes. Nor did I notice any positive effect of *sarvāṅgāsana*. Would you advise increasing the angle or increasing the period for the pose at the present angle?[24]

Nine days later (17 June 1927) Gandhi reports to Swami Kuvalayānanda on further experiments with yogic postures:

---

[22]   Iyer, *The Moral and Political Thought of Mahātmā Gandhi*, 9.
[23]   L. Fischer, *The Life of Mahātmā Gandhi* (repr. ed., New Delhi: HarperCollins, 2006), 52.
[24]   I am indebted to Tamar Bental for informing me of Gandhi's yogic practices.

I have told you that in the physical application of these exercises, I propose to go by faith in you. Whilst I present my doubts to you so long as
I do not understand your explanations, they shall be final for me.

I want to give the practice of these yogic exercises a full trial, if only
because I regard them of all the methods of medical treatment to be the
freest from danger.

After I wrote my letter of the 8th, I took a forward step which I hope
you would not consider hasty. On re-reading your notes, I saw that you
expected me to go up to 30 degrees angle. So, after writing to you, I immediately broadened the angle but limited the duration to five minutes
in accordance with the instructions. But I have my own doubts as to the
angle being 30, because I have not yet secured an accurate measuring
instrument. Not being satisfied with the raising of the cot, I looked
about for a plank which I have now secured. The cot has a wooden
surface. I spread on it not a mattress but a padded rug, and I take the
sarvāngasan on it with the help of the board. It is now infinitely better
than the previous exercises.

The practice of classical (*Pātañjala*) *yoga* consists of many kinds and
dimensions other than the postures and breathing techniques. For the
sages and commentators of old, concentration of mind is of primary importance. *Yoga* is absorption (*yogaḥ samādhiḥ*), says Vyāsa.[25] Gandhi
points creatively to fresh connections between various aspects implied
by Patañjali in the *Yoga Sūtra*. See, for example, the connection he makes
between concentration of mind and *brahmacarya*:

Wandering thoughts can never be a stage in spiritual development.
They do trouble most of us; hence the usual emphasis laid on mental
concentration. What we have to bear in mind is this. We think a multitude of thoughts which involve a waste of energy even as sensuality
results in the waste of vital energy. Just as physical debility affects the
mind, so also mental debility affects the body. Therefore, I understand
brahmacarya in a comprehensive sense and look upon aimless thinking
as a breach of it. We have made *brahmacarya* difficult to achieve by

---

[25] *Yoga Sūtra Bhāṣya, i.e., Vyāsa's commentary* 1.2. Translations from the original Sanskrit are
mine. The text in Sanskrit follows Aranya, *Yoga Philosophy of Patanjali.*

212 GANDHI, TRUTH, AND NONVIOLENCE

understanding it in a narrow sense. But if we accept the broader definition and try to restrain all the eleven organs of sense, the control of
animal passion becomes comparatively very much easier.[26]

Indeed, various types of concentration and meditation are closely associated with the production of the *siddhi*s, supranormal attainments.
However, Gandhi was also somewhat reserved with respect to the significance and meaning of yogic practice. On the one hand, as suggested
above, he thought highly of certain aspects of Pātañjala-*Yoga* (including
concentration and meditation). According to our exposition above, he
was familiar not only with yogic postures and breathing control but
also with the kernel of the science of the so-called supranormal powers,
namely, the inherent connectedness of yogic practice with its results
(connectedness implied by the *siddhi*-character of *ahiṃsā*). However, in
a talk on the sixth chapter of the *Bhagavad-gītā* (16 December 1930), he
explicitly denigrates the *siddhi*s ('miracles'):

> *Prāṇa-yama* (control of breath) and *āsana*s (yogic postures) are re-
> ferred to appreciatively in this chapter, but we should remember that
> at the same time the Lord has stressed the need for *brahmacarya*, i.e.
> keeping the observances calculated to take us nearer and nearer to
> God. It should be clearly understood that the mere practice of *āsana*s
> and the like can never take us to the goal of even-mindedness. *Āsana*s
> and *Prāṇa-yama* may be of some slight help in steadying the mind
> and making it single-purposed, provided that they are practiced to
> that end. Otherwise they are no better than other methods of physical
> training. They are very useful indeed as physical exercise and I believe
> that this type of exercise is good for the soul, and may be performed
> from a bodily standpoint. But I have observed that these practices do
> only harm when indulged in for the acquisition of supernormal powers
> (*siddhi*) and the performance of miracles.

Denigration of the so-called miracles or supranormal powers consequent
upon the practice of *yoga* (according to Patañjali's *Yoga Sūtra*) is also
common among scholarly works relating to the *YS*. For example, such

---

[26] *Selected Works of Mahatma Gandhi*, 452.

*siddhi*s, says Max Müller, are 'of interest for the pathologist' (rather than for philosophers). The *siddhi*s are invariably referred to as dangerous temptations of utterly inferior quality.[27] Scholars such as Mircea Eliade, Jean Varenne, and many others warn of the dangers involved in the alleged production of the 'powers'. The *siddhi*s are thus often considered to be obstacles on the way to true liberation and knowledge and so are to be avoided by all means.[28]

Gandhi was aware, as suggested above, of the general negative attitude towards the so-called miracles of *yoga*.[29] Along with his truly yogic being, he was a practical, down-to-earth, as it were, observer of human behaviour, folly, and self-deception. And yet, an intense level of *yoga*-being such as Gandhi's could generate, even without awareness, a sense of omnipotence such as expressed in his conception of unfailing *ahiṃsā*.

Perhaps the most conspicuous expression of Gandhi's yogic fearlessness and self-confidence is his attitude towards death, particularly his own death. Fear, overcoming of fear, and fearlessness are concepts of major preoccupation of Gandhi's. Hundreds of references to the notion of fear in its relationship with morality, love, nonviolence, true knowledge of self (*ātman*), and so forth are spread throughout his writings and speech. Fearlessness has become for Gandhi inherently associated with the most important notions of his self-understanding, namely, *ahiṃsā* and *satyāgraha*. See, for example, R. N. Iyer's succinct gloss over this matter:

Virtue must be based on *virya*, the dauntless energy that fights its way to the supernal truth out of the mire of terrestrial lies. Gandhi pointed out that if you want to follow the vow of truth in any shape or form, fearlessness is the necessary consequence. 'And so you find, in the *Bhagavad Gita*, fearlessness is declared as the first essential quality of a Brahmin.' We fear consequences and therefore, we are afraid to tell

---

[27] For a description of the invariable attitude of denigration towards the miracles (*siddhi*), see my *Silence Unheard: Deathly Otherness in Pātañjala-Yoga* (Albany, NY: SUNY Press, 2002).

[28] Some scholars emphasize the importance of *YS* 3.37 as a token of Patañjali's own negative attitude towards the 'attainments'. *YS* 3.37: 'These experiences are obstacles in the condition of *samādhi*, but achievements in the condition of outgoing orientation' (*te samādhav upasargā vyutthāne siddhayaḥ*).

[29] We, on the other hand, consider the *siddhi*s as the very heart of Yoga—pristine expressions of yogic imagination and reality.

the truth. A man who has overcome attachment will certainly not fear earthly consequences. 'The trouble is that we often die many times before death overtakes us.' Above all, to Gandhi, 'where there is fear there is no religion.'[30] ... The vow of truth cannot be taken properly without also taking the vow of fearlessness.[31]

Indeed, fearlessness in Gandhi's self-understanding is associated with his central vocabulary, such as *ahiṃsā, satya, brahmacarya,* vow (*vrata*), and so forth. Adequate reflection on notions associated with fear and fearlessness is beyond the scope of this paper. However, one component inherently related to our concept of yogic fearlessness and self-confidence is worthy of closer attention. It is, as suggested above, the fear of death, apparently the primordial fear in man's and woman's life. I refer to Gandhi's fearlessness (also self-confidence) as inherently yogic in its nature and source. Indeed, in my view, Gandhi is a most eloquent interpreter of one of Patañjali's more important *sūtra*s, YS 2.9, which deals with the unending desire for life (and the fear of death).

In Patañjali's *Yoga Sūtra* the fear of death is one of the 'sources of sorrow' (*kleśa*) in everybody's life. The importance of overcoming the fear of death is conspicuous by its inclusion among the five *kleśa*s enumerated in YS 2.3: misrepresentation of reality ('ignorance', *avidyā*), a sense of egocentricity (*asmitā*), attachment (*rāga*), aversion (*dveṣa*), and the desire to live on and on (*abhiniveśa*). These are the sources of sorrow in Patañjali's *Kriyā-yoga* expounded in YS 2.1–2.9. YS 2.9 asserts that the wish for life goes on and on by its own potency and underlies the experience of the wise and the fool. Vyāsa's interpretation of *abhiniveśa*, namely, the desire to live on and on, is noteworthy. He sees this omnipresent desire as 'fear of dying' (*maraṇa-trāsa*). Even a worm just born is afraid of death. And why is this so? Vyāsa suggests that the experience of death is inherently unpleasant. There is misery and suffering in death (*maraṇa-duḥkha*). Men and women like every living creature preserve memories of previous deaths. Thus, in the aversion towards the re-enactment of

---

[30] Iyer, *Moral and Political Thought of Mahatma Gandhi*, 138.
[31] Ibid., 164.

such unpleasant experiences, the wise and the fool, the worm and the tiger are afraid of dying. Vācaspati Miśra integrates Patañjali's reference to *abhiniveśa* as going on and on by its own potency (*sva-rasa-vahi*), with Vyāsa's interpretation of the desire to live as fear of death (*maraṇa-trāsa*). The root of fear of death is aversion (*dveṣa*) (*dveṣa-mūlakatayā dveṣāya paścād abhiniveśaṃ lakṣayati*), which continues endlessly by the force of subliminal impressions (*saṃskāra-matrena*).

Keeping in mind Patañjali's insistence on yogic fearlessness in its association with true knowledge, overcoming the fear of death has been a preoccupation of Gandhi's throughout his life. Engaged in the British war against the Zulus, Gandhi writes to his brother Lakshmidas (on 27 May 1906) about the possibility of dying: 'If I have to face death while thus engaged, I shall face it with equanimity. I am now a stranger to fear.' In the wake of his return to India after a twenty-year career in South Africa Gandhi seems to be acutely aware of possible death. In a cable to G. K. Gokhale (26 December 1913), he says:

No man can hasten or delay my death even by a minute. The best way of saving oneself from death is to go seeking it. It is no doubt our duty to take care of our life in a general way. More than this we need not do. We should rather welcome death whenever it comes.[32]

By March 1914, a few months before his final return to India, Gandhi seems to start thinking hard about death and related anxieties. On 1 March, he reflects on the fear of death in a somewhat abstract manner:

Death should make us think of our duty and fill us with contempt for the body, but inspire no fear. It seems that a man does not suffer excessively even when he is burnt to death. When the pain becomes unbearable, he loses consciousness. Those who cling to the body so very tenaciously only suffer the more. One who knows the truth about the *ātman* will have no fear of death.[33]

---

[32] *Selected Works of Mahatma Gandhi*, 455.
[33] Ibid., 453–4.

Six days later (7 March), Gandhi confesses in a much more personal vein:

> I have not got rid of the fear of death, despite much thinking. But I feel no impatience. I keep on trying and I am sure I shall get rid of it one day. We should not let go a single occasion when we may try. That is our duty. It is for god to produce or will the result. Why worry then? When feeding her baby, the mother has no thought of the result. The result does follow, though. To get rid of the fear of death and to drive away desire, make the effort and keep cheerful; and they will disappear. Otherwise, it will be the same with you as with the man who, resolving not to think about a monkey, kept on thinking of one.[34]

As mentioned above, Patañjali insists on the importance of 'ignorance' in the emergence of the kleśas such as abhiniveśa. Dualist metaphysics (of the abysmal, irreducible difference of the pure subject, puruṣa, from objectivity, prakṛti), which is 'knowledge' in Pātañjala-Yoga terminology, is not identical with Gandhi's eclectic philosophical vision of the one self (ātman) and its freedom (mokṣa). However, the separation of the true self from the body and other entities such as relatives, and the like—the essential spirit of Pātañjala-Yoga—is tangibly present in Gandhi's reflection on the source of his fearlessness of death.

> Death as such leaves little impression on me; I only feel for the bereaved relatives. There can be no greater ignorance than to mourn over death.[35]

Indeed, Gandhi's association of fear of death with ignorance is clear-cut. The impact of the Bhagavad-gītā in this regard is obvious, as the following example illustrates:

> To be afraid of death is like being afraid of discarding an old and worn out garment. I have often thought of death and have the intellectual conviction that it is sheer ignorance which makes us afraid of death.[36]

---

[34] Ibid., 454.
[35] The Diary of Mahadev Desai, vol. 1: 213 (5 July 1932), in Selected Works of Mahatma Gandhi, 456.
[36] Selected Works of Mahatma Gandhi, 459.

As suggested above, Gandhi's perspective of death and the afterlife, nourished by the teaching of the *Bhagavad-gītā*, is eclectic and is not precisely of *Pātañjala-Yoga* metaphysics. However, the spirit of separation (*viveka*) central to the dualist tradition is inherent in dozens (if not hundreds) of Gandhi's statements displaying an awareness of the meaning of death.

> To wish to see the dearest ones as long as possible in the flesh is a selfish desire and it comes out of weakness or want of faith in the survival of the soul after the dissolution of the body. The form ever changes, ever perishes, the informing spirit neither changes nor perishes. True love consists in transferring itself from the body to the dweller within and then necessarily realizing the oneness of all life inhabiting numberless bodies.[37]

In the reference to ignorance as the root of fear of death Gandhi touches upon a major principle of *Pātañjala-Yoga*, a principle pertinent to the sources of sorrow (*kleśas*), among which, as stated above, the wish to live on and on (*abhiniveśa*) is the fifth. Ignorance (*avidyā*) is the ground (*kṣetra*) from which the four other *kleśas* (ego-sense, attachment, aversion, fear of death) emerge.[38]

Integration of spiritual vision and daily experience in life had been a lifelong interest of Gandhi's. His perception of death and its meaning within one's actual realization and behaviour is no exception, as the following examples so amply suggest:

> We are born only to die and we die only to be born again. This is all old argument. Yet it needs to be driven home. Somehow or other we refuse to welcome death as we welcome birth. We refuse to believe even the evidence of our senses, that we could not possibly have any attachment for the body without the soul and that we have no evidence whatsoever that the soul perishes with the body.[39]

I have personally ceased for years to grieve over death at all. The shock is felt when a comrade is torn away from me, but that is purely

---

[37] Bapu's letters to Mira, 156 (6 July 1931), in *Selected Works of Mahatma Gandhi*, 456.

[38] *YS* 2.4: Ignorance is the ground from which all the other sources of sorrow grow, whether dormant, weakened, interrupted, or aroused (*avidya ksetram utaresam prasupta-tanu-vicchinodaranam*).

[39] Bapu's letters to Mira, 260 (4 May 1933), in *Selected Works of Mahatma Gandhi*, 458.

due to personal attachment which in other words is selfishness. But I immediately recover and realize that death is a deliverance and has to be welcomed, even as a friend is welcomed, and that it means dissolution of the body, not of the indwelling spirit.[40]

Death is an event to be celebrated and much more so than birth. For birth is preceded by nine months of life in a solitary cell and is also followed by much unhappiness. But death for some of us spells the attainment of the end of life. To qualify for such a death one should devote one's life to work done in the spirit of detachment.[41]

'Death is but a sleep and a forgetting'. This is such a sweet sleep that the body has not to awake again, and the dead load of memory is thrown overboard.[42]

Many people, men and women, were courageous, unflinching in the face of rivalry and death. Why call fearlessness of death yogic? In my view, Gandhi's yogic fearlessness is of its own hue and flavour. It is rooted in yogic detachment and separation of spirit and body, in yogic practice of postures and breathing exercises, of the value of vows, and staunch faith in the *siddhi*-character of *ahiṃsā* and *satyāgraha*.

And yet, above all, as a matter of course, Gandhi saw himself as a moral agent. However, given Gandhi's yogic style of life inherent in his overt exercise of detachment, austerity, *brahmacarya*, non-possessiveness, conviction of the power inherent in vows (*vrata*), and so forth—also his verbal acknowledgement of a measure of affiliation with *Pātañjala-Yoga* (in particular the *yama*s and *niyama*s)—his complexity of mind and spirit seems to defy simple answers to our preliminary questions. Was Gandhi a saintly person, trusting the victory of goodness over evil? Or does Gandhi's optimism rest upon the discovery of the miraculous, omnipotent force of *yoga*, which is, in a sense *neither good nor evil*?[43]

Now, we cannot disregard Gandhi's own self-understanding as a moral agent. At times he seems, as R. C. Zaehner says, a Christ-like saint. And yet, there is much explanatory power in assuming another source of his

---

[40] *Selected Works of Mahatma Gandhi*, 458.
[41] Ibid., 459.
[42] Ibid.
[43] One recalls in this context *YS* 4.7: The *yogin*'s *karma* is neither white nor black; others' *karma* is of three kinds (*karmāśuklākṛṣṇaṃ yoginas trividham itareṣām*).

exceptional self-confidence. Indeed, although apparently very successful in exercising *ahiṃsā* and *satyāgraha*, being an allegedly promising object of true following and simulation, Gandhi was strictly speaking unique; there is no following to his mode of action, trust, and confidence in times of acute crisis. Roaming in devastated areas of Bengal for about four months (November 1946 to March 1947), present in burning Delhi in the months after independence, he considers himself capable of soothing violence of enormous proportions. Thus, Gandhi's uniqueness implies a measure of inaccessibility. In my view, the inaccessible dimension of Gandhi's life and experience is embedded in the emergence of the *siddhi*-imagination recorded in Patañjali's *Yoga Sūtra*. The fruit, as Patañjali says, resides in the action (*YS* 2.36; see above). In the presence of a *yogin* fully committed to, and successful in unwillingness to injure any being, every type of harmful behaviour ceases (*YS* 2.35; see above). Even the cat and the mouse forgo their so-called natural enmity, as Vācaspati says. Such flavours of omnipotent *satya* and *ahiṃsā* are present in Gandhi's reflection on his life and strategies of conflict resolution. Although an exponent of the forces inherent in saintly, moral behaviour, he was in addition a sorcerer of peace whose undeniably exceptional self-confidence is rooted in the feelings of the old emasculated *yogin*s, those human beings free of the fear of enmity and death.

Considering the course of events in history (in particular the course of the last hundred years), one wonders whether Gandhi-like *yogin*s are not strictly necessary for the survival of our race. Pending other Gandhis whose power of creative imagination emerges from the excruciating discipline of *yoga*, humanity seems on the verge of doom.

9

Gandhi, the Indian National Congress, and the Jewish Question

Vinay Lal

The Indian National Congress was, for decades before the onset of World War II in 1939, the premier nationalist organization in India, one whose structure, mobilization strategies, and modes of resistance to colonial rule would be much studied and even emulated by nationalist movements elsewhere in the world, especially in Africa. Many of its leading figures, similarly, were often men—and not a few women, though this is not often recognized—with substantial experience of the world, a broad international outlook, and, not surprisingly, a considerable sensitivity to questions of colonialism, racism, and the possibilities of a world order which might allow for the redressal of grave global inequities.[1] Mohandas Gandhi, the supreme voice of the Congress for well over two decades, from around 1920 to the mid-1940s, was in his own lifetime recognized as a world historical figure, even if his detractors were legion and opposition to his ideas was widespread among various constituencies, among them Marxists, exponents of Hindu supremacy, and those nationalists who were styled 'armed revolutionaries'. Notwithstanding Gandhi's deep

---

[1] The woman most often cited as an illustration of Indian women's involvement in the freedom struggle and her international outlook is Sarojini Naidu. But one might with equal if not more justification summon Kamaladevi Chattopadhyay, whose lifespan extends across most of the twentieth century. Kamaladevi had an extraordinary engagement with socialist and feminist circles over several decades, well before the war and in the aftermath, and she played an important role in the UN Human Rights Commission; in independent India, she occupied a formidable place in the public sphere, in ways far too numerous to enumerate here. In introducing her memoirs, *Inner Recesses, Outer Spaces* (1985; repr. ed., New Delhi: Niyogi Books, 2014), the eminent writer Raja Rao described her as 'firmly Indian and therefore universal', 'perhaps the most august woman on the Indian scene today' (ix). For a comprehensive selection of her writings and assessment of her life, see Ellen Carol DuBois and Vinay Lal, *A Passionate Life: Writings By and On Kamaladevi Chattopadhyay* (Delhi: Zubaan Books, 2017).

Vinay Lal, *Gandhi, the Indian National Congress, and the Jewish Question* In: *Gandhi, Truth, and Nonviolence*. Edited by: Vinay Lal, Oxford University Press. © Oxford University Press 2025.
DOI: 10.1093/9780198936657.003.0010

immersion in Indian affairs, and the enormous responsibilities that he bore not only as the leader of the anti-colonial struggle but as the principal instigator of a vast programme of social change, he still found it possible to keep abreast of world events. Among his principal associates, Jawaharlal Nehru had long worked to forge links to progressive and anti-imperialist organizations around the world, and he strongly believed that a free India would be a force for good in international politics. 'Though India's voice may be powerless today,' he told an interviewer in August 1945, 'it will not be so in the future. I hope whatever influence India comes to possess will be used to evolve more stable conditions of world peace and freedom.'[2] Subhas Chandra Bose, who rivalled Gandhi in his popularity with Indian masses at one time and rose to the presidency of the Congress, was equally well versed in world politics and was likewise moved by the thought that an independent India would surely play a role in ushering in a world relatively free of the familiar oppressions of colonialism—even if he allowed himself to be led astray by a different school of thought, one which recognized that one might usefully enter into a friendly partnership with the enemy of one's enemy.

In the late 1930s, even as the Congress declared itself neutral in the conflict that would soon consume Europe, North Africa, and much of Asia, stating—if not to the satisfaction of everyone—that though India sympathized with the struggle of democratic nations against fascism, it could not commit to the support of imperialist nations whose own conduct frequently bordered on sheer brutality and naked aggression, another vital question had come to the fore in Europe. The long history of anti-Semitism in Europe was the backdrop to, even if it did not prefigure, the ferocious persecution to which Jews would be subjected in Germany after the assumption of power by the Nazis and Hitler's consolidation of his leadership of a thuggish political party that would eventually commit itself to the project known as the 'Final Solution'. The first laws in 1933 under the new regime of despotism banned Jews from government service, law practice, and the pursuit of a medical career. Dachau came into existence.[3]

---

[2] *The Tribune*, 6 August 1945, cited by Ravinder Kumar, 'Jawaharlal Nehru, The Indian National Congress and the Anti-Fascist Struggle (1939–45)', *Indian Historical Review* 97.

[3] For a succinct chronological outline of, and sourcebook on, the road to the Holocaust, including the passage of anti-Semitic legislation, see Ronnie S. Landau, *Studying the Holocaust: Issues, Readings and Documents* (London: Routledge, 1998).

Two years later, the Nuremberg Laws stripped Jews of their citizenship, an entitlement which they had gained only in 1871, and so banished Jews in Germany from sharing a conception of civic life; and later that year, on 14 November, a law was passed forbidding sexual contact between Jews and non-Jews. Between 1936 and 1938, Jews were gradually stripped of their remaining rights and eliminated from the public sphere, culminating in the seizure of their properties and the terror of the night of shattered glass, *Kristallnacht*, that unmistakably signified the launch of the Nazi annihilationist project and the fulfilment of the dream for expansion, what was indeed sold to Germans as 'breathing space', encapsulated in the term *Lebensraum*. On the night of 9–10 November 1938, SA storm troopers, often ably assisted by civilians, went on an unchecked rampage in Nazi Germany and portions of Austria, setting fire to Jewish homes, businesses, and synagogues, looting shops and killing at will. What is quite distinct about *Kristallnacht*, however, in comparison with later German atrocities, is that the events of this night were at once widely reported throughout the world. 'No foreign propagandist bent upon blackening Germany before the world', the London *Times* commented on 11 November, 'could outdo the tale of burning and beatings, of blackguardly assaults on defenceless and innocent people, which disgraced that country yesterday.'[4]

It is quite likely that Gandhi, ensconced in his ashram in central India at a great remove from Delhi, Calcutta, and Madras, not to mention London or Berlin, had nevertheless read about the events in Germany in the news-papers with which he kept abreast of 'news'. This would seem to be suggested by the fact that on 26 November he published, in the pages of his journal *Harijan*, what would be his most thoughtful and emphatic pronouncement on the Jewish Question—a piece quite simply entitled 'The Jews'.[5] Some scholars have argued that Gandhi was singularly ill-informed about the world's affairs, and even biographers who are favourably disposed towards

[4] 'A Black Day for Germany', *The Times* (11 November 1938).
[5] M. K. Gandhi, 'The Jews', *Harijan* (26 November 1938), in *Collected Works of Mahatma Gandhi* [hereafter cited as *CWMG*] (New Delhi: Government of India, Ministry of Information and Broadcasting, 1952-), 74: 239–42, online at http://www.gandhiashramsevagram.org/gandhi-literature/mahatma-gandhi-collected-works-volume-74.pdf [accessed 17 October 2021]. The online edition replicates the revised or, rather, tampered edition, not the original print edition; but the history of the sordid story behind attempts to tamper with the most authoritative edition of Gandhi's writings does not concern us at present. The original date of publication allows one to search the original print edition as well.

Gandhi have sometimes adopted the view that he was 'not exempt' among the peacemakers and liberals in the 1930s who had 'suffered a loss of contact with reality'. Geoffrey Ashe continues in this vein, averring that Gandhi's 'faith in nonviolence had to endure the test of Fascist aggression, and in that context it rang hollow'.[6] Robert Payne, in his appreciative and thoughtful biography, is equally clear that Gandhi 'had no conception of the menace which Hitler presented to the world', but his critique is more expansive in that he thinks that 'concerning events which took place outside India, South Africa, or England, he would often make judgments which were completely absurd'.[7] Certainly, Gandhi's knowledge of world affairs seems to be put into serious question when we consider that, in May 1940 in a letter addressed to his friend Rajkumari Amrit Kaur, he gave it as his opinion that Hitler did not seem 'to be as bad as depicted. He is showing an ability that is amazing and he seems to be gaining his victories without much bloodshed'.[8]

We need not here be detained at any length by various exculpatory observations—if at all, as many would submit, one can think of any, and none would strike most commentators as even remotely feasible or persuasive. But it is perhaps not impertinent to mention that Gandhi was far from being the only one who was led astray, if that is what happened, in his assessment of Hitler and the threat that he posed to the world. Churchill himself 'had had kind words too for Hitler and Mussolini in the 1930s',[9] and surely one can say that Churchill, said to have a command of world politics and later lionized as the architect of Germany's defeat and the saviour of England and even world democracy, should reasonably be expected to have had greater insights into Hitler than someone such as Gandhi who was far removed from the history of inter-European

---

[6] Geoffrey Ashe, *Gandhi* (New York: Stein & Day, 1969), 340.

[7] Robert Payne, *The Life and Death of Mahatma Gandhi* (New York: Smithmark, 1995 [1969]), 485.

[8] Letter from Sevagram, Wardha, to Rajkumari Amrit Kaur, 15 May 1940, in *CWMG* 78: 218, online at http://www.gandhiashramsevagram.org/gandhi-literature/mahatma-gandhi-collec ted-works-volume-78.pdf [accessed 21 October 2021]. Though the Israeli Jewish writer Norman G. Finkelstein, who is also known for his unflinching critique of Zionism, has advocated for Gandhi and principled nonviolent resistance, he is certain that 'on many counts Gandhi's diagnosis and prognosis appear wanting'. He argues that Gandhi remained 'unrepentant' in his persistent belief both that 'nonviolent resistance could not produce inferior results to violent resistance' and that the Allies in World War II had only triumphed by 'out-Hitlering Hitler' (see his *What Gandhi Says: About Nonviolence, Resistance and Courage* [New York and London: OR Books, 2012], 31).

[9] Martin Greenberg, 'Churchill Revisited: Greatest of Leaders', *Sewanee Review* 119, no. 4 (Fall 2011), 614.

affairs and conflicts. 'One may dislike Hitler's system', to quote none other than Churchill, the vanquisher of totalitarianism and the supreme hero of many cherished fables about liberty, 'and yet admire his patriotic achievement. If our country were defeated, I hope we should find a champion as indomitable to restore our courage and lead us back to our place among the nations.'[10] Gandhi's faint strictures about Hitler in 1940 seem quite benign beside the approbation with which Churchill could speak of Hitler as a 'champion' with 'indomitable' courage and will. One of the 'arch-appeasers of Hitler's increasingly bellicose expansionism' was none other than Lord Halifax,[11] who flew to Germany to meet with Hitler in November 1937 and, in an earlier incarnation as Lord Irwin, had seriously misjudged Gandhi when the latter had written to him declaring his intention to march to the sea to initiate mass nonviolent resistance to British rule.[12] Let me aver again that Gandhi's critics might usefully be reminded, though I suspect to no avail, that his assessment

[10]   Winston S. Churchill, 'Friendship with Germany', *Evening Standard* (17 September 1937). A year later, just days before *Kristallnacht*, Churchill responded in Parliament to an attack by Hitler in the Reichstag upon him as a 'warmonger' with the remark that 'I have always said that if Great Britain were defeated in war I hoped we should find a Hitler to lead us back to our rightful position among the nations. I am sorry, however, that he has not been mellowed by the great success that has attended him. The whole world would rejoice to see the Hitler of peace and tolerance . . . Let this great man search his own heart and conscience before he accused anyone of being a warmonger.' See 'Mr Churchill's Reply', *The Times* (7 November 1938). Churchill's article of 17 September 1937 is, as should be obvious, by no means an anomaly. No amount of subterfuge or dissimulation can obfuscate the fact that Churchill and Hitler, however acute their differences and the adversarial positions they would come to occupy in World War II, were also united by a number of considerations, none more germane for the present discussion than their absolute contempt for what used to be called 'the coloured races'. The argument that Churchill's vindictive racism, and disdain for Indians and more particularly for Gandhi, should be seen as bordering on the genocidal has been advanced in a number of recent studies, among them Madhusree Mukerjee, *Churchill's Secret War: The British Empire and the Ravaging of India during World War II* (New York: Basic Books, 2010). Mukerjee has been attacked by Churchill's acolytes, but Roy Jenkins's highly acclaimed biography *Churchill* (London: Pan Books, 2003) agrees with the substance of the view that he subscribed to a hierarchy of races and was, by inclination and temperament, an imperialist and a monarchist.

[11]   David Arnold, *Gandhi: Profiles in Power* (London: Longman/Pearson Education, 2001), 152.

[12]   M. K. Gandhi, Letter to Lord Irwin, 2 March 1930, in *CWMG* 48: 362–7, online at http://www.gandhiashramsevagram.org/gandhi-literature/mahatma-gandhi-collected-works-volume-48.pdf; also in M. K. Gandhi, *Colonialism and the Call to Freedom*, ed. Vinay Lal, Asian Thinkers Series No. 1 (Penang: Multiversity & Citizens International, 2011), 54–63. The American journalist William L. Shirer, who covered Gandhi's Salt March and came to forge a personal relationship with him, wrote many years later that Irwin 'never quite grasped the revolutionary character of Gandhi nor of the revolutionary force which the Mahatma was marshaling to bring an end to British rule. Later, as Foreign Secretary, he showed an even more appalling ignorance of the revolutionary character of Adolf Hitler and of the forces of destruction which the Nazi dictator was unleashing in Europe towards the end of the 1930's.' See *Gandhi: A Memoir* (New York: Simon & Schuster, 1979), 70.

of 1940, written as a virtual outsider to European affairs, seems unquestionably tame in comparison with the lavish encomiums heaped upon Hitler by his European adversaries. But much else comes to mind: for instance, Gandhi would only have had to consider the supine surrender of the French, and the swiftness with which the Wehrmacht had been able to run over Poland, Norway, Denmark, and the Low Countries by May 1940, to conclude that Hitler 'is showing an ability that is amazing and he seems to be gaining his victories without much bloodshed'. His letter to Rajkumari Amrit Kaur of mid-May 1940, moreover, was written at a time when the Nazi death camp as such was at the planning stage and had not yet come into operation. It was not the Jews alone who had no foreboding of the gargantuan killing machine that the Germans were soon to put into place. Barely anyone in the Western world had any premonition of the Holocaust, even if there were many who were committed to the proposition that German militarism had to be decisively defeated.

There is also the consideration that, contrary to the view that I have thus far entertained of Gandhi as someone who was ignorant of world affairs and utterly naïve in his estimation of what Hitler and National Socialism stood for, there is much to suggest that he was surprisingly well informed about what was transpiring in Europe, the course of Western history, and the nature of anti-imperialist struggles in Asia and Africa. He spoke approvingly, for example, of the Riff tribesmen in Morocco who had waged a war of resistance against French and Spanish forces,[13] and similarly in 1931, on his way to London to attend the Round Table Conference, he expressed solidarity with Egyptian Wafdists in their aspiration for sovereignty.[14] By his own admission, he had little bookish knowledge of Bolshevism, and not until his detention for two years in the Aga Khan Palace after the launch of the 'Quit India' movement did

[13] See *Young India*, 17 February 1925.

[14] See also Yunan Labib Rizk, 'Gandhi in Egypt', *Al Ahram Weekly* 716 (19–25 December 2002). The lengthiest treatment of this subject is Anil Nauriya, 'Soundings in Kindred Struggles: The Egyptian Voice in Gandhi', *Identité, Culture et Politique* 12, no. 2 (December 2011), online at https://www.scribd.com/document/98485964/Soundings-in-Kindred-Struggles-The-Egyptian-Voice-in-Gandhi [accessed 21 October 2021]. 'British statesmanship', an Indian scholar has written, 'was never challenged by circumstances so openly, so aggressively as in the thirties of this century. How did it work out? Appeasement for Hitler and Mussolini, no appeasement for [Saad] Zaghlul [*sic*] and Gandhi, not even moderate concession.' See Nikshoy C. Chatterji, *Muddle of the Middle East* (New Delhi: Abhinav Publications, 1973), 348. Zaghloul was an Egyptian revolutionary who led the Wafd Party.

he finally read Marx and Lenin.[15] Nevertheless, what is striking is that Gandhi had an awareness of the enormous excesses of Stalinism long before most liberals and Marxists in the West could be brought to an acknowledgement of the totalitarian violence of Soviet communism. Gandhi never did visit the United States, but he carried on an extensive correspondence with an astonishing array of Americans. His knowledge of what is ordinarily understood by 'world affairs' cannot consequently be judged by his scholarly reading, nor can it be cavalierly dismissed as insignificant.

Gandhi's statement of 26 November 1938 on 'The Jews' must, however, be assessed against something more than his general awareness of the principal contours of contemporary politics. In an interview given to *The Jewish Chronicle* in October 1931, Gandhi offered a distinction between spiritual and material Zionism. He described Zionism 'in its spiritual sense' as a 'lofty aspiration', urging Zionists 'to realise the Jerusalem that is within' and amplifying his position thus: 'Zionism meaning reoccupation of Palestine has no attraction for me. I can understand the longing of a Jew to return to Palestine, and he can do so if he can without the help of bayonets, whether his own or those of Britain.' But this singular intervention aside, throughout the 1920s and the first half of the 1930s Gandhi had very little to say about Palestine or the Jewish migrations into the Holy Land in the aftermath of the Balfour Declaration. Given his considerable, not to mention controversial, investment in what in India is known as the 'Khilafat Movement', or the agitation against the dismemberment of the Ottoman Empire in the aftermath of World War I and the abolishment of the caliphate, we may reasonably infer that Gandhi kept abreast of the various measures undertaken by colonial powers to reshape the region. His interest in what was transpiring in Palestine was revived by the visit to India in mid-1937 of Hermann Kallenbach, a Jewish architect of Lithuanian German stock with whom Gandhi had shared a close relationship during his long stay in South Africa, where, as Gandhi remarked in 1931, he was 'surrounded by Jews'.[16] Gandhi's long association

---

[15] For further discussion, see Vinay Lal, 'The Russian Revolution in the Indian Nationalist Imaginary', in *The Russian Revolution in Asia: From Baku to Batavia*, ed. Sabine Dullin et al. (London: Routledge, 2021), 155–70.

[16] 'Interview to the "Jewish Chronicle"' (London, 2 October 1931), in *CWMG* 53: 451, online at http://www.gandhiashramsevagram.org/gandhi-literature/mahatma-gandhi-collec

with Jews also made him sympathetic to their plight, and it is through his Jewish friends, among them Kallenbach, that he, in his own words, 'came to learn of their age-long persecution. They have been the untouchables of Christianity'. He was overjoyed at being reunited with Kallenbach after over twenty years when the latter arrived in India in the hope of being able to enlist the Indian leader as a supporter of Jewish claims to Palestine. Nevertheless, Gandhi was not prepared to let his friendship obscure his quest for truth and justice, even as he offered the services of the Indian National Congress in facilitating a 'direct conversation between Arabs and Jews only'. In what would perhaps be a harbinger of the position that he would adumbrate in his statement of November 1938, Gandhi advised Kallenbach and the Jewish Agency that 'the introduction of Jews in Palestine under the protection of British and other arms, is wholly inconsistent with spirituality'. Gandhi was mindful of 'the natural desire of the Jews to found a home in Palestine'; but, adding a caveat to which the Zionist leadership was wont to pay little heed, and which today will be likened by even those few who remain optimistic about the possibilities of a just resolution to the conflict as a fairly distant dream, he stated: 'But they must wait for its fulfillment, till Arab opinion is ripe for it.'[17]

Turning, then, to his statement on 'The Jews' of November 1938, it is not surprising that, even as Gandhi affirmed that his 'sympathies are all with the Jews', he also declared that he could not be blind 'to the requirement of justice':

> The cry for the national home for the Jews does not make much appeal to me. The sanction for it is sought in the Bible and the tenacity with which the Jews have hankered after return to Palestine. Why should they not, like other peoples of the earth, make that country their home where they are born and where they earn their livelihood.[18]

---

ted-works-volume-53.pdf [accessed 21 October 2021]. Subsequent quotations in this paragraph are drawn from the same source.

[17] Cited by Simone Panter-Brick, *Gandhi and the Middle East: Jews, Arabs and Imperial Interests* (London: I. B. Tauris, 2008), 63.

[18] 'The Jews', *Harijan* (26 November 1938), *CWMG* 74: 239–42.

We cannot say, as I have already suggested, precisely what Gandhi knew about the persecution of the Jews then under way in Germany; but it is possible to say with considerable plausibility that, had he been aware of the extent of this persecution, it would not have led to any alteration in his view. He offered condemnation enough, and this when the mass slaughter had not yet commenced, when he pronounced that the 'German persecution of the Jews seems to have no parallel in history. The tyrants of old never went so mad as Hitler seems to have gone. And he is doing it with religious zeal. For he is propounding a new religion of exclusive and militant nationalism . . . .'[19] A militant and material Zionism, backed up by the armed might of the British—and, in the post-World War II order, heavily patronized by the still more formidable American imperial power—could only exist in an adversarial position vis-à-vis the Arabs. Gandhi did not doubt that 'if there ever could be justifiable war in the name of and for humanity, a war against Germany to prevent the wanton persecution of a whole race, would be completely justified'. However, reiterating the position that he had embraced the previous year in his statement to the Jewish Agency, when he had described his opinion on these matters as informed only by 'ethical considerations', 'independent of results', Gandhi added: 'But I do not believe in war. A discussion of the pros and cons of such war is therefore outside my horizon or province.'[20] Yet, as a staunch believer in the efficaciousness of principled nonviolent resistance—measured not merely, as is commonly imagined, by material and political 'results', but as an instantiation of the redemptive power of suffering, the dignity it confers equally on the agent and the recipient of action, and the resoluteness of human courage—Gandhi perforce had just one course of action he could recommend. 'Can the Jews', he asks, 'resist this organized and shameless persecution? Is there a way to preserve their self-respect, and not to feel helpless, neglected and forlorn?' Were Jews not enjoined to offer satyagraha, 'civil resistance', and how could they possibly be 'worse off than now' for doing so?[21]

There was much in Gandhi's position that at once opened him up to vigorous critique. His article invoked, mistakenly as his critics thought,

[19] Ibid.
[20] Ibid.
[21] Ibid.

the position of Indians in South Africa as comparable to the place then occupied by the Jews in Nazi Germany. His further analogy with the Dalits, reduced to pariahs in the Indian polity, is similarly tendentious at best, and many of his critics have suggested that he was seriously crippled in being able to arrive at an independent judgment of the question since he had taken upon himself the task of acting as a custodian of the rights of Muslims in India and had in consequence also accepted some of the premises of a pan-Muslim identity. Martin Buber, an avowed admirer of Gandhi,[22] declared himself deeply disturbed at the Mahatma's 'tragicomic utterance', and expressed astonishment that a man whom he revered should have been so tragically short-sighted in understanding that a 'Jew in Germany could [not] pronounce one single sentence of a speech such as yours without being knocked down'.[23] Buber's letter to Gandhi, which all the available evidence suggests never reached the addressee, is only the most famous rebuke issued in response to Gandhi;[24] but perhaps more poignant yet was the rejoinder of the Jewish pacifist Judah L. Magnes, who reminded him that there was scarcely a people with a 'deeper and more widespread history of martyrdom' than Jews, and 'they need learn but little from anyone in faithfulness to their God and in the readiness to suffer while they sanctify His name'.[25] To his American Jewish admirer Hayim Greenberg, who was similarly baffled by Gandhi's failure to appreciate the totalitarian nature of the Nazi regime,[26] Gandhi

---

[22] Martin Buber, 'Gandhi, Politics and Us' (1930), in Buber, *Pointing the Way: Collected Essays*, ed. and trans. Maurice Friedman (New York: Harper & Row, 1957).

[23] Buber's letter of 1939 is widely available: two reliable sources are Buber, *Pointing the Way*, 139–47, and *The Letters of Martin Buber: A Life of Dialogue*, ed. Nahum N. Glatzer and Paul Mendes-Flohr, trans. Richard and Clara Winston and Harry Zohn (New York: Schocken Books, 1991), 476–86.

[24] For a lengthier discussion of Buber's letter to Gandhi, see Vinay Lal, 'Gandhi and Palestine', *Critical Muslim* 6 (April–June 2013), 171–90, 249–51.

[25] Letter from Judah Magnes to Gandhi, 26 February 1939, available online at Jewish Virtual Library, https://www.jewishvirtuallibrary.org/letter-from-judah-l-magnes-to-gandhi-february-1939 [accessed 24 November 2023].

[26] Hayim Greenberg, 'An Answer to Gandhi', available online at Jewish Virtual Library, https://www.jewishvirtuallibrary.org/an-answer-to-gandhi-by-hayim-greenberg-1939 [accessed 23 November 2023]. Gandhi's reply is instructive for a great many reasons, not least his firm repudiation of the view, which Greenberg was not alone in holding, that like many other Indian political figures he gravitated towards the Arabs and Palestinians as he sought to curry the favour of India's Muslims. 'The second charge of the writer', Gandhi notes, 'is more serious. He thinks that my zeal for Hindu–Muslim unity made me partial to the Arab presentation of the case, especially as that side was naturally emphasized in India. I have often said that I would not sell the truth for the sake of India's deliverance. Much less would I do so for winning Muslim friendship.'

offered a rejoinder of philosophical and moral profundity which points to the distance between him and his detractors:

> It is highly probable that, as the writer says, 'a Jewish Gandhi in Germany, should one arise, could function for about five minutes and would be promptly taken to the guillotine'. But that will not disprove my case or shake my belief in the efficacy of ahimsa [nonviolence]. . . . Indeed the maxim is that ahimsa is the most efficacious in front of the great himsa [violence]. Its quality is really tested only in such cases. Sufferers need not see the result during their lifetime.[27]

No one with any reasonable familiarity with Gandhi's life and writings can doubt that he not only found the violence perpetrated against the Jews deplorable but was pained by the suffering of a people whom he had known intimately since his early adulthood and whom he saw as the inheritors of a great spiritual, cultural, and intellectual legacy. The end of World War II saw the liberation of the concentration camps, and Gandhi, like everyone else, would have heard of the horrific killings that had been taking place there at a frenetic pace. There are at best episodic and fragmentary remarks over the last few years of his life which suggest that Gandhi continued to retain an interest in a conflict which in 1947 he was already describing as nearly 'insoluble',[28] but those who find his silence after the extent of the Holocaust had become known enigmatic may ponder over the fact that he had also very little to say about the three million dead from the genocidal Bengal famine or the atomic bombing of Hiroshima and Nagasaki. What more was there to be said by someone who had always been acutely aware of man's inhumanity towards man and yet remained resolutely attached to the idea of nonviolent resistance? In one of his last reflections on this question, Gandhi reportedly told his American biographer Louis Fischer that 'Hitler killed five million Jews. It is the greatest crime of our time. But the Jews should have offered

---

[27] M. K. Gandhi, 'The Jewish Question', *Harijan* (27 May 1939); also in *CWMG* 75: 415–16, online at http://www.gandhiashramsevagram.org/gandhi-literature/mahatma-gandhi-collec ted-works-volume-75.pdf [accessed 23 November 2023].

[28] Interview to Reuter, *Harijan* (5 May 1947), in *CWMG* 95: 26–8 at 27, online at http://www. gandhiashramsevagram.org/gandhi-literature/mahatma-gandhi-collected-works-volume-95.pdf [accessed 23 November 2023].

themselves to the butcher's knife. They should have thrown themselves into the sea from cliffs. . . . As it is they succumbed anyway in their millions.' On this point, there is near unanimity of opinion that Gandhi was naïve, misguided, ill-informed, and utopian in his thinking; to some, he was foolish, callous, possibly deranged. Gandhi, however, was never one to be deterred by the thought that he might constitute a minority of one; moreover, he claimed as the world's foremost practitioner of nonviolence insights which transcended common understandings of nonviolence and its efficaciousness as the bedrock of human action, reflection, and resistance.

Gandhi's most well-known compatriot in the Congress, Jawaharlal Nehru, came to the Jewish Question from a different if allied perspective. Gandhi had an entire circle of Jewish friends, as has been widely documented;[29] and it is through these friends that he came to acquire some intimate understanding of the Jewish contributions, in a diverse array of fields, to world civilization. There would have been a very small number of Jewish students at Cambridge's Trinity College, where Nehru acquired an undergraduate degree; moreover, he encountered predominantly Indian rather than Jewish students at Cambridge, as may be inferred from his complaint to his father that the university was 'too full of Indians',[30] and there is nothing to suggest that Nehru had any close proximity to Jewish students. Jawaharlal's father, Motilal, was one of the most prominent figures in the nationalist movement, and the younger Nehru was greatly animated by the discussions of politics that were common in the Nehru household. In his autobiography, as well in scores of other pieces, Nehru has like countless other Indians of his generation recounted how the ascendancy of Gandhi around 1919–20 fundamentally altered both his worldview and the course of the nationalist movement. Nehru's own rise through the ranks of Indian nationalism was, however, distinct in that by the late 1920s he had assumed the responsibility for internationalizing, after Gandhi's satyagrahas had introduced a unique vocabulary in world politics of anti-colonial resistance, the Indian freedom struggle—more particularly by forging alliances

---

[29] See, for example, Margaret Chatterjee, *Gandhi and His Jewish Friends* (London: Macmillan, 1982).

[30] M. J. Akbar, *Nehru: The Making of India* (London: Penguin Books, 1989), 78.

globally with socialists, anti-imperialists, and others determined to remove the barriers imposed by race, ethnicity, and poverty. Nehru's first important milestone in this respect was to represent the Indian National Congress at the International Congress against Colonial Oppression and Imperialism held at Brussels in 1927. He made a 'tremendous impression at this conference', notes his biographer, and was appointed a member of the executive committee and honorary president of the League against Imperialism, sharing these honours with Albert Einstein, Madame Sun Yat-sen, and Romain Rolland.[31] Over the next decade, Nehru worked assiduously to develop Congress's relations with other colonized nations and leaders of anti-imperial struggles: though long prison terms, the launch of the Salt Satyagraha, and the escalating political mood in India kept him from travelling overseas, Nehru read widely and followed closely events in Europe, Asia, and Africa. It is striking that some years before independence, when as India's first prime minister Nehru also chose to craft the country's foreign policy, he had already assumed the mantle of directing Congress's relations with the outside world.

If the first generation of Indian nationalists after the founding of the Congress in 1885 were profoundly moved by Japan's triumph over Russia in 1905, stirred by the thought of an Asian awakening, the radicals of Nehru's generation had no doubt that the Bolshevik Revolution of 1917 marked the beginning of the global struggle of the oppressed against forces of imperialism and capitalism. While Nehru's sympathies were with those who were part of what may broadly be characterized as the left, the impress of Gandhi's thinking also moved him in different directions. Unlike Marxists and radicals in Europe, Nehru over time also developed a healthy suspicion of the left's attachment to violence, though he followed the debates over the reconstruction of the Soviet Union along socialist lines well into the 1950s. By the early 1930s, much of his anxiety revolved around political developments that he saw as ominous portents of the catastrophe that was likely to befall Europe. He deplored the tendency of Conservative politicians to appease the fascists who were clearly on the rise in Germany, Italy, and Spain; similarly, Nehru was sharply critical of Japan's aggressiveness in East Asia. A speech he gave in April 1934 furnishes ample testimony to the most distinctive characteristic

[31] Ibid., 193.

of his thinking and of the position that would later be adopted by the Congress, namely his insistence that fascism and imperialism were not so much opposed as bedfellows: 'The world is faced today with two obnoxious movements. They are fascism and Nazism which are prevailing in Italy and Germany, and also in Japan. Fascism is a close relation of imperialism.'[32] Though the leaders of the free world would vehemently deny any relation between imperialism and fascism, Nehru construed the tendency of Conservative politicians in Britain to appease Hitler and Mussolini as a tacit admission of their fear that any stringent demands they placed upon Germany would be countered with the argument that Britain was denying freedom to the peoples of Asia and Africa. Writing just months before the onset of war, Nehru gave it as his view that, had Britain sounded a warning that German militarism would be aggressively resisted,

> Germany would have acted differently. It was within the British power to give this warning in the summer of 1938. Yet it was astounding to behold how safely the whole situation was planned out by Chamberlain's government. The submission and the repeated surrenders to Hitler's demands are not merely accidental. They are the results of a calculated policy of surrender to fascist aggression.[33]

The question of waging or joining a war was never within Gandhi's horizon: in this respect, at least, Nehru was obviously at odds with his mentor's views. They would have parted company in one other respect as well, an exploration of which is well outside the bounds of this chapter but must be noted as germane to the present argument: unlike Gandhi, Nehru had no overarching critique of modernity, and similarly he was also heavily invested, as his tenure as Prime Minister of India after independence would demonstrate, in the project of modernization. Gandhi may not have deployed the language of the academy, but the entire tenor of his thinking suggests that he, anticipating the arguments of scholars such as Zygmunt Bauman, would have seen the Holocaust as but the logical culmination of Enlightenment modernity.[34] We may even say that

[32] Speech by Nehru, *The Leader* (Allahabad) (15 April 1934).
[33] Jawaharlal Nehru, 'British Foreign Policy', *National Herald* (10 January 1939).
[34] Zygmunt Bauman, *Modernity and the Holocaust*, new ed. (Oxford: Basil Blackwell, 1991).

234 GANDHI, TRUTH, AND NONVIOLENCE

Gandhi had some insights into the particular ways in which modernity had informed both European colonialism and fascism. It was, to put it bluntly, well beyond Nehru's ken of thinking to embrace such a radical idea, even if he recognized that one of the most distinctive features of the Holocaust was to visit upon the Jews of Europe the atrocities that had previously been unleashed by European powers in their expansionist mode in Asia, Africa, and elsewhere.

However, on the vexed question of Palestine, and the 'right' of Jews to settle in that land, Gandhi and Nehru moved largely in tandem. Speaking very much in Gandhi's voice, Nehru wrote in 1938 that

> few people can withhold their deep sympathy from the Jews for the long centuries of most terrible oppression to which they have been subjected all over Europe. Fewer still can repress their indignation at the bar-barities and racial suppression of Jews which the Nazis have indulged in, during the last few years and which continues today. Even outside Germany, Jew-baiting has become a favourite pastime of various fascist groups.[35]

And yet, even as Nehru recognized Jews' struggle for recognition and the 'fierce and inhumane persecution' to which they had been subjected, he 'considered the struggle in Palestine as essentially a national struggle for freedom which was suppressed . . . by British imperialism in order to control the route to India'.[36] It was this letter from the same year that pro-voked an appeal to Nehru from a member of the executive of the General Federation of Jewish Labour in Palestine to give 'more sympathetic

---

[35] Jawaharlal Nehru, 'The Arabs and Jews in Palestine', in *Eighteen Months in India, 1936–1937, Being Further Essays and Writings* (Allahabad: Kitabistan, 1938), 133, also cited by Tilak Raj Sareen, 'Indian Responses to the Holocaust', in *Jewish Exile in India, 1933–1945*, ed. Anil Bhatti and Johannes H. Voigt (New Delhi: Manohar, 1999), 55–6.

[36] Cited in 'Jewish Appeal to Pandit Nehru: "More Sympathy for Struggle"', *Times of India* (29 September 1938). In this matter, Nehru hewed to a consistent line throughout the early to mid-1940s and after independence. When probed by the *Newsweek* reporter Earnest K. Lindley in September 1948 to explain if the situation in Palestine was causing him any anxiety, Nehru replied: 'As a government we have tried to play a neutral role. . . . Generally speaking, the Indian people have shown sympathy for Arabs. But they are not anti-Jew. They have sympathy for Jews as victims of persecution in Europe. However, they have a feeling for Arabs as Asiatics. They think nothing should be done to injure the Arabs. Personally I have long felt Palestine should be a federation.' See *Selected Works of Jawaharlal Nehru* (Delhi: Oxford University Press/Nehru Memorial Museum & Library, 1984), 2nd Series, 7: 616–17 [hereafter *SWJN*].

attention' to the struggles of the Jews in Palestine. Regretting that Nehru had no more to offer the Jews 'than an abstract sympathy in their plight', the writer asked whether the Jews did not have a moral basis for their claim that their migration into Palestine was no ordinary migration but, rather, 'a return to the land of their origin, from which their hearts and minds have never been divorced through all the centuries of dispersion and of which they have always dreamed as the eventual scene of their restoration and nationhood'.[37]

The All-India Congress Committee appears to have issued a statement on Palestine for the first time in 1936. The position outlined there was one to which the Congress would, in its essentials, adhere until the advent of Indian independence and beyond. 'While sympathizing with the plight of the Jews in Europe and elsewhere', the statement read, 'the Committee deplores that in Palestine the Jews have relied on British armed forces to advance their claims and thus aligned themselves on the side of British imperialism'. The hope was expressed that the Jews and Arabs would work together to create a 'free democratic state in Palestine with adequate protection of Jewish rights'.[38] In October 1937, the Congress passed a resolution, this time protesting 'against the reign of terror as well as the partition proposals relating to Palestine and assur[ing] the Arabs of the solidarity of the Indian people with them in their struggle for national freedom'.[39] The onset of war did not lead the Congress to alter its position; thus, at the annual session of December 1939, while condemning 'the organized terrorism of the Nazi government against the people of the Jewish race', it also expressed its firm opposition 'to imperialism and fascism alike' and disassociated 'itself entirely from British policy which has consistently aided the Fascist powers and helped in the destruction of the democratic countries'.[40] The war, however, rendered less abstract for Jews in India, where the small Jewish population had never encountered discrimination and where certainly the enormity of what was unfolding in Europe could barely be grasped, the suffering of their compatriots in

---

[37] 'Jewish Appeal to Pandit Nehru: "More Sympathy for Struggle"', *Times of India* (29 September 1938).

[38] A. Moin Zaidi and Shaheda Zaidi, eds., *The Encyclopedia of the Indian National Congress*, 28 vols. (New Delhi: S. Chand, 1977), Vol. 11, 478.

[39] Cited by Leonard A. Gordon, 'Indian Nationalist Ideas about Palestine and Israel', *Jewish Social Studies* 37, nos. 3–4 (Summer–Autumn 1975), 221–34 at 222.

[40] Zaidi and Zaidi, eds., *The Encyclopedia of the Indian National Congress*, Vol. 12, 160.

Europe—and this by bringing to the fore the question of Jewish refugees. The Congress, according to one historian, 'received many applications from those Jews who were desirous of seeking employment in India', and from Prague a certain Dr Fialla wrote to Nehru in 1938 seeking his intervention in finding employment opportunities 'for Jewish experts in Indian economic life'.[41] The Jews of Europe were being displaced and were urgently in need of a new home; India, on the other hand, was on the development trajectory and would be well advised to 'use the opportunity of getting people of the highest knowledge and industrial efficiency for the evolution of Indian national economies'.[42] Might not both Jews and Indians, acting in unison, benefit from such an arrangement?

Nehru had expressed a readiness to admit Jewish refugees to India, though as a policy matter the sole authority in this regard resided with the British government of India—except, of course, in the native states, where, as the Maharaja of Nawanagar famously showed, Jewish children could be sheltered.[43] 'I need hardly assure you', he wrote to a correspondent in London, 'that the sufferings of the Jews in Germany have greatly shocked all the people here. I wish we could help these unfortunate sufferers. To some extent I have been trying to do so. I have received scores of applications and I have sent the information to various provincial governments and industrialists.'[44] But this letter, to a German Jewess in London, suggests why a large-scale emigration of Jews to India could not be contemplated: besides 'the difficulties placed in their way by the British Government [which] are very great', India had millions

---

[41]   Cited by Sareen, 'Indian Responses to the Holocaust', 56.

[42]   Ibid., 56–7.

[43]   The Maharaja of Nawanagar, a princely state in Gujarat, 'adopted' 1,000 orphaned Polish children and quite likely saved the majority of them from certain death. Only a small minority of these orphans were Jewish, though many writers, the present one not excepted, have at some time assumed that they were Polish Jews. The most reliable scholarly source on this matter is Kenneth X. Robbins, 'The Camp for Polish Refugee Children at Balachadi, Nawanagar [India], *The Journal of Indo-Judaic Studies* 4 (2018), 95–113. The Maharaja of Nawanagar is fondly remembered, even venerated, by the survivors: there is a memorial to him in Warsaw in the 'Good Maharaja Square' in the Ochota district, as well as a school that is named after him; and in Israel he is recognized as among the righteous. See Manik Mehta, 'How the "Indian Oskar Schindler" took in 1,000 Polish children during WWII', *The Times of Israel* (17 July 2017), https://www.timesofisrael.com/how-the-indian-oskar-schindler-took-in-1000-polish-children-during-wwii/ [accessed 28 October 2022].

[44]   *Selected Works of Jawaharlal Nehru*, ed. S. Gopal, 1st Series (New Delhi: Orient Longman, 1972–), 9: 224–5.

of its own unemployed, land was scarce, and one could barely think of setting aside 'a large tract of territory for Jewish immigrants'.[45] Nehru could well have elaborated upon other considerations, if he had chosen to be less discreet: Indian Muslims were critical both of Jewish migration into Palestine and of the prospect of Jewish settlement in India. Nazi propaganda in India steered Muslims towards anti-Jewish feelings, and 'Nazi agents tried to cleverly exploit the Muslim sympathy for the Arabs in order to create anti-Jewish sentiments among the Indian Muslims'.[46] Far more critical in fostering sentiments against Jews, however, was none other than the government of India, which had embarked upon a policy of courting Muslim opinion and found, in the circumstances engendered by the war, ripe opportunities to drive a wedge between Muslims and the Congress. The government of India's hostility to Jewish emigration, the opposition from Indian Muslims, little knowledge of the 'Jewish Question' in India, and the Congress's own diffidence on account of the role played by British imperialists in fostering and arming Zionism: these circumstances, among others, conspired to prevent large-scale Jewish refugee settlement in India.

Nevertheless, owing largely to Nehru and the leadership of the Congress, nearly a thousand Jewish refugees found a hospitable home in India—as indeed Jews have over the centuries. But circumstances had also conspired to remove from the scene the one Indian whose patriotism was wholly permissive of opportunism and whose own relationship with the Nazis still staggers the imagination.[47] Subhas Chandra Bose was serving as president of the Indian National Congress in December 1938 when Nehru introduced a draft resolution which simply declared that the Congress Working Committee, the supreme executive body

---

[45] Ibid.

[46] Eugene J. D'Souza, 'Nazi Propaganda in India', *Social Scientist* 28, nos. 5–6 (May–June 2000), 81.

[47] A moving and brave piece has recently appeared from the hand of Sarmila Bose, the grand-niece of Subhas Bose. It is written as an open letter to a number of Jewish organizations, including the Elie Wiesel Foundation for Humanity, New York, and it is honest in its appraisal that Subhas Bose was wanting in his acknowledgement of the sufferings of the Jews and consequently in his denunciation of the Nazi killing machine. See 'An apology to the victims of the Holocaust for the silence of my great-uncle Subhas Chandra Bose', *Scroll.in* (13 March 2023), https://scroll.in/article/1045098/an-apology-to-the-victims-of-the-holocaust-for-the-silence-of-my-great-uncle-subhas-chandra-bose [accessed 24 November 2023].

of the Congress, saw 'no objection to the employment in India of such Jewish refugees as are experts and specialists and who can fit in with the new order in India and accept Indian standards.'[48] Bose's opposition to the draft resolution ensured its defeat. Some months later, Nehru, now back from a trip to Europe, vented his frustration in a letter to Bose, expressing his surprise that the Congress president had formed an opinion that Nehru was keen to 'establish an asylum for the Jews in India'. Nehru sought to explain to Bose that 'it was not from the point of view of helping Jews that I considered this question, though such help was desirable where possible without detriment to our country, but from the point of view of helping ourselves by getting first-rate men of science, industry, etc., on very moderate payment'.[49] Nehru might appear, on a first reading, as being less than humanitarian in his outlook, seeking to help the Jews only to the extent that some of them could have helped India, a country whose manufacturing and scientific potential had barely been realized under two centuries of colonial rule. It is rather beside the point that, even on this crudely realistic reading of his letter, he comes off far better than most of his contemporaries, including those in the West, who remained supremely indifferent to the fate of the Jews when they were not hostile to them; what is instructive, and capable of a more generous interpretation, is that he describes that help to the Jews was 'desirable where possible without detriment to our country'. Writing as he was at the point where communalism was poised to become an all-consuming affair, eroding the patterns of cohabitation, conviviality, and recognition that had marked Hindu–Muslim relations over centuries, Nehru would have been sensitive to the fact that for Indian Muslims their solidarity with their Muslim brethren in Palestine took precedence over the grave difficulties into which Jews had been plunged in Europe, and that granting asylum to Jews was calculated to further inflame Muslim sentiments. It is perhaps not accidental either that the letter is addressed to Bose: even if his willingness to seek assistance from the Nazis in the task of liberating India was not yet a matter of public knowledge, is it possible that Nehru may have sensed his political proclivities and perhaps presented the

[48] Quoted in a letter from Jawaharlal Nehru to Subhas Chandra Bose, 3 April 1939, in *SWJN*, 1st Series, 9: 537.

[49] Letter from Nehru to Bose, 3 April 1939, in *SWJN*, 1st Series, 9: 537.

matter of admitting Jewish refugees into India in a manner most likely to win Bose's approval?[50]

Bose's admirers, especially in his native Bengal, are still legion; and they have been predisposed towards describing his political adventurism as a mere flirtation with Nazism, inspired by nothing more than a patriotism which would stop short at nothing to see India delivered from the yoke of British rule. What better testament to the love for the motherland exists than Bose's stirring inauguration of the Provisional Government of Free India, backed up by a fighting force, the Indian National Army (INA), with which he thought the liberation of India would be at hand: 'In the name of God, I take this sacred oath—that to liberate India

---

[50] Nirad Chaudhuri, always cantankerous and opinionated but never without interest and some insight, had some thoughts on what drove Bose to embrace the Nazis as allies. Gandhi had opposed Bose's re-election to the Congress presidency in December 1939; when it seemed that Bose would prevail after all, having defeated the candidate put forward by the Mahatma, Gandhi made it impossible for him to function in that post and spurred Bose into submitting his resignation. 'This expulsion and the manner of its accomplishment', Chaudhuri notes, 'not only permanently estranged Bose from the Congress but also was the decisive factor in impelling him to seek help from the Axis Powers in liberating India. He left nursing bitter thoughts against the Congress as the betrayer of Indian interests.' But apart from the claim, which can doubtless be disputed, that Gandhi's machinations drove Bose into the hands of fascists, there is the consideration whether Bose had not already experienced fascism as the bosom to which he could retreat when he felt wounded. Chaudhuri continues: 'Nehru regarded himself as a Socialist, while Bose, after many years residence in Germany, took a more tolerant view of totalitarianism. In outlook and ideas Bose was distinctly authoritarian, not only because he had studied German political and social philosophy, but also because the mental constitution of a middle-class Bengali is likely to harbor a perceptible bias in favour of dictatorial regimes.' From this scathing putdown of the Bengali middle class, of which he was every bit as much a member as Subhas Bose, Chaudhuri evidently exempts himself. See Nirad C. Chaudhuri, 'Subhas Chandra Bose—His Legacy and Legend', *Pacific Affairs* 26, no. 4 (December 1953), 355–6. For all his sharpness, wit, provocations, and the elegance of his writing, Chaudhuri puts forward a rather suspect chronology: he claims that it was '*after* many years in Germany' that Bose 'took a more tolerant view of totalitarianism', though there is every reason to argue that it was his predisposition or at least cavalier attitude towards totalitarianism that drove him to Germany in the first place. Whatever the nature of Gandhi's authoritarianism, it was Bose's own failings that led him to the Nazis. Bose made several trips to Germany and Austria in the 1930s and spent a considerable period of time in Berlin and Vienna, and it is possible that Chaudhuri is alluding to these years rather than to Bose's stay in 1941–3; but then it was not Gandhi that drove Bose into the arms of the Nazis. It is in Berlin that he developed a friendship, in 1934, with a couple to whom, in response to a question about how he could stomach the loathsome Nazis, Bose replied: 'But let us not be sentimental. I am doing what I have to do; what must be done. Have you any idea . . . of the despair, the misery, the humiliation of India? Can you imagine her suffering and indignation? British imperialism there can be just as intolerable as your Nazism here, I assure you.' One of Bose's best-known biographers, though an admirer, is nevertheless constrained to admit, 'Since this was only around 1934, Bose and the world did not yet know how the Nazis would work out their program, particularly the Final Solution to the Jewish question. But it was clear that he was willing to work with the devil to free India.' See Leonard A. Gordon, *Brothers Against the Raj: A Biography of Indian Nationalists Sarat and Subhas Chandra Bose* (New York: Columbia University Press, 1990), 282.

and the thirty-eight crores [380 million] of my countrymen, I, Subhas Chandra Bose, will continue this sacred war of freedom till the last breath of my life.'[51] Such a hagiographic narrative is without a shred of credibility: Bose's involvement with fascism ran deep. A cottage industry has developed over the decades since Bose's death in a plane crash in Taipei on 18 August 1945, just days after the atomic bombing of Hiroshima and Nagasaki, devoted to lionizing Bose's role in the 'freedom struggle', but the principal episodes in the narrative of Bose's complicity with Nazism—and, it may be noted at least in passing, Japanese militarism—are equally well established. The narrative begins in the heroic mode, with his escape in disguise from house arrest, under which he had been placed by the British, and moves on to his arrival in Germany in April 1941 and the establishment, later in the year, of the Free India Centre. Bose began broadcasting anti-British messages on Free India Radio; as Goebbels approvingly noted in his diary, 'Bose's propaganda, conducted from Berlin, is extremely embarrassing to the English'.[52] A Free Indian Legion (also known as the Indian Legion), comprised of around 3,000 troops, mainly Indian POWs and a few expatriates and students, was raised, but it saw comparatively little military action during the war. After repeated attempts, Bose, in late May 1942, was finally able to gain a brief audience with Hitler in the hope that he might be able to get from him a German declaration on Indian independence, if not a firm commitment for a German invasion of India—though, once again, his judgment in even wanting a meeting with the Führer, who had nothing but contempt for Indians, must be seriously questioned. It was Hitler who had pompously written in *Mein Kampf* (1925–6),

England will lose India either if her own administrative machinery falls a prey to racial decomposition . . . or if she is bested by the sword of a powerful enemy. Indian agitators, however, will never achieve this. How hard it is to best England, we Germans have sufficiently learned. Quite aside from the fact that I, as a man of Germanic blood, would, in

---

[51] Quoted in Sugata Bose, *His Majesty's Opponent: Subhas Chandra Bose and India's Struggle against Empire* (New Delhi: Penguin Books, 2013), 255.
[52] Cited by Gordon, *Brothers Against the Raj*, 487.

spite of everything, rather see India under English rule than under any other.[53]

Less than a year later, Bose left Germany and eventually made his way to Southeast Asia.

It has often been said of Bose that he had only one love, one obsession, one dream: he longed for the day when India would be free of British rule. He was scarcely singular in nursing that hope; but he was in lonely company in choosing the means that he did. His involvement with Nazi Germany, deplorable as it is, can by no means be construed as uncomplicated. One scholar, while critical of the 'astounding levels of historical revisionism and distortion' with which many Indian historians have written of Bose's truck with the Nazi state, is also dismissive of the view that he should be viewed merely as a fool or quisling. 'Bose did not do the bidding of the Nazis', he writes, adding: 'He certainly served their interests—at times—but it was a complimentary [sic] relationship. It never seemed to have occurred to the Germans to treat Bose as a puppet issuing him with *diktats*. Considering the nature of the Nazi state, Bose acted with remarkable independence, at times even contempt for Nazi policy.'[54] His aspirations for India were indeed bold: he envisioned a truly democratic India and he was resolutely secular and anti-communal. There is virtually no trace of anti-Semitism in his writings. It has been alleged that he once wrote a partially anti-Semitic article for Goebbels's mouthpiece, *Der Angriff* ('The Attack', founded in 1927), but this piece has never been located.[55] On the other hand, one of his Jewish friends in Berlin from the mid-1930s told his biographer many years later that she recalled 'his deep contempt for the Nazis, a feeling which he did not attempt to hide from me'.[56] Nevertheless, what stands out is that in the large corpus of Bose's writings, speeches, and correspondence there is not the remotest expression of sorrow or despondency, much less outrage, at the plight of the Jews. True, he died only months after the liberation of the extermination camps, and one might perhaps feel charitably inclined

[53] Adolf Hitler, *Mein Kampf* (Boston: Houghton Mifflin, 1943), 658.
[54] Romain Hayes, *Subhas Chandra Bose in Nazi Germany: Politics, Intelligence, and Propaganda 1941–43* (London: C. Hurst & Co., 2011), 146–7.
[55] Gordon, *Brothers Against the Raj*, 487.
[56] Ibid., 283.

and suggest that, immersed as he was in his own struggles, news of the Holocaust never did reach Bose. But one might also think that his close proximity to the administrative heart of the killing machine—his last stay in Berlin lasted nearly two years—would at least have elicited a few tears of remorse. Bose's silence in all these respects, one is tempted to say, is deafening. Yet Bose did speak: in one of his last broadcasts, on 25 May 1945, Bose argued that the Nazi state's greatest failing was to have waged a war on two fronts.[57] It is striking if not disturbing that, even at this time, Bose should have passed judgment on the Nazis for their military rather than moral failings—and this is apart from the question whether Bose, who fancied himself a general, really knew much if anything about military strategy. Little did Bose realize that in his assessment he was only echoing his own moral failings.

We find, then, that Bose diverged in very great measure from Nehru in his attitude towards the mass murder of Jews, and the differences with Gandhi are even more striking. Yet, it is true of all three that they were men of international outlook, with wide sympathies, and committed, each in his own way, to the idea of a secular and democratic India. Bose died just months after the surrender of Germany; Gandhi was increasingly drawn towards the immense problems at home and the reconstruction of Indian society after two centuries of colonial rule and plunder. The bloodbath that would ensue in India shortly before the dawn of independence would entail what these days—as millions of Syrians, Iraqis, Kurds, Afghans, Libyans, Ethiopians, Ukrainians, Palestinians, and others find themselves uprooted from their homes—is called a 'refugee crisis' of staggering proportions, and Gandhi was preoccupied in steering the nation to sanity. It is perhaps not surprising that it was left to Nehru to reflect on how he and the Congress had responded to the catastrophe that had engulfed Jewish society, and his letter of 11 July 1947 to Albert Einstein, with whom Nehru had been carrying on a correspondence, may be summoned as the final illustration of the limitations in the Congress response to the Jewish Question and what it hoped to achieve as the party guiding independent India. 'You are quite right in thinking', wrote Nehru, 'that India has mourned the horrors which resulted in the deaths

---

[57] Subhas Chandra Bose, *Selected Speeches of Subhas Chandra Bose* (New Delhi: Ministry of Information & Broadcasting, Publicity Division, 1965), 249–50.

of millions of Jews in the murder machines which were set up in Germany and elsewhere.' But, as Nehru added, nations are generally constrained by self-interest: 'As you know, national policies are unfortunately essentially selfish interests. Each country thinks of its own interest first and then of other interests.' In India, the difficulties were still greater: sovereignty did not reside with the people of India. Thus, 'we in India, engrossed as we have been in our struggle for freedom and in our domestic difficulties, have been unable to play any effective part in world affairs'. These difficulties were not likely to disappear soon; nevertheless, Nehru hoped that India would 'play a progressively more important part in international affairs. What that part will be in future I can only guess'.[58] That, however, is another story, for another time.

---

[58] Nehru to Albert Einstein, 11 July 1947, in *SWJN*, 2nd Series, 3: 394.

10

Satyagraha in America—Gandhi, King, and the Politics of Fasting

James Lawson in Conversation with Vinay Lal

Edited with an introduction and notes by Vinay Lal

Introduction

Most scholarly histories of the American civil rights movement, which has generated a voluminous literature and garnered global attention, recognize the distinct contribution of Reverend James M. Lawson, Pastor Emeritus of the Holman United Methodist Church in Los Angeles's Adams District until his death on 10 June 2024, as one of the most influential architects of the movement and in many respects its most committed practitioner of the idea of nonviolent resistance. In his dense, indeed exhaustive, narrative of the Freedom Rides, Raymond Arsenault recounts how James Lawson, who commenced his nonviolent training workshops in the late 1950s, gathered what would become a stellar group of young African American men and women—Diane Nash, John Lewis, Bernard Lafayette, John Bevel, among others—around him in Nashville. Martin Luther King himself acknowledged Lawson's Nashville group as 'the best organized and most disciplined in the Southland', and King and other activists were 'dazzled' by Lawson's 'concrete visions of social justice' and 'the beloved community'.[1] Andrew Young, another stalwart of the movement and a prominent figure in American public life, similarly speaks of Lawson in glowing terms as the chief instigator of the Nashville sit-ins

---

[1] Raymond Arsenault, *Freedom Riders: 1961 and the Struggle for Racial Justice* (New York: Oxford University Press, 2006), 87.

Vinay Lal, *Satyagraha in America—Gandhi, King, and the Politics of Fasting* In: *Gandhi, Truth, and Nonviolence*. Edited by: Vinay Lal, Oxford University Press. © Oxford University Press 2025.
DOI: 10.1093/9780198936657.003.0011

and 'as an expert on Gandhian philosophy' who 'was instrumental in organizing our Birmingham nonviolent protest workshops'; Lawson was, as Young avers, 'an old friend of the movement' when, in 1968, he invited King to Memphis to speak in support of the sanitation workers' strike.[2]

David Halberstam's hugely engaging and even dazzling foray into civil rights history, *The Children*, lovingly explores the role played by Lawson and his protégés in the most significant attempt since the founding of the Republic to critique and attack racial discrimination in the United States and birth a society organized around principles of justice and social equality.[3] Just as strikingly, the chapter on the campaign for civil rights in the American South in Peter Ackerman and Jack DuVall's global history of nonviolent resistance[4] is not focused on King, James Farmer, A. Philip Randolph, or Roy Wilkins, to mention four of those who have been styled among the 'Big Six', but rather unexpectedly revolves around the critical place of Lawson's extraordinary nonviolence training workshops—most recently featured in the film *Lee Daniels' The Butler*—in giving rise to what became some of the most characteristic expressions of nonviolent resistance, among them the sit-ins, the freedom rides, and the strategy of packing jails with dissenters. Ackerman and DuVall echo the sentiment of Bernard Lafayette, who credited Lawson with creating 'a nonviolent academy, equivalent to West Point'; they pointedly add that, though Lawson was 'a man of faith, he approached the tasks of nonviolent conflict like a man of science'.[5]

It is no exaggeration to suggest that King derived at least as much of his understanding of Gandhi from Lawson as he did from anyone else, though most histories remain insensitive to this consideration and tend to regard Bayard Rustin as the singularly critical person in bringing King to more than a perfunctory awareness of Gandhian thought. John D'Emilio, the biographer of Rustin, affirms what has long been known about King, namely that he 'knew nothing' about Gandhian nonviolence even as he

[2] Andrew Young, *An Easy Burden: The Civil Rights Movement and the Transformation of America* (New York: HarperCollins, 1996), 127, 130, 448. Young served two terms in the US House of Representatives (1973–7), and served as the US Ambassador to the United Nations (1977–9) and as Mayor of Atlanta (1982–90).

[3] David Halberstam, *The Children* (New York: Random House, 1998).

[4] Peter Ackerman and Jack DuVall, *A Force More Powerful: A Century of Nonviolent Conflict* (New York: St. Martin's Press, 2000).

[5] Ibid., 316–17.

246 GANDHI, TRUTH, AND NONVIOLENCE

was preparing to launch the Montgomery Bus Boycott. D'Emilio states that 'Rustin's Gandhian credentials were impeccable', and it fell upon Rustin to initiate the process that would transform King 'into the most illustrious American proponent of nonviolence in the twentieth century'.[6] Though Rustin's command over the Gandhian literature is scarcely in question, Lawson's critical role both in helping King sharpen his understanding of satyagraha, and more generally in inflecting Christian traditions of nonviolence with the teachings of Gandhi and other vectors of the Indian tradition, have been understated.

Uniquely among the great figures of the civil rights movement, Lawson spent three formative years in his early twenties in central India. As a college student in the late 1940s, Lawson discovered Christian nonviolence—both as a consequence of what he learned from his father, who was also a pastor, and his mother, and on account of an encounter with A. J. Muste, who was dubbed 'the No. 1 US Pacifist' by *Time* in 1939 and would go on to be at the helm of every major movement of resistance to war from the 1920s until the end of the Vietnam War. Lawson was a conscientious objector during the Korean War and spent over a year in jail; as Andrew Young remarks, 'His stand on the Korean War was courageous and unusual in the African-American community'.[7] Following his release from jail, Lawson, who had trained as a Methodist minister, left for India, where for three years he served as an athletics coach at Hislop College, Nagpur (originally founded in 1883 as a Presbyterian school). He deepened his understanding of Gandhi and met at length with several of Gandhi's key associates, including Vinoba Bhave. When he returned to the US in June 1956, Lawson uniquely embodied within himself two strands that would converge in the civil rights movement: Christian nonviolence and Gandhian satyagraha, a highly systematic inquiry into, and practice of, nonviolent resistance.

Strangely, notwithstanding the seminal place of Lawson in the civil rights movement and American public life more generally, very little work has been done on his life and, in particular, on his nearly seven decades of experience as a theoretician and practitioner of nonviolent resistance. He was a student of Gandhian ideas and more generally of the literature of

---

[6] John D'Emilio, *Lost Prophet: The Life and Times of Bayard Rustin* (New York: Free Press, 2003), 230–1.

[7] Young, *An Easy Burden*, 126.

nonviolence several years before King's ascent into public prominence; more than five decades after the assassination of King, he remained its most dedicated practitioner in the United States. No American life, in this respect, is comparable to his. Lawson, who settled in the Los Angeles area in the early 1970s and was a legendary figure in certain circles, continued to carry out nonviolence training workshops until just a few months before he passed in June 2024.

Through a fortuitous set of circumstances, Lawson and I met in 1998: in the aftermath of India's nuclear tests, both of us spoke together at a forum in Los Angeles in sharp criticism of India's aspirations to be a nuclear power and the debased culture of militarism. In late 2013, at my behest, Lawson agreed to a short series of conversations with me that I hoped to work into a book. Our conversations concluded only in mid-2016, and in the course of those thirty months I accumulated about twenty-seven hours of dialogue with him on tape. We touched upon Lawson's own life, his experiences of racism, his views on the Korean War, and the various ways in which his three-year stint in India informed his worldview; but there are equally protracted conversations on the anti-apartheid movement in South Africa, the global history of nonviolence, the non-aligned movement, the emergence of the Global South and decolonization movements, and much else. We explored why, unlike in South Africa, where the principal figures of the anti-apartheid movement—Mandela, Ahmed Kathrada, Walter Sisulu, Oliver Tambo, Fatima Meer, Yusuf Dadoo, among others—were not drawn largely from the ranks of the Christian churches, in the United States an overwhelming number of black leaders were churchmen, and the implications of their influence over the movement. We explored, to take another instance, America's uneasy relationships to decolonization and liberation movements all over the Global South. Towards the end of our conversations, we shifted our focus to a consideration of the 'New Jim Crow' in the US, as well as to a very pressing and little-explored question: why is it that the African American intellectual's engagement with the rest of the world has greatly diminished since the end of the civil rights movement? The 1940s to the 1960s were a period of intense intellectual ferment in African American life, and figures such as Paul Robeson, Howard Thurman, W. E. B. Du Bois, Bayard Rustin, James Farmer, Richard Wright, Langston Hughes, the expatriate Josephine Baker, and Lawson himself strove to establish intellectual, cultural, and emotive links between black Africans and the colonized peoples of the Global South.

In the midst of our far-reaching conversations on violence, revolutionary movements, and social change in the twentieth century, I also sought to remain resolutely focused on two questions: first, how are we to understand the history of nonviolence and its revolutionary practices in our times, particularly with reference to the American civil rights movement? How does nonviolence overcome the temptations of violence? What are the implications of forgoing violence, and how do we advance the idea of nonviolence not only within the framework of politics and public life but as a mode of being in this world? Is it possible to deploy nonviolence in tandem with violence, as some have thought, or does that betray a profound misunderstanding of the ethical framework of nonviolence? Secondly, I sought in our conversations to situate the civil rights movement within the larger framework of African American history and the politics and practices of resistance, and examine the relationship of the struggle of black Americans to various articulations of 'Third World' resistance, from the Bandung Conference to the anti-apartheid movement in South Africa. Though comparisons with the Indian independence movement under Gandhi have become inevitable, curiously almost no one has paused to consider that the circumstances under which the civil rights movement was waged were radically different. Gandhi, to take one elementary illustration, put together a movement in a country where by law Indians were forbidden to own guns, while in the American South the culture of guns was pervasive.

The excerpt from our conversation that follows is drawn from two different conversations in 2014–15, and I have merged these conversations. In this excerpt, I probe Lawson on the question of fasting. I brought up this subject more than once: it intrigued me that, though civil rights leaders and activists deployed nearly every 'weapon' in the Gandhian arsenal of nonviolent resistance, they refrained from fasting or what most people, including many scholars, (incorrectly) refer to as hunger-striking. But the conversation veered into a more general discussion of 'satyagraha in America'. The text, though edited, retains the flavour of a conversation, and the syntax and grammar may not always conform to grammar book prescriptions about correct English. It remains to be said that, at the conference where some of the papers published in this book were first presented,

James Lawson gave the inaugural keynote address entitled 'Gandhi and the Long, Bitter, Beautiful Struggle for Justice and Truth'.

LAL: One of the arguments that was advanced in the US among people in the African American community back in the early part of the twentieth century, say around the time when W. E. B. Du Bois first began to write on Gandhi in *The Crisis*,[8] was that there were particular reasons why in India nonviolence was successful or could be practised. It was probably a little bit too early around 1920 to say whether nonviolence was successful in India. But the question nevertheless arose whether it was something that could be carried out in the American South. Du Bois wrote that 'fasting, prayer, sacrifice, and self-torture' had been 'bred into the very bone of India for more than 3,000 years'. The scholar Sudarshan Kapur comments on this and says that Du Bois could not imagine a similar approach succeeding in the United States.[9] On the contrary, it would be regarded as a joke or a bit of insanity. Du Bois went on to caution his readers that African Americans cannot blindly copy others' methods without thought and consideration. Now, the first question that arises for me, when I look at what I call the 'grammar of satyagraha' and King's application of it, is that I do not find any instance where he resorted to fasting—certainly not in the manner in which Gandhi resorted to fasting.

LAWSON: He did not.

LAL: He did not. All right. But he embraced virtually everything else in the grammar of satyagraha. I'm not speaking about the philosophical component of satyagraha as such, but King brought the entire arsenal of nonviolence to the fore—boycotts, strikes, marches, filling up the jails—except the use of the fast. I'll speak of Cesar Chavez in more detail momentarily, but he goes on fasts on numerous occasions to strengthen the resolve of his people. Is that, you think, partly on account of the fact that he's coming from a different strand of the Christian tradition—from Catholicism? You think that has some play in this matter ... What is your understanding of this whole issue? Why

---

[8] See Vinay Lal, 'Gandhi, 'The Colored Races', and the Future of Satyagraha: The View from the African American Press', *Social Change* 51, no. 1 (2021), 151–69.

[9] Sudarshan Kapur, *Raising Up a Prophet: The African-American Encounter with Gandhi* (Boston: Beacon Press, 1992).

is it that King did not resort to this particular part of the arsenal of nonviolence?

LAWSON: All right. Now, I think I want to just add to that a couple of things. One is that Martin King did fast as a Christian. He fasted also before the Birmingham Campaign in 1962 or '63. He fasted for at least three days, thinking primarily about the Birmingham Campaign.

LAL: So, when he fasted for three days, was this a public fast?

LAWSON: No. How many people knew, I don't know. He has written this someplace, that he fasted in preparation for the Birmingham Campaign. He encouraged that from other people. But I think you have to remember that Gandhi saw the fast as more than for personal discipline, and he used it both in the preparations for campaigns and also when he was trying to correct people in the ashram who were messing up. Then I think the most important and significant form of the fast that he used was when he was in the street battling in a concrete struggle. His fast in New Delhi, his fast in Calcutta, he used that then as a major nonviolent weapon to change the scenery.

LAL: Absolutely. And it's that element which I believe is missing in King.

LAWSON: Well, I wouldn't call it missing in King. I would say that, in our case, we did not necessarily see fasting as a nonviolent tactic and weapon in that sense. There was some fasting and praying in jails and there was some fasting and praying at other times. For example, you know, in that period of my life I was trying to fast once a week for twenty-four hours—as a spiritual and moral discipline. I started that in college. I did that continuously. I don't do it any longer. Some of my doctors tell me I should stop it entirely. As a matter of prayer and meditation I've done that for years. But I've never used it as a tactic now for nonviolence.

LAL: That's what I wanted to probe. I fully understand the place of fasting, which is a very honourable religious discipline, within the Christian faith, too.

LAWSON: And within Hinduism. Within Judaism.

LAL: And Islam. Every religion.

LAWSON: Almost, probably so.

LAL: As a form of discipline. As a form of meditation. As a form of the cleansing of oneself. As a form of spiritual preparation for the task ahead. I understand all of that fully well. King may have had fasts of the sort that one might undertake in a Christian tradition, say penitential fasts. But as you're saying, its deployment as a weapon in a nonviolent struggle, that element was not embraced.

LAWSON: That's right.

LAL: It seems to me not only not by King, but very largely within the African American tradition it wasn't. There is one instance only, however, that comes to mind. I recall reading almost thirty years ago a book by the African American comedian and activist Dick Gregory. I recall that he had in fact actually engaged with this weapon explicitly.

LAWSON: That's right, he's the only one I know of. He did do some long-term fasting. He did it partly for purification, but he did it also as protest.

LAL: That's right. But he seems to be an exception within the African American tradition here. Let me press you on this a bit. Why did you and perhaps Martin King not think of this?

LAWSON: Well, all right. I think I want to lift up the fact that Du Bois is mistaken in one respect. Boycotts and strikes and sit-downs and lockouts had been occurring in the United States in the twentieth century by the time that Du Bois wrote. We did not learn, I did not learn, boycotts from Gandhi because these are methods and tactics that had a long history within the United States even, as well as elsewhere.

LAL: Absolutely.

LAWSON: It is Gandhi who is the learner or the practitioner or the social scientist or the religious scientist who has brought all of this into a kind of overall theory of how you achieve self-determination. How you achieve justice. How you dismantle the old and create the new and he calls it satyagraha, nonviolence. Calls it civil resistance. Calls it nonviolent conflict. That's his great contribution, in my mind. He did not utilize all the tactics that the human race has known and that we know now to be nonviolent tactics. He used the ones that were most advantageous to his struggle, which is also what King did.

In that ten-year period where King lived and worked, he was learning all the time. We were in an emerging movement process. We did not understand the full arsenal of nonviolent struggle, and I do not think that we used that many pieces of the arsenal. But I think that very clearly people like John Lewis, Martin King, and others were still discovering from experience what this represented. Whether or not the movement would have continued, in the vein in which it had started, I personally have no doubts that a hunger strike, or a public fast, would have been something that would one day have emerged. I don't know if there was an occasion when non-violence as a hunger strike to change the struggle, to transform people in the movement, if there was an opportunity rife for that. I can't say that. You hear what I'm saying? [*Lal interjects: 'I understand'.*] I'm not sure that I can say there was an opportunity for King or for some of the rest of us.

LAL: I would want to keep in mind the distinction, which is very clear to Gandhi's mind, between hunger striking and fasting . . . while recognizing that there is a sense in which this distinction may collapse. Gandhi did not think of his fasting as intending to co-erce someone, but inadvertently it may have had that effect because people were moved—sometimes moved to do things, which Gandhi will say you shouldn't do unless you're really compelled by the moral argument.

Do you think that Chavez's Catholicism perhaps facilitated his use of fasting in the public domain?

LAWSON: I don't remember how much Cesar Chavez had read Gandhi.

LAL: Oh, he read widely in him.

LAWSON: He did read widely?[10] OK, well, then I would say probably, as an example, that this February fast was more of a Gandhian fast than Roman Catholic.[11] It was an in-house fast for the improvement of the

---

[10] Cesar Chavez, born in 1927, had little formal schooling and only finished junior high school. He subsequently joined the US Navy but, over the years, became an auto-didact. 'Beyond his public Christianity', writes one scholar, 'he was a devotee of St. Francis; he preached a poetic theology that traversed the borders of orthodox religion.' Chavez credited his mother as the fount of his inspiration: as he recalled in an interview, 'When I look back, I see her sermons had a tremendous impact on me. I didn't know it was nonviolence then, but after reading Gandhi, St. Francis, and other exponents of nonviolence, I began to clarify that in my mind. Now that I'm older I see she is nonviolent.' See Luis D. Leon, *The Political Spirituality of Cesar Chavez* (Berkeley: University of California Press, 2015), 30, 41.

[11] Lawson is referring to a twenty-five-day water-only fast commenced by Chavez on 15 February 1968. An article on the United Farm Workers' website refers to Chavez as 'following the example of Gandhi', 'fasting to rededicate the movement to nonviolence', https://ufw.org/today-history-cesar-chavez-began-25-day-water-fast-delano-calif-feb-11-1968/ [accessed 7 March 2024].

struggle. We should all declare ourselves that this unionization going on is going to be a nonviolent process.

LAL: Yes.

LAWSON: That's what he was doing. He was urging everyone to make that decision, so it was an impact upon the organizing people, and the executive branches, and the organizers. It was not as such out there as a weapon in the union for the workers. It was to get ourselves together. And have a common approach that is a nonviolent approach. So that—I think that's one of Gandhi's contributions.

LAL: Yes, absolutely, it's very much in the Gandhian spirit, but let me rephrase the question for you a bit. . . . I'm wondering whether in Christian traditions . . . Catholicism would be more hospitable than the different Protestant denominations to something like the use of the public fast. That's what I'm really asking. There's no question that Chavez's fast of February '68, and many others that he undertook, are very much in the Gandhian spirit, but he's also someone who's profoundly Catholic. If I think, for example, of American activists who have resorted to public fasting, other than Chavez the people I think of are, for instance, Daniel and Philip Berrigan, who come out of the Catholic tradition.

LAWSON: . . . And Dorothy Day.

LAL: And Dorothy Day, indeed. And the only other country in the world, other than India, where fasting for public purposes and as a mode of protest has had a long history is Ireland.

LAWSON: Ireland, that's right, I know.

LAL: I wonder whether it would be plausible to argue that perhaps certain strands of the Christian tradition facilitated the public fast more than other strands of the Christian tradition. That Catholicism is perhaps more hospitable to this . . .

LAWSON: Well, certainly in Ireland that would have been the case. But I'm not sure about the United States. . . . There has been, in Protestant circles, an awareness of fasts for preparation purposes. In the Lenten season, especially. Also in Quaker discipline books and whatnot that this has been true. So, I would say that was partially why King used it primarily for the purposes of getting himself and encouraging others ... getting themselves in the mood to get to engage in the struggle. For him it was more self-purification. What would have happened down the road, I don't know. I think that Chavez was clearly working entirely out of the Gandhian tradition rather than Roman Catholic tradition. In the United States, did we know that much about the Ireland hunger strike back in the sixties? I'm not sure how much we knew about that.

LAL: I don't know how much was known in the US. In India a man by the name of Terence MacSwiney became a legend. He was the Lord Mayor of Cork. When Irish independence and the partition of Ireland took place, Terence MacSwiney went on a hunger strike which lasted some ninety days. He finally died as a consequence of his hunger strike, but his name became legendary. Gandhi and Nehru—everyone knew of Terence MacSwiney. In those days there was an immense discussion in Catholic journals about whether such a form of hunger-striking, leading to one's death, was not tantamount to suicide and therefore unacceptable for Christians to engage in it. Anyhow, that was one of the things that interested me about Chavez ...

Andrew Young, in his history of the movement,[12] says very distinctly that fasting, King felt, didn't impress the American public, and that's one reason why he didn't embrace it. If indeed that's the case, and you may not agree with that, that raises very profound questions, you see, about the nature of American culture. Is there something particular to India which facilitated this? I wonder what bearing the anthropology of food and hunger, which is quite different across traditions and cultures, has on this question. I wonder if, for example, the whole experience of slavery and the deprivation that came out of it makes the African American activist averse to it.

LAWSON: That's an interesting question. I don't know. But I will say that the stroke of the fast on the part of Gandhi in New Delhi and Calcutta was exactly the right strategic move in those circumstances. He fasted with the demand. It's a fast unto death—until you leaders, political and religious, come together, stop the violence against one another, and determine that you're going to maintain a

[12] Young, *An Easy Burden.*

peace. He had a strategic demand and that's something that he could do.[13]

LAL: Yes, but, you see, it's not going to be possible to explain all of his public fasts, and there's a great many more. You're referring to two of the last ones ...

LAWSON: ... and two of the major ones ... that were astonishing.

LAL: But there were a great many other public fasts ... and as regards the fast unto death, only three of them were such—the two last ones, and the epic fast as it's called, of 1932, which had to do with the issue of the Dalits or untouchables as they were then called ...

LAWSON: That's right.

LAL: ... and what kind of representation they were going to receive. In fact, ironically, this is just a little note here, the fasts unto death were in some respects less dangerous because ... when Gandhi went on a fast unto death, then it immediately demanded attention from the others.

LAWSON: There's no doubt.

LAL: None of them exceeded five days. Whereas the twenty-one-day fasts, and some of the other public fasts, were fasts which he pronounced beforehand. They're going to be of a limited duration, twenty-one days, he says, but some of these twenty-one-day fasts are being undertaken by Gandhi in his sixties. He's not a young man anymore.

LAWSON: That's right. And in the last year of his life ...

LAL: Once he's declared that he's going to go on a twenty-one-day fast, he has to complete it. In fact, those were actually much more dangerous because of the duration of those fasts, right?

LAWSON: Absolutely.

LAL: But not all of them can be described as fasts—that is, as a fast which were also strategically useful ...

LAWSON: Why do you say they all cannot be described as fasts?

LAL: Because, for example in 1933, he goes on a twenty-one-day fast where he says very clearly that this fast is not intended really to influence anyone or intended to make anyone do anything.

LAWSON: The untouchables' fast.

[13] See Vinay Lal, 'Gandhi, the Last Fast, and the Call of the Conscience', *APA Studies: Asian and Asian American Philosophers and Philosophies* 22, no. 1 (Fall 2022), 52–7.

LAL: Right, related to the Dalit issue. It seems to me that this matter goes beyond the question of whether it was something that could be strategically deployed as a weapon of nonviolence. I think you're right. But I'm trying to suggest that I think this would not account for all of them...

LAWSON: But I would say, though, that even this latter fast from Gandhi's perspective had a strategic purpose and value. Now, I'm not sure what that would have been from the circumstances, and I don't remember the story that well from my reading... But I would say that even that, because remember, I can't remember the year or the anecdote, but there's at least one short fast where he fasted because of the misbehaviour of somebody in the ashram.

LAL: Oh, yes.

LAWSON: He did that, too. And as I recall, on that occasion and other occasions the ashram person would return in great tears and repentance that Gandhiji had loved him or her so much that he was willing to fast to push the person towards examining themselves and doing whatever correction they needed to do.

LAL: Absolutely. This is recounted in his autobiography. Although I must say again that Gandhi himself would never have conceded, I think, that any of these fasts was designed to have strategic value. In other words, you see, he would have seen that as a form of instrumentalization and Gandhi was very clear in his mind that even if someone else should construe each of his fasts as having strategic value, he himself only undertook the fast because his inner voice told him that he had to do so.

LAWSON: That's right.

LAL: That was the only compulsion he had and none other. There were no other extraneous factors which weighed on it. I think that we'd have to recognize the integrity of his own view on this matter.

LAWSON: Well, there's a comparable matter in King, because critics of course claim that King was slow in speaking about American foreign policy and the Vietnam War. Some of those critics go so far as to say that this is where SNCC [the Student Nonviolent Coordinating Committee] was far in advance of King and SCLC [the Southern Christian Leadership Conference]. But in conversations with King, and I'm sure other people had those conversations, [it became obvious to me that] he was personally dismayed by the development of the Vietnam War and its escalation. But he clearly felt at this time that his words and his behaviour would reflect upon the movement that was emerging. That whatever he did and said had to be done within the context of his understanding of what would take place in the movement and in the country as a whole. He was sure, for example, that when he did speak out on Vietnam, he would have a great amount of hostility expressed from the administration, even the Johnson administration. That is what happened.

I have to say that I may have had a role in this because, from early on, I saw King as the kind of Moses of the emerging movement and pushed him ... to be the key strategist— that on some issues he alone could make the decision. His jail-going decision: my teaching always in the South was that we could not impose on any person civil disobedience—that, in the light of our society anyway, was a serious tactic and everyone had to find in their own lives the decision to go to jail—and when and where. In the controversy over the Freedom Ride, I was opposed to those people in the Freedom Ride who tried to get King to go and take the bus into Mississippi. I myself was committed to going and went. But I was opposed to any effort on the part of anyone in the group and especially among the coordinators, the leadership, to try to impose upon King the demand that he had to do it at this time.

LAL: And why were you opposed to that demand?

LAWSON: One, because with everybody it was their personal decision. If they were going to join the demonstration, which we knew was resulting in jail, and no violence, each person who did that had to do it out of their own deep commitment to the struggle and their own commitment to however they wanted to frame it. I made that clear.

LAL: And, in fact, compelling them to do so or coercing them is a form of violence.

LAWSON: Yes. Trying to demand of them that they lay down their lives was, to me, not allowable. I did that in Nashville from the very beginning.

LAL: All right. But do you agree or not with Young when he says that, according to King, fasting didn't impress the American public.

LAWSON: Well, I can't really address that. I never heard Martin King say that to me, but that's entirely another matter.

LAL: No, but it's not so much a question, I think, of whether King even said it or not. This is Young's interpretation, right? Because he doesn't really put those words in his mouth. He says that that was the impression he got.

LAWSON: I see.

LAL: Do you think that there's some merit to this argument? One is a question of whether King thought that or not, and that's perhaps less important. I'm more interested in the claim that fasting doesn't impress the American public. Is there anything to that, do you think?

LAWSON: Well, the first is I wouldn't agree with it.

LAL: Right. But let's return to Cesar Chavez and take one of his fasts as an example—because he did fast. I've been reading a book by Miriam Pawel, *The Union of Their Dreams* ... In February of '68, when Chavez undertook a fast, he quite rightly made a distinction, which is lost on many people, between fasting and hunger-striking. The two are quite different. When you fast, you are not fasting to use that as a weapon.

LAWSON: Yeah. Right.

LAL: The idea is that you are not fasting for some political ends, as such; it's not a negotiating tactic. But let me read out a passage from Pawel's book: 'Only a handful of people knew that Chavez was already fasting when he called the Delano strikers and union staff to Filipino Hall on February 19th. He announced that he would fast until everyone in the union agreed to embrace nonviolence. Anything less, Chavez warned, would endanger the whole movement. Impassioned arguments broke out as soon as Chavez left the room. Some objected to the religious overtones. Leftists found the idea particularly distasteful. [*Lawson laughs heartily.*] His own family urged him to abandon the protest.' The author continues and cites someone who says, 'he told us that he was fasting as a prayer'. And here is someone in the movement speaking: 'It was not a hunger strike, and its purpose was not strategic but as an act of prayer and of love for us. He felt that he was responsible as a leader of the union for all the acts of any of us ... The most important thing he said ... was that we as a union and as a movement have aroused the hopes and aspirations of poor people, and we have a duty and a responsibility to those people. We cannot, by resorting to violence, crush their hopes and destroy what we have done. He said that even if all of us in the room were to disappear the movement that had been started would still go on, but that did not mean that we could sacrifice the aspirations that we had aroused.'

Do you think, then, that fasts left a visible impression on people in the United States?

LAWSON: Fasting left a visible impression upon the folk who were trying to organize the struggle. There's no doubt about that.

LAL: That perhaps matters more ...

LAWSON: ... There are folk right now, activists in the labour movement, who remember his [Chavez's] fasting, remember it vividly. They're still impressed and inspired by it in their work today. I would not be prepared to agree that in the right historical context and circumstance of a struggle, that people will not be impacted by this or that tactic or methodology. Especially such a thing as a hunger strike.

LAL: I think you've added an important modification which I think is probably crucial and that is that in the right circumstances, in the right historical context, there's no reason to suppose that people might not embrace it and that it might not have been embraced by African Americans ...

LAWSON: The non-pacifist fifty years ago insisted that nonviolence worked in India because the British had a humane perspective. [*Laughs loudly.*]

LAL: Well, we can rubbish that view.

LAWSON: [*Still laughing heartily.*] I didn't accept it back then and I don't accept it now. You really cannot know in some ways what tactic will impact people when you're operating from inside a movement that's an effective campaign. I mean, that does require a certain amount of serious searching and work and wrestling. In the United States, I think, I've heard too many activists talk as though if they don't have a guarantee of success, they won't do it. Some nonviolent practitioners teach that your tactic must be measured as you plan it from the role of its effectiveness on the public.

I don't teach that. I don't agree with that. I don't think Gandhi organized his mind that way. You work from the inside of a campaign and not primarily from the outside. You work from the inside out, not from the outside in. You try to have as learned an understanding of your social, political, economic, spiritual context as you can, but you still work from the inside. The Montgomery Bus Boycott would not have happened if there were not a few people who were not only outraged but said, 'Let's do a boycott'. They were outraged as most black folk in Montgomery were over the buses. But you had Mary Jo Robinson and Ed Nixon and Rosa Parks and a number of other people who felt, for a couple of years, that a bus boycott would be an effective way to go after it. So they mobilized and made it happen—on Friday, Saturday, and Sunday. So, Monday it was 90 something per cent effective. That could not have happened if some people were not thinking of a specific tactic that they felt could be effective.

LAL: At that particular juncture.

LAWSON: At that particular moment, that's right. A part of the problem in the black community, as in the white activist community, or intellectual community, is the fact that we have not given due study to strikes and boycotts—the abolitionist campaigns prior to the Civil War, or the eighteenth-century nonviolent campaigns that went on that led up to July 4th, 1776. We haven't given enough attention to that. Some of that indication of American history only has a passing word in the history text that I read in high school, like the refusal to pay taxes. Well, most Americans don't know that there were colonists who wouldn't pay King George's taxes in 1774. They don't know that.

LAL: And some who do know would now use that argument for very different purposes. I'm speaking here about extreme right-wing Republicans who obviously want to disavow the role of the state as taxman and would rather not see the rich pay any taxes at all. But that's a different element of the story.

LAWSON: That's an extremism, an ideological extremism that is among the most dangerous extremist positions in Western civilization.

LAL: To speak of fasting is to speak of the body. One has to have a relationship to one's body and understanding of one's body—and what the body can or cannot tolerate, what are its limits. What Gandhi did, of course, was to insert his own body into the body politic. He was very attentive in every respect to his body. There are some biographers and commentators who have chosen not to pay too much attention to that; they think it's either trivial or irrelevant or perhaps embarrassing. For example, he would take enemas constantly—often while giving an interview or while conversing with a visitor. He was very particular about what he ate, and at what time he ate.

LAWSON: Oh, yes, he's very meticulous.

LAL: Personal hygiene, sanitation, all of that—very meticulous. It is also indubitably the case, I think, at least from Gandhi's own standpoint, that there is some—an intricate—relationship between how one takes care of one's body and one's ability to adhere to the principles of nonviolence. Let me stress that I'm not speaking only about something like vegetarianism. That might even be a little bit of a red herring, frankly. For example, Gandhi was very clear in his mind that when he had a visitor who had come from overseas to his ashram, the visitor should get meat if he wanted it. You don't simply impose your particular lifestyle or your ideas about what constitutes good nutrition upon others; but there's also some conception of 'hospitality' in the most generous sense of the term, being 'hospitable' to another's mode of living and thought. If a person who has been bred in England is used to having meat three times a day, and you insist on a vegetarian diet, that's an imposition. I think also of his friendship with Badshah Khan, also known as Frontier Gandhi—a gigantic figure. He was a Pathan, and he was not a vegetarian by any stretch of the imagination.

LAWSON: That's right.

LAL: Gandhi was also of the view that Badshah Khan was the perfect practitioner of nonviolence. Bearing all of that in mind now, my question to you is this. When I look at the life of King, we find something very different here—at least with respect to, for example, things like his relationship to food and relationship to the body. The biographies I've read suggest to me that King was someone who loved food. It's even been suggested that, in some respects, he was actually a glutton.

LAWSON: I doubt that.

LAL: OK. But it's very clear that that part of Gandhi's worldview does not seem to really resonate with King.

LAWSON: Yeah. I agree.

LAL: What would you say about Gandhi's own views on this, then? Do you think that he was mistaken about that? About the relationship between what one...

LAWSON: No. I continue to teach bodily health and care and discipline if you want to participate in serious nonviolent struggle.

LAL: You do?

LAWSON: Oh yes. And I've done that for years. I did that in the fifties as well. Personal discipline of your body so that you can do the work is an important attribute of nonviolence. You do not, I think, have to be a vegetarian or a meat eater or this or that to be a nonviolent practitioner.

LAL: Or even a teetotaller?

LAWSON: Or even a teetotaller. I'm not convinced of that, even. But you do have to have a way of discipline. And when you're in a movement, that personal discipline so that you are ready and able is even more critical. I strongly push that. From my perspective, Gandhi was the kind of learner and teacher and provides the kind of leadership in which he would not say to Jim Lawson, 'You have to become a Hindu to be a practitioner. You have to be a man of prayer to become a practitioner of nonviolence.'

LAL: Yes.

LAWSON: 'You have to do it my way.' It's very, very important, it seems to me, to teach, especially beginners, that you do not have to be religious like Gandhi was religious in order to develop a strong practising perspective of nonviolent struggle and conflict. Those are all, those are in some ways Gandhi's specific details for himself, for his life, that represented a way in which he responded to his make-up and to his experience. In some ways each person has to do their own work. Gandhi's work cannot become your work personally, in that sense.

   ... In terms of nonviolence as soul force? Yes. In terms of nonviolence as discovering how you manage your own anger and fear and all the rest of it? Absolutely. In terms of seeing in the midst of conflict nonviolent tactics that can make a difference and that can work? Absolutely. In terms of even some of the theories, absolutely. You cannot create a better society using instruments of hatred and destruction. You can't dismantle racism by practising racism. Simply cannot be done. His [Gandhi's] notion goes back to all kinds of ancient thought that you cannot grow grapes out of a thistle bush, which is the way Jesus put it. You have to grow grapes out of a vineyard. Those kinds of major themes of Gandhi, I think, are mandatory. It seems to me that's one of the reasons why I call Gandhi the father of nonviolence. It is not because Gandhi invented civil resistance conflict or nonviolent conflict, but because he pulled it all together and tried to give it a direction. He gave it new names, which I think we ought to use. Nonviolence, satyagraha. He said terms like pacifism and non-resistance are inadequate. I agree with that. I think we need to be saying that. I think that his insistence upon thorough evaluation of your situation and wrestling with it from a theoretical and a strategic practical perspective is absolutely critical. In my judgment, this can be done from any culture. I refused some years ago to go to Rwanda and East Congo to do workshops on nonviolence because I felt that the scenery was so violent that it could not be understood. I would not go. And a second reason I wouldn't go, technically, was that I wanted to have some serious experience in African history and development from which I could have some anecdotes and understandings that could be used in a nonviolent workshop in Africa. I think that Africa, for nonviolence, they have to put this in their own language, in their own thoughts. Putting it from my perspective would not be that helpful.

11

On Being Impervious to the Discreet Charms of M. K. Gandhi

Tridip Suhrud

I.

At 6.30 a.m. on 12 March 1930, M. K. Gandhi, accompanied by seventy-eight[1] marchers, left the Sabarmati Ashram for Dandi, a coastal village in South Gujarat. He did not ever return to live in the ashram that he had created and nurtured since 1917.[2] It is evident that the self-imposed exile applied not only to the Ashram but also increasingly to the city of Ahmedabad and Gujarat itself. In the remaining eighteen years of his life, Gandhi was to spend 301 days in Gujarat.[3] His last visit to Ahmedabad was on 2 November 1936. His exile from Ahmedabad is reminiscent of a *tap* [penance]. He did not visit Gujarat after January 1942.

If we understand something of this obvious turning away from Gujarat on the part of Gandhi, we might be able to capture something of the relationship that present-day Gujarat has with him.

---

[1] The figures vary between seventy-eight and eighty. Thomas Weber adds Kharag Bhadur Singh Giri and Satish Kalekar to the 'official' list of seventy-eight marchers. But they joined the march on 14 March 1930. See Thomas Weber, *On The Salt March* (New Delhi: HarperCollins, 1997), 495.

[2] He visited the ashram on 31 July 1931 and again on 19, 20, and 21 August 1933. On neither visit did he stay the night at the ashram.

[3] Eighty-eight days in 1931, thirteen days in 1933, seven days in 1934, ten days in 1935, forty-one days in 1936, thirty-one days in 1937, eighty-one days in 1939, and thirty days in 1942.

Tridip Suhrud, *On Being Impervious to the Discreet Charms of M. K. Gandhi* In: *Gandhi, Truth, and Nonviolence*. Edited by: Vinay Lal, Oxford University Press. © Oxford University Press 2025.
DOI: 10.1093/9780198936657.003.0012

II.

Gandhi chose to establish his ashram in Gujarat, and specifically in Ahmedabad, on his return from South Africa. He hoped to render service to the country through the Gujarati language. He had hoped that Ahmedabad, an ancient centre of handloom weaving, would be the most favourable site for its revival, not just as a craft but as a way of living. Gandhi also had hoped that the wealthy merchant-capitalists of Gujarat would extend monetary help to his ashram and its activities. About twenty-five men and women became the first inhabitants of the Satyagraha Ashram at Kochrab. They lived in a hired bungalow, unsuitable for the ashramic life. Gandhi and his ashram were soon put on the anvil in September 1915 the first 'untouchable' family of Dudabhai, Danibehn and their daughter Lakshmi, joined the ashram community.[4] His closest associates, including Maganlal Gandhi, a man described as the 'soul of the ashram', were deeply distressed by this. All monetary help from the Jain and Vaishnav mahajan of Ahmedabad ceased, and just when Gandhi was to move the ashram to the 'untouchables'' quarters, monetary help from Sheth Ambalal Sarabhai saved the ashram. But the internal rumblings in the ashram did not stop, nor did the opposition from the citizens of Ahmedabad.

In 1917, the ashram shifted further away from the city, to the banks of river Sabarmati. A plague in Kochrab was the immediate reason for the hasty move to a barren piece of land, bereft of tress, where the inhabitants lived under canvas tents and cooked in a tin shed for a kitchen. The fact was that Kochrab had become inhospitable after Danibehn's family moved into the ashram. Search for a more suitable site away from the inhospitable neighbours had commenced in 1916, and the purchase of 36 acres of land was completed during the plague. The ashram community could not have been sustained without the ashramites contributing their physical labour. Gandhi was attracted to the site because of its proximity to the Sabarmati Central Jail. He wrote in his autobiography: 'Its vicinity to the Sabarmati Central Jail was for me a special attraction. As jail-going

---

[4] For the full text of Dudabhai Dafda's letter to Gandhi seeking admission to the ashram, see M. K. Gandhi, *An Autobiography Or The Story of My Experiments with Truth,* A Critical Edition, Introduced with Notes by Tridip Suhrud (New Delhi: Penguin, 2018), 611–12. Henceforth referred to as *An Autobiography.*

was understood to be the normal lot of *Satyagrahis*, I liked this position. And I knew that the sites selected for jails have clean surroundings.'[5] What Gandhi did not mention was that the site had a far deeper symbolic resonance. It was close to the ancient ashram of Sage Dadhichi, known for his sacrifice.[6] It was an ever-present reminder of the mythical sacrifice for the ashram community. Furthermore, what he chose not to disclose was that the site was situated near a *smashan*[7] (crematorium), ritually one of the most impure locations for a Hindu. The only two communities that traditionally lived in proximity to the *smashan* were the *doms*, who cremated the dead, and a community of 'transgressive' renunciates known as *Aghoris*, who seek sublimation through internalizing the impure. Gandhi could not but have grasped what it meant for a Hindu to live in the proximity of a *smashan*. It was not just a constant reminder of mortality and the precariousness of human existence but also a reminder of what it meant to live as an 'outcaste', outside the pale of city and *civitas*. It also signifies the liminal position that Gandhi and his followers had come to occupy in the caste hierarchy of Ahmedabad.

Notwithstanding its liminality, the ashram soon became the centre of the city's political economy, with Gandhi's arbitration and subsequent fast in the dispute involving the mill owners and millhands of Ahmedabad.[8] Gandhi was required to oppose Ambalal Sarabhai, the same man whose gift had saved the ashram from certain financial ruin. The dispute resulted in the creation of a permanent institutional arrangement, the Textile Labour Association, that sought to arbitrate in disputes between the workers and the mill owners through the principles of truth and nonviolence.[9]

---

[5]   *An Autobiography*, 661.

[6]   It is said that Sage Dadhichi gave up his life so that Indra could fashion an infallible weapon—the *Vajra Ayudha*—from the spinal bone of the sage. The area around the present-day Sabarmati Ashram is called Dudheshwara, indicating that the memory of this myth is alive even today.

[7]   This *smashan* is still operative today.

[8]   The economy of Ahmedabad in 1918 revolved around textile mills. Of the estimated total population of 250,000, nearly 100,000 comprised textile labour and their dependents. The mills had roughly 100,000 spindles and 20,000 looms. Mahadev Desai's account of the strike and the fast remains the most authoritative chronicle. See Mahadev Desai, *A Righteous Struggle*, trans. Somnath Dave (Ahmedabad: Navajivan, 1951). Erik Erikson based his psychoanalytical study of Gandhi on this event. See Erik Erikson, *Gandhi's Truth: On The Origins of Militant Nonviolence* (New York: W. W. Norton & Co., 1969).

[9]   The salience of Gandhi's intervention can be judged by the fact that after his assassination a trust was formed in 1951 to preserve his memory and the buildings of his ashram. The corpus fund for this trust was created by the millworkers and mill owners of Ahmedabad. The

While Gandhi was still negotiating the labour dispute in Ahmedabad, he was called by the peasants of the neighbouring Kheda district to lead their struggle against the British on the question of payment of land revenue. It was the success of the two local agitations in Gujarat, besides his success in the struggle of indigo growers of the Champaran region, that paved the way for Gandhi's first nationwide, non-cooperation movement in 1919.

Gandhi's stated objective in selecting Gujarat to establish his ashram was that he would be able to serve the nation through the Gujarati language. In 1909, Gandhi had written a philosophical dialogue, *Hind Swaraj*, and published it in his journal *Indian Opinion*.[10] A century later *Hind Swaraj* remains not only a key text of Gandhi's but also perhaps the most salient philosophical work in the modern Gujarati language. Gujarati language scholarship has shown remarkable indifference to this work.[11] Gandhi wished to reach out to the weaver and the farmer and to women through his writings. The vehicle chosen was *Navajivan*, which commenced publication as a weekly under Gandhi's editorship on 7 September 1919 and continued publication until 10 January 1932. In his first editorial, Gandhi made a remark about the Gujarati language that his journal would adopt: 'India lives in farmers' huts. The weaver's skill is a reminder of India's glory, and so I feel proud in describing myself as a farmer and a weaver. I wish to see *Navajivan* reach the farmers and weavers in their huts and dwellings. I want it to be in their language.'[12]

He was to repeat this idea that writing must be such that it can be understood by the farmer and the weaver with much greater force in his presidential address to the Gujarati Sahitya Parishad in 1936. But in 1919 an event took place that remains unexplained and largely erased from

millworkers donated one day's earning, amounting total of 2.3 million rupees, to the trust. The mill owners' association made a matching donation.

[10] This work was written on board the *Kildonan Castle* between 13 and 22 November and was published in two instalments (11 and 19 December) in the *Indian Opinion*. It was rendered in English by Gandhi as *Indian Home Rule* and published in South Africa by the International Printing Press.
[11] Kishorelal Mashruwala's *Gandhi Vichar Dohan* is imbued with the presence of *Hind Swaraj*, but there are only two book-length studies or commentaries on the text in Gujarati. They are Kanti Shah, *Hind Swaraj: Ek Adhyayan* (Vadodara: Yajna Prakasahn, 2007), and Tridip Suhrud, *Hind Swarajya Vishe* (Vadodara: Purva Prakash, 2008).
[12] *The Collected Works of Mahatma Gandhi* (New Delhi: Publications Divisions) 16: 94.

official histories. On 22 August 1919, Gandhi was defeated in an election for the position of president of the Gujarati Sahitya Parishad. This body, created in 1905, is an autonomous body of *littérateurs*. The man who defeated Gandhi in this election was Hargovind Kantawala.[13] This clearly shows that the educated and literary classes of Gujarat felt a deep ambivalence towards Gandhi, as also towards his claims to serve the nation through the Gujarati language.[14] It is true that Gandhi's national prominence was some years away, and so were his celebrated books in Gujarati, *Dakshin Africa Na Satyagraha No Itihas*[15] and *Satya Na Prayogo*.[16] The mode adopted to deal with this ambivalence and even embarrassment—as the same body repeatedly invited him to be its president, which he accepted in 1936—was silence and erasure. With the sole exception of the extraordinary chronology of Gandhi's day-to-day life by C. B. Dalal,[17] no other history, including that published by the Gujarati Sahitya Parishad, even mentions this fact.[18] This curious omission is more startling because the person who wrote the chapter on Gandhi in the Parishad's history was C. N. Patel, who along with Professor Swaminathan edited the hundred volumes of the *Collected Works of Mahatma Gandhi*.

The deep ambivalence becomes more pronounced because in the same volume of Parishad's history the editors—Umashankar Joshi,

---

[13] Hargovind Kantawala (1849–1931) was Director of Public Instruction, Baroda State.

[14] One of the persons who voted against him was Narhari Parikh, who was to become an ashramite and a close associate.

[15] He began to dictate this account to his fellow prisoner Indulal Yagnik in Yeravda Central Prison on 26 November 1923. By the time he was released, due to ill health, on 5 February 1924—earlier than his stipulated term of six years—he had completed thirty chapters, which appeared serially in *Navajivan* from 13 April 1924 to 22 November 1925. The rest of the remaining twenty chapters were written after his release. They appeared in book form in two parts, in 1924 and 1925. The English translation by Valji Govindji Desai, *Satyagraha in South Africa*, which was seen and approved by Gandhi, was published in 1928 by S. Ganesan of Madras. A second revised edition was published by Navajivan Press in December 1950.

[16] The autobiography appeared serially in the issues of *Navajivan*, beginning on 29 November 1925 and ending on 3 February 1929. An English translation of these chapters, by Mahadev Desai, appeared simultaneously in issues of *Young India*. The first English edition of the *Autobiography* came out in two volumes. The first, containing three parts, was issued in 1927, and the second, containing parts IV and V, in 1929. The second revised edition, in one volume, was released in 1940. For a history of the revised edition and a concordance of changes between the first and second edition, see Tridip Suhrud, *An Autobiography Or The Story of My Experiments with Truth: A Table of Concordance* (New Delhi: Routledge, 2009).

[17] C. B. Dalal, *Gandhi Ni Dinwari* (Gandhinagar: Government of Gujarat, 1990, 2nd rev. ed.), 85.

[18] Volume IV of *Gujarati Sahitya No Itihas* published by the Gujarati Sahitya Parishad has a large chapter on Gandhi, but no mention is made of this event. See Umashankar Joshi, Anantrai Raval, and Vishnu Shukla, eds., *Gujarati Sahitya No Itihas* (Ahmedabad: Gujarati Sahitya Parishad, 1981). Specifically, C. N. Patel, ch. 6 'Gandhi', 257–308.

Anantrai Raval, and Yashwant Shukla—decided to name the period of Gujarati writing between 1915 and 1948 as Gandhi *Yug* (the Age of Gandhi). Anantrai Raval, in his overview of the volume, gave a justification for this naming:

> After the arrival of the British, the other most significant development in the period under consideration is the advent of Gandhi in the universe of thought and action of India. The period of over three decades, after his triumphant Satyagraha in South Africa – which enhanced India's prestige – and his subsequent return to India in 1915 till the time of his death in 1948, is filled with the influence of his ideas, especially Satyagraha movements for national independence of 1920–22, 1930–32 and 1942 that people fought under his leadership and resultant attainment of freedom. This period, therefore, can without hesitation be called Gandhi *Yug*, both in history as in literature. It is a matter of joy and pride for Gujarat that most of Gandhi's work was done in Gujarat and through Gujarati language.[19]

He does mention Gandhi's 'straight, simple, unadorned, sparse and yet direct' prose and his contribution to Gujarati discourse through his *Dakshin Africa Na Satyagraha No Itihas* and *Satya Na Prayogo*. Raval concedes that these two works 'have luminous creative sections'. He takes note of Gandhi's discursive essays and letters, without mentioning any specific details. The one contribution that is specifically mentioned is Gandhi's contribution to the standardization of Gujarati orthography. Clearly, for Raval and his fellow editors, Gandhi's Gujaratiness and his politics are far more salient than his contribution to Gujarati language and literature.

III.

From 17 June 1917 to 12 March 1930 Gandhi spent a total of 1,520 days at the ashram, of which 685 days were spent during the time he wrote substantial parts of his *Autobiography* between 25 November 1925 and 3

---

[19] Anantrai Raval, 'Bhumika', in Joshi, Raval, and Shukla, eds., *Gujarati Sahitya No Itihas*, 4.

February 1929. The sudden death of Maganlal Gandhi on 23 April 1928 in faraway Bihar had also forced Gandhi to contend with desolation at the ashram and to pay greater attention to the administrative details of the ashram's functioning, including the normative aspects of following of ashram observances. On 14 June 1928 Gandhi published a revised constitution of the ashram.

The ashram had a constitution that was drawn up after consultation in 1915. But Gandhi found it 'desirable to recast the constitution in view of the many changes and ups and downs that the Ashram had undergone'.[20] Explaining the need for a revised constitution, he wrote:

> The Ashram represents a prayerful and scientific experiment. The observances are many, but they have been tested for the past 13 years of the existence of the Ashram whilst, it is impossible to claim their perfect fulfilment by any one of us, the workers have in all humility tried to enforce them in their lives to the best of their ability and with more or less success.[21]

But by 4 November 1928 Gandhi announced that the Satyagraha Ashram would no longer be an ashram, as vital changes were introduced in ashramic life. He admitted that the name Satyagraha Ashram was suggestive of its qualities and claimed, 'It has always been our endeavour to stick to truth and to rely on its support alone. It cannot be said that we have always succeeded in our efforts. It cannot be claimed that all the inmates of the Ashram have worshipped truth. It can definitely be said that on the whole truth has been adhered to'.[22] Gandhi was not concerned with adherence to vows but with the comprehension of their subtler meaning by all ashram inmates. He admitted, 'We did not find ourselves capable of coping with subtler meanings to the rules, a fact which we gradually realize. Hence we arrived at the decision to keep those very rules intact but change the name'.[23]

This change of name, he hoped, would allow for a greater leniency in the ashramic observances. He decided to maintain the Satyagraha

---

[20] *CWMG* 36: 398.
[21] Ibid.
[22] *CWMG* 38: 22.
[23] Ibid, 23.

Ashram as an ideal and carry on its activities under another name. An ideal does not require a location; it is something that he hoped he could carry within himself. He kept for that ideal only a small prayer ground. He instead decided to rename the ashram Udyog Mandir (Temple of Industry), as 'Industry and Physical work have always been the outward manifestations of the Satyagraha Ashram and we can claim that they have brought considerable credit to it.'[24] Gandhi said that the term Udyog had to be read in light of the *Gita* as a *yajna* (sacrifice) or *kurbani*. The change was necessary because consciousness of the name 'made us conscious of our unworthiness to bear it.'[25]

The churning within the ashram and its impact on society outside is evident from rumours that Mahadev Desai had been made chairman of the managing committee, as 'inmates having lost confidence in me'.[26] Gandhi revealed the innermost reasons to Devadas in two hitherto unpublished letters. On 18 September 1928 he wrote to Devadas, who was unable to attend a meeting at the ashram called to discuss these changes:

> Implementing the new changes in the Ashram, I have got drained out. You know well how the advancement of women is dear to me. And yet, with the exception of two or three, none of the women living in the Ashram do so of their own choice. Even those who do cannot be said to have grasped even the surface meaning of Ashram observances. Do all the men in the Ashram know them? What then is one to say of the subtler meaning of these observances? For that matter, even I, who have formulated the observances, do not know their subtle forms in their fullness. But the inner value of these observances reveal themselves to me, each successive day, with ever-increasing clarity. Seeing all this and holding discussions on it I saw that while following the observances and ensuring their observance and thus building the Ashram, there was an aggression being committed, both unrecognised and entirely unintended, on the Ashram woman. She could leave neither her husband, nor the Ashram. There was a full desire to stay but the strength needed to adhere to observances was just not there. If the Ashram were

---

[24]   Ibid.
[25]   Ibid., 38.
[26]   Ibid., 34.

to maintain its inherent character any softening of Ashram observances seemed like it would be sinful. I consider the observances that
have been brought into being to be an indispensable part of Satyagraha.
To make these observances correspond to everyone's nature would be
good, true, but the closer we get to truth the stricter should the observances become. Considering this I felt that if women are to be equal
participants in the Ashram, the Satyagraha Ashram should adopt a new
character. Thus, hereafter, the Ashram, divesting itself of all symbolisms
of an exterior kind, will be as a regenerative seed commemorating the
original. The agency of the Ashram is to be with the newly formed body.
Even the Ashram lands would be given to it on rent. Thus, the Ashram
would become almost invisible. But, as the burden of the others is reduced, so will the burden on those who have taken a vow of Ashram
observances increase. This is because even in the newly formed Udyog
Mandir they would be principal workers. They would have to contribute to the Udyog Mandir while becoming sentinels of the observances. The hope underlying this is that if the Ashram inhabitants are
true ashramites the Udyog Mandir would ultimately come to life as a
mature form of the Ashram.[27]

Devadas, clearly unsatisfied, must have sought further clarifications,
and Gandhi responded on 29 September:

That Satyagraha Ashram is, to a major extent, to become Udyog
Mandir has pained you. I understand that but the reasons for the pain
are not correct. It does not imply that the co-workers have failed and
that I have been disappointed in them. If we take it that they have failed,
we should conclude that I have also failed. The change has been necessitated by a clearer perception of the prevailing situation. It is a sign
of affectionate consideration for the ashram's women. Certain liberties
were necessary to secure justice for them; liberties, which can neither
be taken nor given in the Satyagraha Ashram. Its rules are an inviolable
part of its constitution. Therefore, we should adopt a name wherein the

[27] M. K. Gandhi to Devadas Gandhi, 18 September 1928, unpublished correspondence, in
Gopal Krishna Gandhi and Tridip Suhrud, *Scorching Love: Letters from Mohandas Karamchand
Gandhi to His Son, Devadas* (New Delhi: Oxford University Press, 2022).

imperative for such rules is not felt. This is the principal reason for the change. It is no doubt a bitter draught to swallow but in the language of the *Gita* it is a *Satvika Karma*. Though, to begin with, this seems like poison, its results are very likely to be ambrosial.[28]

If the ashram was an ideal and the only location that it required was the prayer ground and the act of congregational prayer, the ashram could be anywhere; later in his life Gandhi claimed that the ashram was where he travelled. It went with him on his barefoot pilgrimage of Noakhali and to Bihar, which he described as his Karbala.

IV.

If the Ashram's ideals were so subtle that they could not be followed by anyone in their fullness, what of his other ideas? Let us consider them around four public and political ideals, all of which were also among the ashram observances.

The idea of the congregational living required two observances, *asteya* and *aparigraha* (non-stealing and non-acquisitiveness). Gandhi and the ashram stood as a challenge to the mercantile culture of Gujarat. It eschewed both private property and personal inheritance. If it were to remain an ascetic ideal, the mercantile capitalists who welcomed Gandhi in the city and in some instances into their homes would not have been unduly perturbed by it. Gujarat had a long tradition, like the rest of the Indian subcontinent, of ascetic renunciation. The ascetic re-nouncer stood outside the framework of the householder. Gandhi and the ashram were not renunciates in the traditional sense. Gandhi was a householder and was soaked into 'family matters' throughout his life of nearly eight decades. 'Both he and Kasturba as she came to be known very early into her married life widened the walls of their homes raised its roof, opened its doors to admit and welcome not just cousins, nephews and nieces and their spouses, but host of those many from all over the world who joined their energies into his life's missions.'[29] While

[28]   Ibid.
[29]   Ibid.

'[n]o special privileges were reserved by him for his biological descend-
ants and no hardship withheld from them. And yet there was that space
he carved out of the borderless province of his public life, the room he
cleaned out of the vast lodging-house of his public endeavours where
family was, simple family.'[30]

Gandhi and his ashram were composed of individual family units,
with some notable exceptions such as Vinoba Bhave and Mirabehn/
Madeleine Slade. It was while remaining a householder that Gandhi
espoused *asteya* and *aprigraha* as ideals. All societies have cultural
resources to deal with such challenges, and Gujarati society was
no exception. The Gujarati mercantile class would have known of
other exemplars who as householders held up the ascetic ideal. Kavi
Shrimad Rajchandra is a fine example. But there was a vital difference between Gandhi and others: Gandhi was eager to 'interfere' in
both the business and family affairs of the mill owners of Ahmedabad.
Even before he led the Ahmedabad millworkers' strike and fasted
to hold them steadfast to their pledge, Gandhi wrote an unusual
letter to Ambalal Sarabhai, a pioneering industrialist and generous
philanthrope.

Ambalal's sister, Anasuya Sarabhai, had been pleading the case of the
millworkers to her brother and other mill owners for both enhanced
wages and better working conditions. Gandhi chose to intervene in
this situation when he came to know of this from a public worker of
Ahmedabad, Krishnalal Desai. He wrote to Ambalal:

> I think you should satisfy the weavers for the sake of Shrimati
> Anasuyabehn at any rate. There is no reason to believe that, if you sat-
> isfy these you will have others clamouring. . . . How could a brother be
> the cause of suffering to a sister? and that too a sister like Anasuyabehn?
> I have found that she has a soul which is absolutely pure. It would be
> nothing strange if took her word to be law. You are, thus under a double
> obligation: to please the workers and earn a sister's blessings. My pre-
> sumption, too, is doubly serious in a single letter I have meddled in your
> business and your family affairs. Do forgive me.[31]

---

[30]   Ibid.
[31]   *CWMG* 14: 115.

This tendency to meddle both in the business and family affairs of others made Gandhi distinct. The wealthy merchant capitalists of Gujarat—Hindu, Jain, and Parsi—were not strangers to *dharmada*, what one is obligated to give to others from one's wealth. In fact, they were inheritors of a long tradition of *dharmada*, but their *dharmada* and the trusteeship that Gandhi had begun to articulate had some crucial differences. The tradition of *dharmada* has either been centred around religious institutions or been aimed largely at a specific community to which the donor belonged. It created public good, but its beneficiaries belonged to an exclusive group.

Gandhi's trusteeship sought to go beyond the idea of *dharmada*. He wanted the wealthy to decide what part of their wealth could justly belong to them and what portion was held by them in trust. The difference between *dharmada* and trusteeship is not in degree or intended beneficiary. *Dharmada* is a voluntary act; obligation is self-imposed. For Gandhi, trusteeship was an obligation, an obligation that had a large degree of self-volition, but it had to be understood as a duty. Gandhi's aspiration and expectation were that all surpluses should be treated as trust, even when that surplus was used as accumulated capital. Gandhi wanted the trustees to act as trustees of their wealth for all society and not a section of it.

Gandhi felt that non-stealing and non-acquisition had to be for all society, and not just the wealthy. This he sought to explain through the twin ideas of *yajna* and bodily labour. The latter came to him from Christianity and the former through the *Gita*. He developed the idea of physical labour as *yajna,* sacrificial work done for others. His insistence on the daily observance of *Sutra-Yajna,* sacrificial spinning, embodied this idea. In a society that had deep structures of hierarchies of ritual purity and impurity and of engagement with materiality of productive work, Gandhi's insistence—not only for himself and the ashramites but for *all* Indians— created cultural and social anxieties. Gandhi and his ashram co-workers worked with their hands with materials that were considered polluting— sanitation work, including removal of night soil and work with leather— which sought to challenge the cultural fears around touch and specially polluting touch. Gandhi's aspiration was rarely shared by caste Hindus, the emerging merchant-capitalist class, and classes of professionals who had freed themselves from bodily labour.

Gujarat was and remains permeated with Jain ethos, with its belief in ahimsa, nonviolence, as a supreme duty and an obligatory personal observance. Gandhi's satyagraha had placed ahimsa at the centre of resistance to all forms of injustice. Ahimsa for him was a means to truth; it was attainable. It was what made us human. This was true not only of the political realm but also of the spiritual realm. Gandhi believed that the more we take to violence, the more we recede from the self, from truth. Violence foreclosed the possibility of self-realization, of seeing *Satyanarayana,* truth as God face to face and the attainment of moksha. Gandhi argued that it was his unceasing search for nonviolence that enabled him to hear his 'inner voice', his *antaratma,* the dweller within or the 'small, still voice', as he called it. He constantly sought to hear this voice, sought its guidance, and submitted himself to it, surrendering his self-volition. Ahimsa made self-search and self-realization possible. Ahimsa, by creating the possibility for self-knowing, also made possible the quest for swaraj. Swaraj is when we learn to rule ourselves. This swaraj is both self-rule and rule over ourselves. This capacity for self-rule and rule over ourselves requires bringing all senses in harmony with each other. This give us the capacity for performance of our duty. Gandhi said that performance of duty and observance of morality are convertible terms, and so doing we know ourselves. The ashram observances for him were the key to both swaraj and self-realization. Gandhi's ahimsa and his incessant advocacy of the moral superiority of non-vegetarianism created a ground from which middle-class and middle-caste Gujarati Hindus could engage with him. His advocacy of the harmful effects of all toxicants both on the body and morality should have created a shared ethos with the dominant structures of belief and observance in Gujarat.

Gandhi sought to expand the ambit of ahimsa as non-killing and non-injury. He sought to establish it not only as personal virtue but as political ethics. In the realm of the satyagraha it became an active force as nonviolent resistance. At the same time, he began to think of ahimsa as not just nonviolence or non-injury but as love. In the English translation of the ashram observances the term that he preferred for ahimsa was not nonviolence but love. Ahimsa in this sense became an active force of compassion, of empathy, of *daya.* Ahimsa dharma became daya dharma; daya was both the root of religion (*Daya dharam ka mool hai*) and a path to an egoless state and moral conduct.

Two of Gandhi's actions—one taken in the ashram domain and the other in the civic domain—completely shattered the ground that he and the ashram had hitherto shared with Gujarati society on the stead-fastness to ahimsa. Between 25 and 30 September 1928 Gandhi got a doctor to administer a quietus, by means of a poison injection, to an ailing calf at the ashram. Gandhi advanced the argument that ahimsa demanded that agony should be ended by ending life itself. Responding to 'great commotion' and 'angry letters', Gandhi wrote in *Navajivan* a two-part essay, 'Pavak ni Jwala' (Fiery Ordeal), in which part one examined 'Ahimsak Pranharan' (When killing may be ahimsa) and part two 'Himsak Pranharan' (When killing may be himsa). We should note that the Gujarati title does not have the caveat 'may', which was introduced by Pyarelal in the English translation. Gandhi described the circumstances and the process by which he helped the ashram's managing committee, and the entire ashram community, arrive at the decision.[32] Gandhi said that he was aware that public opinion in Ahmedabad would see this action as 'himsa', but he contended that performance of duty, dharma, cannot be subject to public opinion.

Gandhi asserted that the path of ahimsa, like the path of love, is lonely; often one treads all alone. He answered the question that would inevitably be asked of him: would he apply the same principle to human beings? To himself?' He replied, 'same law holds good in both the cases', so long as the ultimate objective was 'to relieve the suffering soul within from pain'. He insisted that in such an instance, 'not to kill would spell himsa, while killing would be ahimsa'. He challenged the votaries of ahimsa that they had made it a 'blind fetish and put the greatest obstacle in the way of the spread of true ahimsa in our midst'. He charged them that their conscience was drugged and that had made them insensitive to the more insidious forms of himsa, including starvation, exploitation, and selfish greed. 'It is this fundamental misconception about the nature and scope of ahimsa, this confusion about the relative values, that is responsible for our mistaking mere non-killing for ahimsa and for the fearful amount of himsa that goes on in the name of ahimsa in our country.'[33] He agreed that to cause pain to, wish ill to, or take the life of any living being out of

---

[32] *CWMG* 37: 310.
[33] Ibid, 313.

anger or selfish intent is himsa. But he asserted, 'after a calm and clear judgment to kill or cause pain to a living being with a view to its spiritual or physical benefit from a pure, selfless intent may be the purest form of ahimsa'.[34]

If this challenge to the votaries of ahimsa were not enough, in the same article he wrote of the serious consideration that he was giving to the question of killing the monkeys that were wreaking havoc in the ashram. He did not make any attempt to pass off this clear breach of ahimsa as nonviolence. But he took the argument in what appears to be philosophically the opposite direction. He argued about the inevitability of himsa. The one that lives in the body is bound in a chain of destruction. Is there a measure, can there be a measure, of the extent of himsa one must commit to live? As a seeker after truth, he may make a ceaseless endeavour to reduce his needs and hence the circle of himsa, but as a peasant he must chalk out a path for himself.

His action and, more importantly, his advocacy of killing as an act of ahimsa and the clear expression of the inevitability of himsa brought upon him the ire of many incensed critics, who cast aside all decorum and propriety and poured upon him 'the lava of their unmeasured and acrimonious criticism'. He summarized their objections and criticisms. The critics said that he should retire from the field of ahimsa and that his views about ahimsa were imported from the West. He contended that as a satyagrahi it was his bounden duty to express his views openly and freely, even at the cost of incurring popular displeasure or even worse. One could give up what one perceives as a right, but one cannot forsake that which is a duty. He dismissed the charge of his ahimsa being Western in philosophical disposition. He was certain that, no matter what the inspiration was, his views on 'ahimsa have now become a part and parcel of my being'.[35]

The letters that he received confirmed for him his belief that, in our effectiveness over matters of no particular significance, 'We forget the elementary duty of kindness, are led away from the path of true love, and discredit our ahimsa'.[36]

---

[34]   Ibid.
[35]   Ibid., 339.
[36]   Ibid., 341.

Starting on 10 October 1926, Gandhi wrote eight essays in *Navajivan*, which were translated into English by Mahadev Desai for *Young India*. The Gujarati essays were called 'Aa te Jivdaya?' (literally, 'Is this compassion to all life?') and in English they carried the title 'Is this Humanity?', which, while including the idea of compassion, does not foreground it.

This series was occasioned by what could be called the Great Ahmedabad Dog Massacre. The Ahmedabad Municipality, following their own notion of ahimsa and compassion, decided that rabid dogs should not be put to sleep but conveniently placed outside the limits of the Municipality. The textile mills and colonies of millworkers were in many instances outside the city limits. This was certainly true of the mills of Seth Ambalal Sarabhai, himself of Jain lineage. There were sixty such rabid dogs on his mill premises, and he in consultation with Gandhi decided to have them killed. Retribution was swift. Ambalal Sarabhai was no longer to be regarded as a Jain. The Humanitarian Society compelled Gandhi to enter a public discussion. Gandhi said that he had indeed advised Ambalal and that he had upon reflection found no need to revise his opinion. He argued that Hinduism and all other religions agree on the principle that killing any living being is sinful. But the difficulty arises while putting it into practice. The problem arises when imperfect beings are required to put in practice a perfect principle; he argued that a city dweller responsible for other lives under his care is required to make a choice between the sin of killing a rabid dog and a greater sin of not killing it. He claimed to be imbued with ahimsa. 'I believe myself to be saturated with ahimsa non-violence. Ahimsa and truth are as my true lungs. (In Gujarati it is more evocative *prana*, life's breath.) I cannot live without them.' He was convinced that many votaries of nonviolence were propagating himsa in the name of nonviolence owing to deep ignorance of the great principle and failed to recognize that often the so-called 'himsa to be truest form of ahimsa'.[37]

Many advocates of ahimsa—quite often Jain—met him with a view not to understand his position but to correct him. He told his visitors and wrote politely that Jains have no monopoly of ahimsa. He reminded his visitors and readers alike that Mahavir was the incarnation of ahimsa, compassion. Gandhi wryly remarked, 'How I wish his votaries were

---

[37] *CWMG* 31: 488.

votaries also of his ahimsa!'[38] He did not hesitate to say that ahimsa in his times had become a monopoly of the 'timid vaisyas'; what he wished to establish instead was the ahimsa of the brave.

'Ahimsa', he said, 'is the extreme limit of forgiveness',[39] which was an attribute of the brave. He cited figures of rabid dog bites obtained from the city's Civil Hospital and cited the example of how the city of London had tackled the problem of both stray and rabid dogs head-on and solved it. He reminded his readers that the West was not innocent of humanity. He advanced an argument that his compassion made it impossible for him to allow rabid dogs to die a slow, painful death.

Gandhi's open challenge to the dominant and widely shared notion of ahimsa as simply non-killing or non-injury created deep unease both among Hindus and the Jain communities of Gujarat. They could not have but seen that even the mahajan leaders of community and industry such as Ambalal Sarabhai were willing to be led by Gandhi and forsake their ancestral religion. The rupture on the question of both principle and practice of ahimsa would never be healed.

One of the most painful occurrences in Gandhi's life was the disruption of his prayers. This became almost a routine feature during his last months when he was prevented from taking the name of Allah. Those who gathered to hear him speak in Delhi would object to the utterance of Auzubillah. Gandhi made it a practice to ask if someone in the gathering had an objection to the verses from the Quran being recited.

But the episode that occurred in Ahmedabad was very different in nature. Gandhi was on a 'sabbatical' from public activities and had decided to inhabit the ashram to write the *Autobiography* at the prompting of his *Anataryami*, the dweller within. Every morning during this year he gave a discourse on the *Gita* to his associates at the ashram. The students and teachers of Gujarat Vidyapith that he had founded, and whose chancellor he was, made a claim on him. They wanted him to teach a regular class. After deliberation it was decided that he would read with them the New Testament, and specifically the Sermon on the Mount, and provide a commentary.

---

[38] Ibid., 505.
[39] Ibid., 524.

Gandhi's attraction for the Passion of Christ, his intimate contact with Christians, and his deep, scholastic reading of the Bible and the Sermon were well known. He had during his early years in South Africa read both widely and deeply on the life of Christ and Christian theology. He had read Anna Kingsford's esoteric Christianity, had worked as an agent of esoteric Christian union in South Africa. His early essays included a series on the life of Christ, wherein he had described Christ as a 'Prince' among satyagrahis. Christ was constantly on his mind as he discoursed on the *Gita* to his ashram associates. During the morning discourse Gandhi was asked by an ashramite as to who is a yogi. Gandhi replied that the exemplar was Jesus, his life and death being the embodiment of the life of a yogi as envisaged by the *Gita*. Thus, it was not unexpected that the community at Vidyapith should ask him to read the New Testament with them.

What happened on that fateful afternoon remains opaque, even with the aid of Mahadev Desai's diary. What we know is that Gandhi stopped giving the lectures after that day, as there was opposition to discourses on the Bible both within Vidyapith and the city of Ahmedabad. Gandhi had to face allegations of being a closet Christian and using the opportunity to discourse to the students of his own institution to proselytize them. Gandhi responded to this charge publicly, as was his chosen mode.[40] Though deeply pained, his reply is philosophically and personally very nuanced.

He dealt with the change of being a closet Christian simply. All those who were even in the slightest acquainted with him would know that he had both personal and public courage to own up to his conviction and practise his deeply held beliefs. He also thanked his critics for admitting or acknowledging that he had the capacity to both comprehend and be moved by the sublime beauty and truth of Christ's life and message.

The memory of this clearly stayed with him. We do not have any record of Gandhi offering to discourse on any scripture hereafter at Vidyapith. The response of the post-independence administrators of Gujarat Vidyapith has been very telling. They decided to commemorate the un-delivered discourse by designating a space in the Pranjivan Chhatralaya,

[40] This was published as 'Crime of Reading Bible' in *Young India* (2 August 1926). See *CWMG* 31: 350–1.

where the congregation had gathered. Keenly alert to the price of real estate, they designated one of the smallest rooms in this sprawling building with a vast quadrangle in the centre as the Bible Room. This intellectual and spiritual closure on the part of a community that he had helped create and nurture would have deeply perturbed Gandhi. Gujarat Vidyapith had a long history of inviting as teachers some of the leading scholars on various religious traditions, such as Muni Jinvijayji, who apart from establishing the department of Jain philosophy pioneered the study of Indology, and Dharmanand Kosambi, an expert on Buddhist philosophy. This objection in view of this intellectual and spiritual engagement with scriptural and religious traditions would have shaken Gandhi, especially on the part of a community that had sought to prepare itself and others for swaraj and freedom of ideas in the widest possible sense. This objection was clearly a result of deep-seated cultural anxieties regarding Christianity. It should be mentioned that there is no record of the ashram community objecting to the inclusion of either Christian or Islamic prayers in the congregational prayers at the ashram, and the community even innovated the Vaishnava Jana to include a Parsi Jana, Khristi Jana, and Muslim Jana in their renditions.

After Champaran, as the ashram inmates were making efforts to create a habitat out of a barren land and foster a sense of community both within the ashram and with the city of Ahmedabad, Gandhi hastened to Kheda, responding to the call of the peasantry. Despite Gandhi's 'Mahatmaship', even though the landed peasantry in Kheda was willing to be led by him in their struggle for deferment of the payment of land revenue, Gandhi's insistence upon stopping the pernicious, violent, and sinful practice of untouchability was rarely afforded hearing space. The Patidars of central Gujarat accepted Gandhi's political leadership but resisted his message of social reform, both within the caste—especially concerning their treatment of women—and in their relationships to other 'weaker' castes.

Gandhi and his colleagues decided to make a camp in Nadiad town, as they had done in Motihari in Champaran, and travel to the interior villages, at times spending nights there or, if convenient, returning to the camp. The landed, affluent, organized, and dominant Patidar community would have been expected to provide hospitality—a place to stay and sparse meals, which Gandhi was willing to cook. That had been his experience in Champaran where he went as an unknown, curious, and

sympathetic outsider. The indigo tenant farmers of Champaran, following generations of oppression and penury, had opened themselves
to Gandhi and his vakil associates. They not only spoke in thousands
to Gandhi and his associates but also invited them into their homes.
Gandhi did not speak their language, and yet they allowed him to 'pene-
trate' the villages. He would have expected a similar openness, especially
because he had been invited by persons like Narhari Parikh, who had
deep roots in the community, and he was accompanied by his new associate, Vallabhbhai Patel, who had shed his reluctance about barrister
Gandhi's ways.

In Nadiad, Gandhi lived not as a guest of any person or in the facility
created by the community but in an orphanage. During the entire duration of the agitation Gandhi stayed at the orphanage whenever he was
required to spend the night at Nadiad. Even when he stayed the night, in
some villages his resting place was often the village dharamshala, a place
for wayfarers where the village community was unlikely to be polluted by
their proximity. The Patidars of Kheda showed a way for many in Gujarat,
including the landed peasantry of Bardoli, that while Gandhi's political
leadership would be accepted, even sought, especially when the community stood to benefit directly from it as in non-payment of land revenue,
his social message, especially regarding untouchability, the exploitation
of landless labour, and the treatment of women, could easily be ignored.
There appeared a divisible Gandhi: a Gandhi of satyagrahas, a Gandhi
of vegetarians, an ashramic Gandhi, and an 'untouchable' Gandhi who
need not be given much hearing space or followed.

That many in Gujarat had come to regard him as an 'untouchable'
became apparent during his visit to Kutch. The presence of Lakshmi,
daughter of Danibehn and Dudabhai, who had been recently placed
in his and Kasturba's care, added a new dimension. Gandhi not only
was unwilling to obey customary norms of untouchability and to observe prohibitions on interdining in his ashram but also had begun to
care in public for the daughter of an untouchable as one would care for
one's own. This sharp divide between the political following of Gandhi
and resistance to the social reform agenda was evident even during the
Dandi March, a meticulously planned and expertly executed mobilization that reaffirmed Gandhi's confidence in the power of nonviolent
resistance and our capacity for collective nonviolence. During what

was hitherto Gandhi's most successful political mobilization in India, Gandhi's intertwining of the social reform agenda as a necessary condition for the attachment of swaraj remained unheeded. Many villages had ceremoniously welcomed him along with his co-marchers, but in several places after he and his co-marchers had left the village, they with equal enthusiasm set fire to the 'hut' that was specially made for him. This was borne out in the recent commemoration of the Dandi Memorial by the government of Gujarat and India. The aspiration was to create an appropriate memorial at Dandi and a highway (a particular fascination for us Gujaratis), with each resting place being marked with an appropriate facility for night stay. In village after village, the team in charge could not find the place where he and the marchers had stayed.

V.

Gandhi might have turned away from Gujarat, but his presence left a lasting and indelible impression on Gujarati mind and society. The combination of older forms of societal responsibility expressed by *dharmada* and Gandhi's idea of trusteeship combined to create an exceptionally enriching tradition of institution building. This tradition has made the city of Ahmedabad home to some of modern India's finest academic and intellectual institutions. They include the Ahmedabad Education Society (AES), Indian Institute of Management Ahmedabad (IIMA), National Institute of Design (NID), Ahmedabad Textile Industry's Research Association (ATIRA), Physical Research Laboratory (PRL), CEPT University, and the Calico Museum of the Sarabhai Foundation. The city also nurtured a remarkable tradition of modern institutional architecture that saw Claude Batley, Louis Kahn, Le Corbusier, Charles Correa, B. V. Doshi, and Achyut Kanvinde build in Ahmedabad.

Gandhi's intervention created the Majoor Mahajan Mandal, a unique institution of modern India where the millworkers and mill owners were represented and resolved all industrial disputes, not just wages and bonuses, in a spirit of dialogue and arbitration without taking recourse to strikes, lockdowns, or litigation. This institution worked alongside the Textile Labour Association (TLA) and the Ahmedabad Textile Mill Owners' Association (ATMA). Together they laid the foundation of industrial dispute resolution in Gujarat. Until 1980 the three organ-izations and their leaders also played a significant role in civic affairs, especially in times of communal strife and natural disaster. This had an-other implication in the political field. The spirit of dialogue, collabor-ation, arbitration, and participation in civic affairs meant that Gujarat did not develop a left-wing or communist labour movement. The ab-sence of the left both politically and culturally in one of the most in-dustrialized states of modern India has been a result of this movement. Even as the textile industry declined in the mid-1980s, other institu-tional innovations inspired by the TLA and Majoor Mahajan Mandal emerged to play a large role in empowering workers in the informal economy. Ela Bhatt's Self Employed Women's Association (SEWA) or-ganized and empowered women labourers in the informal economy. Bhatt and SEWA self-consciously trace their intellectual, practical, and organizational legacy to the TLA and its leaders Anasuya Sarabhai and Shankarlal Banker.

The political mobilization of the Patidars of central Gujarat during the Kheda Satyagraha and the Salt Satyagraha allowed the community to emerge as not only a dominant caste but also a powerful political force. The community's own enterprise and strong diasporic linkages also helped it to reduce its dependence on land and agriculture. The emer-gence of the milk cooperative movement soon after independence in Kheda district, which over time came to be emulated in other parts of the state and the country, owed its emergence and the deep roots it cast to the political mobilization of the Kheda and Salt Satyagrahas. One criticism that the milk cooperative movement has faced bears this out. The demo-cratic processes by which the leadership was elected and the political-economic benefits of a cash economy around milk further consolidated the Patidar dominance.

Gandhi's engagement with coastal communities was surprisingly little. He and his family came from the coastal town of Porbandar, and he himself was a seafarer. He was acutely aware of the contribution that merchants had made through sea trade. Yet none of his political mobil-izations in Gujarat or his constructive activities paid any special attention to the coastal communities. This even though salt and salt tax preoccu-pied his thoughts and action for several decades. This vast coastline and many coastal communities and seaboard economy have remained outside the institutional awareness of Gandhian organizations in the post-independence period.

The eastern belt of Gujarat is a pre-dominantly tribal area. According to the census of 2011, 14.75 per cent of the population of Gujarat is tribal. Gandhi had very limited understanding of and affinity with the tribal society, language, culture, or arts. His only meaningful intervention in the life of *dubla* (literally, 'feeble') tribal people of South Gujarat was to rename them *halpatis* ('those who husband the plough'). His close associates Jugatram Dave and A. V. Thakkar ('Thakkar Bapa') worked among tribal communities of the eastern belt. That work has continued. The compulsory primary education introduced by the Gaikward state and the 'ashram schools' (residential schools) started under the influence of Jugatram Dave, and A. V. Thakkar created among the tribal people an educated class, which, aided by the affirmative action policies of the post-independence Indian state, entered the modern institution space. But the legacy of the so-called Gandhian institutional and constructive work in the tribal area is not that of Gandhi but, largely, of Dave and Thakkar.

Gandhi's work on the removal of untouchability remains contested. It has come under acute political, cultural, and scholastic scrutiny. Gandhi's failure to seek the destruction of the caste system, his unwillingness to accept that at the root of the varna system is a notion of ritual purity and impurity and that it cannot be seen as mere division, and the claim that all forms of labour are equal have brought questions about the authenticity and genuineness of his endeavour.

Gandhi's work with Harijans had one lingering impact on the consciousness of the community in Gujarat. The Dalit community took much longer to acquire a political consciousness. The empowering ideas and mobilizations around the inspirational figure of B. R. Ambedkar have been slow in coming to Gujarat. This despite Dr Ambedkar's personal biography, which linked him to Baroda and the linguistic, practical, commercial ties that Gujarati has with Maharashtra. And despite the fact that Gujarat has witnessed 'anti-reservation' mobilizations of caste Hindus that led to caste riots, the incidence of violence against the Dalit community remains deeply entrenched in the social and economic interactions between/among caste Hindus and Dalits.

One aspect where Gujarat has rejected Gandhi's striving is in Hindu–Muslim relations. The historical and present-day communal violence and practical and cultural mobilization of Hindutva politics around this violence that has led to both the ghettoization of Muslims and marginalization of Muslims in Gujarat are well documented and do not bear repetition.

It is, however, necessary to retell one story from this long history of macabre celebration of violence. With Gandhi came Abdul Qadir Bawazir from South Africa. Imam Saheb, as he was called, was neither a member of the extended Gandhi family nor a native of Gujarat. Imam Saheb and his family came to India and Satyagraha Ashram Sabarmati out of pure conviction concerning Gandhi's ideas. Imam Saheb and Gandhi were also bound by deep bonds of personal affection. Invitations to the wedding of Imam Saheb's daughter Amina and Gulam Rasul Kureshi were sent by Gandhi, wherein he described Iman Saheb as a 'Sahodara' born of the same womb. The Imam-Kureshi family continued to live in the ashram even after Gandhi left it. Their house, built by Imam Saheb—a beautiful, well-appointed cottage called Imam Manzil—was their home till 1969. During the 1969 riots the Imam Manzil and the Kureshi family came under fierce and sustained attack by Hindu violent mobs. The family was saved but had to move out of the ashram precinct to a 'safer' area. This move has been permanent. Amina and Gulam Rasul Kureshi's son Abdul Hamid Kureshi wrote a monograph on their experience of the riots and called it *Agnipariksha*.[41] The ever so genteel and courteous Hamid Kureshi did not even once mention that it was really a fiery ordeal of the Gandhian institutions and Gandhians in which they failed miserably, and remain unrepentant.

---

[41] Hamid Kureshi, *Agnipariksha: An Ordeal Remembered,* trans. Rita Kothari from original Gujarati (New Delhi: Orient BlackSwan, 2018).

12

Exemplary Citizens and the Symbolic Politics of Nonviolent Protest

Karuna Mantena

I.

In December 2019, a wave of mass protest swept across India. Remarkable in speed and spread, it was arguably the largest popular upheaval since the Emergency.[1] Triggered by the passing of the Citizenship Amendment Act (CAA), three months of sustained anti-government protests were eventually stymied by the combination of a harsh COVID lockdown and government repression. The COVID lockdown became an alibi for the assertion of police power and the criminalization of dissent. The ferocity with which the activists involved in the nationwide anti-CAA agitations were targeted with violent harassment, arrest, and detention attests to the political significance of the movement. It represented a direct challenge to prime minister Narendra Modi, his ruling Bharatiya Janata Party (BJP), and the ideology of Hindutva—the distinct brand of Hindu nationalism promoted by them. Moreover, it was precisely those constituencies—students and Muslims—who had been directly attacked and stigmatized by the government that led the boldest action.

Mobilization against Hindutva and its project of transforming the Indian polity into an assertive Hindu majoritarian state was not new. Since the destruction of the Babri Masjid in Ayodhya in December 1992, Hindu nationalism has been a core fault line of Indian politics. Creating and exploiting divisions between majorities and minorities have

---

[1] As Rahul Rao noted, 'numbers cannot adequately convey the scale and ferocity of the agitation ... Within three weeks of the passage of the CAA, protests had taken place in 94 of India's 732 districts across 14 of its 29 states.' Rahul Rao, 'Nationalisms by, against and beyond the Indian state', *Radical Philosophy* 2, no. 7 (Spring 2020), 17.

Karuna Mantena, *Exemplary Citizens and the Symbolic Politics of Nonviolent Protest* In: *Gandhi, Truth, and Nonviolence*. Edited by: Vinay Lal, Oxford University Press. © Oxford University Press 2025.
DOI: 10.1093/9780198936657.003.0013

undergirded the rise to power of the BJP. Activists aligned to progressive secular forces have for nearly three decades tried to expose and counter the threat of Hindutva politics to civil liberties, religious pluralism, and minority interests. But there was something novel in the spontaneity, spread, and especially rhetoric of the anti-CAA movement.

At one level the intensity was born of sheer necessity. Buoyed by another robust electoral victory in May 2019, the BJP advanced its most ambitious political and legislative agenda. From altering the constitutional status of Kashmir, criminalizing the so-called Muslim practice of 'triple-talaq' or oral divorce, planning the construction of a Ram temple on the disputed site in Ayodhya, to proposals for a universal civil code—the BJP was trying to actualize some of the most provocative elements of its platform. The new CAA Act was of a piece with its long-term goal of reversing the Indian commitment to secular citizenship. The Hindu right had for years maligned this commitment as nothing more than 'pseudo-secularism'. Rather than strict equality, they alleged that previous Congress governments had instead extended privileges and exceptions to the Muslim minority in exchange for political support.

The CAA's stated purpose was to make available a path to citizenship for non-Muslim illegal migrants from Afghanistan, Bangladesh, and Pakistan, countries in which it was claimed these migrants faced religious persecution. In doing so, the CAA introduced a religious classification for citizenship. When taken in tandem with measures for verification of citizenship status under the newly proposed National Register of Indian Citizens (NRC), it called into doubt the legal status of every Indian Muslim. Following quickly on the heels of the assault on Kashmir, the new CAA act was perceived, and rightly so, to be an existential threat to the political rights and security of Indian Muslims, a community that has become one of India's most marginalized and vulnerable. Realizing that the BJP were attempting to 'transform citizenship from a right into a privilege', Muslims felt that the stakes of resistance were nothing less than a 'fight for survival'.[2] This was surely one of the reasons for the

---

[2] Ali Khan Mahmudabad, 'Indian Muslims and the Anti-CAA Protests: From Marginalization Towards Exclusion', *SAMAJ: South Asia Multidisciplinary Academic Journal* 24/25 (2020), 2, 11. Note here the resonance of Aamir Aziz's protest poem *'Mere hi mulk mein mujhe haq ke bajaye bheekh, diya jaaye mujhe manzoor nahi* (I refuse to accept that in my own land, instead of rights I will be given alms like a beggar)'. Quoted in Fathima Nizaruddin, 'Resisting the Configurations for a Hindu Nation', *HAU: Journal of Ethnographic Theory* 10, no. 3 (2020), 728.

unprecedented mobilization of Indian Muslims, the largest ever since independence.

What lent further poignancy to the movement were the ways in which protesters deftly appropriated symbols of the state to their cause. The Constitution and the flag came to stand for another nationalism, a prior and more plural nationalism associated with India's founding. As Rohit De and Surabhi Ranganathan noted, one innovative form of protest to emerge was the solemn recitation of the Preamble to the Constitution.[3] In choosing the pithy Preamble as opposed to any particular provision or fundamental rights clause, the Constitution was evoked not as a legal document as much as the embodiment of political identity, of what it means to be an Indian citizen. Reciting the Preamble was thus a simple, performative reminder that the CAA and NRC threatened to negate a core feature of Indian self-understanding as established in its secular Constitution: that citizenship was not to be determined by blood, religion, or ethnicity.

Such acts of appropriation were especially daring when led by those citizens—most prominently students and Muslims—whom the regime had repeatedly branded as anti-national and targeted as seditious. These so-called 'breakers of the nation', as the noxious slur 'tukde tukde gang' maligned, came forth most assuredly to speak for the nation. In another telling scene in the early days of protest, Asaduddin Owaisi, leader of the All India Majlis-e-Ittehadul Muslimeen (AIMIM), led the chanting of the Preamble in Urdu and English at a mass demonstration in Hyderabad. An intelligent and powerful orator, over the last ten years Owaisi has emerged as the most prominent and astute defender of secular nationalism in Indian politics. At this rally, the first of many, Owaisi asked all who opposed the new citizenship amendment to hoist the Indian flag— the Tiranga or Indian tricolour—atop their homes. The flag became a ubiquitous feature of the protest marches.

Crucially, bathing oneself in the flag was neither a sign of defeat nor a test of patriotism but became a proactive assumption of identity with the nation and the assertion of the right to speak in its name. Muslims raised

---

[3] Rohit De and Surabhi Ranganathan, 'We are Witnessing a Rediscovery of India's Republic', *New York Times* (27 December 2019).

the flag alongside placards that read 'Indian by choice, not blood'.[4] This was a brave assertion at a time when every Indian Muslim's birthright citizenship status was coming under severe scrutiny. But Owaisi outlined an even more profound implication. It was precisely because Muslims had made a 'conscious political choice' to stay in the country after partition that India could legitimately claim the mantle of secularism.[5] In this respect, Indian Muslims were the Republic's exemplary founders and exemplary defenders; their presence and protection were key to realizing the promise of Indian democracy.

It is hard to overstate how radical and courageous a claim this was. To declare oneself 'Indian by choice' was a precise counterpoint to the Hindu nationalist assertion that India is first and foremost a state of and for Hindus. In their vision, Hindus are entitled to rule as a permanent majority, and minorities should live in deference to this claim. The new documentation regime to be imposed by the CAA and NRC is a mechanism intended to induce de facto deference to Hindu power by rendering precarious the existing rights and status of religious minorities. By forcing everyone to prove their status, in one stroke citizenship is no longer an entitlement but a concession or favour to be granted or withdrawn at the pleasure of the majority.

In capturing symbols of the state, the protestors were bringing to the fore a clash of competing visions of Indian political identity. They attempted to recall the meaning and ambition of secular democracy, an ideology and identity that had lost coherence and lustre through decades of political sloganeering and capricious implementation. This crisis of

---

[4] Bhatia and Gajjala record a 68-year-old Muslim woman at Shaheen Bagh arguing, 'each woman here has held a tricolor and sang the national anthem and said—again and again—that we chose India, and we will continue to choose it'. Kiran Bhatia and Radhika Gajjala, 'Examining Anti-CAA Protests at Shaheen Bagh: Muslim Women and Politics of the Hindu India', *International Journal of Communication* 14 (2020), 6293.

[5] Hilal Ahmed interprets Owaisi's long-standing emphasis on choice as foregrounding 'a kind of contract between Muslims as a collective political entity and the Constitution-based sovereign Indian state'. But I think Owaisi is pushing a more profound centring of Indian Muslims— not just as one community among others contracting with the Constitution for liberty and protection. Rather, Indian Muslims are uniquely positioned to protect the Constitution and its secular credentials. Hilal Ahmed, 'Politics of Constitutionalism: Muslims as a Minority', in *Minorities and Populism – Critical Perspective from South Asia and Europe*, ed. Volker Kaul and Ananya Vajpeyi (Cham: Springer, 2020), 98. See also Soumya Shankar, 'Asaduddin Owaisi's Bid to Redefine Indian Secularism', *Foreign Policy* (13 April 2021), https://foreignpolicy.com/2021/04/13/asaduddin-owaisi-muslim-india-secular-party.

Indian identity was now laid bare for reflection and reassertion but also reimagining on new terms.

This essay investigates how techniques of nonviolent protest were used to dramatize a crisis of Indian identity. I hope to show that such a staging of identity is in fact a key but often overlooked feature of the theory and practice of nonviolent protest. This essay recovers this aspect of nonviolence by analysing modalities of performance and identification in the campaigns led by M. K. Gandhi and Martin Luther King, alongside those enacted during the anti-CAA protests, in order to better understand and theorize the nature, limits, and possibilities of the symbolic politics of nonviolence.

II.

That such monumental protests should have arisen in the 150th anniversary of Gandhi's birth and the centenary of the first mass satyagraha against British rule is almost too apt. Indeed, the very scene of satyagraha's invention in South Africa uncannily mirrors the coordinates of India's current citizenship politics. Gandhi first enacted the novel technique of mass 'jail-going' against a strict new registration regime in the Transvaal which was similarly justified on grounds of rampant illegal migration. Likewise, the demand for re-registration immediately nullified existing documentation and made the legal status of all Indians instantly precarious. Gandhi discerned that the predicament was not strictly legal but political. The threat to legal rights was a demonstration of power, 'the power possessed by a strong party over helpless men . . . and it shews a desire to wield that power with the greatest rigour and in total disregard of the feelings of the helpless victims'.[6] This is what made the law 'so insulting and humiliating', such that 'no self-respecting Indian' could submit to it.[7] Hence protest could not be limited to law courts or legislative assemblies but had to be conducted in the street. Only through

---

[6] M. K. Gandhi, 'Letter to Colonial Secretary (25-Aug-1906)', *The Collected Works of Mahatma Gandhi* (New Delhi: Publications Division, 1999), Volume 5: 313–14. References are to *The Collected Works of Mahatma Gandhi* (E-Book/CD-ROM), 98 vols., and are cited hereafter as *CWMG*, followed by volume and page number.

[7] M. K. Gandhi, 'Interview to *Rand Daily Mail* (6-Jul-1907)', *CWMG* 7: 46.

concerted public action could Indians assert their rights and challenge the assumed balance of power.

Disobedience as the means to enact and assert one's identity as a free person was also at the core of Gandhi's first all-India campaign, the Rowlatt Satyagraha of 1919, which challenged the legal extension of wartime emergency restrictions on civil liberties. For Gandhi, rights of speech and assembly were fundamentals rights. To restrict such elemental freedoms was an affront to 'one's self-respect and human dignity', requiring 'defensive' disobedience in response.[8] Under such conditions, people have not only a right to resist but a peremptory and sacred *duty* to disobey.

The global history of nonviolent protest has shown that organized disobedience to objectionable laws and mass demonstrations that stage public disaffection can fundamentally challenge a regime's legitimacy. In rallying around slogans such as 'when injustice becomes law, resistance becomes duty', Indian protesters invoked and participated in this century-long tradition. But the protests in India also forefronted an equally significant but often unmarked register, namely the rhetorical register of nonviolence. Specifically, I want to highlight the ways in which nonviolent protest creates scenes of exemplary citizenship. Nonviolent activists are often seen as moral exemplars, for example, in the common portrait of the Gandhian satyagrahi as a model of self-sacrifice and ascetic self-mastery. Here, I want to consider the idea of the satyagrahi or activist as a different kind of exemplar, a political exemplar. Protesters enact and disclose what they see as a more desirable, attractive political identity—in this case, a more inclusive and egalitarian model of citizenship. And Indian Muslims, and perhaps especially Muslim women, became the embodied carriers of that identity. For it is through the realization of *their* freedom, dignity, and equality that such an ideal itself comes into being.

The symbolic politics of nonviolence have garnered less attention and analysis than the disruptive power of mass protest. In the growing academic and activist scholarship on nonviolence, it is understood primarily as a powerful way to convey dissent and discontent. And when channelled into programmes of disobedience and non-cooperation, mass

---

[8] M. K. Gandhi, 'Notes (9-Feb-1922)', *CWMG* 26: 122–3.

nonviolence has proven to effectively immobilize repressive states. Erica Chenoweth and Maria Stephan argue that it is precisely their capacity to mobilize populations on a mass scale that has made nonviolent uprisings comparatively more successful at overthrowing authoritarian regimes than their armed counterparts.[9] Another prevalent view of how nonviolence works emphasizes confrontations between nonviolent crowds and the state. When protestors are subject to coercion or brutality, they expose the violence of the state and win the moral battle over public sentiment. This is what radical activists tend to infer as the lesson of Gandhi's Salt March and the 1963 Birmingham campaign led by Martin Luther King and the Southern Christian Leadership Conference. Both campaigns have furnished salient images and accounts of protesters enduring violence that sometimes activists seek to provoke state violence in order to discredit it.[10]

To focus on such confrontations as the necessary or primary catalyst for moving public sentiment, however, can be distorting and not wholly true to the theory and practice of nonviolence. To be sure, Gandhi and King insisted that protesters be prepared for repression, that they should be willing to risk bodily injury, even death, when assuming direct action. But the idea of necessary violence was never as central to their understanding of the dynamics of nonviolent persuasion as is often supposed. Neither was it the focal point of the majority of demonstrations, boycotts, and marches they organized and led. Likewise, Gandhi and King celebrated the material and performative power of mass protest, the political force inherent in its numerical scale. And yet, this dimension did not exhaust the ideological work of nonviolent politics. Real political impact certainly depends on sustained mass protest. Just as important as the size of protest was the *who* and *how* of protest. That is, the meaning of nonviolent direct action is embedded in how a constituency is enacted and called forth, how it is enunciated in *the form of protest itself*.

In this respect, what was as important as the mass scale of protest was the ways in which nonviolent action effects a public drama of enactment and subversion, appropriation and reimagination. The ingenuity of

[9] Erica Chenoweth and Maria Stephan, *Why Civil Resistance Works: The Strategic Logic of Nonviolent Conflict* (New York: Columbia University Press, 2014).

[10] Mark Engler and Paul Engler, *This is an Uprising: How Nonviolent Revolt is Shaping the Twenty-First Century* (New York: Nation Books, 2016).

Indian protest has foregrounded the possibilities of this often-overlooked dynamic in new and powerful ways. As protesters speak for the nation and project themselves as its exemplary citizens, they simultaneously undermine the state's attempts to depict dissent as criminal and, at the same time, rework the moral and political ideals that define the nation.

III.

For Gandhi and King, the politics of nonviolence, like all politics, were symbolic contests that involved perception, narrative, imagination, and identification. Rational argumentation and criticism were not enough for resolving political controversy. Decades of activism had taught Gandhi that political opponents often shut their ears 'to the voice of reason'.[11] People cling tightly to their beliefs. When challenged, they try to vindicate and protect them as aspects of their identity. King likewise thought that reason often served to 'justify man's defensive ways of thinking'.[12] Reason rationalizes; it gives succour to existing prejudices and convictions. To shake the hold of these settled beliefs one had to move beyond words to deeds, to the sphere of direct action. Nonviolent action in the form of coordinated, powerful displays of dignity and discipline, suffering and fearlessness, would, in Gandhi's words, 'move the heart' and awaken 'the inner understanding in man'.[13] By *directly* targeting affective registers— the passions and emotions unearthed in political contest—satyagraha would *indirectly* 'strengthen' our capacity to perceive and reason about justice.[14] Affect produced in and through nonviolent action is what compels attention, subverts expectations, chastens psychological resistance. The hope is that this will in turn open a path for the reconfiguration of identities, affiliations, and commitments.

When the marginalized and oppressed speak as exemplary citizens, they immediately assume and perform the status they have been denied.

---

[11] M. K. Gandhi, 'Speech at Birmingham Meeting (5-Nov-31)', *CWMG* 54: 48.

[12] Martin Luther King, Jr., 'Pilgrimage to Nonviolence', in *A Testament of Hope: The Essential Writings and Speeches of Martin Luther King, Jr.*, ed. James M. Washington (New York: HarperOne, 1986), 36.

[13] Gandhi, 'Speech at Birmingham Meeting', 48.

[14] M. K. Gandhi, 'Talk to Inmates of Satyagraha Ashram, Vykom (19-Mar-25)', *CWMG* 30: 382.

Participation in nonviolent protest—what King sometimes called 'dignified social action'[15]—is a declaration of moral and political agency, of freedom with subversive implications. Enacting public presence, the centring of a once-marginalized constituency, is the first necessary act that exposes a crisis of political identity and imagination. In the political controversy that mass protest provokes, such acts of free and dignified action also work as a tactical counterpoint to the state's disparagement of political mobilization from below. Reinhold Niebuhr was the first to fully recognize and articulate this distinctive dynamic at the heart of nonviolent politics. In *Moral Man and Immoral Society*, Niebuhr contended that the political advantages of nonviolent action derived from its unique capacity to blunt prejudice against insurgent movements.

We have been accustomed to the following dynamic: in the wake of mass demonstrations, the state and its political allies respond instinctively with insinuations of criminality on the part of protestors. They demand that the protestors remain nonviolent, though the state never suggests it might itself be held to reciprocal standards or make a similar promise. Niebuhr argues that the rote and relentless rhetoric of law and order is typical of what he calls the 'moral conceit' of the state and the classes who see their interests as aligned with the existing structure of social and political power.[16] Today we call this privilege; it marks the easy way in which dominant groups identify with the state. They see the police as on their side; when they appeal for law and order, they do so in part because they are confident that the police will side with them.

The state—and those who benefit from the status quo—relegate dissenters to 'the category of enemies of public order, of criminals and inciters to violence'[17] to discredit them. In both the Rowlatt Satyagraha and the Non-cooperation Movement which followed quickly upon its heels, Gandhi was accused of unleashing anarchy and eventually tried under the sedition act for exciting 'disaffection' against government. To be labelled an anarchist invoked an image of the cosmopolitan terrorist, someone who detested all authority and sought its violent destruction.

---

[15] Martin Luther King, Jr., *Stride Toward Freedom: The Montgomery Story* (Boston: Beacon Press, 2010 [1958]), 206.

[16] Reinhold Niebuhr, *Moral Man and Immoral Society: A Study in Ethics and Politics* (Louisville, KY: Westminster John Knox Press, 2001 [1932]), 250.

[17] Ibid.

Likewise, civil rights activists were regularly dismissed as communists and 'outside agitators', a depiction coupled with racist overtones of primitive criminality and rage. The Indian government's litany of derogatory epitaphs given to the anti-CAA protestors falls neatly into this depressing genealogy. They are routinely smeared as gangs of 'urban naxals', jihadis, traitors and anti-national extremists bent on fomenting sedition. In Niebuhr's view, nonviolent action, through a willingness to suffer insults and violence with dignified defiance, immediately, pre-emptively, thwarts such attempts to equate protest with unruliness and criminality. This unique 'temper' and 'method' punctures the moral conceit of dominant and entrenched groups, and allows the protesters to win the initial battle of public perception.[18]

To counter such dismissals, Gandhi insisted that satyagrahis take a vow to comport themselves nonviolently in thought and deed. Fulfilling a self-imposed vow showed them to be self-ruling lawmakers and not the anarchic or criminal lawbreakers they were repeatedly accused of becoming and emboldening. The commitment to nonviolence also had to be conveyed through the tactics of protest itself. Nonviolent pickets and boycotts eschewed all forms of intimidation, such as physically blocking patrons from entering shops or schools. Another evocative example was the hartal. A proper hartal would be announced in advance, and no attempt would be made to secure compliance from shopkeepers on the day itself. Indeed, it was a 'a matter of pride . . . from the satyagraha standpoint, that some shops were open. This fact proved the voluntary character of the hartal'.[19]

In this way, satyagrahis proved themselves to be 'the best constitutionalists', and civil disobedience would be 'the purest type of constitutional agitation'.[20] 'Under the British Constitution,' Gandhi contended, 'obstruction is a perfectly legitimate and well-known method for securing rights.'[21] Satyagraha was emulating—indeed it was *perfecting*—a tried and tested method of English political reform to realize the promise of political liberty. From his time in South

---

[18] Ibid.
[19] M. K. Gandhi, 'Satyagraha Leaflet No. 21', *CWMG* 18: 41.
[20] M. K. Gandhi, 'Notes (12-Dec-21)', *CWMG* 25: 260; 'Evidence Before the Disorders Inquiry Committee (9-Jan-20)', *CWMG* 19: 217.
[21] M. K. Gandhi, 'Speech at Public Meeting, Bombay (17-Jun-18)', *CWMG* 17:71.

Africa through to the Jallianwala Bagh massacre of 1919, Gandhi had consistently argued for the rights of Indians as subjects of the British Empire. He spoke as an exemplary British subject, instructing the British that in respecting *his* rights they would be living up to *their* values. Gandhi was appealing to the ideal of liberty as a core feature of British identity.

The Indian regime responded ferociously to the first wave of anti-CAA protests. From attacking universities to police brutality against Muslim citizens, especially in states under BJP control, the government chose to openly assert brute power against dissent.[22] Its aims were simple—to intimidate its citizens and directly coerce obedience from them. But it also unleashed more insidious tactics, using vigilantes and proxies to both throw a light veil over state complicity and provoke counter-violence. The purpose was to implicate protesters in violent encounters, to depict them as perpetrators and not the victims of state power, and then arrest and detain them on charges of rioting or outright sedition. Thousands of protesters were detained and arrested in the initial months of protest. During the COVID crisis and after, this led to a coordinated campaign to formally charge those involved in protests—a broad array of civil liberties activists, academics, students, and members of opposition parties—as terrorists and/or conspirators in sedition.

The protesters were savvy and bold in the face of government provocation. They not only appropriated the symbols of the state, the Constitution, the flag, and national anthems; the protests also displayed their dignity through scripted rituals and performances of silence. Candlelit vigils for the slow repetition of the Preamble and the collective recitation of patriotic poetry and nationalist anthems were particularly affecting ways to stage disciplined defiance, and a perfect rejoinder to the frenzied scenes of counter-violence orchestrated by the government. The most dramatic display of this aesthetic power was the months-long sit-down protest led by Muslim women in the Shaheen Bagh neighbourhood of Delhi. Surrounded by flags and banners with slogans of peace

---

[22] Bharat Bushan, 'Citizens, Infiltrators, and Others: The Nature of Protests against the Citizenship Amendment Act', *South Atlantic Quarterly* 120, no. 1 (January 2021), 205.

and fraternity, continuous silence took centre stage, conveying nobility, resilience, and strength.[23]

The movement as a whole retained an inventive, self-organizing, and affirmative spirit and demeanour which, despite all the attempts to distract public attention through violence, kept the central issue—the existential threat to core notions of citizenship—front and centre. Nonviolence is often described as a way to occupy the moral high ground. But that can make it sound too much like a form of self-regarding righteousness or virtue signalling. The point of performing dignity is not to effect superiority but, rather, to cut through the partisan clamour so as to see and hear the message of the movement. Indeed, the meaning is to be embodied in the very bearing and presence of the protester. It is in this imbrication of the act with the identity of the actor that nonviolence is so invested in questions of comportment. And why Gandhi elaborated a myriad rules and rituals for nonviolent protest. Throughout his career he offered continuous instruction on how to ensure that boycotts, pickets, and hartals were truly nonviolent in the sense of avoiding all appearance of intimidation and direct coercion. King likewise insisted that nonviolent struggle had to always be conducted 'on the high plane of dignity and discipline'.[24] These rules and rituals that came to comprise the discipline of nonviolence were not just about modelling an ethical code but were techniques meant to control, intensify, and manifest the movement's political message.

King was acutely aware that in the context of the politics of protest, and perhaps especially so in democracies, public wrangling about whether the means of protest match the grievance was inevitable. Opponents have clear incentives to question the motives and methods of protesters and stir controversy to obfuscate public debate. Minimizing frenzy and aggressive intent while also insisting on the necessity of disruption is the fine line that nonviolence must navigate. This is ultimately why, for Gandhi and King, a protest is nonviolent not only because it abjures physical violence but because it dramatizes discipline and dignity in such

---

[23] Bhatia and Gajjala, 'Examining Anti-CAA Protests at Shaheen Bagh;' Aarti Sethi, 'One Year Later: Reflections on the Farmer's Protest in India', *HAU: Journal of Ethnographic Theory* 11, no. 2 (2021), 869–76.

[24] Martin Luther King, Jr., 'I Have a Dream', in *A Testament of Hope*, 218.

a way as to keep the public sharply tuned to the moral and political stakes of the protest.

IV.

Without doubt, the political aims of nonviolent movements have been diverse. Yet there is a rhetorical style distinctive to nonviolent protest, a distinct way of persuading or moving public opinion. I suggest that the ideological work of nonviolence appeals to and redefines political identity, and it does so through opening up creative fissures in processes of identification. This is what is at stake in the staging of exemplary citizenship. Its aim is to dramatize and provoke a crisis of identity as the means by which to shift the foundations of belief and renovate political ideals.

Some of the boldest actions against the CAA were undertaken by those who were targeted by the state as 'breakers of the nation'. When they appropriated the symbols of the state, they were not asking for inclusion or legal safeguards. Instead, they declared *themselves* to be the true inheritors of the nationalist project and the protectors of the Constitution. Varun Grover's poem, which became a key slogan of resistance, captured this defiant agency: '*Hum samvidhan ko bachaenge / Hum kagaz nahin dikhaenge / Hum jan gan man bhi gaenge / Hum kagaz nahin dikhaenge*' ('We will save the Constitution / We will not show papers / We will sing Jan Gan Man [the national anthem] / We will not show papers').[25] Anti-CAA protests were also striking in their unapologetic display of portraits of such nationalist-era icons as Gandhi, Abul Kalam Azad, Jawaharlal Nehru, Bhagat Singh, Subhas Chandra Bose, and B. R. Ambedkar. They chanted freedom slogans, poems, and songs to remind Indians of the radical promise of secular egalitarian citizenship and the long and plural history of struggles to secure it.

The flag featured prominently in many demonstrations. By law, the Indian flag is only meant to be displayed in officially sanctioned state spaces and events and is not freely available for private use except on certain national holidays. In 2016, the BJP government mandated flying the flag in central universities in their battle against what they decried

---

[25]   Quoted in Rao, 'Nationalism by, Against and Beyond the Indian State', 20–1.

as growing sedition on campuses. This charged backdrop made the insurgent performances of flag-waving by protestors especially resonant. On Republic Day, January 2020, while the official parade on Rajpath displayed military pomp and might, a very different celebration was taking place at Shaheen Bagh. Here, the flag was raised by the elders or *dadis*—Bilkis, Asma Khatoon, and Sarvari—who had been leading the sit-in along with Radhika Vemula, mother of Rohith Vemula, whose suicide in 2016 occasioned nationwide protests against caste discrimination in higher education. The two contrasting scenes conveyed a sharp sense of competing meanings of patriotism, one in which citizens exult in collective power versus another that takes pride in the promise of community and equality.

That a contestation over identity was at stake was even clear in how the Constitution came to play a central role in the political repertoire of dissent. When Indian protesters appealed to the Constitution, they did not do so in a legalistic way. Having lost faith in the courts to save the Constitution, they sought to revivify the commitment to secular and plural citizenship through direct action on the streets. And rather than refer to any specific rights provisions, they focused on reciting the Preamble and its broad invocation of the principles of secular citizenship. Even here, secularism and equality were evoked not as abstract principles but as core features of Indian identity.

Identity in nonviolent protest works in a double register. Firstly, the identity of the actors matters; it is their agency and presence that bring forth a new constituency. This is what Papia Sengupta helpfully delineates in terms of 'acts of citizenship'.[26] Building on the work of Engin Isin, Sengupta suggests that such acts create new scenes of citizenship. Rather than confirming and fitting into pre-existing identities, they originate a new script. Secondly, in performing exemplary citizenship, the emergent constituency calls forth a new public and invites them to rethink their identity. It challenges them to reconsider what being an Indian means to them.

[26] Papia Sengupta, 'Making (Ab)sense of Women's Agency and belonging in Citizens Debates in India: Analysing the Shaheen Bagh Protests as "Act(s) of Citizenship"', *Social Change* 51, no. 4, 523–37.

Gandhi and King both thought of political beliefs as affective attachments bound up with identity. That our deepest commitments are intimately tied to how we see ourselves as individuals and as members of a community. To motivate people to re-examine and shift these core commitments, one had to trouble the process of identification, to expose a contradiction or discrepancy between how we view ourselves and the kinds of injustices we give succour to and perpetuate. This is what Gandhi tried to do in pointing out the hypocrisy in celebrating political liberty as a core British value and, at the same time, denying it for Indian subjects. In a similar vein, Gandhi argued that Indian swaraj should not simply re-enact 'English rule without the Englishman'.[27] Indians should strive to be better rulers, to forge a new and superior form of rule. For this, Indians would have to not only reject the industrial civilization which underpinned British rule but build a swaraj that would secure the freedom, security, and dignity of its overwhelmingly poor majority. Exemplary citizenship and true patriotism here meant working towards a truer swaraj, a swaraj 'in terms of the masses'.[28]

With every successive phase of nationalist mobilization, Gandhi became increasingly concerned that, 'in the consciousness of strength we are daily acquiring', Indians were in danger of repeating 'the wrongs of the rulers . . . in our relations with those who may happen to be weaker than we are'.[29] He would continually insist that true swaraj was neither simply a transfer of power from one elite to another nor simply the assumption of power by a demographic majority. Rather, the goal was to make self-rule a possibility for even India's most vulnerable citizens. For Gandhi, a perfect or true democracy was one that 'fully protects the weakest amongst its subjects'.[30]

Such a demanding vision of swaraj underlay some of Gandhi's most arresting proposals to shift political power downward. In the 1920s, Gandhi tried to institute a khadi or spinning franchise, in which membership and office-holding within the Indian National Congress would depend on fulfilling a minimum quota of daily hand-spinning. In a similar

---

[27] M. K. Gandhi, *Hind Swaraj* (22-11-1909), *CWMG* 10: 255.
[28] M. K. Gandhi, 'In Fulfilment of Promise (24-7-1924)', *CWMG* 28: 345. Italics in original. Also M. K. Gandhi, 'Speech at Meeting of Deccan Princes (28-7-1946)', *CWMG* 91: 372.
[29] M. K. Gandhi, 'Fraught with Danger (26-1-1922)', *CWMG* 26: 15.
[30] M. K. Gandhi, 'Insanity (30-5-1920)', *CWMG* 20: 375.

vein, Gandhi's ideal form of village democracy was one in which suffrage would be tied to the performance of 'bread labour', of manual labour equivalent to basic consumption. This was an idea that Gandhi adopted from Tolstoy, who himself picked it up from the philosophy of labour developed by former serf Timofei Bondarev. The most realized attempt to implement such egalitarian aspirations of swaraj was the constructive programme, in which constructive work involved concrete practices of service, friendship, and toleration. Khadi, arguably the programme's centrepiece, was envisioned as a form of manual labour and social service through which the elite would unlearn privilege and actively identify with the poor. For Hindus, as the newly empowered majority, the burdens of voluntary service were placed even higher. It was incumbent on them to allay Muslim fears of political marginalization through unconditional acts of friendship. Most famously, Gandhi exhorted upper-caste Hindus to create and cultivate a new ethical horizon in which being a Hindu required the abolition of untouchability and atonement for it.

Gandhian swaraj was reinventing Indianness through the projection of a set of aspirational identities, such as the progressive Hindu or the exemplary Indian building up swaraj from below. These identities were in turn given form through embodiment in daily rituals of social service. Constructive satyagraha, through creativity and discipline, was meant to sustain radical social change. It would disorient existing identities and commitments enough to make way for the possibility of new attachments, motivations, and alignments. Rhetorical framing, and the calling forth of aspirational identities, aimed to motivate people to transform themselves and their political worlds.

Gandhi often invoked the unusual term 'conversion' in reference to these hoped-for shifts in identification and affiliation. I say unusual because Gandhi was critical of religious conversion and consistently objected to proselytization. And yet, he was keen to describe nonviolent persuasion in the sphere of politics in the provocative language of conversion. Why? On the one hand, conversion signalled attention to beliefs and sentiments that are not wholly rational. But perhaps most importantly, it evokes an analogy between political persuasion and religious conversion. That a shift in political commitments might take the form of a recovery or revision of identity, which is confirmed by and through new rituals and practices. For Gandhi, political persuasion was something more than a political compromise or calculation of interest; it was marked by an invitation to self-transformation, to see oneself in a new way.

In the 'Letter from Birmingham City Jail', King aimed to provoke a similar crisis in the self-understanding of liberal America.[31] King was often criticized for trying to appeal to a white conscience that simply did not exist. King, however, did not assume that reliable white support was always already there; indeed, he became increasingly sceptical of this in his final years. Rather, King sought to *activate* it by positing or projecting an aspirational figure—the white liberal ally, the true American in sympathy with the movement's goals. He offered an account, often a scathing and demanding account, of what someone ought to think and how they ought to act if they identified as a white moderate or liberal American, as someone who saw themselves to be on the side of justice. To foreground this truer version of their identity was a way to promote introspection and, hopefully, adjustment and emulation. When Americans as individuals are 'personally confronted'[32] with the problem of race, this begins the ethical transfiguration of what it means to be American.

Something analogous is at work in King's recurring invocation of what he called 'the American dream'. In substance this was the dream of democracy, the promise of true equality. King was well aware that it was an illusion, a dream in the literal sense of having 'never been fulfilled'.[33] Indeed, African Americans had acutely experienced the underside of the American dream; the horrors of slavery, oppression, and violence had made them its paradigmatic victims. But King also pointed to the dream's 'amazing universalism',[34] which afforded a template upon which one could press the claims of racial empowerment and integration. African Americans were thus uniquely positioned to 'bring into full realization of the American dream'.[35] They were America's conscience, its troubled soul, but also its exemplary founders. The ordeal of the civil rights movement was a historic opportunity to simultaneously 'transfigure' themselves and American society.[36]

---

[31]   Martin Luther King, Jr., 'Letter from Birmingham City Jail', in *A Testament of Hope*, 289–302.
[32]   King, *Stride Toward Freedom*, 193.
[33]   Martin Luther King, Jr., 'The American Dream', in *A Testament of Hope*, 208.
[34]   Ibid.
[35]   Martin Luther King, Jr., 'An Address Before the National Press Club', in *A Testament of Hope*, 105.
[36]   King, *Stride Toward Freedom*, 216.

V.

Effectuating the promise of democracy was not simply the fulfilment of pre-existing norms of equality. King rendered a challenge to create a new script, to expand the meaning of equality. Full integration, in King's vision, was a far-reaching ethical and political ideal; indeed, it served as the equivalent of emancipation.[37] To be fully integrated is to freely participate in the 'total range of human activities', to know and realize 'one total capacity'. This was only possible in a polity that confirmed 'the dignity and worth of every human personality'.[38] In this respect, integration as completing 'the process of democratization'[39] would of necessity redefine the very nature of American democracy. In his late years, King was even more explicit that the project of redeeming America required a 'radical revolution of values'.[40] The tragedy of Vietnam and the backlash against King's pivot toward questions of poverty showed how quickly the commitment to equality—the dream of democracy—dissipated if not reconfirmed through innovative, sustained political struggle.

The prominent place of Ambedkar, both as a Dalit leader and the drafter of the Constitution, attests to the fact that anti-CAA protests were enacting a politics that was quite different from nostalgic veneration. Saving the Constitution, reclaiming nationalism, demonstrating a truer patriotism, all held out the promise of a genuine refounding, not a return but a pointing forward towards a novel configuration. The hope was to disclose an identity that is more demanding and more universal, rejecting existing forms of nationalism that draw the boundaries of the nation in the narrowest sectarian terms.

Constitutional imagination in India has never assumed the model of conservative veneration prominent in US political discourse. Nevertheless, appealing to the Constitution is always a double-edged sword. On the one hand, the Indian Constitution serves to legitimate the state and its various powers, including its military and police powers.

---

[37] Danielle Allen, 'Integration, Freedom, and the Affirmation of Life', in *To Shape a New World: Essays on the Political Philosophy of Martin Luther King, Jr.*, ed. Tommie Shelby and Brandon Terry (Cambridge: Harvard University Press, 2018).

[38] Martin Luther King, Jr., 'The Ethical Demands for Integration', in *A Testament of Hope*, 118, 121; King, 'An Address Before the National Press Club', 105.

[39] King, 'The Ethical Demands for Integration', 117.

[40] Martin Luther King, Jr., 'A Time to Break Silence', in *A Testament of Hope*, 240.

On the other hand, it also promises to be a charter of liberty, outlining mechanisms by which individuals and groups can contest state power. An ongoing worry for Indian constitutionalism is how and to what extent access to the Constitution and the appeal of its values—from secularism, rights discourse, to legality itself—have moved beyond its elitist origins and statist orientation.

Legal scholars have tried to pinpoint and unearth alternative, more popular, and insurgent forms of constitutionalism. Rohit De has shown that ever since the Constitution came into force in 1950, a much wider range of ordinary Indians used the tools of writ petitions and rights litigation.[41] This underscores the fact that public consciousness of, and investment in, constitutional imagination were never simply elite phenomena. Moreover, fundamental rights provisions have been the focal point of various movements and struggles seeking to expand and extend protections to historically oppressed, marginalized, and dispossessed populations.

Given the extreme hierarchy of Indian society, there is arguably an inherent radical potential in the recourse to a liberal discourse of rights. Kalpana Kannabiran's pioneering work has shown how anti-discrimination jurisprudence can interpret fundamental rights clauses to reimagine the democratic potential of citizenship rights.[42] Kannabiran tethers these possibilities to an important reworking of Ambedkar's notion of constitutional morality. Many scholars gloss Ambedkar's call for constitutional morality in terms of the need to cultivate moral habits around legality. For Kannabiran, the idea of constitutional morality should also be seen as a counter to entrenched habits of discrimination. In this, it points to a more capacious practice of liberty, where the tools of civil liberty are exercised to free oneself from dependence and domination, especially majoritarian domination.[43] Suryakant Waghmore, in a similar vein, suggests that current invocations of the Constitution are not just aimed at reviving secular citizenship but also at recovering the Constitution's 'humanizing potential'. A humanist ethics in this

---

[41] Rohit De, *A People's Constitution: The Everyday Life of Law in the Indian Republic* (Princeton: Princeton University Press, 2018).

[42] Kalpana Kannabiran, *Tools of Justice: Non-discrimination and the Indian Constitution* (New Delhi: Routledge, 2012).

[43] Ibid., 8–11.

context involves activating the Constitution's promise of social justice and equality 'against the spirit of hierarchy'.[44]

In an editorial marking the 150th anniversary of Gandhi's birth, Owaisi argued that the true legacy of Gandhi's secularism for independent India is bound up with the 'courage to stand up to majoritarian fervour, and to stand by those who are most vulnerable'.[45] Owaisi is right to note Gandhi's prescient appraisal of the problem and appeal of majoritarianism, dangers he thought would plague even a democratic and independent India. 'Swaraj necessarily means the rule of the majority'. But, he warned, when a majority 'acts in total disregard of any strongly-felt opinion of a minority', its 'numerical strength savours of violence'. When newly empowered majorities 'misuse their increased power', that form of rule 'will not be swaraj, that will be oppression or tyranny'.[46] The larger ethical and political lesson Owaisi draws is that secular parties must ally themselves with those groups, such as Indian Muslims, that face 'widespread majoritarian exclusion and violence'.[47]

The challenge then, in this moment of contesting and reinvesting in nationalism, is to move towards more substantive ethical and institutional transformations. And to ensure that its symbolism is not merely a cover for the re-enchantment of the state and its legal institutions. The anti-CAA protests provided a glimmer of how to cultivate a new ethos and popular attachment to it. By centring the Constitution as the site of collective action and resistance, Kannabiran suggests that the protests shifted power—the power and legitimacy of constitutional interpretation and deliberation—from the courts to the public square. Such a shift opens the way to rethinking the 'constitution-as-commons'.[48] The enactment of this kind of alternative, subaltern constitutionalism, such as the use of the Preamble as an anthem of resistance, was prefigured in the Pathalgadi movement. In 2017 and 2018, in dramatic and solemn acts of defiance,

---

[44] Suryakant Waghmore, 'Humanizing Citizenship: Constitutional Principles and the Protests against the CAA', *PS: Political Science & Politics* 54, no. 4 (October 2021), 641.

[45] Asaduddin Owaisi, 'When Gandhi Took on the Mob', *Indian Express* (23 October 2019).

[46] M. K. Gandhi, 'Speech at Bardoli Taluka Conference (29-1-1922)'. *CWMG* 26: 45; 'Khadi Franchise (9-6-1927)'. *CWMG* 29: 30.

[47] Owaisi, 'When Gandhi Took on the Mob'.

[48] Kalpana Kannabiran, 'Constitution-As-Commons: Notes on Decolonizing Citizenship in India', *South Atlantic Quarterly* 120, no. 1 (January 2021), 232–41.

stone slabs inscribed with extracts of articles of the Constitution and legislative acts were erected across villages in Jharkhand.[49]

Here what comes to the fore is again how the very form of protest can begin to vivify new affective ties and ethic commitments. The Shaheen Bagh protests were remarkable in centring the agency of Muslim women, who enacted their citizenship as Muslims. Their religious identity was part and parcel of their invocation of Indian identity. The presence and hyper-visibility of the female body in protest enacted agency and power in direct opposition to prominent figurations of vulnerable and hidden Muslim women in need of rescue from Islamic patriarchy.[50] Moreover, the staging of women in their everydayness, in situations of care and suffering, dramatized and enlarged practices of hospitality and empathy. In this way, in Shiv Viswanathan's words, they were 'inventing democracy with a vigour which is both vernacular and cosmopolitan'. In 'fighting for their rights, these women through empathy, sensed the suffering of others and fought for them in a language that went beyond rights'.[51]

The insistence on peace and nonviolence at Shaheen Bagh served as a poignant counterpoint to the violence of state repression. What was on display was not the angry mob, the kind of volatile crowd often mobilized by state supporters and vigilantes, but a 'caring crowd'.[52] Aarti Sethi notes that in the Shaheen Bagh encampments as well as the more recent farmers' cities on the borders of Delhi, 'living crowds' emerged that did not 'produce fear' but instead offered 'security, relief, sustenance, and solace to those who came'.[53] These scenes of 'forbearance and joy' embodied acts of care that create an 'ethical vision of citizenship'.[54] In weaving protest politics into daily life, domestic work with political agency, popular and affective sentiments were seamlessly anchored to the practice of democracy.[55] In both form and content, it is through

---

[49] Nandini Sundar, 'Pathalgadi is Nothing but Constitutional Messianism So Why is the BJP Afraid of It?' *The Wire* (16 May 2018); Eva Davidsdottir, 'Our Rights are Carved in Stone: The Case of the Pathalgadi Movement in Simdega, Jharkhand', *International Journal of Human Rights* 25, no. 7 (2021), 1111–25.
[50] Bhatia and Gajjala, 'Examining Anti-CAA Protests at Shaheen Bagh'.
[51] Shiv Visvanathan, 'The Symbolism of Shaheen Bagh', *Seminar* 729 (2020).
[52] Sethi, 'One Year Later', 870.
[53] Sethi, 'One Year Later', 873.
[54] Sethi, 'One Year Later', 870; Visvanathan, 'The Symbolism of Shaheen Bagh'.
[55] Visvanathan, 'The Symbolism of Shaheen Bagh'.

such practices that constitutional ideals will have to be energized and reclaimed.

VI.

The COVID crisis, as well as the ongoing government crackdown on dissent, effectively stymied the anti-CAA movement. The BJP government, emboldened by their electoral successes, is unlikely to give way on the CAA and NRC anytime soon. Even though political repression is escalating in alarming ways, the deeper challenge for contemporary Indian protest against Hindu majoritarianism is that what is being contested is not just a regime and their policy agenda but an ideology that is supported by a significant number of the population. The protests took place in a deeply polarized political world, in which dissent came face to face with a population mobilized in opposition. In this sense, the protesters face a situation much more akin to what King and the civil rights movement were up against in the United States of the 1950s and 1960s than the satyagrahis of the independence movement.

Many recent studies of nonviolent resistance have rightly celebrated it as a mechanism to undermine state legitimacy and, especially, its success in overturning authoritarian regimes. But these instances tell us very little about the distinct challenges nonviolent protests face in democratic regimes, and in conditions of extreme polarization. From his very first campaign in Montgomery, King astutely observed that achieving racial integration was going to be much more difficult than anticolonial independence. The civil rights movement was not just fighting against an oppressive state or a distant power. It was a struggle with and against neighbours and fellow citizens. The oppressors and oppressed had to find some manner of living together in dignity and equality. This is an extraordinary challenge; in such circumstances King insisted that the philosophy and discipline of nonviolent action were both harder and more urgent.

The Montgomery Bus Boycott—the campaign that brought the young King into the limelight as a political leader—was an astonishing and unexpected triumph. After 381 days of continuous boycott, integration was upheld in a federal circuit court. But the court decision was met with massive resistance and a sharp wave of vigilante violence. This push and pull would be repeated throughout the period, with legal and political victories punctuated with reactionary violence. Unfortunately, this is a very likely scenario for India today—a long campaign that will proceed in fits and starts and be marred by state and vigilante violence. In the United States, the federal government—not consistently but in key moments—gave support to the civil rights campaigners. In India, the hope is that some of the state governments, led by non-BJP parties, will provide some protection and resistance to the federal political agenda. At the beginning of the anti-CAA protest, a dozen states refused to implement the NRC, with many joining constitutional challenges to it.[56]

In such a polarized context, the appropriation, expansion, and reconstruction of Indian identity will be equally important. Gandhi and King believed that truly transformative action can only come about when the largest coalition of people can be motivated to invest themselves in the project of radical reform. This is not by any means an uncomplicated task. The aspirational identity being posited in and through Indian protest is a constitutional identity. While it has served the purpose of reminding people of what that founding entailed and symbolized, something more substantive will have to be articulated. Constitutional ideals have to be reimagined and revivified in new terms so that they can speak to the demands and aspirations of younger generations and marginalized citizens who have only ever experienced those ideals as limited or compromised at best.[57]

[56] Loraine Kennedy, 'Federalism as a Moderating Force? State-level Responses to India's New Citizenship Law', *SAMAJ: South Asia Multidisciplinary Academic Journal* 24/25 (2020).
[57] I owe a great debt to Vinay Lal for his extraordinary patience and insight in helping me revise this essay. I also would like to thank the Berkeley Institute for South Asia Studies for hosting an early discussion of this essay, and Shaunna Rodrigues and Giulia Oskian for their careful reading and discerning advice.

13

Advocate Gandhi

Race, Role, and Transformation?

Charles R. DiSalvo

Who *Is* Mahatma Gandhi?

The world knows him as an old, thin, bespectacled man with a walking cane. Amidst his campaign for Indian independence from British colonial rule, he campaigns across India for better Muslim–Hindu relations, for spiritual uplift, for a move away from cities and toward village life. He conducts nonviolent civil disobedience against the British. He leads his movement's defiance of British law in the Salt Campaign of 1930.[1]

In recent years the world has also come to know the South African Gandhi, the Gandhi who spent the better part of two decades practising law in the British colonies of Natal and the Transvaal in South Africa. In the early 1890s, after Gandhi finishes his law studies in London and after he fails to establish a successful legal practice in India, he accepts an offer to do some low-level legal work in Durban, South Africa, then the commercial capital of the coastal colony of Natal.

There the British have large sugar and tea plantations that require enormous amounts of manual labour. When the British fail to attract native Africans to work in these fields, they turn to their colony in India for a solution to this problem. They import tens of thousands of manual labourers from India, many of whom stay on in South Africa after they

[1] The author thanks Thomas Weber and Kathleen Kennedy for their helpful comments. The author also thanks the Arthur B. Hodges Fund for its kind support. The point of departure for this essay is a book review written by the author; see Charles R. DiSalvo, review of Ashwin Desai and Goolam Vahed, *The South African Gandhi: Stretcher-Bearer of Empire*, in *South African Historical Journal* 68, no. 4 (2016), 672–4. This essay borrows some phrasing from that review.

Charles R. DiSalvo, *Advocate Gandhi* In: *Gandhi, Truth, and Nonviolence*. Edited by: Vinay Lal, Oxford University Press. © Oxford University Press 2025. DOI: 10.1093/9780198936657.003.0014

have served their period of indentured servitude.[2] A sizeable Indian population in South Africa results. Eyeing an opportunity, Indian merchants move in to serve this community.[3] These merchants are wildly successful, and they expand; in fact, they begin to serve the European community in Natal as well.[4] The newcomers soon outcompete their established European merchant rivals[5] and, as a consequence, make themselves highly unpopular with the European merchant and political establishment.[6]

In response to this rising tide of Indian economic power, the colonial legislature in Natal begins to enact draconian legislation intended to drive the Indian merchants out of business. In addition, the legislature also moves to interfere with Indian immigration and make life difficult for Indians already in the colony.[7]

Enter Mohandas Karamchand Gandhi, barrister at law.

Gandhi arrives on the scene in South Africa just as the legislature is starting its anti-Indian campaign against the rights of Indians to trade, to own property, to vote, to travel, and more. The Indian merchant community turns to Gandhi—the only Indian lawyer in all of South Africa—to be its political organizer. He accepts this role, discharges it, and also leverages his relationships with the merchants who are his political clients to develop a very successful law practice.

This, then, is another Gandhi with whom the world is becoming familiar.

There is, however, a third Gandhi, one whose life has now come under a good deal of scrutiny because of a very specific charge made against him. The charge is harsh.

The charge is that this Gandhi is a racist.

[2] Maureen Swan, *Gandhi: The South African Experience* (Johannesburg: Raven Press, 1985), 20. See also Mabel Palmer, *The History of the Indians in Natal* (Cape Town: Oxford University Press), 58.

[3] Swan, *The South African Experience*, 1.

[4] 'European' here refers to colonists of British and other European descent who had settled in South Africa.

[5] 'Access to exploitable family labor, suppliers, and distributors, and working long hours helped Gujarati traders outperform their white counterparts.' Goolam Vahed, 'Passengers, Partnerships, and Promissory Notes: Gujarati Traders in Colonial Natal, 1870–1920', *International Journal of African Historical Studies* 38, no. 3 (2005), 449 at 478.

[6] See 'Merchant Politics I: Natal, 1895–1906', ch. 2 in Swan, *The South Africa Experience*.

[7] Charles R. DiSalvo, *M. K. Gandhi, Attorney at Law: The Man Before the Mahatma* (Berkeley: University of California Press, 2013), 105.

The charge is legitimate. It can be substantiated. As I will demonstrate, there is no debate about that. The debate, the controversy, the question is what does the charge *mean* for our understanding of Gandhi? Who *is* Mahatma Gandhi? What do we *make of* the Mahatma in the wake of this charge? In an attempt to offer a response, I will set the charge against a broader picture. In the process of doing that, and with an awareness of the irony involved, I will widen the charge. I will place this expanded charge in context, and, lastly, provide one answer to the question, 'Who is Mahatma Gandhi?'

Gandhi as a Lawyer

If we are to answer the question about the ultimate identity of the person who has been charged with racism, we must first confront the question 'Who was Gandhi the lawyer?', for the grounds for the racism charge arise from Gandhi's time in South Africa—which is to say, during the time Gandhi practised law.

Gandhi's life in the law begins in 1888. In that year, Gandhi's family sends him off to study law in London. With Gandhi's father having died, the family needs a new source of income. Young Mohandas is going to be the family's meal ticket. He takes his studies seriously, passes his examinations, and is called to the bar in Britain in June 1891. Returning home, he tries to set up practice in India, but he fails in the attempt.

His acceptance of an offer to work in South Africa in 1893 is the start of an almost uninterrupted period of eighteen years practising law in South Africa.

Now, during this entire time, Gandhi is a lawyer for the poor, yes? Gandhi dedicates all his professional expertise to uplifting the oppressed, yes?

No.

For several years, his practice is almost exclusively a commercial law practice—he represents the interests of powerful businesses. These businesses have an extensive presence throughout South Africa. They have wholesale and retail operations in foodstuffs, jewellery, cloth, household goods, and more, they run international shipping lines, and they have substantial real estate holdings.

Gandhi acts the part. He dresses like a business lawyer; he wears three-piece suits and silk ties. He lives in the best part of town. He negotiates for his business clients, he sues other businesses for them, he helps them buy property, he helps them deal with the government's usual regulatory demands upon them. He does what his clients ask him to do. He is an instrument not of his wishes but of his clients' interests.

Two of Gandhi's 1894 cases make the point, each in a different way. The first is the Balasundaram case, familiar to anyone who has read Gandhi's autobiography.[8] Some business lawyers will do *pro bono* cases on the side.[9] Balasundaram's case is a *pro bono* case for Gandhi.

Balasundaram is an Indian indentured servant who has been viciously beaten by his European master. The master has actually driven Balasundaram's teeth through his lip and beaten him so badly that his turban is soaked with blood. After being discharged from the hospital, he heads straight to the Durban office of Barrister Gandhi. He asks Gandhi to get him freed from the control of his master and placed under a new and better master.

Gandhi sinks a good deal of time in the case, first in unsuccessfully negotiating with the master who had beaten Balasundaram, then in suing the master with some initial success, and finally in resuming negotiations with him. In the end, Gandhi gets what Balasundaram wants—a transfer to another, kinder master.

This is not a case Gandhi takes for money. It is a case he takes because he believes in his client's cause.

Back at Gandhi's business law office, that is not the situation in another case Gandhi's office is handling at just about the same time. One of the biggest Gandhi clients is a very large Indian merchant company, Dada Abdulla and Company. Abdulla and Company's interests are far-flung and extensive. The company has a shipping line, it has stores, it has rental properties. It is one of the most powerful business entities in South Africa, European, or Indian.[10]

---

[8] Mohandas K. Gandhi, *An Autobiography or The Story of My Experiments with Truth: A Critical Edition*, trans. Mahadev Desai, introduced and annotated by Tridip Suhrud (New Haven: Yale University Press, 2018), 264 *et seq.*

[9] *Pro bono* is short for *pro bono publico*—for the public good. A lawyer who takes a case *pro bono* normally does so without charging a fee.

[10] Referring to the decade 1890 to 1899, Gandhi's newspaper, *Indian Opinion*, would later describe Dada Abdulla and Company as 'probably ... the largest Indian business throughout South Africa during the last decade of the past century. [The] firm had at one time no fewer than fifteen branches, their transactions with England, Germany and India running into thousands of pounds sterling. [It was the first Indian firm to have] gone in for ship owning in South Africa, ... having bought the *Courland* and the *Khedive*.' 'Late Mr. Abdoola Hajee Adam', *Indian Opinion* (3 February 1912), 40.

Max Scheurmann, a tenant in one of Dada Abdulla and Company's commercial properties, is the owner of a combination bakery and restaurant in Durban known as the German Café. Scheurmann struggles to make a success of his mom-and-pop enterprise, but he cannot keep up with the rental payments to his landlord. Dada Abdulla and Company orders Gandhi to evict Scheurmann from his shop. Gandhi brings suit against Scheurmann and gets what his client wants—a court order removing Scheurmann from the premises. For good measure, Gandhi also gets a money judgment, along with the costs of the suit.[11]

This was a complete win for Gandhi and his client.

Scheurmann? Scheurmann is out on the street. His business is finished.

Scheurmann has been broken by the same lawyer who represented Balasundaram. In this instance, Gandhi was doing whatever was necessary to serve his client's interests. There would be no negotiated settlement, as there was in the Balasundaram matter. There would be no extension of his tenancy offered to Scheurmann. There would be no forgiveness of Scheurmann's back rent. Shortly after the eviction, on 13 December 1894, this beleaguered and now impoverished man is in Durban Circuit Court, going belly up.

He's there to file for bankruptcy for himself and his wife.[12]

Advocate Gandhi has pushed him over the cliff.

Gandhi's Problematic Arguments

Arguments Based on Race

Before we discuss the professional ethic that would have the lawyer serve as a willing tool of his client's interests, let us briefly examine the record of Gandhi's racist statements.

---

[11] 'Durban Civil Court – Dada Abdoola &Co. v. Max Scheurmann', *Natal Advertiser* (4 December 1894), as cited in Charles DiSalvo, *The Man Before the Mahatma: M.K. Gandhi, Attorney at Law* (Noida: Random House India, 2012), 76.

[12] 'Durban Circuit Court – Civil Session – Applications', *Natal Advertiser* (14 December 1894), as cited in DiSalvo, *The Man Before the Mahatma*, 76.

Gandhi was far from alone in his consciousness of race. In advocating for Indian rights in South Africa, Gandhi faced a major difficulty: the racism of his opponents that predated the arrival of Indians in South Africa. The elites in Natal's European power structure had every interest in repressing the native population, by whom the Europeans were greatly outnumbered; Africans had to be kept powerless for Europeans to maintain their social, economic, and political superiority.

This was a problem for Gandhi and the Indian community. If the Europeans recognized the civil rights of Indians, what defence would the Europeans have against the arguments for rights from another disenfranchised community, the African community? The continued dominance of the European colonial elite over all non-whites depended on uniform resistance to the entreaties of both communities.

Gandhi appears to have understood, and responded to, this dynamic. He set about identifying Indians with Europeans as loyal members of the same empire and, significantly for our current discussion, distinguishing Indians from Africans. To the Europeans, Gandhi argued, 'We are like you, not like them.'

In my examination of Gandhi's time in South Africa,[13] I catalogued five instances of this approach on Gandhi's part.

- In a letter to the Natal legislature in 1894, Gandhi states:

  A general belief seems to prevail in the Colony that the Indians are little better, if at all, than savages or the Natives of Africa. Even the children are taught to believe in that manner, with the result that the Indian is being dragged down to the position of a raw Kaffir.[14] [The word 'Kaffir' is understood today to be an offensive reference to African blacks.]

- In 1895, Gandhi quotes approvingly from an editorial in a South African newspaper, the *Cape Times*, that condemns those who would lump Indians together with native blacks, those who, in the words of the editorial with which Gandhi agreed, would put Indians

---

[13] DiSalvo, *The Man Before the Mahatma.*
[14] 'Open Letter to the Legislative Council and Legislative Assembly', before 19 December 1894, Mohandas K. Gandhi, The *Collected Works of Mahatma Gandhi*, 100 vols. (New Delhi: Publications Division, Government of India, 1969 (hereinafter *CWMG*), 1: 170.

'in the same category as the half-heathen Native . . . and subject [them] to the harsher laws by which the . . . Kaffir is governed.'[15]

- In 1896, Gandhi is temporarily in India, where he gives a set of speeches. The first is in Mumbai:

Ours is a continual struggle against a degradation sought to be inflicted on us by the Europeans, who desire to degrade us to the level of the raw Kaffir whose occupation is hunting, and whose sole ambition is to collect a certain number of cattle to buy a wife with and, then pass his life in indolence and nakedness.[16]

- Later that same year, he speaks in Madras (now Chennai), where he again refers to the policy of the Natal authorities of 'degrading' Indians 'to the level of the raw Kaffir'.[17]

- In an 1899 petition to the Secretary of State for the Colonies, Gandhi states that Indians were 'undoubtedly infinitely superior to the Kaffirs.'[18] In that same year he protests government action that treated Indian businesses as if they were 'raw Zulus'.[19]

I was shocked to learn that Gandhi had spoken and written these things.

It pains everyone who admires him to learn of Gandhi's racism.

The charge brought against him, however, cannot be denied. It was brought to greater public attention with the 2016 publication of Ashwin Desai and Goolam Vahed's indictment of Gandhi, *The South Africa Gandhi: Stretcher-Bearer of Empire.*[20] Desai and Vahed roundly criticize Gandhi for placing 'African below Indian in the imagined racial hierarchy'.[21] They argue that 'Gandhi sought to ingratiate himself with

[15] 'Petition to Lord Ripon', before 5 May 1895, *CWMG*, 1969, 1: 201, at 202–3.
[16] 'Speech at Public Meeting, Mumbai', 26 September 1896, *CWMG*, 1976, 2: 50.
[17] 'Speech at Meeting, Madras', 26 October 1896, *CWMG*, 1976, 2: 69 at 74.
[18] 'Petition to Secretary of State for Colonies', before 27 May 1899, *CWMG*, 1979, 3: 87 at 89.
[19] 'Indians in the Transvaal', 17 May 1899, *CWMG*, 1979, 3: 79 at 80.
[20] Ashwin Desai and Goolam Vahed, *The South African Gandhi: Stretcher-Bearer of Empire* (Stanford: Stanford University Press, 2016). The subtitle is a reference to Gandhi's service in the 1899 South African War and the 1906 Bambatha Rebellion; in each he headed up an ambulance corps for the British.
[21] Desai and Vahed, *The South African Gandhi*, 61.

Empire and its mission during his years in South Africa. In doing so, he not only rendered African exploitation and oppression invisible, but was, on occasion, a willing part of their subjugation and racist stereotyping.'[22]

The charge of racism against Gandhi is well founded. What, however, are we to make of it? How are we to read it? What post-criticism picture of Gandhi should emerge?

Before we can answer these questions, we have more to consider.

Role-differentiated Behaviour

When Gandhi agreed to serve as the political representative of the Indian merchant community in South Africa, he made it a condition of his service in that role that the merchants agree to send their legal business his way. They did, and, as a result, Gandhi and the merchants had two relationships—an organizer–constituency relationship and an attorney–client relationship. Gandhi was the merchants' political representative at the very same time that he served as the lawyer for these same merchants.

So strongly did Gandhi identify as a lawyer during his time in South Africa that when he spoke and wrote words on behalf of the merchant community that reflected a racist point of view, he did so as if he were acting in his capacity as the merchants' legal advocate—even when he was dealing with issues that were overwhelmingly political rather than legal. When Gandhi did this, he approached his political work for his merchant clients using the framework provided by the ethos of the legal profession.

That ethos contains within it an uncommon trait that is a peculiar characteristic of lawyers—role-differentiated behaviour.

The predominant understanding in the profession in Gandhi's time and ours is that it is the lawyer's job to play a role—the role of

---

[22] Desai and Vahed, *The South African Gandhi*, 22. 'The task that Desai and Vahed have set themselves is to question [the] adulation [of Gandhi], wherever it occurs, intent as they are in "demystifying" Gandhi and the way Gandhian iconography has developed, progressed and gathered momentum over the decades. Desai and Vahed's main complaint is against the mythology or "saintliness" that has gathered around Gandhi, and of the subsequent "heritage mythmaking" by his acolytes, and they feel compelled, as a matter of duty, one that becomes an all-consuming mission and crusade, to set the record straight.' Betty Govinden, 'Gandhi – of the Earth, Earthy: A Critical View of Gandhi in South Africa', *English Academy Review* 34, no. 1 (2017), 71–84, at 72.

representative of his or her client. In this role, the lawyer does not speak for him- or herself. The lawyer as person, as independent moral agent, is suppressed and quite intentionally absent. Rather, the lawyer speaks for the client. Because the lawyer's responsibility is to speak zealously for the client, it is the lawyer's obligation to make for the client the most powerful arguments that the law permits.

Professor Richard Wasserstrom, then a professor of both law and philosophy at UCLA, described role-differentiated behaviour in his seminal article 'Lawyers as Professionals: Some Moral Issues':

[W]here the lawyer-client relationship exists, the point of view of the attorney is properly different – and appreciably so – from that which would be appropriate in the absence of the attorney-client relationship. For where the attorney-client relationship exists, it is often appropriate and many times even obligatory for the attorney to do things that, all other things being equal, an ordinary person need not, and should not do. What is characteristic of this role of a lawyer is the lawyer's required indifference to a wide variety of ends and consequences that in other contexts would be of undeniable moral significance.[23]

Wasserstrom continues:

[A]n attorney may have, as part of his or her duty of representation, the obligation to invoke procedures and practices which are themselves

---

[23] Richard Wasserstrom, 'Lawyers as Professionals: Some Moral Issues', *Human Rights* 5, no. 1 (1975), 1–24, at 5. Professor Wasserstrom explains: ' [T]he professional as professional has a client . . . whose interests must be represented, attended to, looked after by the professional. And that means that the role of the professional . . . is to prefer in a variety of ways the interests of the client . . . over those of individuals generally' (5). Professor Wasserstrom adds: '[I]t is in the nature of role-differentiated behavior that it often makes it both appropriate and desirable for the person in a particular role to put to one side considerations of various sorts – and especially various moral considerations – that would otherwise be relevant if not decisive' (3). Wasserstrom's essay produced an enormous response from the profession and from some of the leading thinkers in the legal academy. For a collection of these responses, see Stephen L. Pepper, 'The Lawyer's Amoral Ethical Role: A Defense, A Problem and Some Possibilities', *American Bar Foundation Research Journal* 4 (Fall, 1986), 613–35, nn. 2, 3, and 7. Much of the debate centres around the value to be placed on client autonomy. See, e.g., David Luban, 'The Lysistratian Prerogative: A Response to Stephen Pepper', *American Bar Foundation Research Journal* 4 (Fall, 1986), 637–49, and Craig Taylor, 'Morality and the Role-Differentiated Behavior of Lawyers', *Australian Journal of Professional and Applied Ethics* 6, no. 1 (2004), 36–46. Others see the problem through the lens of loyalty to the client. See, e.g., Eli Wald, 'Loyalty in Limbo: The Peculiar Case of Attorneys' Loyalty to Clients', *St. Mary's Law Journal* 40, no. 4 (2009), 909–66.

morally objectionable and of which the lawyer in other contexts might thoroughly disapprove.[24]

Wasserstrom questions this conception of the lawyer's role.[25] So do I. It is, however, generally unquestioned in the profession.[26] In this role of advocate and representative, the lawyer's own morality, politics, and spirituality do not matter. They are of no consequence. They are, in a lawyerly word, irrelevant.[27] The lawyer takes up the *client's* cause. The lawyer does everything and anything the law permits to advocate for the *client*. The person of the lawyer recedes, the interest of the *client* emerges. The lawyer cannot be charged with moral responsibility for the arguments the lawyer makes on behalf of the client because they are not the lawyer's arguments; they are the *client's* arguments. The lawyer, as lawyer, serves, in Wasserstrom's phrase, as an 'amoral technician',[28] one 'whose peculiar skills and knowledge in respect to the law are available to those with whom the relationship of client is established'.[29]

Professor Wasserstrom paints a stark but accurate picture of how the profession regards morality. He states that matters of morality

are just of no concern to the lawyer *qua* lawyer. . . . The lawyer's task is . . . to provide that competence which the client lacks and the lawyer, as professional, possesses. In this way the lawyer as professional comes to inhabit a simplified universe which is strikingly amoral – which regards

---

[24] Wasserstrom, 'Lawyers as Professionals', 6.

[25] Wasserstrom, 'Lawyers as Professionals', 12.

[26] It is a conception that, in its most extreme form, manifests itself in figures like attorney Roy Cohn, who decades ago instructed his client—a young real estate magnate in New York City who was later elected to high office—to always attack and to never apologize. Robert O'Harrow, Jr., and Shawn Boburg, 'The Man Who Showed Donald Trump How to Exploit Power and Instill Fear', *Washington Post* (17 June 2016). Film-maker Matt Tyrnauer explains: 'Donald Trump is Roy Cohn. He completely absorbed all of the lessons of Cohn, which were attack, always double down, accuse your accusers of what you are guilty of, and winning is everything. And Trump absorbed these lessons and has applied them in every aspect of his life and career.' Matt Tyrnauer, *Documentary: 'Where's My Roy Cohn?'*, interview by Sacha Pfeiffer, *All Things Considered*, National Public Radio (13 October 2019), audio, 5:50, https://www.npr.org/2019/10/13/769946862/documentary-wheres-my-roy-cohn.

[27] Professor James R. Elkins puts it in straightforward terms: 'Lawyers sometimes act as if they are not bound or limited by the most basic tenets of ordinary morality.' James R. Elkins, 'The Moral Labyrinth of Zealous Advocacy', *Capital University Law Review* 21, no. 3 (Summer 1992): 735–96 at 735.

[28] Wasserstrom, 'Lawyers as Professionals', 6.

[29] Wasserstrom, 'Lawyers as Professionals', 6.

as morally irrelevant any number of factors which nonprofessional citizens might take to be important, if not decisive, in their everyday lives.[30]

It is very easy to go from this standard conception of the lawyer's relationship to morality, politics, and spirituality to say that, in the lawyer playbook, the ends justify the means.[31] The end is winning *the client's* case, achieving *the client's* goal. The range of possible means, to anyone concerned with conscience, is extraordinary: it is made up of *all possible* arguments, except those the law forbids. Accordingly, there is virtually no scrutiny of means.

It is in light of this traditional understanding of the lawyer's role—one which Gandhi seemed to embrace—that I argue that the attack that has been made on Gandhi for his racist statements, while not at all inaccurate, is, however, misleadingly incomplete.

Arguments Based on Class

Gandhi's arguments on behalf of his Indian constituents are not limited to arguments based on race. A separate set of arguments relies on *class* distinctions. Gandhi's critics either understate this point or miss it altogether.

In 1900 Gandhi is still practising in Durban, the commercial capital of Natal province. At that time, Durban is teeming with rickshaws—more than 1,700 hand-pulled carts that carry paying customers from one place in town to another. Who could ride these rickshaws? By order of the Durban Town Council 'Europeans only'.

Gandhi did not initially oppose the Durban by-law governing ridership because some rickshaws operated without 'Europeans only' signs. Well-dressed Indian customers had no trouble getting rides.

Soon enough, however, the city ordered the strict enforcement of the 'Europeans only' by-law. Now Indians found themselves without access to what was then a basic form of transportation in Durban.

---

[30] Wasserstrom, 'Lawyers as Professionals', 8.

[31] Thomas Weber takes up the question of ends and means in Gandhi's law practice in Thomas Weber, *Gandhi, Gandhianism, and Gandhians* (New Delhi: Roli Books, 2006), ch. 5, 'Legal Ethics/Gandhian Ethics'.

The Europeans had an image of Indians as dirty.[32] Gandhi went to the Town Council and asked that the law be changed—not to allow all Indians to ride but to allow clean, well-dressed Indians to ride. Gandhi was prepared to serve his monied constituency—his business clients—even if it meant throwing lower-class Indians under the bus—or, in this case, under the rickshaw.

The Town Council turned him down flat.[33]

Here is a photograph that is no laughing matter. It is from Gandhi's time in South Africa. It is disturbing. If Gandhi's critics had wanted to encapsulate their argument that Gandhi identified with Empire in one photograph, this would be it.[34]

Gandhi did not look upon this Durban scene with twenty-first-century eyes. Gandhi did not identify with the person pulling this

---

[32] Untitled article, *Natal Mercury*, (12 July 1900), as cited in DiSalvo, *M. K. Gandhi, Attorney at Law,* 134.

[33] 'Petition to Governor of Natal', prior to 24 December 1900, *CWMG* 3, 1979, 191 at 192, as cited in DiSalvo, *M.K. Gandhi, Attorney at Law,* 134.

[34] Photo used with the permission of Sally Leventis. Ms Leventis, whose grandfather appears in the photograph as the rider, states that this photograph was taken in 1912.

rickshaw. Gandhi did not identify with the childcarer in the centre of the photo. Rather, Gandhi, and the wealthy, male, and small but relatively powerful part of the Indian community that he represented, identified with the rider.[35]

Durban is not the only locale in which Gandhi mounts an argument based on class. In 1906, when Gandhi is practising in Johannesburg, the city brings into service an electrified system of tramcars[36] the equal of any system in Europe at the time. This appearance of transportation modernity, however, is accompanied by an artefact of cultural modernity— racism. As in Durban, Indians are forbidden to ride.

Gandhi initially argues that all Indians should have the right to ride. When that argument fails, however, he changes his position, and argues only—futilely, in the end—that 'well and cleanly dressed' Indians should be allowed to ride.[37]

In both cases—1900 in Durban, 1906 in Johannesburg—Gandhi is willing to surrender what should have been his principles to serve the interests of his monied clientele—those at the upper reaches of the Indian social and economic ladder.

So, we see arguments based on race.

And we see, too, arguments based on class.

That is not all. We also see purely procedural arguments that come from what Wasserstrom would call an amoral technician.

Arguments Based Purely on Procedure

On more than one occasion, Gandhi devises from whole cloth arguments to defend the behaviour of his clients that they had not—and would have never—devised on their own. These arguments did not relate to the substantive merits of the clients' cases but were made on the basis of what non-lawyers would call 'technicalities'.

During the time Gandhi practised in Natal, Frederick Laughton was a leading member of the South African bar and a member of a distinguished

---

[35] Note the sign on the side of the rickshaw: 'Europeans only'.
[36] A type of trolley car or streetcar.
[37] 'A Reply to "The Leader"', 16 February 1906, CWMG, 1961, 5: 191, as cited in DiSalvo, The Man Before the Mahatma, 210.

European law firm in Durban.[38] He often represented Indian interests, sometimes in tandem with Gandhi. He perfected the art of ferreting out and attacking the procedural weaknesses in the opponent's case. Laughton schooled the less-experienced Gandhi on how to seize on the procedural errors of the opponent to achieve victory.

Gandhi learned well from his teacher. When the Transvaal colonial government requires Indians to register with the government, Gandhi urges Indians to refuse to register and to burn registration certificates already issued. When an Indian resister, Sorabji Shapurji, is arrested for having refused to register, it is Gandhi who is at his side—armed with Laughton's technique.

Gandhi argues that his client is not guilty because the government has failed to introduce into evidence the relevant portions of the *Government Gazette* that set out the requirement to register by a certain date—a purely technical defence having nothing to do with the merits of the case and an argument that obviously could not have been in the head of Sorabji or any of the other resisters whom Gandhi represents when they disobey the registration law. Gandhi's defence of Sorabji is built on considerations that had provided no motivation whatsoever for the behaviour of the client that was at issue in the case—the failure of his client to register with the government.[39]

This move irritated the judge trying the case:

The Magistrate: It is this, in short – we must bring the accused up again, and give the Government as much trouble as possible?
Mr. Gandhi: That's the point.[40]

Another egregious example of a technical defence is one Gandhi adopted from his law office colleague Henry S. L. Polak, who had argued on behalf of another non-registrant that resisters could not be convicted of the failure to register because the government had not properly appointed a Registrar of Asiatics. Gandhi borrows this purely technical

---

[38] Peter Spiller, *A History of the District and Supreme Courts of Natal, 1846–1910* (Durban: Butterworths, 1986), 60 and 123.
[39] DiSalvo, *The Man Before the Mahatma*, 234.
[40] 'Law and Police: Law and Asiatics – The Registration Problem – Test Case from Charlestown', *Johannesburg Star* (9 July 1908), cited in DiSalvo, *The Man Before the Mahatma*, 234.

argument wholesale from Polak. Surely no resister had refused to register on the grounds that the government had failed to properly appoint the Registrar. This is a purely utilitarian argument devised after the fact by lawyers. But Gandhi picks up this argument from Polak and uses it.[41]

In both these cases, Gandhi makes arguments on behalf of his clients that have nothing to do with the merits of the cases, that are made up from facts that emphatically have nothing to do with the resisters' refusals to register, and which, in the end, fail to keep Gandhi's clients out of jail.

All of this brings to mind the passage in Gandhi's tract *Hind Swaraj*, in which Gandhi states that lawyers are duty-bound 'to side with their clients and to find out ways and arguments in favour of the clients, to which they (the clients) are often strangers'[42]—a point I will take up in a moment.

First, we must ask, what do these three sets of behaviours by Gandhi have in common? What do his arguments based on race, his political positions based on class, and his technical arguments based on procedure share?

In each set, Gandhi makes arguments as an amoral legal technician or, in the instance of his race arguments, possibly as an immoral legal technician. They are arguments made with one purpose, and only one purpose, in mind: to win.[43]

It would be helpful in understanding the larger professional context in which Gandhi was operating to remember instances of other lawyers who also went astray when they embraced the win-at-all-costs role of legal technician. Recall, for example, the Watergate scandal and the involvement of numerous lawyers whose crimes helped Richard Nixon and his associates cover up their unsavoury behaviour.[44]

---

[41] DiSalvo, *The Man Before the Mahatma*, 251–2.

[42] Suresh Sharma and Tridip Suhrud, *M. K. Gandhi's Hind Swaraj: A Critical Edition* (New Delhi: Orient BlackSwan, 2010), 51.

[43] Some would chalk up Gandhi's use of racist arguments not to his being a lawyer but to his being a *British-trained* lawyer. See Mary Elizabeth King, 'How South Africa Forced Gandhi to Reckon with Racism and Imperialism', *Waging Nonviolence* (2019), https://wagingnonviole nce.org/2019/10/south-africa-forced-gandhi-reckon-with-racism-imperialism/, and 'Can We Celebrate Gandhi's Achievements while Also Learning from His Errors?', *Waging Nonviolence*, https://wagingnonviolence.org/2019/10/can-we-celebrate-gandhis-achievements-while-also-learning-from-his-errors/.

[44] 'The Lawyers of Watergate', *American Bar Association Journal*, undated, https://www.aba journal.com/gallery/watergate.

Professor Wasserstrom notes that the Watergate lawyers acted in their professional role, exhibiting role-differentiated behaviour:

> Having been taught to embrace and practice the lawyer's institutional role, it was natural, if not unavoidable, that they would continue to play that role even when they were somewhat removed from the specific institutional milieu in which that way of thinking and acting is arguably fitting and appropriate. The nature of professions . . . makes the role of the professional a difficult one to shed even in those obvious situations in which that professional role is neither required not appropriate. In important respects, one's professional role becomes and is one's dominant role, so that for many persons at least they become their professional being.[45]

What happened to the Watergate lawyers, happened to Gandhi. They were all overtaken by their professional identities.

Gandhi: Saint or Sinner?

What are we to make of this Gandhi who acts as an amoral or immoral legal technician?

I spend a good deal of my time teaching students how to try cases to juries and judges; one of my principal courses is entitled 'Trial Advocacy'. If Gandhi the amoral or immoral technician were a student in my class, here is what I would tell him:

Speak and write only words you believe.

Take only positions consistent with who you are.

Be prepared to defend the morality of your representation of the client.

---

[45] Wasserstrom, 'Lawyers as Professionals', 15. Seven years after Gandhi quits the practice of law, he engages in activity that opens him to another charge of allowing the ends—in this case, Indian independence—to justify the means. Gandhi conducted, on behalf of Britain, a military recruitment campaign in India during World War I, a campaign seemingly at odds with his devotion to nonviolence and one that caused much consternation among his friends and co-workers from South Africa. Gandhi defended himself, in part, by arguing that the Indians' plea for self-government would be aided by defending the Empire during the war. Judith M. Brown, *Gandhi's Rise to Power: Indian Politics, 1915–1922* (Cambridge: Cambridge University Press, 1972), 147; Ashwin Desai and Goolam Vahed, *The South African Gandhi*, 292. Is this, too, the lawyer at work?

I rest this advice on two foundations:

- The advocate who speaks from the heart is the more effective advocate. Audiences can usually tell the difference between the lawyer who is speaking from the heart and the lawyer who is making an argument simply because it appears to be useful to do so in the moment. Gerry Spence, the noted trial lawyer, explains:

  The form and the content of the winning argument may stem from the logical, intellectual, linear progeny of the mind. But the energy, the power, the stuff that excites and moves, that makes us credible and eventually convinces, is born of the soul. Because an argument from the soul is truthful, it bears the ring of truth.[46]

- When a lawyer makes arguments that are in contradiction to the lawyer's own morality, politics, and spirituality—in other words, in contradiction to who the lawyer is and what the lawyer believes—the lawyer is damaging his or her soul.[47] That's obviously bad for the soul and an evil in its own right, but it also leaves behind a deformed human being to plead the case, and a more deformed human being to plead the next case, and an even more deformed human being to plead all the cases after that.

Professors Thomas Smith and Eduardo Lindemann put it well: 'We become what we do.'[48]

---

[46] Gerry Spence, *How to Argue and Win Every Time* (New York: St. Martin's Griffin Edition, 1996), 66.

[47] 'To tell your client's story well, you must believe in the truth of the case .... Otherwise, you are not just fighting the other side, but your conscience as well.' Joel ben Izzy, '10 Ways to Know if Your Story Is Ready to Tell in Court', *Trial Magazine* 34, no. 7 (July 1998), 91. 'Just as a good cause can be sullied by the means used to achieve it – "The ends pre-exist in the means", said Emerson – so a man can be contaminated by his actions. To manipulate others, he must become an actor, and to be an effective actor of this sort requires that he manipulate his own emotions. He must learn to appear sincere when he is not, to be friendly when he is hostile, to seem angry when he feels no anger. Several years of such acting and he longer knows who he really is or what he really feels. He is nothing but a set of masks, and even he does not know which mask he prefers .... He is a slave of the same game to which he subjects others.' Franklyn S. Haiman, 'Democratic Ethics and the Hidden Persuaders', *Quarterly Journal of Speech* 44, no. 4 (1958), 385–92, at 391.

[48] 'A person's character finally takes on the pattern of his acts, not his wishes ... We become what we do.' Haiman, 'Democratic Ethics and the Hidden Persuaders', 391, quoting T. V. Smith and Eduard C. Lindeman, *The Democratic Way of Life*, rev. ed. (New York: Mentor Books, 1951), 126.

Gandhi eventually comes to understand this dynamic.

The evidence is in the arc of his time in the law. There are three phases to it.

In the first phase, there is a clear separation between, on the one hand, Gandhi's practice and, on the other hand, his morality, politics, and spirituality. I write now about the nature of the cases Gandhi took. Business is business. Business is not politics. And Gandhi is a business lawyer. He does not directly use his practice of law to advance the Indian cause in South Africa. He does not litigate in defence of Indian civil rights. He simply does not see or make a connection between his work inside his office and his work outside his office. He practises business law in his professional sphere and attempts to advance the interests of the Indian community in the political sphere. Never do the two overlap.

In the second phase, we see the two realms coming somewhat closer together as he begins to take on some civil rights cases as part of his practice. While the majority of Gandhi's practice most assuredly remains a business practice, he is making some room in this phase for cases that reflect his morality, politics, and spirituality. His professional life and the rest of his life, particularly his political life—these are slowly, but inexorably, moving toward each other.

Allow me to make a brief interruption of the analysis here—between phases two and three.

It is 1909. Gandhi is making the transition from phase two to the briefest, but most meaningful phase, phase three. Just sixteen months before he ends his legal career in 1911, Gandhi writes and publishes *Hind Swaraj* or, as it was also titled, *Indian Home Rule*. It is many things, of course, but, as Professors Tridip Suhrud and Suresh Sharma have described it, fundamentally it is a 'categorical and unqualified' condemnation of modern civilization.[49] Gandhi devotes one section of his tract to a discussion of one of the aspects of modern civilization that this essay touches on—the behaviour of lawyers. His thesis is that lawyers 'have

---

[49] Sharma and Suhrud, *M. K. Gandhi's Hind Swaraj*, xxiii. Professor Anthony Parel adds that *Hind Swaraj*'s critique of modern civilization 'is one of its main contributions to modern political thought'. M. K. Gandhi, *Hind Swaraj and Other Writings*, ed. Anthony J. Parel (Cambridge: Cambridge University Press, 1997), xvii.

enslaved India, have accentuated Hindu-Mahomedan dissensions, and have confirmed English authority'.[50]

In support of this thesis, Gandhi makes a very broad attack on the profession. He says that 'the profession teaches immorality; it is exposed to temptation from which few are saved'.[51]

Is Gandhi thinking of himself? Is he thinking of his work against Max Scheurmann? Perhaps.

Is he thinking of role-differentiated behaviour? Likely.

Is he thinking of his race-based arguments? His class-based arguments? Probably not at this juncture of his life. He first needs the distance of time.

'[The duty of lawyers]', Gandhi writes in *Hind Swaraj*, 'is to side with their clients and to find out ways and arguments in favour of the clients, to which they (the clients) are often strangers. If they do not do so, they will be considered to have degraded their profession.'[52]

Is his thinking about his technical arguments based on procedure? Likely.

Hind Swaraj sets the tone for the third, and last, phase of Gandhi's practice. After Gandhi's litigation on behalf of Indian rights in phase two is largely unsuccessful, he completely gives up his practice of business law. In the final stage of his practice, he only engages in movement work; he represents Indian resisters in court who are being tried for civil disobedience, for refusing to register with the colonial government.[53]

There is now a great unity between who Gandhi is as a human being and who he is as a lawyer. His professional activity mirrors his morality, politics, and spirituality. He is integrated. He is one Gandhi.

Gandhi is not a lawyer who believes his professional activity, on the one hand, and his politics, morality, and spirituality, on the other, are separate spheres, one the alien of the other. In the end, we have a Gandhi who is a different kind of lawyer and a different kind of person. This is a turning point in Gandhi's development.

---

[50] Sharma and Suhrud, *M. K. Gandhi's Hind Swaraj*, 50.
[51] Sharma and Suhrud, *M. K. Gandhi's Hind Swaraj*, 50.
[52] Sharma and Suhrud, *M. K. Gandhi's Hind Swaraj*, 51.
[53] For a description and analysis of the cases Gandhi litigated in this phase, see DiSalvo, *The Man Before the Mahatma*, especially Appendix, 'Resistance Cases Litigated by Gandhi', 313 *et seq.*

As he completes this journey of reconciliation between the professional and the personal, Gandhi abandons the practice of law in April of 1911. He leaves South Africa in 1914 and arrives home in India in 1915.

What picture of Gandhi does this leave us? Who *is* Gandhi?

There have always been those who perceive Gandhi as a sainted figure, coming down from above as a perfect being without need of redemption.[54] This view of Gandhi readies the ground for the critics to implicitly square the actual, far-less-than-perfect, human Gandhi against an imagined, flawless, sanctified Gandhi, the idealized Gandhi of statues and portraiture. Thus, they are ensnared in a trap set by the popular culture—a trap these very same critics recognize but cannot manage to escape.

I would suggest that so strong, so unqualified, is the current attack on Gandhi—one that centres on, but goes beyond, race[55]—that we are in danger of losing our bearings.

It is the South African advocate who takes his South African legal and political experience and begins to build a philosophy and practice of nonviolence. *It is that same Gandhi* who takes his philosophy and practice of nonviolence to India with great effect. He deeply influences the late Gene Sharp, the leading nonviolence theorist of our era. Sharp's work inspires the activists who overthrow the strongman, Slobodan Milosevic, in Serbia and the dictator, Ben Ali, in Tunisia. Sharp's work inspires Erica Chenoweth and Maria Stephan, whose book *Why Civil Resistance Works* is changing the way people around the world think about how revolutions ought to be conducted.[56]

The critics take no account of this influence Gandhi has had on the twenty-first century.

The critics also take no account of the contradictions in Gandhi's own life.

The *same South African advocate* whom the critics fault for not pressing for women's rights in South Africa would come to host his female

---

[54] See, for example, Dorothy Day, 'We Mourn the Death of Gandhi Non Violent [*sic*] Revolutionary', *The Catholic Worker* (February 1948), in which Day (who herself is being considered for canonization by the Catholic church) refers to Gandhi's 'divinized humanity'.

[55] Desai and Vahed, for example, attack Gandhi for not advocating for the rights of women and the lower classes.

[56] Erica Chenoweth and Maria J. Stephan, *Why Civil Resistance Works* (New York: Columbia University Press, 2011).

secretary as an articled clerk in his office in support of her application for admission to the bar as South Africa's first woman lawyer.[57]

The *same South African advocate* who paid scant attention to the interests of the impoverished classes would later ally himself with striking Indian millworkers and poor peasants, and, on occasion, mobilize lawyers to volunteer in their struggle.[58]

The *same South African advocate* who belittled Africans to elevate Indians would later unreservedly voice his sympathy with, and understanding of, the problems of the African American community,[59] offer encouragement directly to the African American community,[60] advise prominent African Americans,[61] condemn the prohibition of intermarriage and the exclusion of African Americans from public accommodations,[62] and warmly receive and meet with leading African American intellectuals of the 1930s and 1940s.[63]

---

[57]   *Schlesin v. Incorporated Law Society*, Transvaal Supreme Court Reports 363 (23 April 1909); George Paxton, *Sonja Schlesin: Gandhi's South African Secretary* (Glasgow: Pax Books, 2006), 14. The application was unsuccessful. Shortly after Gandhi witnessed Schlesin's articles of clerkship, the Transvaal Supreme Court ruled against her, stating that women were not to be admitted to practice. George Paxton, *Sonja Schlesin*, 14.

[58]   J. M. Brown, 'Chapter 3: Satyagraha, 1917–18', in *Gandhi's Rise to Power: Indian Politics, 1915–1922* (London: Cambridge University Press, 1972), 52–122, cited in DiSalvo, Book Review, *The South African Gandhi: Stretcher-Bearer of Empire*, 674.

[59]   Sudarshan Kapur, *Raising Up a Prophet: The African-American Encounter with Gandhi* (Boston: Beacon Press, 1992), 125.

[60]   Kapur, *Raising Up a Prophet*, 39.

[61]   Kapur, *Raising Up a Prophet*, 134 *et seq.*

[62]   Kapur, *Raising Up a Prophet*, 141.

[63]   'Gandhi habitually hosted foreign visitors, but when the Negro Delegation arrived on March 14, 1936, he ventured outside to meet them. Mahadev Desai, Gandhi's secretary, told Thurman he had never seen the Mahatma do this.' Sarah Azaransky, *This Worldwide Struggle: Religion and the International Roots of the Civil Rights Movement* (New York: Oxford University Press, 2017), 41. The delegation included Howard Thurman, then professor of religion and future dean of Rankin Chapel at Howard University and Marsh Chapel at Boston University, and Sue Bailey Thurman, a social historian and future editor of the *Aframerican Women's Journal*. They met with Gandhi in 1936. Kapur, *Raising Up a Prophet*, 81 *et seq.* See also 'About Howard Thurman', The Howard Thurman Papers Project, Boston University School of Theology, https://www.bu.edu/htpp/thurman/. Thurman describes his meeting with Gandhi in his autobiography; see Howard Thurman, *With Head and Heart* (New York: Harcourt Brace & Co., 1979), 130–5. The visit of the 1936 delegation was followed the next year by a visit by Benjamin Mays, who had just received his PhD from the University of Chicago and was then serving as dean of Howard University's School of Religion. In 1940 Mays would assume the presidency of Morehouse College, where he was a major influence on one of its students, Martin Luther King. Kapur, *Raising Up a Prophet*, 93 *et seq.* See also Jason Kelly, 'Benjamin Elijah Mays: The Conscience of the Civil Rights Movement', *University of Chicago Magazine* 105, no. 3 (2013), 62; Sarah Azaransky, *The Worldwide Struggle*, 68 *et seq.*; John Herbert Roper, Sr., *The Magnificent Mays: A Biography of Benjamin Elijah Mays* (Columbia, SC: University of South

Gandhi's current critics either avoid mentioning these contradictions in Gandhi's life or write them off as unimportant. Rather, the critics' well-founded dismantling of the image some have of Gandhi as a near deity is performed so single-mindedly as to leave the critics no room to accurately and fully portray the historical Gandhi.

The resulting danger is that the critics may diminish our hope that, as a society suffering from the sins of racism and more, we can transform ourselves. If our society is to move from racism to equality, it must believe that history is not destiny but that change is, in fact, within its power.

Is belief in the power of society to make such a change reasonable?

The historical Gandhi's story of growth over time responds to that question with a measure of hope—hope that society can, in fact, move beyond its past to its future.

Like the historical Gandhi whom we all mirror, human society is flawed.

Like the historical Gandhi whose limitations we all bear, human society is guilty of having stained its soul.

And like the historical Gandhi who transcended transgressions of which we are all guilty, we, too, have it within our power to rise above the sinfulness of our time.

Carolina Press, 2012), 192 *et seq.* Sarah Azaransky observes that neither visit with Gandhi was without tension; see Azaransky, *This Worldwide Struggle*, 42 *et seq.* and 68 *et seq.*

William Stuart Nelson, editor of the *Journal of Religious Thought* at Howard University, was another African American intellectual who met with Gandhi; his visit occurred in 1947. Kapur, *Raising Up a Prophet*, 7 and 134 *et seq.* During World War II, Gandhi also spent time with African American reporters Deton Brooks, Jr., and Frank Bolden; Deton noted that Gandhi expressed a 'keen sympathy and understanding' of the problems of African Americans. Kapur, *Raising Up a Prophet*, 124 *et seq.*

Anil Nauriya argues that the 'widening of Gandhi's outlook on racial matters goes back to his South Africa years and was not merely a later occurrence as is sometimes erroneously assumed'. Anil Nauriya, 'The Making of Gandhi in South Africa and After', *Deccan Herald* (23 June 2020).

Notes on Contributors

Editor

Vinay Lal is a writer, blogger, cultural critic, public commentator, and Professor of History and Asian American Studies at UCLA. His twenty-some authored and edited books include *The History of History: Politics and Scholarship in Modern India* (Oxford University Press, 2005); the two-volume *Oxford Anthology of the Modern Indian City* (Oxford University Press, 2013); and *Insurgency and the Artist: The Art of the Freedom Struggle in India* (Roli Books, 2022). His intellectual interests include nonviolence, Gandhi, resistance movements, Indian history, global politics, historiography, cinema, and the politics of knowledge systems. He maintains an extensive academic YouTube channel, now with over 3 million views, at https://www.youtube.com/user/dillichalo. He is the founding editor of the Backwaters Collective on Metaphysics and Politics series from Oxford University Press, Delhi. Volume I appeared as *India and the Unthinkable* (with Roby Rajan, 2016), Volume II as *India and Civilizational Futures* (2019), and Volume III as *India and Its Intellectual Traditions* (2023).

Contributors

Leilah Danielson is Professor of History at Northern Arizona University, where she traces a range of courses on modern American politics and culture and US/World. She is the author of *American Gandhi: A. J. Muste and the History of American Radicalism in the Twentieth Century* (University of Pennsylvania Press, 2014) and co-editor (with Doug Rossinow and Marian Mollin) of *The Religious Left in Modern America: Doorkeepers of a Radical Faith* (Palgrave Macmillan, 2018). Her current research examines the history of the workers' education movement of the 1920s and

1930s, exploring its pedagogical, organizational, and cultural interventions and influence on the labour movement.

Faisal Devji is Professor of Indian History and Fellow of St Antony's College, Oxford. He is the author of four books, including *The Impossible Indian: Gandhi and the Temptation of Violence* (Harvard University Press, 2012) and *Muslim Zion: Pakistan as a Political Idea* (Harvard University Press, 2013).

Charles R. DiSalvo is the author of *M. K. Gandhi, Attorney at Law: The Man Before the Mahatma* (University of California Press, 2013) and the Woodrow A. Potesta Professor of Law at West Virginia University. He teaches one of the few American law school courses on civil disobedience. He has represented disobedients, written widely on disobedience, and lectured internationally on the subject. Professor DiSalvo attended St. John Fisher College, Claremont Graduate School, and the University of Southern California, where he was a member of the *Southern California Law Review*. After holding a teaching fellowship at the University of Chicago Law School, he came to WVU, where he has won university, state, and national teaching awards.

Yohanan Grinshpon was born and raised in Kibbutz Yagur, Israel. He studied philosophy, sociology, and comparative religion at the Hebrew University, Jerusalem. He wrote his MA thesis on Shankaracharya's theory of language and freedom under David Shulman and his PhD thesis on Patanjali's theory of meditation and powers under Wilhelm Halbfass (University of Pennsylvania). He has taught in the Department of Asian Studies at the Hebrew University of Jerusalem for many years. His English-language works include *Silence Unheard* (SUNY, 2000); *The Upanishadic Experience and Story-Telling* (Oxford University Press, 2003); and *The Secret Shankara* (Brill, 2016).

Sudipta Kaviraj has had a long academic career at some of the leading universities in the world, including Jawaharlal Nehru University, SOAS, and the University of Chicago. He is presently Professor of Indian Politics and Intellectual History at Columbia University. His research interests are in the fields of political and social theory, Bengali literature, and Indian aesthetics. Several volumes of his essays on politics, political theory, and history have been published in recent years by Columbia University Press and Permanent Black, including *The Imaginary Institution of India: Politics and Ideas* (2010), *The Invention of Private Life: Literature and Ideas* (2015), and *The Enchantment of Democracy and India* (2018).

Rev. James M. Lawson (1928–2024) was Pastor Emeritus of Holman Methodist United Church in Los Angeles. He was one of the principal architects of the American civil rights movement and the initiator and principal strategist of the Nashville Sit-ins. He played a critical role in the creation of the Student Nonviolent Coordinating Committee (SNCC) and over the last four decades was a major force in the labour movement in Los Angeles. His life and work are discussed at some length in David Halberstam's book *The Children* (1998), and a collection of his speeches and interviews has appeared from the University of California Press as *Revolutionary Nonviolence: Organizing for Freedom* (2022).

Karuna Mantena is Professor of Political Science at Columbia University and co-director of the International Conference for the Study of Political Thought (CSPT). She is the author of *Alibis of Empire: Henry Maine and the Ends of Liberal Imperialism* (Princeton University Press, 2010), which analysed the transformation of nineteenth-century British imperial ideology. She has recently published articles on Gandhi's political realism, the nonviolence of Martin Luther King, and the theory and practice of nonviolence in the twentieth century. She is currently finishing a book tentatively titled *Gandhi and the Politics of Nonviolence*.

Uday Singh Mehta is Distinguished Professor of Political Science at the Graduate Center of the City University of New York. He is the author of two books, *The Anxiety of Freedom: Imagination and Individuality in the Political Thought of John Locke* (Cornell University Press, 1992) and *Liberalism and Empire: Nineteenth Century British Liberal Thought* (University of Chicago Press, 2000). He was an undergraduate at Swarthmore College, where he studied mathematics and philosophy. He received his PhD in political philosophy from Princeton University. He has a forthcoming book titled *A Different Vision: Gandhi's Critique of Political Rationality*.

Sumathi Ramaswamy is James B. Duke Professor of History and International Comparative Studies, and Chair of the Department of History, at Duke University. She has published extensively on language politics, gender studies, spatial studies and the history of cartography, visual studies and the modern history of art, and, more recently, digital humanities and the history of philanthropy. Her recent writings on Gandhi include *Gandhi in the Gallery: The Art of Disobedience* (Roli Books, 2021) and the digital project *B is for Bapu: Gandhi in the Art of the Child in Modern India* (https://sites.duke.edu/bisforbapu/). She is currently working on a new project on educational philanthropy in British India.

Neelima Shukla-Bhatt is Professor of Religion and South Asia Studies at Wellesley College. Her work focuses on devotional literature of medieval north India, goddess traditions in Gujarat, South Asian models of religious pluralism, and Gandhi's thought and life. She is the author of *Narasinha Mehta of Gujarat: A Legacy of Bhakti in Songs and Stories* (Oxford University Press, 2015) and co-author (with Surendra Bhana) of *A Fire that Blazed in the Ocean: Gandhi and the Poems of Satyagraha in South Africa, 1909–1911* (Promilla, 2011). She has also published on the woman poet Mira, *garba* (the goddess worship dance of Gujarati women), and Hindu approaches to religious pluralism.

Ajay Skaria teaches History and Global Studies at the University of Minnesota. He is the author of *Hybrid Histories: Forests, Frontiers and Wildness in Western India* (Oxford University Press, 1999) and *Unconditional Equality: Gandhi's Religion of Resistance* (University of Minnesota Press, 2016), as well as of many articles on environmental and intellectual history. As a member of the Subaltern Studies Editorial Collective, he was one of the editors of *Subaltern Studies Vol. XII*. He is currently working on two books, one tentatively titled *Ambedkar's Revolutions* and the other attempting a history of secularism from India.

Tridip Suhrud is a scholar, writer, and translator who works on the intellectual and cultural history of modern Gujarat and the Gandhian intellectual tradition. As the director and chief editor of the Sabarmati Ashram Preservation and Memorial Trust (2012–17), he was responsible for creating the world's largest digital archive on Gandhi—the Gandhi Heritage Portal. His books include the critical edition of *Hind Swaraj*, a translation of Narayan Desai's four-volume biography of Gandhi, *My Life is My Message*, and an English translation of the four-volume epic Gujarati novel, *Sarasvatichandra*. His recent works include a critical edition of Gandhi's autobiography *My Experiments with Truth* in two languages, Gujarati and English, *The Diary of Manu Gandhi* (1943–4), and a compilation *The Power of Non-Violent Resistance*. He is working on an eight-volume compendium of testimonies of indigo cultivators of Champaran, the first volume of which has appeared as *Thumb Printed: Champaran Indigo Peasants Speak to Gandhi* (2022). He is Professor at, and Provost of, CEPT University, Ahmedabad, and also Director of Lalbhai Dalpatbhai Institute of Indology, Ahmedabad.

Index

For the benefit of digital users, indexed terms that span two pages (e.g., 52–53) may, on occasion, appear on only one of those pages.

European 35
Evil 201, 202, 206–7, 218

Farmer, James 102
fasting 249–62
    and African Americans 249–50, 251, 254
    and the American public 257–58, 259
    and the body 260–62
    and Cesar Chavez 258–59
    different from hunger-striking 252
    see also Gandhi, Mohandas Karmachand:
        and fasting
fearlessness 201–2, 213–14, 215, 216, 218
Fellowship of Reconciliation (FOR) 93–94,
    96, 99–100, 101–4
First World War 40–41, 94
    as Great War 41
Fischer, Louis 210, 230–31
Foucault, Michel 77–79
Freedom Rides 257
Freud, Sigmund 59, 60, 61, 62, 78–79, 82,
    83–84, 85, 85–86n.28
Frydman, Maurice 145–46

Gadamer, Hans-Georg 117
Gandhi, Devdas 143n.33, 155–57, 158–62,
    271, 272
Gandhi, Kanu 155–58
Gandhi, Kasturba 140–41, 143–44n.37, 273–
    74, 283–84
Gandhi, Lakshmidas 140–41
Gandhi, Maganlal 144n.38, 153–54,
    265, 269–70
Gandhi, Manu 142
Gandhi, Mohandas Karamchand 23, 24, 25,
    26, 27, 28–30, 31, 32–39, 40–43, 89–90,
    91–92, 96–97, 98–101, 114–34, 292–94,
    295, 296–98, 300, 302–3, 307, 310
    and American views of 89–90, 96–102,
        109–10, 113
    as amoral technician 323, 325, 326
    on aparigraha 128–31
    and assassination 3–5, 136, 155–57, 158–
        60, 170–71
    as author of Hind Swaraj 32–33, 37–38
    autobiography of 27, 30, 34–36, 37–38,
        176–77, 178–79
    and Balasundaram case 314, 315
    on the Bihar earthquake 123–28
    and charge of racism 12–13, 312, 313, 318
    charisma of 10–11

and Christians 11–12
on conversion 303–4
and Dada Abdulla and Company
    case 314–15
disavowal of normal politics by 16–
    17, 18–19
on disobedience 293, 297–98
on equality 115n.2
and fasting 249, 250, 251, 254–56
and footwear 142–43, 149–50, 151–52,
    153–58, 164–66
and goal of selflessness 174
and Harijan 42–43
on Hindu-Muslim unity 60
his inclusiveness 11–13
and his mother's Pranami faith 69, 70
historical Gandhi 332
and Hitler 6–7, 222–25, 228
and idea of non-possession 137–38,
    141, 148
Indian Home Rule 32–33
as Indian merchants' lawyer 318
indifference to Bolshevism 225–26
knowledge of world affairs 222–26
legal training 313
in London 137–39, 144–45, 146
as Mahatma 24, 25, 26, 28–29, 30, 32, 33,
    35, 37–38, 39, 40, 42–43
on majoritarianism 307
and material life 135–36, 140–41, 142–44,
    162, 164–66, 168
and memorialization 157–62
in museums 145–46, 149, 160–62, 163–
    66, 168–69
in Nazi Germany 239–40,
    239n.50, 241–42
and neighbours/neighbourliness 60–88
on nonviolence 259–60, 262–63, 294, 295
and pen 142–43, 144–46, 149, 157–58,
    164–66, 168
on persuasion 303–4
as a player of infinite games 7, 15, 21
as political organizer 312
and Rabindranath Tagore 114–34
and racist statements 315, 316–17, 321
relations with Jews 226–27
and relations with the British 10–12
on rules of protest 297, 299–300
on the search for truth 20
and secularism 21
and segregated rickshaws 321–23

342   INDEX